The Antirevolutionary

"In a compact historical biography of Groen van Prinsterer, Roel Kuiper has the quality of highlighting his ideological significance in his context. He masters his subject like few others and convincingly presents Groen as one of the first Protestants who fervently unmasked the ideas of the revolution of 1789 as a rival worldview of Christianity. Kuiper describes Groen vividly as he develops his antirevolutionary ideas, that have been an inspiration to many."

—**GEORGE HARINCK**, professor of history of Neo-Calvinism, Theological University Utrecht and Vrije Universiteit Amsterdam

"This captivating biography brings to life Groen van Prinsterer's enduring legacy and pivotal role in shaping modern Christian political thought. A must-read for those interested in European history, faith, and the roots of Neo-Calvinism."

—**JOHN CHOI**, professor, Handong Global University, South Korea

"Roel Kuiper's biography of Groen van Prinsterer shows clearly why the life of this extraordinary Hollander meant so much to those who knew him personally and why it came to mean perhaps even more through his legacy as founder of the Antirevolutionary Party. Insights that van Prinsterer gained through his work as a historian, service as a politician, and faithfulness as a lay Christian shaped his writings about the character of Christian faith and the hope of Christian civilization. That life and those writings would, in turn, inspire Abraham Kuyper and a host of others who shared his vision that the Christian gospel pointed the way to social health now as well as to everlasting life."

—**MARK NOLL**, co-author of *Turning Points: Decisive Moments in the History of Christianity*

"Groen van Prinsterer (1801–1876) provides inspiration worldwide to public intellectuals offering principled critiques and alternatives to ruling ideologies. He also inspired the social entrepreneur, public theologian, and statesman Abraham Kuyper (1837–1920), whose global influence is growing. But in contrast to Kuyper, relatively little is known about Groen's life. This authoritative biography tells its fascinating story and places Groen's writings in context. It will be welcomed by audiences of thinkers and change-makers around the world."

—**Peter S. Heslam**, University of Cambridge

"Groen van Prinsterer was a brilliant scholar-statesman who had a profound influence on nineteenth-century Dutch political and religious thought. Unfortunately, little has been known about him in the English-speaking world. Now we have the much-needed corrective in this impressive study of Groen's life and thought, authored by Roel Kuiper, himself a gifted Dutch scholar-statesman!"

—**Richard Mouw**, former president, Fuller Seminary

"This biography of Groen van Prinsterer, who faced the challenges of rationalism and liberal theology in his time with a Christian spirit, is a great inspiration and encouragement to modern Christians. The result of Dr. Kuiper's professional study of Groen van Prinsterer's letters adds greater trust and expectation to readers. In the present age, where human desire and reason are still absolutized and the created world is being destroyed, Christians around the world in the twenty-first century—especially Christians in various Asian countries suffering from growing pains amid rapid economic growth—will be able to gain valuable insight into how Christian faith can reform the areas of politics and education."

—**In-Sub Ahn**, Chongshin University and Theological Seminary, Seoul, South Korea

"This biography of the unique and influential character of Willem Groen van Prinsterer is as urgent as it has been long overdue. A true 'whisperer behind the throne' of the new Dutch king, Groen stood out by his intellectual contribution to the politics and history of conservative, Protestant, and constitutional thought alike. Thus, this lucidly written book is an excellent contribution to the current historiographical trend of highlighting not just the post 1815 revolutionary networks but also the cosmopolitan, conservative, and transnational Christian ones."

—**BEATRICE DE GRAAF**, distinguished professor of history of international relations and global governance, Utrecht University

The Antirevolutionary

Life and Works of Groen van Prinsterer (1801–1876)

Roel Kuiper

PICKWICK *Publications* · Eugene, Oregon

THE ANTIREVOLUTIONARY
Life and Works of Groen van Prinsterer (1801–1876)

Copyright © 2025 Roel Kuiper. All rights reserved. Except for brief quotations in critical publications or reviews, no part of this book may be reproduced in any manner without prior written permission from the publisher. Write: Permissions, Wipf and Stock Publishers, 199 W. 8th Ave., Suite 3, Eugene, OR 97401.

Pickwick Publications
An Imprint of Wipf and Stock Publishers
199 W. 8th Ave., Suite 3
Eugene, OR 97401

www.wipfandstock.com

PAPERBACK ISBN: 979-8-3852-2456-2
HARDCOVER ISBN: 979-8-3852-2457-9
EBOOK ISBN: 979-8-3852-2458-6

Cataloguing-in-Publication data:

Names: Kuiper, Roel [author].

Title: The antirevolutionary : life and work of Groen van Prinsterer (1801–1876) / by Roel Kuiper.

Description: Eugene, OR: Pickwick Publications, 2025 | **Includes bibliographical references and index.**

Identifiers: ISBN 979-8-3852-2456-2 (paperback) | ISBN 979-8-3852-2457-9 (hardcover) | ISBN 979-8-3852-2458-6 (ebook)

Subjects: LCSH: Groen van Prinsterer, G., 1801–1876. | Netherlands—Church history. | Christianity and politics—Netherlands—History—19th century. | Christianity and politics—Calvinism. | Anti-revolutionaire Partij (Netherlands)

Classification: JN5985.A6 K85 2025 (paperback) | JN5985.A6 (ebook)

VERSION NUMBER 05/30/25

Scripture quotes are from New Revised Standard Version Bible, copyright 1989, Division of Christian Education of the National Council of the Churches of Christ in the United States of America. Used by permission. All rights reserved.

Contents

Preface | vii

1 Childhood, Youth, and University | 1
2 Employment and Discoveries | 17
3 Near Death's Door and a Decision for Life | 48
4 The Salt of Education, the Salt of the Earth | 82
5 Public Trials | 118
6 Martyr and Popular Tribune | 162
7 The Old General | 195

Endnotes | 219
Images | 245
Bibliography | 271

Preface

WILLEM GROEN VAN PRINSTERER is one of the key figures in modern Dutch political and religious history. In the national parliament in The Hague there is still a public meeting room named after him. Many schools bear his name. But Groen van Prinsterer's influence was not limited to national borders. He was a Protestant leader in Europe of his time, the founder of a Christian political movement that was copied worldwide, and an inspiration to many political and religious leaders. One of them was Abraham Kuyper (1837–1920), the man who fruitfully built on Groen van Prinsterer's legacy. Abraham Kuyper founded the Antirevolutionary Party and the Free University of Amsterdam and shaped an international Neo-Calvinist movement inspired by the ideas of Groen van Prinsterer.

When Groen van Prinsterer died in 1876, nothing of what would become of his legacy was yet visible. At his grave, many thanked him for his life and remembered all his struggles. He died as a general without an army, as was said at the time. However, many obituaries compared him to another key figure in modern Dutch history, Johan Rudolf Thorbecke (1798–1872). Indeed, these two men determined to a considerable degree the shape of Dutch political life and society. Thorbecke was able to do so during his lifetime, during which he served three times as prime minister; Groen never held that office. His greatest influence would come after his death.

Groen knew that in his lifetime he was against the "spirit of the age." He borrowed this phrase from his brother-in-arms, Isaac da Costa (1798–1860). He saw this spirit in the advance of a rationalistic worldview and the encroachment of a liberal Christianity, both based on the progress of modern science. He saw this secular spirit, which also found expression in political life, as dangerous—religiously dangerous—to the well-being of man and society. According to Groen, this spirit was not in harmony with the true character of European history. This history was shaped by Christianity. It was the breakthrough of unbelief in Enlightenment thought that concerned him most, as he would explain in his magnum opus, *Unbelief and Revolution*.

Groen van Prinsterer observed what was changing at the heart of Western civilization. He was therefore an "antirevolutionary" spokesman of protest, pointing to the gospel to show what Christian politics was about. His concerns were international, but at the same time he saw something dear and special in Dutch history. The true nature of the Dutch people had been forged in the struggle for the Christian faith that had established the Netherlands as a free and independent Protestant nation in the sixteenth century. Calvinism had secured constitutional liberties. Throughout his life, he was a champion of those freedoms. This Christian faith, Groen believed, was still alive among the common people. It was a discovery that Groen made throughout his life, even though he himself came from an aristocratic background. The common people were to be trusted, even more than the conservative and liberal leaders of his day. When the common people began to gain influence after Groen's death, they recalled Groen's tireless struggle against the secular spirit of his time. Those who were not his followers recognized in him a noble figure who stood head and shoulders above his contemporaries.

This biography paints a picture of Groen's life and work against the background of his times. Naturally, we will focus on his public career. As we shall see, he was a pioneer in Dutch historiography, a leader of the "antirevolutionary" faction in Parliament, a leader of the religious revival in the Netherlands, a leader of the international Réveil movement, and a prominent layman in the Dutch Reformed Church.

According to his pastor in Wassenaar, Van Rhijn, four souls were united in Groen's breast: a child, a gentlewoman, a scholar, and a hero. Such characterizations bring us closer to Groen as a person. How did he view his own work? How did he feel when he was ignored or misunderstood? How did he cope with his defeats? Where did he find the strength to continue working without bitterness on a project that seemed fruitless until his last breath?

It was Groen's whole approach to life that impressed many during his lifetime and later became an example to others as a paragon of self-sacrifice and principled behavior. Groen's popularity cannot be attributed solely to

Preface

his writings, which contained brilliant aphorisms but were never easily accessible. Groen's works cannot be understood without reference to his life story. Groen has remained relevant, and not just as a name on streets and school buildings. He is relevant as a model of a man of the modern world who has never stopped witnessing to his faith. "You will always be an example." This was the prediction of the poet and publicist Isaac da Costa in 1854, when Groen's political career seemed to have come to an untimely end. Da Costa was referring to Groen's example of parliamentary struggle for Christian politics.

It seemed important to me that this biography should appear, an intellectual biography that would emerge from the story of his life. For about thirty years, in various smaller and larger publications, I have been dealing with the leading personalities and ideas of the antirevolutionaries in the Netherlands. This biography is dedicated to the antirevolutionary. The name of Groen van Prinsterer is also known internationally. There are various biographical notes and introductions, and there are translations of *Unbelief and Revolution* in several languages. However, a comprehensive biography has been lacking. I am delighted that at last there is this English edition of the Dutch original, written for a new generation and, in the case of this English translation, for a new audience altogether.

I would like to thank a number of people for their advice and critical comments. First of all, I would like to commemorate the late Ludi van Essen, who has spent her professional life editing and publishing Groen's voluminous correspondence, and who has shown an abiding interest in everything that is written about her "friend" Groen. Next my thanks go to Andries Boertien, Guido Sneep, Machteld Siegmann, and Merijn Wijma of Buijten & Schipperheijn, the Dutch publishers who also supported this English version. I am grateful to Harry Van Dyke for the care he took in translating the book into English. Harry also translated *Unbelief and Revolution* and introduced Groen van Prinsterer to an English-speaking audience in our time. I thank Pieter Kwant and the publishers at Wipf and Stock for making this publication possible. The final editing by Dana Carrington proved invaluable. I am, of course, solely responsible for the text. I hope the book will reach many readers who share my fascination with a figure who never received a monument, but who lived with a soul of fire and as such was a monument in the eyes of many.[1]

---

1. This was the judgment of the Roman Catholic statesman-priest H. J. A. M. Schaepman, "Mr. G. Groen van Prinsterer," *Onze Wachter* 3 (1876) II, 65–74; reprinted in G. Puchinger, ed., *Aandacht voor Groen van Prinsterer* (Kampen: Kok, 1976), 34–43.

1

Childhood, Youth, and University

HOME AND UPBRINGING

"My beloved wife, Adriana Hendrika Caan, by the goodness of God, was today successfully delivered of a healthy son. *Vreugd en Rust*, near Voorburg, August 21, 1801."[1] This was the first public attention paid to the main character of this book, who acquired a copy of the advertisement from a relative after his public debut. He saved the clipping, just as he saved everything related to his public life. Public life was this man's natural environment. He played his role in the public arena through the spoken and written word. His word was always carefully prepared in private and sometimes met with positive, but more often negative, response in public. It was a life without great public accomplishments, and yet it became exemplary. Many have appealed to it or explicitly distanced themselves from it. One cannot avoid this life if one wants to understand something of the societal, political, and philosophical attitudes of many Christians in the centuries after his death.

Our protagonist has not made it difficult for us. His life can be traced from his birth, beginning with the newspaper advertisement written by Doctor Petrus Jacobus Groen van Prinsterer. The father and level-headed doctor hid his joy behind the matter-of-fact announcement that the newborn was healthy and his mother had had a successful delivery. The family also experienced less fortunate births; a few babies died at birth. In 1801 there was already a girl of three years, called Keetje. In 1806 a second daughter was born, Mimi.

The Antirevolutionary

The heir who would grow up between Keetje and Mimi was known in the family circle by the simple Dutch name of Willem. When he was baptized in the French-speaking Walloon church in Voorburg, he was given the name Guillaume. This was the official name he used throughout his life. But whether he was called Willem or Guillaume, the fact remained that the eldest son bore a name that had not been used by his ancestors. Cornelis, Petrus, Jacobus—these had long been the customary first names for the male members who carried on the family name. Was it a touch of modern pragmatism that moved the parents not to name their son after his ancestors? Or did they want to make a new dynastic start, now that the Groen family had established itself in high society with the fashionable addition of "van Prinsterer"?[2]

It is unlikely that the choice of name is evidence of resistance to French power and influence, which had underpinned the vassal-like government of the Netherlands during the years of the Restoration 1795–1813. The deliberate Gallicizing of Willem's name argues against this, but even more so the attitude and behavior of the parents. Mother Caan was a cousin of the brothers Jan and Nicolaas Staphorst, Amsterdam bankers who played a prominent role in the Batavian Revolution of 1795 and thereafter. These circles regretted the revolution mainly because of its economic consequences.[3] Her family came from Rotterdam and was well-to-do. Whatever the circumstances, the Caans continued to enjoy life to the full. Mother preferred to speak French and participated in the social life of the elite in The Hague, the administrative center of the country. Father Groen was still busy advancing his career during these years. He was an ambitious man with a strong sense of social responsibility and an eye for the demands of the times. Thus, the parents showed anything but a rebellious attitude toward the established order.

In 1805 the family moved into a stately mansion built in 1635 and situated on what was then a slight rise (*berg*) along the Korte Vijverberg, catercorner to what is now the Mauritshuis Museum and overlooking the length of the pond (*vijver*) that nestles against the parliament complex. Even then, the house was one of the finest in the city center. The large estate of *Vreugd en Rust* ("Joy and Rest"), a property that had belonged to the Caan family, remained their country home during the summer months. Adriana Hendrika Caan brought a great deal of money into the marriage, and this enabled the Groens to occupy a prominent position in society. Their status as a patrician family was confirmed by the purchase of this substantial house in the heart of The Hague, which they had rented since 1797.⁴ All this wealth did not go to the head of the family. To be sure, father Groen remained a hard worker for the public good. He played a role in provincial governments and medical boards and became a prominent figure in Dutch society. From 1805 he served as "commissar for the affairs of the medical government regulation," that is, he was in charge of organizing the public health inspection. There he gained a reputation as a progressive man, and he would remain active in this field until 1822. Shortly after taking up permanent residence in The Hague, we find him associated with the court of the chief executive officer of the Republic, Grand Pensionary Rutger Jan Schimmelpenninck, and after 1806 with the court of King Louis Napoleon. Dr. Groen had a special relationship with Schimmelpenninck, who needed a lot of medical care because of an eye disease.

The family's rise was well deserved, but it also had something to do with opportunism. In those turbulent times, the behavior of many citizens was characterized by a smooth adaptation to the new political and social circumstances. Revolutionaries became moderates within a few years, and fiery Orangists reconciled themselves to another period in which no member of the House of Orange would serve as head of the executive or commander-in-chief of the armed forces.⁵ In this so-called "French period," there was nothing like the resistance movement that emerged during the Second World War. Between 1795 and 1806, the country was still ruled by the Dutch. Especially after 1801, an ideological thaw set in and social conditions were gradually normalized. One of the clearest signs of this was the return from exile of the poet Willem Bilderdijk. In 1806, this Orangist eccentric set foot on Dutch soil again. He even managed to sing the emperor's praises in his "Ode to Napoleon" and to give lessons in the Dutch language to Napoleon's brother, King Louis Bonaparte. In those years, many Dutch people personally experienced the truth of the saying "*Het kan verkeren*"— "Times change and people change with them." People chose to live in the knowledge that a new world offered new opportunities. So did the parents of the newborn child. They steered clear of the shoals and rode the waves of history that were sweeping across the European continent.

This willingness to adapt to new social conditions was balanced by a disciplined lifestyle. In this way, the turbulence of the world was reduced to the manageable dimensions of everyday tasks. In the social circles of Groen's parents, the virtues of decency and decorum, industry, duty, diligence, modesty, and religious observance were practiced. The motto on the family crest expressed the dominant idea: *Virtus nobilitat* (virtue ennobles). The young Groen did not lack instruction in virtue. Father Groen personally took charge of his son's education. He saw to it that the boy was encouraged and disciplined at every step. He selected the best schools, hired the most prominent clergyman for religious instruction, and chose reading materials that were both educational and morally edifying. In this way, Willem's education became a reflection of his father's various competing aspirations. Until his eighth year, the child was privately educated at home according to strict standards. For example, a visit by Dr. Groen to Schimmelpenninck, who had retired from politics and now lived near the eastern city of Deventer, was the occasion for their father to send a letter to seven-year-old Willem and his ten-year-old sister in which he instructed them to trace his journey on a map and calculate the distances.[6]

Father Groen's approach to education has been described as "schoolmasterly."[7] A father who educates his son at home is, of course, open to being called pedantic. But that judgment can also obscure the merits of a father who teaches his son discipline, responsibility, and leadership in a rapidly changing society. The paternalistic management of his youth, however rigid and bookish, served Willem well, as we shall see. For a long time, however, it gave the father a central role in decisions about his son's future. Even after Willem graduated from college, Dad's opinion still mattered a great deal. Father Groen was practical enough to bend to the facts so that his will did not ultimately become an iron law. In any case, he was wise enough to respect Willem's personal preferences and talents. In this way, Willem, whose characteristic trait in his youth was to be accommodating, did not suffer from his strict upbringing. The fact that his path was always neatly laid out for him is probably the reason why he matured relatively late. As an adolescent he showed very little self-confidence, and throughout his university years he was still reluctant to speak his mind about people and issues. This did not change until after his marriage, although modesty would remain his enduring trait. What was to become characteristic of the later Groen was the urge to express himself openly and to communicate his thoughts orally and in writing. It should also be remembered that the ambitious and disciplined approach of Father Groen was counterbalanced by the sunny and sociable outlook of Mother. She provided a happy and carefree home, a haven that meant a great deal to Willem and to which he was always happy to return.

Childhood, Youth, and University

SCHOOL YEARS

From the age of eight, Groen attended primary school. The school was run by the local chapter of the so-called Society for the Common Good.[8] This private organization, steeped in modern ideals, was dedicated to improving education and enlightening the middle class. Beginning in 1795, the Society became increasingly popular. To avoid competition with public schools, the Society's schools held classes in the evenings. The school in The Hague was located at the Buitenhof and had more than two hundred pupils. From the Korte Vijverberg you could see the lights go on at five o'clock in the school across the city pond. According to his mother, Willem could hardly be contained. At school he met boys of his own age, like Jaap Dermout and Gerrit van Limburg Brouwer, who became his best friends. Jaap was the son of the still young pastor Isaac Dermout, while Gerrit came from a prominent merchant family.

The classes met four evenings a week and were devoted to the general education of the children. The curriculum included penmanship, arithmetic, geography, and history. At home, Willem also received lessons in modern languages from Miss Lufneu, the governess, and in mathematics and Dutch from his father. The pedagogical maxim was to teach children as much as possible while they were young and receptive. The evening school was to lead to a certificate that would give access to secondary education. To encourage the children to do their best, they were constantly rewarded with bonuses, promotions, and even public awards. The "real competition" that resulted from this practice made the children strive for the highest praise. The system was not wasted on Willem, for he always competed with Jaap Dermout for first place in their age group. In May 1813, Willem graduated "with distinction" from the Society school. The regents noted in the student's certificate that "during his three and a half years of attendance at the aforesaid school, he has conducted himself so excellently and praiseworthily in diligence and virtue, as to make considerable progress, and to fill them with confidence that this will serve as the foundation of increasing cultural refinement and thus of true happiness."[9]

There was no question in the Groen family that Willem should go to university. After all, a university degree gave access to all the higher positions in society. Dr. Groen desperately wanted his son to follow in his footsteps and become a doctor. To gain admission to a university, one had to prepare oneself by attending the highest level of secondary education. In those days, it was the Latin schools that prepared young boys for academic studies. Like the universities, the Latin schools devoted the bulk of their curriculum to the study of the classics. In both institutions, Latin was the language of instruction and studies focused on the writings of classical antiquity, the only difference being the level at which this was done. Graduates of a Latin school became the "educated classes of society," while university graduates earned doctorates. The common focus was the classical tradition. The debates of those years about whether these schools and universities should be given a more practical curriculum, one oriented toward the professions, did not lead to any adjustments.[10] Higher education continued to be devoted to the education of the whole person through the study of the classics. For the time being, the general appreciation of this type of curriculum prevailed over more modern views of socially relevant education. Thus, a thorough grounding in the humanities was to be the next phase in Willem Groen's formative years.

In the summer of 1813, due to some of father Groen's objections to the Latin school in The Hague, Willem was sent to a prestigious boarding school in Haarlem whose pedagogy followed modern insights. It was an unfortunate choice. The school's director died suddenly, and when political tensions in the Netherlands rose that summer, father Groen sent for Willem to come home. That fall, however, there was no possibility of organizing regular schooling at home. The country had been annexed by France in 1810, but now it was in open revolt against the crumbling regime, which oppressed the population with increasingly arbitrary measures. Demonstrations and riots became more frequent, especially in the cities. In the late fall of 1813, Russian and Prussian armies crossed the eastern border of the Netherlands after defeating Napoleon at Leipzig. Twelve-year-old Willem witnessed the national liberation when it reached The Hague in the early weeks of November. Gijsbert Karel van Hogendorp proclaimed the independence of the Netherlands in a short proclamation, and the Prince of Orange returned from exile in England, landed on a beach near The Hague, and took up residence in the city. These events made a great impression on Willem. Many years later he still remembered the "unanimous rejoicing" in The Hague.[11] He must have realized that for the first twelve years of his life he had grown up as a war child. For the rest of his life, he saw the liberation of 1813 as a high point in modern Dutch history.

The last years of the French regime had seen an increase in pauperism, the decay of the cities, and a general decline throughout the country. Widespread unemployment and the depopulation of cities such as Leyden and Haarlem contrasted sharply with the prosperity of earlier times. Young Willem began to understand that his country's mounting political, social, and economic trials were related to a struggle that was raging most violently beyond its own borders. In the very days that he was living a regulated and protected life, somewhere out of sight, a hotbed of action was setting the world on fire. Somewhere a political force was at work that was shaking the world to its core. The French emperor Napoleon had to be conquered with the greatest possible effort by an alliance of the great European powers. The international dimensions of this all-consuming conflict were brought home to Willem when the Prussian commander, von Bülow, and the Cossack general, Marklay, were quartered in the Groen's house on the Korte Vijverberg. Willem played many a game of chess with Marklay, with the general's mind probably wandering to less peaceful battlefields. The peacefulness of the game contrasted with the mighty struggle that was still required to bring Napoleon to his knees. The realization that there can be peace at home while revolutions rage abroad would accompany Groen throughout his life.

By the beginning of 1814, life was back to normal for Willem. This time, however, he ended up at the Latin school in The Hague, where he remained for nearly two years. Reunited with his friend Jaap Dermout, he made good progress, mastering Latin and becoming a promising young scholar. Of some importance to Willem was the arrival of a new rector, Dr. Johannes Kappeyne van de Coppello. Until his untimely death in 1833, this classicist befriended the young Groen, especially during Willem's university years.

Willem's precociousness prompted his father to consider other options, and in the fall of 1815, he sent his son to a boarding school in Utrecht. Again, the choice was guided by the idea that Willem should have the best school-education that was available in the Netherlands. It was at the Hieronymous School that Groen completed his secondary education. The core of the curriculum was the study of the classics, but the entire curriculum was modernized in Utrecht. It was here that Groen laid the foundation for his great ability to speak and write Latin, which later gave rise to the university saying "To speak Latin like Willem Groen." Groen's contact with the classicist Philip Willem van Heusde, who had been a professor at the University of Utrecht since 1809 and who invited Groen to his home, was stimulating in this respect. Van Heusde awakened Groen's interest in Plato and the Greek classics.

The main contact with home during these years was by mail. The letters that have survived give us an idea of the family's concerns and social relationships. The catechism lessons with Rev. Dermout in The Hague were continued by correspondence. Father and mother Groen's appreciation of their pastor Dermout, who was known as a pulpit orator, was so great that they had made this special arrangement with him. Sister Keetje acted as a courier, relaying the pastor's questions and delivering her brother's answers at the next catechism session. In Utrecht, Groen also received several letters from Gerrit van Limburg Brouwer in Rotterdam. This old school friend was now standing behind a desk in the office of a large trading firm, from which he could see the first steamboats, "the newest wonders of the world," entering the harbor. Gerrit expressed the hope of seeing "my old friend" again soon in The Hague.[12] Mother Groen, for her part, told her son about her own vocation: in January 1816, the Groens had attended a reception at court on the occasion of the marriage of the crown prince. Society was well represented, she wrote. The line of carriages was *"très grande"* and the queen and princess wore *"un grand nombre de diamants."* It was *"vraiment triste"* in this company, she added with some feeling, to see the blind Schimmelpenninck shuffling on the arm of a chaperone.[13]

Willem was deprived of such scenes in Utrecht, but his letters do not suggest that he regretted it. The life of "high society" never appealed to him. His sister Keetje derived more pleasure from Mother Groen's world, and in the few letters we have of her she proves to be a real chatterbox. The difference in interests and outlook between the two eldest children gradually widened as they grew older. Mimi was quieter and more like Willem in manner. Whatever else happened in the family circle is not known, since Groen removed most letters of a personal nature from his archives.[14] His years in Utrecht still show the family unity intact. What is clear is that all members considered Willem's progress important. Toward the end of 1816, he returned home to prepare for the final examinations. When the exams were held, he was allowed to give a speech in Latin as one of the top students. Under Kappeyne's supervision, he prepared a speech on the relationship between Cicero's personality and his politics. In the spring of 1817, he completed his Utrecht period and at the age of sixteen was officially enrolled in the University of Leyden.

UNIVERSITY YEARS

Starting with his university years, Groen's personality begins to emerge more clearly. First of all, we must note his choice of studies. He enrolled in both the Faculty of Letters and the Faculty of Law. This meant that he would not become a medical doctor like his father. Willem followed his own special interest, the study of literature. Father Groen, of course, knew of this interest and approved of his son's choice. Willem's abilities in Latin had been so convincing in previous years that his enrollment in the Faculty of Letters was almost a foregone conclusion. However, literature was not a way to make a living. The study of law therefore served as a fallback position for later. Many students kept their options open in this way. Of the approximately 450 students enrolled at Leyden in those years, about 40 percent studied law. Enrollment in the Faculty of Arts accounted for only 6 percent of the total student body.[15] Groen's interest lay in this small faculty, where professors taught the literature and history of the ancient world. "History was always my favorite subject," he would later write. "Everything else in the academy was subordinate to it."[16] In the years 1818–23, Groen was able to pursue the love of his heart.

Second, we should take note of his decision regarding religion. The first year of his enrollment actually marked the completion of his catechism instruction. Until the beginning of 1818, Willem still lived at home because he was too young to go to Leyden and rent his own rooms. Still under the guidance of Rev. Dermout, he prepared to make his profession of faith in a public service. Groen was attached to the man from whom he received "excellent and orthodox" instruction in the faith—"evangelical teaching on a biblical basis," he called it.[17] The catechetical instruction was entirely in the spirit of his parents. It avoided the rocks of radicalism and focused on what was attainable. Later, with pain in his heart, Groen would disagree with Rev. Dermout, a church leader who for thirty years had served as secretary of the synod, the denomination's governing body. Groen spoke out on behalf of the Seceders and argued for the maintenance of the confessional standards in the Dutch Reformed church. In Dermout's eyes, those standards contained expressions that were hard to swallow, an opinion he made no secret of at the bicentennial celebration of the Synod of Dordt in 1817, much to the indignation of the uncompromising Calvinists in the national church. At the time, this went unnoticed by the young Groen. In 1818, at Dermout's suggestion, he read a popular treatise tinged with pious rationalism, *Groundwork of My Faith*, by the poet and magistrate Hieronymus van Alphen.[18]

On Easter Sunday 1818, Willem Groen made a public profession of faith. It signified his coming of age in the matter of his Christian faith. From now on he would be responsible for his own spiritual life. At least that is how Willem himself felt. During his college years, it was his habit to read half a sermon every morning by Van der Palm, the university chaplain and professor of oratory.[19] He also continued to read devotional literature by Van Alphen. In the diary that Groen kept for a few months in 1822, he reported on the services and the scriptural texts on which the sermon was based.[20] On October 20, 1822, Groen witnessed the baptism and profession of faith of Isaac da Costa and his wife Hannah and their cousin Abraham Capadose in the Pieterskerk.[21] It was not an everyday event, this initiation into the Reformed church of three young Jewish people who had been raised in the Sephardic synagogue of Amsterdam. The service, led by Rev. Lucas Egeling, made a deep impression on Willem, and that same day he wrote to his parents about it: "The beautiful way in which the minister conducted each part of the service; his prayers; his sermon; his warm personal address; the delicate way in which he spoke about the Jews; the weight of the step these three people had taken; the universal reverence that was present everywhere—all this made such an impression . . . !"[22] The young academic Willem Groen took the Christian faith very seriously. He made it his own.

So, we immediately get to know Willem Groen as a well-balanced and thoughtful young man—definitely not the superficial type. He disliked boisterousness and extravagant behavior. He preferred not to join either the Concordia or the Minerva fraternities, rather than become involved in their violent feud. Toward the end of his studies, we see him on a few occasions representing the student body to the city authorities of Leyden; but it was not his intention to play a prominent role in the student world. Willem devoted himself to his studies with great regularity. His schedule was as follows: mornings were devoted to study, and afternoons to attending lectures, social visits, and recreation, so that the evenings could again be spent in reading. Not that youthful pleasures were lacking. Willem had a riding horse and took pleasure rides in the area. He also took many walks, a habit he had acquired in Utrecht, and played golf with his friends. But he never lost sight of his goal: academic studies.

Several times during the second half of his Leyden period, he increased his pace to the point where he was forced to stop working. What contributed to his overwork, in addition to his concentration on his studies, was his involvement in student clubs and his participation in essay contests. Groen was a member of four different fraternities, both literary and legal, but he was most active in *Graecis litteris sacrum* (Sanctuary of Greek Literature) and *Suum cuique* (To Each His Own). In the first group, to which Johan Rudolf Thorbecke also belonged for a short time, the main activity was the reading of Plato. The second group read modern literature, especially French writers such as Rousseau and Madame de Stael. Meanwhile, essay competitions whetted Groen's appetite. He entered several, always going for gold. In 1820 he won a prize with Thorbecke for an essay on the hegemony of the Athenians. In 1821 an essay on Cicero won a prize. Thus, in the years 1818–21, Groen devoted himself to further study of classical antiquity, with a preference for the ancient Greek world.[23] From Utrecht, he continued to be encouraged by Professor Van Heusde, who followed Groen from a distance and sent him a book now and then. When, in 1821, Groen was urged by his fellow students to become chairman of *Suum cuique*, he initially refused, arguing that he had been studying mainly the classics.

Interaction between professors and students was more intimate at the beginning of the nineteenth century than it would be later, when universities became degree factories for the masses. It stands to reason that in a literary faculty of about thirty students and a handful of professors, contact could be much more personal. Students would go to a professor's house for tea, and all sorts of close relationships flourished. Willem Groen was a very popular student because of his dedication, his achievements, and his modest character. After winning his first prize, he caught the attention of Professor Elias Borger, the thirty-five-year-old wunderkind of the faculty. To the great dismay of the entire academic community, Borger died suddenly in 1821. Willem now completed his studies at the Faculty of Letters under the guidance of Professor Jan Bake.

A special bond developed with Johan Melchior Kemper, professor of law. Groen referred to him as a "fatherly friend." Kemper wanted to see Groen in Leyden as a professor of history; a year of study at a German university would prepare him for this position. When this plan began to take shape, Groen's father put a spoke in the wheel. He considered his son too young and his health too fragile to accept the position. Willem agreed, although a note of regret can be heard when he looks back on the decision: "In view of my then fragile health, I was dissuaded from going through with it by a party to whom it would not have been proper to contradict."[24]

Nevertheless, Groen sensed that a tenured position at the University of Leyden would not have given him the change of direction for which he would later be grateful. In his autobiographical sketch, he describes the milieu in which he moved as follows: "I grew up in a liberal atmosphere, especially at the Academy."[25] This liberal atmosphere was not the product of an ideology, but of the political correctness observed by the professors. They wanted nothing more than to confirm and support the existing order established in 1813. In that year, Kemper had been one of the founding fathers of the constitutional monarchy under the House of Orange. Van der Palm—once firmly in the camp of the anti-Orangist patriots in the twilight years of the Dutch Republic—was now the much sought-after spokesman to give voice to national sympathy for the new political order. Groen felt at home in this atmosphere, which could be right-of-center liberal or progressive conservative. It was the atmosphere he knew from home.

There were, however, two dissenting voices that he took with him from Leyden without being able to process them. The first was that of Willem Bilderdijk, who had been giving private lessons in Leyden since 1817. For about a year and a half, starting in January 1820, Groen attended these tutorials with his father's permission. Papa Groen could see some usefulness in them, although at the same time he warned his son not to get carried away by the poet and his paradoxes. Groen must have been on his guard, for later he regularly protested that he had never been a follower of Bilderdijk. Nevertheless, Bilderdijk, with his sharp criticism of everything that came out of the "liberal atmosphere," was of special importance to Groen. As he would later say, Bilderdijk taught him to doubt much that had previously seemed unquestionable.[26] Bilderdijk's view of monarchy as absolute, his rejection of Rousseau and the doctrine of the social contract, his criticism of popular sovereignty and the desire to legitimize authority through written constitutions—these were ideas that gave Groen a different perspective on the issues of the day. The ideas of Bilderdijk had a strong impact on him; they made him think hard and critically. Groen did not become an opponent of the constitutional order like the brothers Willem and Dirk van Hogendorp and Isaac da Costa. But neither was he finished with Bilderdijk's ideas when he finished his studies. They stayed with him, as did Bilderdijk's poetry, which he read for relaxation for the rest of his life.

Groen did not remain aloof from the struggle that Bilderdijk's students waged against the academic establishment in Leyden. Without openly taking sides, he defended Bilderdijk's right to his views. He was grateful to Bilderdijk for his teaching, and although a boy from a class-conscious social background, he was not put off by the unconventional lifestyle and living conditions of the famous poet. In fact, Bilderdijk's ascetic example of globetrotting, his principled attacks on what the majority approved of, his calm resignation to vilification and neglect, all gave Groen pause. Bilderdijk not only taught Groen to think for himself, but sometimes the shadows that fell over the man also fell over him. During his time in Leyden, Groen was not embarrassed to associate with some of Bilderdijk's most devoted and controversial followers. Nor did he distance himself from Da Costa's *Objections Against the Spirit of the Age*, which appeared in 1823, the year of Groen's graduation. He was willing to consider these views as well. It is a sign of Groen's impartiality that he was willing to consider anything that seemed worthy of consideration.

The second dissenting voice was found not outside but within the walls of the university. It came from Cornelis Jacobus van Assen. Professor Van Assen was Groen's doctoral thesis supervisor. A traditional conservative, he was strongly opposed to any further liberalization of the political arrangements in the Netherlands. Van Assen was a man of old-fashioned habits and manners, but with a keen eye and sense of humor. He drew Groen's attention to the Historical School of Law, co-founded by the German scholar Friedrich Karl von Savigny. Thus, in 1822, we find Groen reading Von Savigny "with unusual pleasure."[27] There he discovered a counterweight to the legal and political theories of the French philosophies. According to Von Savigny, law results from a process of growth that is realized only gradually in history. Laws are not made in an instant; they develop in the consciousness of a nation. Law and justice draw their vital sap from the habits and customs of a people, and they create political institutions that must be able to withstand the political storms of the day. With this vision, Von Savigny opposed the idea of creating law out of nothing, on the basis of reason alone. Law-making is not a purely rational activity, but must take into account existing historical rights. Groen embraced this view of law, a view that corresponded to his own historical approach to things. It ultimately led him to set aside Rousseau, whom he had previously "devoured." The historical nature of political institutions would remain a cornerstone of his thinking. His plan to write a dissertation on the Historical School of Law had to be abandoned, but in his second dissertation, on the Justinian Code, the same point of view is prominent.

The Antirevolutionary

GRADUATION

In January 1823 Willem Groen passed his qualifying examination in the Faculty of Letters, and in April he repeated the examination in the Faculty of Law. In between, his parents celebrated their twenty-fifth wedding anniversary. The three children, now twenty-three, twenty-one, and sixteen, were warmly united at this family celebration. The year before, Keetje had married Mari Hoffmann, a member of the Garde d'Honneur who, even before Willem's years in Utrecht, had occasionally visited the Groen home, where he made quite an impression in his smart uniform. In 1813–15 Mari had served with the cavalry in Germany and France. After the Napoleonic Wars he had joined the Rotterdam Rifles. After his military years he had joined the trading house of J. F. Hoffmann and Sons in Rotterdam. In the summer, Mari and his young wife liked to stay in *Vreugd en Rust*. He is hardly mentioned in Willem's letters or diary, for the two had few interests in common. The little that bound Mari to Willem was not enough for them to work together in later years. Their difference in tone and temperament manifested itself decades later in the Second Chamber: Hoffmann never joined Groen's antirevolutionary group. But in March 1823, the entire Groen family was still together in cordial harmony.

It was to this happy family occasion that we owe the first portrait of Willem. Apparently, it had been decided that the entire family should pose for portraits by the well-known English-born painter Charles Howard Hodges to celebrate the event. So, we also have portraits of father and mother Groen from that year. Willem's face is painted as a narrow oval and has a distinctly boyish expression, the eyes uncertain rather than confident as they look out into the world. It must have been very different from that of Mari Hoffmann, who was six years older and had already had a military career. During the silver jubilee celebrations, Willem fulfilled his duty as the eldest son by reciting a long poem in which he did not forget to praise his father's hard work and sense of duty.[28] Some of the lines were as follows:

> Where the father, daily toiling
> for his children and the land,
> owed his peace and true joy
> to his happy marriage bond.
> What has become of mortal bodies?
> love sinks not into the grave:
> offspring of a higher order,
> Love is the gift that heaven gave.

Love as "offspring of a higher order" is a Platonic element in this poem: mortal bodies perish, love is eternal. It was indeed his beloved Plato who must have been running through Willem's mind at that moment. During these same months, he had begun writing a dissertation to fulfill the requirements for a doctorate in letters. It was to be a *prosopography*, describing the Greek philosopher's personal judgments of the people who appear in his dialogues. It would deal in turn with the Sophists, the Socratics, and the Pre-Socratics. Groen had long nurtured this idea, beginning in 1819 when the Utrecht Provincial Society offered a prize for the best essay attempting such a *prosopography*. After discovering that the Society had received no submissions, Groen felt free to devote himself to the subject. His desire to complete a literary dissertation once again revealed Willem's ambition. It was certainly not necessary. Admittedly, a PhD was the normal conclusion of academic studies at that time (only a doctorate gave access to a career in law or medicine, for example), but Willem could have confined himself to defending a thesis in the field of law. However, he wanted to graduate from both faculties and put most of his emphasis on the literary dissertation.

Groen demanded a great deal of himself. In late spring, he suffered a minor breakdown and briefly toyed with the idea of abandoning the literary dissertation. But by the summer, the dissertation on Plato's *prosopography* was finished. Its basic thrust was that Plato's philosophy is not as timeless as is often assumed. In his philosophy, Plato is in dialogue with his contemporaries, and this gives his views their peculiar color and stamp. Plato has been judged too much in terms of his philosophy, Groen later wrote, and too little as a historical figure.[29] Thus, Groen's dissertation, which he dedicated to his teachers, Kappeyne and Bake, made a contribution to the history of philosophy. Then, starting that summer, he began to work on the law thesis. This was shorter and was completed in the late fall. It dealt with "the excellence of the Justinian Code as manifested in its principles." December 17 was the day of Groen's "double promotion," as he defended his two theses in succession before a public meeting of the University Senate before noon. The room was filled with students and professors. Willem was calm, answered the questions in his proverbially fluent Latin, and was awarded his degrees magna cum laude. His dissertation on Plato, in particular, attracted much attention and would find its way to recognized authorities in the field in Holland, Germany, and France. It soon led to contact with the renowned French philosopher and Plato scholar Victor

Cousin. Groen's supervisor, Bake, long kept the work handy and quoted from it in his lectures.

In the midst of all the recorded praise—from the Leyden professors, from Kappeyne in The Hague, from Van Heusde in Utrecht, from Bilderdijk, who had come to the reception afterward, and from many fellow students—one piece is missing that might have given us a clue as to the feelings of the parents. Willem's double honor must have been for them, and especially for Groen's father, the crowning of all the efforts he had made for his son. However, the only evidence we have of this is an undated letter, written shortly before the day of the defense, in which Dr. Groen expressed his reservations about some of the wording in the preface to the legal thesis. Willem wanted to dedicate this work to his parents and had submitted the text to his father. Father Groen wanted to see some changes. Some things, he warned his son, might not come across in the right way.[30] Indeed, duty and propriety ruled the doctor's world. Moreover, he did not want to spoil his talented son by lavishing praise on him. His focus on what needed to be accomplished through hard work prevented him from resting on his son's brilliant laurels. He was already thinking about the next phase: a position in society. In the years that followed, anxiety and nervous ambition about Willem's career opportunities would often determine father Groen's attitude.

2

Employment and Discoveries

AN UNCERTAIN FUTURE

WELL INTO THE NINETEENTH century, the University of Leyden was the gateway to the higher echelons of Dutch society. It overshadowed the other two academies, Utrecht and Groningen, both of which were more closely identified with their regional function. Nor could the universities in the southern Netherlands, which had been part of the United Kingdom of the Netherlands since 1815, compete with the country's oldest university. The academies of Brussels, Ghent, Louvain, and Liege did not fully develop until after the establishment of the United Kingdom. Leyden's professors advised and assisted the king in constitutional and legislative matters. Leyden was the guardian of the Dutch language and its spelling. Leyden provided the leading Protestant theologians. It was useful for career prospects to have studied at this leading "national" university. The path to a job in the civil service, at home or in the colonies, or to a position in the judiciary was shorter if you came from Leyden. Families who felt connected to the country's administrative elite preferred to send their sons to Leyden.

Nevertheless, the job market for young graduates was not rosy in the 1820s. The economy was expanding only modestly, and the number of jobs in this moderately differentiated society was limited. Doctors and preachers sooner or later found their way to a practice or a parish, but it was more difficult for lawyers. The civil service and the judiciary were small, so the only way to be gainfully employed was to open an office as a lawyer. This is what Willem Groen van Prinsterer did. Five days after graduating, he was sworn in as an attorney at the Supreme National Court. He was admitted to the bar of The Hague and assigned to an experienced attorney to mentor him in the intricacies of the profession. At university, one learned some knowledge of law, especially general legal principles; one's professional training began after graduation. At that point, a person still had to learn everything about the profession itself. A family meeting had led to the conclusion that Willem should be trained in this profession for the time being. The father's opinion that one had to gain a position in society undoubtedly influenced this result.

Willem now had to read cases and attend trials and occasionally had the opportunity to argue a case himself. He practiced law for almost four years and certainly gave the impression at the beginning that he was serious about what he now began to refer to in his letters as "my career." At first the work did not disappoint him. He wrote to Thorbecke that he found satisfaction in his work.[31] More than a year later he informed Van Assen that a law practice was better than he had thought when he was at university. But it is clear that during these years Groen made the best of the inevitable out of a sense of duty. He did not enjoy his work with heart and soul. To Thorbecke he spoke of "rigorous work" to make progress on the thorny path to legal expertise, which unfortunately left little time for literary pursuits. However, since clients were not exactly flocking to the new lawyer, he began to fill the idle hours with "historical literature."[32]

In Leyden, the young doctor had certainly not been forgotten. Was Groen quietly hoping to be appointed to the literary faculty? After the death of Professor Kemper in 1824, the Faculty of Law made Groen an offer in early 1825. Leyden's professors did not want to see their alumnus lost for the academy. In his reaction to their offer, we see a side of Groen that he would show more often during these years: he was uncertain and hesitated to accept. He was aware, he replied in a polite but wordy letter of thanks, that he would not be able to meet the demands of the position. After some flattery from Van Assen, he changed his mind and withdrew his initial refusal. His teaching assignment would be natural law, criminal law, and legal history. By the end of June, he had heard nothing, so he wrote a panicked letter to Van Assen: "What if I am appointed and have to start in September? I would not be properly prepared!" The uncertainty was a daily torment and prevented him from concentrating on his work. In the summer of 1825, however, no appointment came. The king passed him over because of his youth and because he had not yet made any significant contribution to the field of law.³³ This outcome was probably a relief, but also a sign that despite the best plans of the tenured professors, he was not destined for a chair in Leyden. Next came the Atheneum in Deventer, but Willem did not care much for living anywhere but The Hague. While Thorbecke, after moving from one German university to another, was appointed to the new University of Ghent in 1825, Groen preferred to stay at home.

For a short time, he dutifully continued his legal practice. He completed a treatise on mortgage law—unique among Groen's publications—and it looked as if the young lawyer was developing a taste for writing in the Dutch language. The subject matter, however, was to change. Groen began to publish on the political issues of the day: on an appeal to support the Greeks in their revolt against the Turks; on political factions in France; on the war in Portugal. He seems to have read the newspapers and journals of the day thoroughly. He wanted to be part of the public debate and thus strengthen "the public spirit," as it was called at the time. What had aroused his interest in politics were international affairs. The pieces he composed were first submitted to his father and Kappeyne, and sometimes to Van Assen. At a time when freedom of the press was still being debated, an error in print could have dire consequences. Leading circles in the Netherlands strongly objected to anything that suggested division and partisanship, recalling the discord of the Patriot era. But Groen had a knack for expressing his opinions without antagonizing people.

And yet these early writings expressed very personal views. Their author republished them many years later, describing them as "my first contributions to the periodical press." They reveal that the twenty-five-year-old political commentator was already thinking within intellectual frameworks that would remain his trademarks. His discussion of "constitutional Portugal," which was in danger of being annexed by Spain, focused on the duty of the European powers to nip the revolution in the bud. Revolution had brought war to Europe; now everything should be done to keep the peace. "The days of revolutions are not over, and the world faces new storms. The electric charge fills the firmament, and it is uncertain where and when the thunderbolts will strike."³⁴ Groen could still speak this way many years later, only in less swollen language. In 1826, however, he is still very much a child of his time in the positions he takes and the remedies he offers. He called on his countrymen to unite around the "constitutional throne." He identifies "ultra-liberals and ultra-royalists" as the true polarity in Europe; these are the parties, he writes, that are constantly at loggerheads and causing unrest everywhere. But why, asks the young Groen, do people not learn from history? "Such conflicts of opinion have so often plunged the world into misery, and yet, after trying every extreme, men have always had to resort to moderate positions." Our small country has always been great at practicing moderation, and that is why the Netherlands is unmistakably a safe haven amid "the revolutions that rage around us."[35] Thus the essay concludes with the self-satisfaction that the moderate elite of the day always welcomed.

With all this passion for political issues, it became increasingly clear that Willem's future did not lie in the legal profession. Groen's father also began to realize this and began to look for new opportunities. His thoughts turned to the king's cabinet, where officials carried on preparatory work for the benefit of the monarch. Shortly after the summer of 1826, Dr. Groen, having heard that there would be vacancies in the cabinet as a result of a reorganization, had a conversation with Secretary of State Jean Gijsbert de Mey van Streefkerk. He told Streefkerk that his son would be "very happy" to consider an appointment. Whether Willem himself saw it that way was another matter. He had no particular ambitions, and civic responsibilities did not appeal to him. He would just as soon devote himself to subjects of his own choosing, studying and writing about them. He left things to his father and took few initiatives himself. In the fall of that year, he returned in high spirits from a visit to Paris, where he had met Victor Cousin, attended the opera, and paid his respects at Rousseau's tomb. That fall, he returned to his hobby of reading books. He enjoyed living at home on the Korte Vijverberg or staying at *Vreugd en Rust*. He now began to focus on modern Dutch history, on which he gave occasional public lectures, the most important of which was entitled "Reasons for Making the History of the Nation Known." These lectures were imbued with the spirit of Romanticism, and in particular the ideas of Johann Gottfried Herder: the past speaks the language of great deeds, and knowledge of them binds a people together. Groen's new orientation reflected the growing cultural interest in one's own national past. Modern historiography was gaining ground in Germany and France, and Willem believed that an active program of historical study would be an important aid to national consciousness in the Netherlands.

But Willem had to get a position, father Groen thought, and time was pressing. A talented young man who, at the age of twenty-five, was already majoring in what others considered hobbies could not possibly earn the respect of society. A great opportunity presented itself when, in December, the king issued a public invitation to "all historical and literary scholars in the fatherland" to submit "by Easter next" a sketch of how a "general history of the Netherlands" should be composed. Such a work would have to be based on "the most authentic documents," i.e., primary sources, which would still have to be made accessible. Groen threw himself into the task and by February had completed a draft of more than two hundred pages, which he discussed with Kappeyne. He was able to submit his draft well before the Easter deadline. From that moment on, he was consumed by the prospect that was likely to open up for him. What could be more wonderful than becoming an official historian in the service of the country? He and his sister Mimi often talked about it as they walked the avenues around *Vreugd en Rust*. Before spring was out, he requested an audience with the king and spoke to him about his interest in Dutch history. Meanwhile, the law practice was nominal and the university world quite distant. When Van Assen invited him in April to collaborate on a book in "good Latin," he was alarmed and hoped he could politely decline. "I am really afraid of writing in Latin," he confided.[36] There it was again: hesitation and fear of failure.

It was not until 1829 that a decision was made about a national history. No fewer than forty submissions had been received, and the king was a man who took his time to weigh the pros and cons and did not rush into a decision. This did not, of course, come as a complete surprise to Groen, for two years earlier the slow decision-making process at court had been precisely what had tormented him in connection with the vacancy left by the late Kemper. On that occasion, Van Assen had reminded him that, in his experience, the king did not tire of asking for advice and reading reports. In the summer of 1827, Groen again realized that his patience was likely to be severely tested. During these days of waiting, a short letter arrived at the Groen home. It came from Secretary Streefkerk and contained the news that His Majesty intended to appoint Willem to his cabinet in the position of clerk. It was a surprise for everyone and a bit of a disappointment for father Groen. He would have preferred to see his son appointed to the higher rank of secretary. Since Willem was in the northern town of Steenwijk at the time, courting a young woman with whom he had fallen in love, it fell to father Groen to answer the letter. He pointed out, of course, that the decision was Willem's, but he could not resist reminding the sender that in earlier contacts there had been talk of a job in the "quality" of a secretary. And while he was at it, he tried to convey another message. He mentioned that his son had "with great enthusiasm" devoted much time to the study of "his favorite subject: Dutch history," and that a combination of tasks would probably prove "unworkable."[37] By exerting this not-so-subtle pressure on the secretary of state to force a decision in the other pending matter, the Groen family betrayed their influence; but otherwise, it was a wasted effort.

Willem accepted the appointment to the cabinet, even though he was afraid of an office job of modest rank in the civil service. People think highly of it, but it is perhaps "the most slavish post" in the whole country, he wrote before his first day on the job. He had to give up his independence in exchange for working "until all hours of the night," being "tied hand and foot," and following the king "wherever he goes."[38] Nevertheless, as unpleasant as it might have been for someone who cherished his hours of quiet study, Willem had to do his duty. The post had been offered at his request; it would be ungrateful for him to decline. And there was another reason for finally overcoming his many hesitations: in the summer of 1827, Groen had found the love of his life. With her, he would have to start making a living for himself.

ENGAGEMENT AND MARRIAGE

Betsy van der Hoop was twenty years old when Willem asked for her hand in marriage. It came at the end of her visit of several weeks to *Vreugd en Rust*. Betsy attended a school in The Hague and was friends with Groen's younger sister, Mimi. She visited the Groens regularly and had most likely been courted by Willem before the extended stay at the country house. Following her positive response, events unfolded rapidly, suggesting that the cautious Willem had not been swept off his feet by a momentary infatuation. Within a fortnight he traveled north, engagement ring in pocket, to the country estate of De Bult near Steenwijk to introduce himself to the Van der Hoop family. The engagement was sealed in early August. Nine months later, in May 1828, the young couple was married in the city of Groningen. In October of the same year, Mimi married Johan Antoni Philipse. Mimi and Betsy were able to continue their friendship in The Hague.

Elisabeth Maria Magdalena van der Hoop was the daughter of Abraham Johan van der Hoop, a Groningen alderman who had died the previous year.[39] Her mother, Arnoldina Thomassen à Thuessink, was a strong personality and a deeply devout woman. Betsy had an older sister and three brothers, whom Willem got to know during the seven happy weeks he spent at De Bult. In many ways, Betsy was the opposite of Willem. She wore her heart on her sleeve, expressed herself spontaneously, and was deeply sensitive to the social needs of those around her. As a young woman, she had a tendency to be blunt and direct, which she later regretted as "rash."[40] She admired Willem's patient and quiet character, while she considered herself rather impatient. Although born and raised in a "respectable" family—there was no difference in social class between the Van der Hoops and the Groen van Prinsterers—she disliked excessive etiquette and outward show. She often violated the social codes and was quite comfortable with people from the lower classes. In the vicinity of Steenwijk, she showed an interest in the children and families of the neighboring farmers. Her relationship with the domestic servants in her own household would be informal and friendly. Betsy was not a woman of harsh and reproachful words. She had a distinct aversion to authoritarian behavior and was very grateful that Willem showed absolutely no signs of it as she got to know him.[41]

In this period of history, there was a great social divide between men and women. For women from the patrician classes, it was important to get an education, but without career prospects. A solid education was considered desirable for girls so that they would be culturally informed and valuable conversation partners for their husbands. Betsy was an intelligent woman who could write and converse in French. The range of women's knowledge could be as broad as that of men, but it was seldom very deep. It generally did not occur to women to become personally involved in politics, science, or public administration. They lacked the university education to be taken seriously in these worlds. The mere abundance of Latin words and phrases with which men peppered their speech marked the distance between them. Nevertheless, women were not merely passive. They played a large role in the running of their households and could have much to do on a practical level. This independent role sometimes formed the basis for sound judgments about the great issues of the world. Women who felt involved in what was going on in the world formed their own independent opinions about it. Betsy was such a woman. She was stimulated by her marriage, but also by her religious faith.

Betsy inherited a strong interest in matters of faith from her mother. The Bible, church attendance, spiritual conversations, and reading Christian literature were very important to her. She began to dislike the social intercourse of the circles to which she belonged, circles that had no place for these elements. A tea party or a soirée, where time was spent exchanging gossip, was a waste of time in her eyes. She shared this serious trait with

Willem, who could be terribly bored during the long dinners he had to attend at court. Her aversion to such occasions would, in the long run, keep her at home most of the time. Indeed, in the early years of their marriage, they themselves would receive few visitors. In contrast, interaction with a small circle of like-minded friends and relatives was intense. Some people complained about their lack of sociability, but Betsy and Willem were quite content to spend their days that way.

"Groen arrived where he arrived on a woman's hand," is the well-known opinion of a younger contemporary, Allard Pierson. This opinion is an exaggeration. At least it is not the case that Willem let himself be guided in everything by his wife. It also contradicts the view of the historian Elisabeth Kluit, who has intimate knowledge of the period and its characters; she writes that Betsy was a "convinced Christian without self-complacency."[42] This sounds correct in light of Betsy's rather frequent self-analysis of her shortcomings—shortcomings in zeal and faith. Willem also engaged in such self-analysis, as many Christians do from time to time. It is clear that she was a committed Christian. Betsy believed that every decision had to be made in faith, and so she did, not always foreseeing the consequences. She could not, of course, advise Willem on matters of science or politics. It was Betsy's earnest nature and her fearlessness that would become and remain Willem's guide in life as he deepened his insights and made the decisions that would determine the course of his life and career.

The news of Willem's engagement to Betsy was greeted with joy in the Groen household. The letter in which Willem told them about it caused a "sensation," his mother wrote, adding that she had shed many a tear for "a mother's happiness."[43] Willem already knew what she thought of Betsy; his mother's fondness for her was well known in the family. Father Groen was also pleased. He knew the Thomassen à Thuessink family, and an uncle of Betsy's was a professor of medicine at the University of Groningen. His usual brevity was enriched in those days by the unusually warm "Dear Willem" with which he expressed his pleasure. In other words, the son had done well. This was also the opinion of Willem's friends, whom he told the good news in letters sent from Steenwijk. Kappeyne was quick to congratulate him on this love, which was "based on rational, moral, and religious grounds."[44] Willem's old friend Jaap Dermout, now a doctor of theology and aspiring pastor, openly confessed that they had sometimes wondered if this happiness would ever fall to Willem's lot. "Whenever we talked about you and your future happiness at home or among friends who thought they knew you and your circumstances, the fear crept up on us, perhaps more than on you, that you would not easily see your heart's desire fulfilled."[45] Willem received this letter while he was still in Steenwijk. He would soon have to rush home to report to the royal cabinet.

IN THE SERVICE OF THE KING

Since 1815, King William I had reigned over two countries which, in his eyes, were united in a new union under the sovereignty of the House of Orange. At his request, the powers had added the southern Netherlands to the territory of the former Dutch Republic. The justification for this merger was a common history that began with the revolt against Spain in the sixteenth century. But as early as 1579, the Union of Utrecht and the Union of Arras had parted ways, and 236 years of separation had left their mark on the two countries. The South was predominantly Catholic and more industrial than commercial. The North was predominantly Protestant. Holland had large commercial interests and extensive overseas possessions in both the East and West Indies. Even after unification, the two populations continued to differ in interests and outlook. They remained oriented toward the cultural life of either the northern or southern Netherlands. Any intermingling occurred only with great difficulty.

In 1815, the king decided to administer his new kingdom alternately from Brussels and The Hague. This annual change of residence emphasized the duality within the kingdom, a feature that was also visible in the arrangements for parliamentary representation: the First Chamber, or Upper House, was appointed by the king, while the Second Chamber, or Lower House, was an elected body. The number of northern and southern seats in the latter was exactly the same, fifty-five each, so that the two countries remained identifiable here as well. Parliament also met alternately in Brussels and The Hague. Parliament's powers were few. In addition to reviewing bills, its most important instrument was to vote on a five-year budget. The influence of the executive, on the other hand, was considerable. William I's style of government, a blend of modern pragmatism and old-fashioned paternalism, resembled that of an "enlightened despot."[46] Paternalism and enlightenment in this case resulted in a highly centralized and top-down approach to government. The most prominent figure in this political administration was Cornelis Felix van Maanen, a man who had matured during the Napoleonic regime, served as minister of justice during the French period, and would remain in that post almost continuously from 1814 to 1842.

William I was undoubtedly a king of great insight. His efforts to modernize the economy and infrastructure of the United Kingdom of the Netherlands were considerable. He personally pushed the industrial development of the South. William thought in terms of investment projects, canals and dikes. Thanks to him, the South modernized at a rapid pace. A Protestant prince himself, he was less fortunate in his dealings with Catholics in the South. His language and education policies, which were an attack on the position of the Catholic clergy, met with great resistance from the church. In 1828, an opposition movement began to emerge, calling for more liberal measures and greater attention to "Belgian" culture.

As soon as the king encountered opposition, he began to hesitate and lose his momentum. It was his habit to let everything pass over his desk. Sixteen hours a day he worked his way through piles of documents. Not infrequently, he would get lost in the details or end up following the dictates of circumstance. His highly personal style of government was insufficient to avert the disruption of the kingdom in 1830. By doing everything himself, he failed to create the kind of political life or national enthusiasm that might have welded the two countries into a true unity. The period in which Willem Groen van Prinsterer worked at the court included the most critical years of King William I's reign.

Initially, Groen had little influence. The royal cabinet consisted of two secretaries and a few lower-ranking officials. Groen was one of the latter. The cabinet was responsible for the papers presented to the king. These could be memoranda or bills from the various government departments, called ministries; they could also be newspaper articles or other political writings. In other words, the cabinet kept the king's agenda in order for him to make decisions and keep abreast of developments. The cabinet did not initiate action itself; that was reserved for the ministries. The link between them was Secretary of State Streefkerk, the powerful head of the much larger State Secretariat, an office staffed by no fewer than ten civil servants. They saw to the implementation of the king's decisions. There was thus a close link between the Secretariat and the cabinet, although their functions remained distinct.[47] The cabinet ensured a daily flow of information to His Majesty, requiring all sorts of documents to be selected, summarized, and copied. Copying in those days was done by hand, of course, and during

Employment and Discoveries

Willem's first eighteen months in the cabinet he wore out many a quill. The salary was not bad, so Willem earned his own living.

The office work, however, was anything but appealing to the young clerk. The mechanical side of it tired him out. The hurried pace, the copying itself—he did it with great reluctance. Some days he would come home feeling "squeezed like a lemon." After a good year, he had had enough and was thinking of throwing in the towel. The only post he really wanted was that of national historian, for which he still held out hope. In a long letter to Papa, he summed up the disadvantages of his work in the cabinet: the obligation to do a lot of copying, the deterioration of his health, the sacrifice of domestic bliss, the total neglect of serious study.[48] He added that the honor and respect attached to the post were of little value to him, and that Betsy agreed with him. Father Groen clearly saw things differently. His reply began by listing the positives and concluded: "Knowing how much the advantages of the present position are appreciated by you, we trust that you will not leave it without the prospect of another, which you would consider even more preferable to yourself."[49] This was language of a different kind, and so father and son exchanged many a sigh behind the scenes. Meanwhile, Willem's activities do not betray his ambivalence about his situation. During these years, he has gained a wealth of knowledge and professional skills. In addition to his office work, he pored over the works that were crucial to the further development of his mind. His views on political and constitutional matters acquired a firmness that was at the same time deepened by personal observations and experiences while working in the nerve center of the government. In addition, he was free to publish. Toward the end of his life, he would say that the six years he spent in the royal cabinet, though spent against his own inclinations and needs, had been an indispensable training school for him.

In the late summer of 1828, shortly after his marriage, Willem Groen experienced the move to the alternate capital, from The Hague to Brussels. This always happened in October, just before the opening of the new session of Parliament. As a newly married couple, Willem and Betsy took up residence in the civil servants' quarters near the Schaarbeek gate, a short walk from the Parliament building and the Royal Palace. Here they would live until September 1829. This one year in Brussels would be of immense importance to their personal lives. They were plunged into an atmosphere of political unrest and tension that seemed remote in the North but was palpable in the South. At the same time, they became acquainted with the

Réveil, the spiritual awakening movement that was spreading throughout Europe from Switzerland. Within a few months of arriving in Brussels, Willem and Betsy discovered a young pastor, Jean-Henri Merle d'Aubigné, who was associated with the local Walloon church while serving as court chaplain. Merle d'Aubigné had been trained in Geneva, where he and a small group of theology students had been influenced by the Scotsman Robert Haldane. Merle's pastorate was characterized by biblical preaching, an appreciation of Calvin's theology, and above all, an intimate personal spiritual life. Willem and Betsy lived in the same neighborhood as the Merles and began a lifelong friendship with them. It was Merle who introduced Groen to the philosophers, historians, and theologians who wrote in the Christian tradition.

From the beginning of 1829, Willem was allowed to do most of his work at home. He had petitioned the king for this privilege. In Brussels, the workload of the cabinet was less than in The Hague, and more time could be devoted to private study. The hours that Groen worked for the cabinet were largely spent in the public gallery of the Second Chamber. Here he listened to the deliberations and prepared a written report for the king. But even here there were slow moments and empty hours, times he spent reading the books he had brought with him. Here, on Merle's recommendation, he read Edmund Burke's *Reflections on the Revolution in France*. Burke placed the Revolution in a broad historical context; his *Reflections* further deepened Groen's perspective on the Revolution, which he had gained from studying historical law. Another favorite author of his Brussels days was the Christian thinker Blaise Pascal. In addition to Pascal's *Pensées* (*Thoughts*), Groen studied *The Restoration of Constitutional Law* by the Swiss legal scholar Carl Ludwig von Haller, a work that severely criticized the political theorists of the French Enlightenment, especially Rousseau, who viewed the state not as a natural order but as a human construct.[50]

Groen developed his view of political events in the South in part with the help of this literature. Out of a strong desire to elaborate his "personal vision,"[51] he attempted to formulate premises, principles, and opinions that would help him understand the historical events unfolding before his eyes. The elaboration of a vision, the development of an interpretive framework, did not come easily to a man who always studied things from many angles: old views were never abandoned, but were covered, layer by layer, with fresh nuances. This is how he would continue to work in later life. It is not difficult to trace the growth of Groen's political and constitutional views during these years.

CALLING FOR NATIONAL CONSCIOUSNESS

To underscore his undiminished historiographical ambitions, Groen published the text of the public lecture he had given two years earlier: *Reasons for Making Known the History of the Nation.* Then, in March 1829, he sat down in his Brussels home to compose a work that addressed a burning issue of the day: *National Consciousness and Public Spirit.* He had been prompted to write this pamphlet by his growing irritation with the opposition of liberal and Catholic newspapers and parliamentarians in the South. More specifically, he was provoked by a Belgian member of the Chamber, G. J. A. Baron de Stassart, who earlier that year had attacked the idea that Dutch, the language of the Netherlands, should be the national language. According to De Stassart, French had always functioned as the national language in Belgium, even though French was dominant only in the southern, Walloon part of the country.[52] De Stassart was in direct opposition to the language policy of William I, who wanted Dutch to become the accepted language throughout the United Kingdom and who personally spoke Dutch as a rule, even in the South.

As opposition to the king's policies and person grew in the South, Groen became increasingly concerned about the lack of a strong response from the North. If the goal was to truly weld the Netherlands into a national unity, the Dutch would have to shed their provincialism and political apathy. The German theologian Tholuck once exclaimed after a visit to Holland: "The Dutch are all sleepyheads."[53] Does this also apply to politics? As a Hollander living in Brussels, Groen had a good sense of the difference in mentality between North and South, and of the lack of interest on the side of Hollanders in what was happening in the new parts of the kingdom. In correspondence with Van Assen and Kappeyne, he gathered information about the mood in The Hague. "What do people say about the political questions? Are they being discussed at all, or could people care less that we must gradually bow under the scepter of a couple of Brabantish demagogues and fanatics?"[54] Indeed, Groen wrote his *National Consciousness and Public Spirit* to protest against the "lukewarmness" of the Hollanders.[55] He issued a call to give form to a common policy and a truly national life.

Groen begins his essay with an important distinction: political unity is not the same as national unity. A state is formed by a "collection of people subject to the same administration."[56] It is therefore an external bond that does not yet say anything about the nature and quality of national life. How can both be strengthened? National unity is strengthened by the sense of belonging to a community of fellow citizens. Political unity is strengthened by the consciousness of belonging to a "union of subjects and citizens." The first, Groen calls "national consciousness" or "national spirit" (*volksgeest*); the second, he calls "public spirit" or "civic spirit" (*burgerzin*). Both should work together to create a national unitary state that is strong and durable. In the present United Kingdom of the Netherlands, however, both are weak. This is the conclusion of Groen's analysis. The purpose of his pamphlet is to identify the means of strengthening both the national and the public spirit.

As Groen goes on to discuss the national spirit that should permeate the United Kingdom, he expresses his firm belief that there is a Dutch nation living in both parts of the country, and that a "Dutch nationality" is not limited to the northern territories. The Dutch and the Belgians are descended from "the same Dutch people." This is Groen's strongest argument. He defines Dutch nationality in terms of a common blood relationship or common ethnic roots. This is the natural and necessary basis of any nation, he posits, and this basis is identifiable here. The Dutch people, however, were divided; the southern half was unable to develop in accordance with its own nature, while the northern half had the opportunity to do so. Holland—as Groen meant the Seven United Netherlands or the Dutch Republic—achieved an "unparalleled height of prosperity and glory, and preserved and refined what belonged to its distinctive character." It must also be made to flourish again in the South. There, the Dutch nationality has been preserved in the language spoken by a large part of the population. Whatever belongs to the national character must therefore be nurtured in the North and strengthened in the South. And how? By maintaining the Dutch language, promoting Dutch literature, publishing the history of the Netherlands, and preserving national customs.

The pamphlet was an appeal to the national spirit of the northern Dutch. They were flattered to be told that they belonged to the "refined Dutch nation."[57] The work was less flattering to the southern Dutch. The French spoken by the leading circles of the South stood in the way of a healthy national development: by their orientation toward French culture, Groen's message went, the upper classes were prejudiced against the Dutch nationality. This was undesirable for several reasons. First, it was no way to foster a common national life: the "body politic" would be without a "soul."[58] Second, French culture was not so innocent. French culture aspired to supremacy. Soon the French language and customs will be the vehicle of French arms. This, Groen writes, we have learned from the experience of the

Revolution. Thus, according to this reasoning, the defense of the kingdom begins with the preservation of truly Dutch customs and morals. In the Second Chamber, therefore, Dutch should be the only official language, and not French, as is currently the case, at least in Brussels. By accommodating the language of the southern deputies, Groen argued, the northern deputies had already capitulated. Full of sarcasm he remarked that for those "who one day wish to become statesmen in the Kingdom of the Netherlands, a long stay in Paris will be the best preparation; saturated with French literature, they need not be acquainted with Dutch literature."[59]

But Groen also took the "Hollanders" to task, by which he meant the inhabitants of the northern Netherlands. They have little public spirit. They like to leave public administration to others and are reluctant to get involved in public affairs unless they are asked to do so. "When one thinks of the difference between the Belgians and the Hollanders in public spirit, one cannot help wishing either for more life among the Hollanders or for more moderation among the Belgians."[60] But how to stimulate public spirit in the North? A newspaper would help. But while several newspapers in the South contain inflammatory editorials every day, there are none at all in the North. Moreover, scholars should pursue their erudite learning "in much closer relation to daily life."[61] These things are to be found among the English, with their practical inclinations, but not in the Netherlands. Groen concludes his essay by emphasizing once again that "national consciousness," if it is to survive and flourish, cannot do without "public spirit."

Was Groen aware that his pamphlet, unmistakably addressed to his compatriots in the North, was itself a voice from the North? To describe Holland as the most refined part of the Dutch nationality was not exactly a compliment to the South, which was already under the impression that it was dominated by the North. Even less complimentary was the remark that, unlike the South, the nation in the North had not "callously and passively" bowed under "the scepter of Napoleon" and had not waited for the yoke to be removed in 1813, but had thrown it off of its own accord.[62] Did Groen not realize that he was using northern prejudices against the South? In any case, he was only passing on the view that prevailed in the circle around William I and that Groen took for granted. Unity of language was essential for the kingdom established in 1815. Groen was not the first to publicly advocate this view. In 1818 it was Jan Frans Willems, the future leader of the Flemish movement, who in his poem "To the Belgians" had argued strongly for the restoration of the Dutch language in the South:

> The language of the subject and the language of the state
> will be the same again, for the good of the whole.
> The villagers will no longer be asked in French for
> their hard-earned pennies for the good of all.⁶³

Jan Frans Willems would soon discover that unity of historical interpretation was just as difficult as unity of language. In August 1829 he delivered a public lecture in Leyden and Amsterdam in which he blamed William of Orange and the uncompromising Calvinists of the sixteenth century for the schism of 1579.⁶⁴ His audience was shocked, and northern indignation was his lot.

The pamphlet on public spirit was better received in Holland. Although it appeared anonymously, a small circle knew who the author was. Van Assen had sent the manuscript to the printers and then, at Groen's request, sent review copies to certain newspapers in the North.⁶⁵ The pamphlet received positive reviews in a number of newspapers. Thorbecke, who lived in Ghent, also entered the public debate, read Groen's pamphlet, and resumed his correspondence with Groen. *National Consciousness and Public Spirit* marks Groen's breakthrough into the world of political journalism. It also indicated that his own public spirit was now more strongly aroused than ever. When it soon became clear that the king would award a prize for his treatise on "The History of the Nation" but would not appoint a national historian, Groen shifted his attention to political and constitutional issues. This shift was confirmed around this time by his appointment as secretary to the cabinet. The promotion helped Groen to reconcile himself for the time being with his career as a civil servant. As secretary, he was in direct contact with the king, for it was the secretary who personally delivered the documents to the king and could add verbal explanations if His Majesty so wished. In this capacity, Groen was directly involved in the affairs of state, albeit mostly as a spectator, since his status required the utmost discretion. His free time for study was gone again, and some days Groen worked the same long hours as the king. But he was happy to be one of the men directly behind William I's chair.

BACK IN THE HAGUE

In October 1829, Willem and Betsy moved back to The Hague. This time it was for good, for after August 1830, when the Belgian Revolt broke out, the government would never return to Brussels. Father Groen had

Employment and Discoveries

bought a house on the Korte Voorhout. In the fall of 1832, Willem and Betsy would make their own choice and move to a house on Plein Square. At that time, The Hague was a city of about fifty thousand inhabitants. It had wide avenues and spacious squares, but nothing very monumental. To foreigners, the city seemed rather dull and monotonous.[66] There was no cultural life with entertainment such as opera and concerts, as there was in Paris and Brussels. The bourgeois lifestyle was domestic, and when people went out, it was usually to attend a lecture or sermon, rarely anything else. The level of musical life was low, and attempts to improve it went unnoticed by the Groens. By his own account, Willem had little ear for music and never seemed to long for it. What The Hague did have was a royal museum, the Mauritshuis, with Italian, Spanish, German, and Dutch masters.

For the young couple, returning to The Hague meant, above all, being reunited with the family and friends they had so eagerly anticipated. In August, Mimi gave birth to their first child. It was a boy, Pieter, named after father Groen. Almost two years earlier, Keetje had given birth to a daughter, Jacqueline, whose other names honored mama Groen. Betsy became very involved with the children as they grew up, helping out with Mimi's family from time to time. It was at this time that the prospect of remaining childless began to dawn on her. "I don't think I've ever waited so long to answer one of your letters," she wrote to her friend Marianne van Hogendorp shortly after her return to The Hague.

> But there was something toward the end of your letter that made me realize, dear Marianne, that you do not yet know me. Do you really think that with all the happiness I enjoy now, I feel entitled to even greater happiness? . . . There are moments when I think that it must bring great happiness to have children; but to tell the truth, I never had an unpleasant feeling when I saw Mimi's baby. . . . When I hear Madame de Stael speak of her father, it makes me want to have a child, to have it brought up by one who would make such an excellent father in my eyes. Whenever I see that truly angelic child of Keetje's, I could wish to have such a child myself. . . . But the greater happiness of another will never, I hope, cause me any trouble or make me unhappy. I am fully persuaded of God's love, not because I am entitled to it, but only because of the blood of Christ, in which alone I place all my hope; and I believe, by God's Holy Spirit, that not only my head is persuaded, but that my heart also feels His love. Whether children always increase the happiness of life, I will not decide; I do not need to know, as long as God's love is sufficient for me. But if having children really brings

such great happiness, I think I should not want them for that reason, since I already have so much, and too much happiness is often a very great temptation.[67]

She seems to have resigned herself early to remaining without children of her own. We do not know what Willem's feelings were about this; not a single utterance of his has survived in which he comments on it.

During these years, a special bond would develop between Willem de Clercq and his wife, Caroline. Since 1824, Willem de Clercq had been the executive secretary of the Dutch Trading Company (*De Nederlandsche Handelmaatschappij*) at its headquarters in The Hague. There had been contacts before the Groens left for Brussels, but the relationship would not be solidified until after their return. That this friendship could develop had everything to do with Willem and Betsy's experiences in Brussels. It was there, in the Walloon church with Merle d'Aubigné, that their faith life had deepened. They also found the intense spiritual life that was so dear to them with Willem and Caroline de Clercq. Willem de Clercq came from a Mennonite family in Amsterdam. He was a very sensitive man who carefully recorded the state of his inner life. A poet with the extraordinary gift of improvising in rhymed verse, he came into contact with Isaac da Costa, who played a major role in his spiritual development. In The Hague, he finally followed his wife and joined the Walloon church. It was here, in the fall of 1829, that they were reunited with Willem and Betsy. The Groens were greatly blessed by the ministry of Isaac Secrétan, the Swiss pastor who had come to the church in 1828 and soon attracted large crowds.[68] A shared appreciation for the Walloon Rev. Secrétan would strengthen the bond of friendship that was beginning to grow between the Groen and De Clercq families, a bond that became very close and intimate. After the De Clercqs moved back to Amsterdam in 1831, the couple maintained an intense correspondence. Betsy, whom Willem de Clercq called "my soul mate," was the champion, with 371 letters in fourteen years. Her husband wrote another 211 letters over the same period.[69]

In 1831, Betsy and Caroline de Clercq founded a sewing school for girls from underprivileged families. There was room for twelve girls whose parents were "unable to pay for any of their education." Classes included Bible reading, prayer, and singing. In addition, once established in The Hague, Betsy put time and effort into purchasing housing for the elderly. The many concerns in her own household as well as outside her home kept her busy, as evidenced by comments such as "I have little time today" in letters that took several days to complete or were abruptly signed off. Because of their many activities and their fastidiousness in making new acquaintances, Willem and Betsy's circle of friends remained small. Willem spoke with some self-deprecation of the "domestic habits" that made him such a couch potato.[70] Through the De Clercqs, they came into contact with a number of Réveil people from Amsterdam, men and women who were participating in the religious revival that was sweeping Western Europe in those years, with its emphasis on Bible reading and personal devotion. Da Costa and Koenen were particularly prominent among them. Koenen visited Groen in The Hague, and in the fall of 1829 the Groens first met Da Costa at the De Clercqs' home while they were still living in The Hague. According to De Clercq, Betsy was "very animated" with the ladies that evening, telling them with delight about Merle d'Aubigné.[71] The men, who sat apart, talked about historical subjects and the royal family. Groen later remarked that it had been somewhat risky, in his capacity as cabinet secretary, to meet the author of the anti-constitutional *Objections Against the Spirit of the Age*.[72] But after his resettlement in The Hague, he immediately demonstrated that he wanted to steer his own course. The time available to him in addition to his official activities in The Hague was used to work out a new plan: the publication of a political journal.

NETHERLANDIC REFLECTIONS

In *National Consciousness and Public Spirit*, Groen had already expressed the need for political newspapers in the North. In the South, journalism had become a force that threatened the government. Government circles were upset and angry about the "attacks" on the king's administration. Several southern Dutchmen were fined or imprisoned for writing newspaper articles that were deemed seditious or libelous. Minister of Justice Van Maanen considered the possibility of restricting the freedom of the press while at the same time responding to the opposition newspapers with a countervailing journalistic voice. A government-sponsored newspaper, the *Gazette de Pays-Bas*, appeared in the South from 1827, but it was filled with official announcements and summaries of parliamentary debates and was unable to parry the attacks of the free Belgian press. Van Maanen, always an advocate of a firm line, therefore wanted to intervene and replace the *Gazette*'s editorial board, but he met with resistance from the southern Dutch ministers. The king vetoed the plan, but Groen, who had been appointed cabinet secretary, revived the issue. In November 1829, he surprised the king with a memo on the "dangerous situation" in which he said, among other things, "In view of the pernicious influence of the journals, we must have well-appointed government dailies. The government must have its recognized defenders, because they can speak with greater authority and credibility in many respects."[73] This idea, which was shared by others, would lead to the creation of the government newspaper *Journal of The Hague*.

But there was another possibility. It was alluded to by the king when he told his ministers in late 1828 that he thought "private newspapers" were better suited to defend "the actions of the government."[74] In this way, the king hoped to create a free press that would be supportive of the government. This was also Groen's hope—if possible, even more so. The kingdom was in a "very precarious position," he wrote to Van Assen; "the most important thing now is to keep the Dutch and Protestants united."[75] The "private newspaper" that Groen launched in October 1829, and of which he was the editor-in-chief, sought to accomplish this very goal: *Netherlandic Reflections*. The plan was first born in Brussels. There Groen had discussed it with Anthony van Rappard and Johan Hora Siccama. He knew Van Rappard as an official in the Ministry of Education. Hora Siccama was employed at the High Military Court in Utrecht. Groen had tried to recruit Siccama as editor-in-chief of the new journal in April. He and Van Rappard would contribute articles—anonymously, of course. Groen was well aware of the restrictions under which he would have to work: "A civil servant intent on anonymously censuring the government whose trust he has, I do not, as a rule, consider commendable and he who does it openly usually deserves to be dismissed."[76]

However, the idea of having Siccama in a leading role never came to fruition. Siccama admired Groen because of his Leyden reputation, but Groen himself was unsure and hesitant. Groen, however, did not give up his plan. After a few months, the secretary of the royal cabinet overcame his scruples. He was now ready to take the lead himself, and toward the end of August he outlined to his friends his final plan for a journal "in which we would examine the events in our country according to firm principles, with a definite aim and according to a definite plan."[77] These principles were the defense of constitutional monarchy; the preservation of Protestantism ("not as a cloak, either for a fainthearted deism, or for a Christian morality that omits the essence of Christianity"); and "the preservation and strengthening of all that is Dutch." Two of these principles came as no surprise to the readers of *National Consciousness and Public Spirit*. It is doubtful that the friends realized the significance of Groen's Protestant principle, which was even supposed to be rooted in a return to "the purity of revelation." From now on, however, Groen would include this principle in *Netherlandic Reflections* to be disseminated.

The first issue of the journal appeared on October 2, 1829. For the first few years, it was printed about twice a week in The Hague and could be ordered "at the principal booksellers and all the post-offices in the kingdom." The first issue set the tone for the polemic. It had begun:

> For some time now, the south of the kingdom has been dominated by a very dangerous faction. . . . Liberalism has become the common rallying point. . . . The Dutch nation is being distorted in the image of the French nation. . . . The constitutional throne, the religion of Protestantism, and the Dutch character are equally endangered. . . . The Netherlands must defend itself against the threat from the south. To this end a fixed course must be followed.

The paper had two guiding ideas about the course to be followed. It was clear to Groen that the government had to take a firm stand against the "faction" of Catholics and liberals in the South from the beginning. The government should not waver or give in, but should stand firm. This was the line of thought that people identified with Van Maanen, whom some people in the South suspected of being the author of *Netherlandic Reflections*. The second guiding idea was that the government's own approach could only be strong and confident if it was guided by clear principles. The call for ministerial responsibility and the slogan of popular sovereignty had to be countered by the fundamental principle of constitutional monarchy. The demands of the Catholic clergy had to be answered with Protestantism and religious freedom. French culture and language had to be countered with what was truly Dutch.

Groen went to great lengths to keep his editorship a secret. The opposition press would howl if it learned that the paper was actually conceived in the bosom of the government. Keeping it a secret from the king, who probably preferred not to see his secretary involved in press activities, caused Groen some headaches. What would be the consequences if the king ever found out? Meanwhile, with the boldness of youth, he explained his point of view to Van Assen, who soon became more of a supporter than his two fellow editors:

> I am defending principles which, in my personal conviction, I believe to be essential. The general tenor of these principles is to support and strengthen the government, and therefore, so far from being incompatible with my present position, I seem to me to be fulfilling a duty which rests equally upon officials and the rest of the citizens. It is a real pleasure for me to enjoy the King's favor, but my aim is above all to do what I believe to be true and beneficial for the fatherland. There is much in my office that pleases me; but if I cannot work there for the purpose, I have set for myself, I am not much attached to it.[78]

Given the mood in government circles, Groen had seized his chance. The civil servant, who had to observe his place every day, was also a personality with an independent mind, who created for himself a platform from which to advise the government on the course it should take. The *Netherlandic Reflections* were a stimulus for Groen to develop his own political ideas. These ideas also began to guide his work in the cabinet. The memoranda he now submitted to the king on the increasingly threatening situation in domestic politics did not deviate from the insights he had conveyed to his press.[79] Even more forcefully, Groen urged the king to act in accordance with these insights. "The opinion is growing in the North," he wrote in November 1829, "that the government must act as the protector of true principles." This was the only way to calm revolutionary spirits. "The fatherland can be saved by national spirit, patriotic enthusiasm and Dutch energy—by these means alone; and it is not difficult for Your Majesty to arouse these feelings."[80]

Groen did indeed succeed during these months in getting the king to issue a public proclamation in this vein. This became the oft-quoted royal proclamation of December 11, 1829, which accompanied the new, stricter press law. The press law was the work of Van Maanen; the proclamation was inspired by Groen. The king proclaimed that the Netherlands was a monarchy, that the desired ministerial responsibility would not strengthen public authority, and that the government would uphold the constitution. Every official in the realm was required to sign the proclamation. Groen regretted that the king's Declaration of Principles had been accompanied by the Press Act, which dealt a blow to the free press in the South in particular. Groen himself was not an advocate of restricting the press, but rather of making good use of it. Groen blamed the fact that the Royal Proclamation ultimately bore little fruit on the government's own failure to abide by it.

He never tired of proclaiming in the *Netherlandic Reflections* that the king's message had been a good start, but that it needed to be followed up.

The strong language of *Netherlandic Reflections* was met with criticism and resentment in the South.[81] It inflamed passions even further. Southern administrators blacklisted the journal and complained that the press in the South was being restricted while this northern paper continued to publish. Groen received a warmer reception from a circle of readers in the North. It was not a large circle. People in general showed little interest in politics. Only a small part of the elite read such journals. As early as January 1830, while Groen was still busy writing the first of the agreed forty issues, the publisher informed him that the subsidy had to be increased. It was Van Rappard who then agreed to try to improve the financial arrangement, apparently to everyone's satisfaction, for after this episode Groen managed to get two more series of forty issues each from the same publisher by the spring of 1832.

Soon, however, Groen's collaborators began to disappear from view. The issues were mainly filled by Groen. The other two men were only too happy to acknowledge that it was Groen's paper. They submitted their articles from time to time, but it soon became apparent that their editor-in-chief did not always publish them, preferring to do everything himself. He wanted to give his *Netherlandic Reflections* a clear profile. This profile was also recognized. Siccama reported how the paper was received in Utrecht: "It is monarchist; it is pro-government; or sometimes: it is Bilderdijkian."[82] That the paper was not liberal became clear when its pages declared that it opposed the "liberal theories" that separated religion from politics. *Netherlandic Reflections* aimed to "recommend a Christian Netherlands under the scepter of the House of Orange."[83] These were words that warmed the hearts of Koenen, De Clercq, and Da Costa. They had learned of the editor's identity through the grapevine and, along with Van Assen, were among the subscribers who sent in their reactions.

This response was important for Groen's own development. The issue that launched the second series, begun in April 1830, was entirely devoted to the religious foundation of the state. "God, King and Country! Let religion be our beginning. The Netherlands must be Christian."[84] Shortly before, Da Costa had written him a long letter expressing his approval and wishing that *Netherlandic Reflections* would bear even stronger witness to the Christian principle.[85] Groen apparently took this to heart. Burke's emphasis on religion as a pillar of the state was probably also on his mind. In any case, the second series, more than the first, emphasized religion and religious belief as a defense against the "errors" of the "faction." Groen's interest in Bilderdijk was also rekindled. Bilderdijk's fulminations against the thinkers and ideas behind the French Revolution took on a prophetic air for Groen in the days of the Belgian Revolt. Meanwhile, southern parliamentarians were beginning to raise serious questions about the content of *Netherlandic Reflections*. Willem de Clercq noted in his private diary that people in Brussels scoffed at the "religious nature" of the paper.[86]

THE BELGIAN REVOLT

The bomb exploded in the South in the summer of 1830. Toward the end of August, in an echo of the July Revolution in Paris that had put the citizen-king Louis Philippe on the French throne, riots broke out in Brussels. Other cities soon followed. The homes of ministers and civil servants and government buildings were attacked. Windows were smashed and large crowds filled the streets. The riots were quelled by the installation of vigilante committees, which in this way gained a position of power. It soon became clear that these committees were harboring well-known Belgian opponents, who began to demand, in French of course, that the government redress their grievances. Indeed, power was now in their hands. Within a few weeks, the first signs of Secession began to appear. William I, unable to assert his authority in the South by military means, made some concessions, including the dismissal of the hated Van Maanen. But these concessions could not turn the tide. In mid-September, the king's two sons were sent to the South at the head of an armed force, but Prince Frederick failed to gain control of Brussels. The army's shameful retreat from the capital was a victory for the Belgians. By the end of September, the Belgians had formed a provisional government. The talk of the day quickly turned to the terms of Secession, the future of the dynasty, and the role of the Alliance of the Great Powers—Britain, Prussia, Austria, Russia.

Groen felt that events were confirming his predictions. "After the revolution in France, it was easy to foresee similar upheavals in other countries, and neighboring Belgium, so largely Gallicized, was soon bound to be swept off its feet by a seductive example, even if there had been no conspiracy of any kind."[87] That the king's authority had been undermined and ignored was the result of liberal views that the government had failed to oppose. Groen's recommended course of action for the time being was also along the lines he had outlined earlier. The government should exude "moral strength" and be firmly united. It should not negotiate with the "rebels," because that would mean recognizing the principle of popular sovereignty. The dismissal of the "loyal and honest" Van Maanen was already a questionable concession in this direction. Until mid-September, Groen believed that the rebellion could still be put down. But the king wasted time gathering advice and ordering conflicting measures. It bothered Groen that the king continued to do everything personally, and that he now wrote in his journal in clear terms that what was needed was a "Ministry" that could act with unity and force.

It was this public criticism that prompted Groen to tender his resignation as cabinet secretary. The letter was written and submitted on the evening of September 18. Groen had come into conflict with his own basic rule that no civil servant had the right to criticize the government, even anonymously. His letter explained that "principles which he could neither conceal nor deny" compelled him to resign.[88] That same Saturday night, in a letter justifying his decision to his parents, he wrote that staying on would put him in a "totally wrong position."[89] The very next day, however, his request for an honorary discharge was off the table. Between the two services that day, Groen was invited to a brief conference with Streefkerk, who was able to tell him that the king would very much regret his departure. Groen, who was always grateful for a personal favor from the king, felt his conscience had been cleared, and that Monday he resumed his work as before. He never learned what the king thought of *Netherlandic Reflections*. He got the impression that they had no influence on the course of events. A few months later, in one of his memos to the king, Groen alluded to his close relationship with the paper. Again, there was no reaction.

What did the cabinet secretary think of the events that followed? As soon as Prince Frederick and his troops had left Brussels, it was all over as far as Groen was concerned. "Let no one entertain any more illusions," he wrote; "the Kingdom of the Netherlands is torn in two."[90] Under the terms of the Vienna settlement of 1815, the Great Powers (England, Austria, France) were obliged to intervene. But they, too, accepted the *fait accompli*. For Groen, the important thing now was for the Netherlands, pushed back into its old territory, to declare its independence, protect the constitution, and rally around the throne. Groen, however, did not come up with any concrete proposals, and in the fall of 1830, he resigned himself to the inevitable sooner than Thorbecke. During these months, Thorbecke, who had fled Ghent in September, repeatedly contacted Groen. According to Thorbecke, the South should not be abandoned so quickly. He believed that the United Kingdom of the Netherlands should be preserved and that the Great Powers should intervene on the basis of international law. In principle, Groen shared this view, but he considered it totally unrealistic. "The thinking that dominates our age," he wrote, "nullifies the correct conclusion of many logical arguments."[91] There are spiritual forces that cannot undo history. "The fight against false ideas has been waged weakly; now we are dealing with armed mobs." The following year, the North continued to hope for help from the Great Powers, but many were relieved to finally be rid of the troublesome Belgians. Groen realized that after 1830 his *Netherlandic Reflections* no longer commanded a circle of Great Netherlanders. He did not change his message to the smaller Netherlands.

ANTIREVOLUTIONARY PRINCIPLES

As the flow of events from the Belgian-Netherlands front gradually slowed, the content of Groen's correspondence changed. In 1830 it was dominated by political activity, knee-jerk reactions to the latest news, and excited letters from Groen's circle of friends. From 1831 on, the phase of processing everything that had happened in the past years began. Groen himself increasingly took stock of his spiritual development. In letters to Siccama, Van Rappard, and also Thorbecke, he mentions the Christian faith and asks them where they stand in relation to it. It seems to be the dominant theme in Groen's own mind at this time. Everything he has ever learned and experienced he now wants to look at from this new perspective. He explains what he is seeking by saying that he wants to exchange the conviction of his mind, his "historical faith," as it was then called, for the assurance of faith in his heart. The word "seeking" is not just a spiritual stopgap for notorious doubters. Groen is aware that he has undergone a transformation and has come to a defining moment in his personal development.

He described this change in a long letter to his friend Van Rappard in November 1831. After recounting how he had been privileged to have had a "very religious education," the aim of which had been "to convince the understanding and the desire to be virtuous in order to serve and gain respect," he moved on to his formative years after university.

> After leaving the Academy, I continued to observe the outward forms of religious obligation, but without any particular interest,

and engaged in various studies, always considering religion as something separate rather than as a principle of life which should be united and interwoven with our whole existence. In the last three or four years, a number of circumstances have combined to give me an entirely different perspective on the matter. Among these circumstances, you will feel, I include my marriage, the acquaintance and fellowship with men like Merle, Secrétan, and De Clercq, and finally the publication of the *Netherlandic Reflections*, which forced me to think more and more about the causes of evil, until finally the main cause, the systemic apostasy from Christianity, became clear to me. Since then, thousands of things have become clear to me that I once regarded as insoluble mysteries, and all of history has become for me one continuous confirmation of the truths revealed in Scripture.[92]

Groen here speaks of a discovery that caused him to see many things differently. If we try to locate this discovery, it must have been in the summer of 1831. In the spring of that year the Merles were in The Hague. They had fled Brussels because it was becoming unsafe for them; the district where they and the Groens had lived was the scene of the most violent disturbances. Naturally, the conversation that summer revolved around the question of how to make sense of the revolutionary events. What were the motives and forces that drove people to such actions? It was at this time that Groen came to the personal conclusion that the liberal theories, which he had so often characterized as revolutionary propositions in mitigated form, were not only incompatible with the Christian faith but were themselves rooted in unbelief.

Groen's discovery was now that the antithesis between faith and unbelief had to be seen as the preeminent conflict in history. He discovered that unbelief, too, is a dynamic force that sets everything on fire—no less dynamic than Christian faith when it is a principle of life. In the spring of 1831, concluding the second series of the *Netherlandic Reflections*, he wrote, "Terrible, but also wonderful and majestic is the world crisis that has lasted for more than forty years. What is the main cause of the calamities under which so many nations are now sighing? That God . . . has been excluded from the State."[93] Half a year later, he wrote of an even deeper cause: unbelief as the motivating force that compelled its adherents to make different political choices.

Once Groen had made a decisive choice, he wanted to see it reflected in his surroundings. He was more successful with Van Rappard than with

Siccama or Thorbecke. Van Rappard stayed in contact with Groen and met Secrétan at his instigation. Siccama found more comfort in philosophy than in religion. Groen had a conversation with Thorbecke that taught him that "on the main question" they did not agree.[94] For Groen, the Bible was "God's revelation." Thorbecke admitted that he found it difficult to discuss these matters, even with his most trusted friend, because "differences of opinion disturb the most tender chords." But he stated his conviction that divine truth is not to be found in Scripture alone. Trained in German philosophy, Thorbecke believed that there was also an independent "law of order" in reality. In order to know what to do in the political realm, one had to begin with the state, not with Scripture. So, his method was different from Groen's. Moreover, Thorbecke wrote, he was not attracted to Protestant Christianity. Protestantism still seemed to him to be "much too limited and much too backward." The difference in perspective expressed here did not lead to a rupture in their relationship. It did, however, later lead to opposing positions in the political arena. From 1831 on, this would no longer surprise the two protagonists.

Groen articulated his new insights in a series of articles in the *Netherlandic Reflections* from late September to late November 1831 under the collective title *Overview*. When he reprinted these articles many years later, he noted that they were a "sketch" of what would later be set forth in his book *Unbelief and Revolution*.[95] The extent to which *Netherlandic Reflections* were seminal for Groen's convictions is evident from the curious announcement at the top of the opening article that *Overview* was intended to provide greater insight into "the whole system of *Netherlandic Reflections*." In other words, the "system" was not there to begin with, but could be assembled like the pieces of a puzzle at the end of the whole enterprise. The *Overview* articles were cast entirely within the framework of his new discovery: behind the "erroneous idea" of popular sovereignty lay a dominant trait of an entire age: namely, unbelief. It was unbelief that gave rise to a "false philosophy" in the eighteenth century, and from it flowed the ideas that men have sought to apply to state and society since the French Revolution. But they produced chaos and violence. There are no soft solutions. What is needed is to attack the "fatal doctrine" at its source. This requires taking a stand on the basis of the Christian religion. The revolutionary principles must be opposed by "antirevolutionary" principles! The truth was out. Groen had come clean. It was mentioned almost in passing, this reference to "antirevolutionary principles"; readers of Groen's later works would hear much more about it.

In light of this "system," should we not conclude that Groen was essentially a conservative? Was he not, when he began his *Netherlandic Reflections*, defending the monarchy and Dutch traditions in the areas of religion and culture? Had not Savigny, Haller, and Burke pushed him further in a conservative direction? These questions have never been absent from debates about Groen's intellectual roots. But the discovery that Groen made in the summer of 1831 was nothing less than the beginning of an entirely new approach to politics. To get there, he was now convinced, one had to go "one step further" than most political thinkers.[96] There are dynamic religious motives behind the ideas, and therefore it is not enough to criticize concepts like popular sovereignty and the social contract without taking this background into account. Nor is it enough to declare that public religion is a pillar of the state or to note that the common foundations are being attacked by a "religious war." These last words Groen had earlier quoted from Burke.[97] However much he owed to this "father of conservatism," the Burkean "utilitarian view of religion"[98] did not go far enough for Groen. The "one step further" that he wanted to take led to the insight that unbelief is a dynamic driving force, a new principle of life that is opposed to faith or the Christian religion. Accordingly, Groen arrived at a position that was fundamentally different from that of the conservatives. This independent position would enable him to accept a future political renewal that passed for liberal. Groen never turned against the coming liberal constitution as such. He supported freedom of the press, freedom of religion, and other civil liberties. As early as 1830, he welcomed the idea of ministerial responsibility in the face of the autocratic government of William I. Groen was not so conscious of all these things in 1830, but later it became clear that he approved of the constitutional legacy of the Enlightenment, while always rejecting the legacy of the Revolution. Thus, Groen remained a modern thinker in his time, not a counter-revolutionary like Bilderdijk, but an *antirevolutionary*.

A NEW ASSIGNMENT

If Groen himself had given up his historiographical ambitions, the king had not forgotten them. The departure and death of two superintendents of the Royal Family Archives made it necessary to find a successor. At the end of October 1831, the king appointed Groen to the post. The Royal Family Archives had been established in 1825 to collect, inventory, and make accessible the archives of the House of Orange-Nassau. William I had a vision of the importance of archival collections. The 1826 essay competition on the history of the nation did not come out of nowhere. In this respect, the nation and the dynasty were mutually exclusive. The close relationship between the two made the organization of the family archives a complicated matter. The archival records of the members of the House of Orange were not easy to distinguish from the archival records relating to the history of the Netherlands since the sixteenth century. The two members of the court—one of whom was even head butler—who were appointed to this task in 1825 performed their duties efficiently. By the time the Belgian uprising interrupted the work in 1830, a considerable amount of sorting had been done, various collections had been assembled, and an initial inventory had been taken.[99]

When Groen was appointed, little progress had been made for some time. The clerk of the archives, W. Häberling, had been called up for military service in the fall of 1830 and would not return to his post permanently until the spring of 1833. The family archives had a number of upper rooms in the palace on Plein Square at its disposal. Groen went to look every day, but soon realized that he could devote little time to his new task for the time being. In any case, there were three issues that would require his attention. First, a permanent solution had to be found for the separation of family and national documents. Secondly, the royal decree of 1828 had to be followed, which had stipulated that important parts of the family archives should be published in the interest of scholarship. Thirdly, the housing conditions of the Royal Family Archives needed attention. The archival documents were scattered in various palaces and the rooms on Plein Square would not be sufficient in the long run. This triple agenda certainly made it clear that the supervision of the family archives could no longer be considered an honorary post for some court dignitary. Groen was pleased that the king had entrusted him with this task, even though he initially saw it as an extension of his work as cabinet secretary.

Van Assen understood that this new position could become something important for Groen, and he congratulated him with his appointment. "May these archives give you material to work on" was his encouraging comment. "Thanks to your quick mind and easy comprehension, you are able to do what is not given to others."[100] For the time being, however, Groen had no concrete plans for working at the archives. It was shortly after the ultimately unsuccessful Ten-Day Campaign against the rebels in the South. The political reality of each day demanded all his attention, and the *Netherlandic Reflections* consumed all his free time. Issue 40 appeared in May 1832, concluding the third series. A trickle of issues followed, but then it stopped. Despite encouragement from Koenen and De Clercq, Groen did not continue the journal. He enjoyed expressing his views on politics, but for some time he felt that the tide had gone out. What he would rather do now was to expound his newfound understanding of the connection between faith and unbelief in a more elaborate study. It would include philosophy, religion, and history. It was not the questions of the day that needed to be clarified, but the underlying principles. This was the new task he set himself. Were Van Assen's words running through his mind? "Willem should not regret," the Leyden professor wrote, "that his appointment to the university in 1824 had fallen through, because with his free time for study he could make a much better contribution outside the university." Indeed, Groen would develop into a scholar in his own right. But before he could proceed with his plans, he suffered a serious setback.

3

Near Death's Door
and a Decision for Life

DEATH GIVES PAUSE

Like the distant boom of cannons creeping ever closer, death entered Groen's life. Beginning in 1832, death first entered his environment, then his family, and finally his own life. Whenever people died, it touched a sensitive chord in Groen, who was always so in control of himself on the outside. He was rarely thrown off balance, but when he was, it was often related to the death of a friend or loved one. This emotional side of him first emerged in December 1831, when he recorded his reaction to the death of Bilderdijk. Upon hearing the news, he was "terribly shocked."[101] The following week, he honored Bilderdijk with an "In Memoriam" in *Netherlandic Reflections*. According to the (still anonymous) author, a great man had died. The anonymity was not intended to conceal the author's sympathy: in other contexts, Groen was not ashamed to admit his affinity for Bilderdijk.

In the summer of 1832, Holland was struck by a cholera epidemic. It was the first outbreak of "Asiatic dysentery" in the Netherlands, and the disease would claim some seven thousand victims throughout the country. The hotbed of the epidemic was Scheveningen, the seaside village that hugged The Hague, and doctors' carriages rattled through the city's streets. These carriages usually passed over the doors of the wealthy, but death was everywhere, as was deep sympathy for the victims of cholera. People who contracted the disease died quickly, sometimes within a day. Deeply moved by the epidemic, Groen, on an impulse, wrote a tract for distribution among the affected people. He called it *Is It Right Not to Be Afraid of Cholera?*[102] It was a *memento mori*, "remember your death," written in simple language. "Many people are dying of cholera, and they are dying quickly. You may also die soon. It is always good to remember that, but especially when our lives are in extraordinary danger."[103] The first of several popular tracts Groen would write during his lifetime, it focused on the heart of the Christian faith, assuring readers that they need not fear the epidemic if they believed in Christ:

> Christ says: I am the resurrection and the life. Those who believe in me, even though they die, will live, and everyone who lives and believes in me will never die. Do you believe this?[104] Happy are you, my friend! Then you don't need to be afraid of the cholera anymore.[105]

The cholera epidemic subsided after half a year, but Groen did not stop thinking about death. He had never seen death with his own eyes until his mother died on December 28, 1832. At sixty, she was not yet old. She had been ill since the summer, and the family worried about her severe nosebleeds and deteriorating condition. By mid-December, things were going rapidly downhill. Willem, Betsy, and Mari Hoffmann took turns sitting up with her the last few nights. Her death shook Willem to the core. He was distraught with grief. She had been a loving mother to her only son, and Willem had felt very close to her. When it was all over, he was "extremely upset and overcome with grief," Betsy wrote to the De Clercqs.[106] We can assume that Groen was present at his mother's funeral. On the first of January he wrote his customary New Year's letter to the king, but immediately afterwards he was confined to bed with a severe attack of bronchitis. For a month and a half, he himself had to struggle with a serious illness. *Memento mori* now applied directly to him personally.

Groen's health had already proved fragile in previous years. During the winter season, he suffered from colds and other illnesses. He would complain at home, but at the same time he would push himself with piles of work. By the summer of 1832, Betsy was concerned about his "thinness and pale cheeks."[107] By the end of the year, his reserves were exhausted and he collapsed. It soon became apparent that something was seriously wrong with him. He ran a fever and coughed incessantly, robbing him of sleep. This condition lasted for more than a month and was exacerbated by the fact that he had to cough up a lot of phlegm. Betsy saw him deteriorate, and in her letters to the De Clercqs, whom she updated almost daily, she spoke of "unimaginable suffering."[108] Willem lost a lot of weight, and his slender body looked emaciated.[109] There was little the doctors could do. During the first week that Groen was bedridden, they subjected him twice to bleeding with leeches, and after that they made regular visits to pronounce his condition "highly critical." This was also the growing concern of Groen's father, who, though still mourning the death of his wife, was very concerned about his son and visited his children's new home on Plein Square as often as four times a day.[110]

Willem and Betsy had a few anxious weeks where the thought of death was ever present. Betsy walked through the house, wringing her hands in despair and praying for her husband's life, which she could not let go of. She wrote to the De Clercqs in Amsterdam:

> When I read what you have written to me, I can only say: Lord, I believe; help me with my unbelief. Willem will be better off if his soul is taken away from the troubles and struggles of this life. I often try to think that way; but I will be comforted, God willing, if it is not yet to be. Here the spirit is willing, but the flesh is too weak. The bond is so close. I had as much in him as any woman can ever have in a husband; my relatives and first friends, all were forsaken for his sake, and he made it up in so double measure. But I firmly believe that the strength of faith will surely be given to me under all circumstances, so I am waiting in prayer.[111]

The letters she received from her friends gave her great comfort. As for Willem, he prepared for the possibility that he might die. Outwardly, he remained calm. He barely spoke, and when the coughing stopped, he lay very still. "He never complains," Betsy wrote. "He just takes his medicine and lets us treat him like the gentlest child. . . . I have never seen a sick person so patient." What little energy he had left, he spent on spiritual care. "Just say a few more words, especially short ones, because I can't think." Every day, his wife read to him from the Bible, especially from the Gospel of John, which became very precious to them during this time, and she prayed with the patient. Pastor Secrétan also made regular visits to the sickbed—"such good visits," she reported. The conversations with the pastor were much appreciated by Willem and Betsy and formed the beginning of a close relationship. Willem was aware that something was happening to him as a result of this illness. He indicated this by the short sentences he would utter: "Give thanks to God for everything. I have great reason to do so on this sickbed." And: "God is good. . . . My hope is in Christ alone." One morning

Near Death's Door and a Decision for Life

he called for Betsy and reassured her, "Don't be afraid. I believe in Christ, without much influence on my life, it is true, but still, in these last weeks, with a greater influence on my heart, so that there is no reason in this respect why I should be excluded: the statements of the Bible are sure."[112]

Toward the end of January, the fever broke and there were signs of recovery. The relief was great, but for a long time the patient remained extremely weak. By mid-February, he was able to stay up only a few hours a day. But the fact that Willem had come through and was out of danger filled the house with gratitude and joy. There were many visits from people who had been very concerned, and Willem and Betsy enjoyed the time immensely. "I have never had such days in my life," Betsy wrote to the De Clercqs.[113] Groen enjoyed sitting upstairs in his room, looking out over the square, reading a little, and thinking a lot. On March 8, he picked up his pen for the first time—"I still cannot write much"—and thanked his friends in Amsterdam for the support they had given Betsy during the past few difficult weeks. After Betsy gave him the letters that had been exchanged, he wrote, "I was very moved to read these good words. God has given us many good things during our suffering."[114] His sickbed had been a confirmation of his faith. Now that he was back in the land of the living, he wanted to devote the limited strength he had left to "the glory of God." Having searched and tested the Christian faith over a wide terrain in recent years, he now focused it on a single point: Christ alone. Willem and Betsy were one in experiencing this as a precious fruit of this sickbed, and they felt blessed by it. Christ had to be number one in their lives; everything else was subordinate.

From that sickbed onward, Groen's unconditional focus on "the one thing needful" would determine his life. His Christ-centered faith began to determine his decisions and color his relationship to his surroundings and his work. His analyses of the background of the Revolution in previous years, which had led to his discovery of "unbelief" as an active driving force in history, were now bathed in the clear light of a heartfelt evangelical conviction. In 1833 we see a different Groen, a man who subordinated his tendency to analyze and understand in favor of a desire to be a witness of Christ. This is how we see him from now on. His habit of pointing out what was wrong in his eyes was now coupled with a boldness and confidence in speaking about matters of faith that he had not had before. The year 1833 was a year of transition in the life of Groen van Prinsterer. It marked his final conversion to the Réveil. It also marked a change in his view of his work in the royal cabinet, which he now felt like a heavy burden on his shoulders. After his illness, the relative importance of his official position had diminished even further in his estimation. Personally, he wanted to leave the cabinet, but it was his father's judgment that prevented him from following his heart's desire for the time being.

OUT OF THE CABINET

The inevitable return to the cabinet after his illness became an obsession for Groen. He saw the approaching bureaucratic treadmill as a threatening storm. He began to think about it as early as March. A month later he wrote to De Clercq, "Soon I will have to resume my duties in the cabinet and I am rather reluctant to return to the cares and pressures of everyday life."[115] He resumed his duties at the palace at the end of April, but his health remained fragile. The death of his old teacher, Kappeyne, that month again caused him distress, and the coughing attacks returned. Father Groen thought they were caused by "the nerves," not "the chest." His son's nerves were indeed strained by the situation, so plans were made for a travel cure. Willem eagerly embraced the medical indication for such a trip to extend his period of reflection and relaxation. The destination was quickly decided. Betsy and Willem wanted to go to Geneva, where the Merles had lived for two years. Their friend was teaching at the newly founded École de Théologie, where students were being trained for spiritual, pastoral, and missionary work. As early as December 1832, Groen had succeeded in persuading the king to make a personal gift to this new theological school, which was free of both state and church.

Geneva would therefore be the main destination of their journey. Willem was granted three months leave for the journey. From the end of May to the end of August, Betsy and Willem were abroad. They traveled to Southern Germany and northern Italy, and by mid-July they were in Switzerland, where they stayed for several weeks. Their letters home were written in high spirits. Among the many contacts they made was a visit by Groen to Carl Ludwig von Haller, the Swiss scholar of constitutional law whose analysis of the French Revolution was of particular importance to Groen. In Geneva and Basel, they met the leading figures of the Swiss Réveil. The spiritual life around the theological school, the Bible lectures, and the worship services made a deep impression on Betsy and Willem. Their letters to the De Clercqs contain ecstatic accounts. Father Groen, who at first had mistakenly thought that they would stay for two months instead of three, was kept informed of their spiritual experiences in smaller doses. Here, too, his opinion had to be taken into consideration. At the instigation of Willem and Betsy, a contact was established with Rev. Secrétan, but this relationship did not flourish. The spiritual development of his children remained alien to Dr. Groen senior, whose attachment to the ecclesiastical establishment would last to the end.

When Willem and Betsy resumed their lives in The Hague in early September, Willem resumed his work as cabinet secretary. For a short time, it looked as if he was back in the saddle. At least during that month, he prepared a position paper on the political situation regarding Belgium, a situation that had reached a complete impasse: the king had signed an armistice, but refused to make peace. To give in to the Great Powers and the Belgians, or to stand firm and insist on historical rights—that was the dilemma facing the government, on which Groen now advised the king. Groen examined both sides of the question, but could not come up with anything concrete. He would "not presume to make any recommendations, since we see no solution except a complete change of policy."[116] In this way, Groen shifted the question back to his own area of interest. The situation called for a general turn in political thought, the paper concluded, revealing that Groen was already preoccupied with a philosophical study of fundamental political principles. After showing how both constitutional and international law had been poisoned by a new, unbelieving philosophy, he told the king that it was necessary to return to "a Christian, historical and genuinely philosophical politics, while completely abandoning liberal theories." This could be done by applying the constitution in a way that was in line with "the Christian religion, the historical constitutional law and the Dutch nationality."[117]

A peculiar component of Groen's recommendation was that the southern Dutch province of North Brabant should be administered separately. At the time, there was much speculation about the future of this Catholic province. To avoid a repeat of the difficulties that had arisen between Belgium and Holland, Groen advised that "heterogeneous elements" should be kept separate rather than forced into organic cohabitation. The historic rights of the Roman Catholic church, "subject to evangelical toleration," should be recognized, so that North Brabant would become, in comparison with the Belgian territories, a small "model state" that would show the world the difference between "a revolutionary fusion and a proper respect for provincial rights and liberties."[118] All in all, it was a highly theoretical paper, as Van Assen let him know. "Your proposal for North Brabant appeals to me, but try to implement it! . . . And don't forget that in order to administer a model farm, the tenant must also be a model."[119] A governor who was both Catholic and "antirevolutionary" in Groen's sense of the term was nowhere to be found throughout the country, according to Van Assen. Nevertheless, Groen did not abandon the idea and later revived it when Catholic Limburg joined the Netherlands.

For the time being, this paper would be Groen's last contribution to the political deliberations of the day. His influence on the king's policy was, in view of these considerations, very limited. It is certainly not the case that Groen's work at court as a man of the Réveil can be compared to the influence of Prussian Réveil figures at the court in Berlin. Groen was a lone figure, whereas in Berlin there was a group of prominent ministers, officials, and pastors. Groen took his cue from what was beginning to grow in Berlin, precisely because the opportunities there looked better than in The Hague. He followed with interest and approval the emergence of the *Evangelische Kirchenzeitung* and the *Berliner Politisches Wochenblatt*. In his own country, however, Groen's personal development had relegated him to the periphery of the king's corps of advisors. Any influence that Groen's advice had was greater in 1829 and 1830 than after his return in 1833. He did, however, retain the ability to offer his contributions orally. While the king valued Groen's opinion, this meant little, since it was in his paternalistic nature to value the opinions of many people.

From the first weeks after his return, Willem began to hint at resignation. The occasion came a few months later, when his health began to deteriorate again. By mid-November, Groen was not well. Betsy's heart sank as the long coughing spells returned. By the end of November, the doctor's diagnosis was that Groen was "suffering from nerves." He had to be at the palace but was unable to go. At night, compresses were applied to his chest. This gave him temporary relief, but the worries remained. Willem fell back into his role of patient and stayed in his room upstairs, looking out over the square. Faced with this situation, even Groen's father agreed to the inevitable. On December 6, Groen was able to write to Willem de Clercq that he could not remain at his post. "As this is now also the opinion of my father, I have, for a variety of reasons, seen little objection to tendering my resignation."[120] He received what he had asked of the king: an honorable discharge, with the title of cabinet secretary retained; there would be no change in his function as superintendent of the Royal Family Archives.[121]

Near Death's Door and a Decision for Life

Groen was naturally satisfied with this outcome, but he was not entirely at peace. His deep sense of duty told him that he had fallen short. Since he had not spoken to the king personally, he presented himself at the next audience as soon as he felt better. To his great relief, the king was kind to him. It was as if a weight had been lifted from Willem's shoulders. At last, he was the master of his own time and his own agenda.

GROEN'S WORLDVIEW

"The words *memento mori* should also and especially be inscribed above the door of one's study."[122] Life is short, and therefore one must make the most of one's time and talents in order to exchange "pseudo-wisdom" for that which "retains its value."[123] If we did not know the autobiographical background of these words, we would be surprised by the youthful age of the author. Groen recorded them as thirty-three years old in the preface to the first book he published after his illness. Although his work for the cabinet had come to an end, there was no lack of plans. Two areas remained in which Groen wanted to be active. The Royal Family Archives naturally attracted him, and he began to work there in earnest. At first, however, another project took precedence over the archives. For several years, Groen had been working up the courage to systematize and further elaborate his "reflections on constitutional and international law." Meanwhile, some of his regular correspondents urged him to round up his work on *Netherlandic Reflections* with a final treatise. "Why don't you work out some of these ideas?" Van Assen had written him repeatedly. Groen was slow to formulate his philosophy, but given the new circumstances, he would finally take the plunge. The "one talent" that a person has been given, the preface modestly observes, should also be used "for the benefit of others."[124]

To this end, Groen planned a multi-volume work under the grand title *Considerations on Constitutional and International Law*, of which only the first volume was ever published. That first volume was an introduction subtitled "Essay on the Means by Which Truth Is Known and Confirmed."[125] That truth is found in the Bible was beyond doubt for the author. The book is concerned with the means by which truth can be known, confirmed, and applied. This essay contains Groen's chosen starting point for all intellectual and scientific questions. For a long time, this work would have the status among contemporaries of an orthodox view of religion, learning, and politics. As such, it enjoyed a strong reputation in Christian circles. Shortly after its publication, his Réveil friend Carel van der Kemp waxed lyrical, "This work, I believe and hope, will make history not only in the disciplines of constitutional and international law, but also in those of religion, philosophy, and history. It offers a new and at the same time a correct perspective, while being hitherto unique in its kind."[126] When Rev. Otto Heldring had Groen's abridged edition reprinted in 1858, he did so out of respect for its reputation.[127] Doing so, he overlooked the work that had appeared in the intervening years, *Unbelief and Revolution*, which Groen himself by that time considered a more important articulation of his basic worldview.

Essay on Truth gives us a window into Groen's intellectual universe. We learn which contemporary authors he read and what he thought of their ideas. In a plethora of notes, loose thoughts, and polemical passages, the work oscillates between past and present, displaying an enduring characteristic of Groen's style. Within a clear framework, many lines of inquiry converge that are not always completed or elaborated. Already in this work, Groen, echoing Victor Cousin, recognizes that the Christian who holds to the truth of the gospel can find something good in every system and need not be ashamed of eclecticism,[128] a point he would reiterate in *Unbelief and Revolution*.[129] He did not see this eclecticism as a chink in his armor, nor did it ever become one. He never copied others uncritically and always forced his readers to take note of what he had to say. Rarely, however, did any of his writings amount to a sustained, systematic treatise. More often they were defenses of a limited number of powerful ideas that he developed with a panoply of arguments. In this way, he made a virtue of necessity, and it was on this basis that he would later defend himself when his critics complained that his own system was so difficult to grasp.

The main ideas of the essay, however, are clear. First of all, Groen feels it is essential to explain what he means by "principles." He has used this term many times in the past, but what does he mean by it? What he will say now is no different from what he said about principles in *Netherlandic Reflections* two years ago.[130] He begins with the common usage: principles are those truths that constitute one's *principia* or starting points. They are the presuppositions of any inquiry or argument. Every science, including the sciences of constitutional and international law, begins with such principles. But these, in turn, come from somewhere else: they are derived from higher truths. "And so one ascends from higher to still higher principles, until at last one reaches the highest truths—truths that are unquestionable, but also not susceptible of further analysis and argument; objects of faith, but of a faith that is the beginning of knowledge. These are called principles par excellence; they are based on the will and nature of God."[131] Thus, Groen distinguishes two types of principles: more "subordinate" principles, which are still hypothetical and need to be further investigated, and supreme principles, which are the very criteria by which other principles are tested. Science advances by testing lower principles against higher ones, and so "the whole chain of human knowledge is, if one may use the expression, connected with God."[132] One of the causes of the abandonment of principles, which Groen claims many people deplore as a sickness of the age, is "the abandonment of God." It was the philosophy of the eighteenth century that no longer sought the "touchstone of truth" in the Word of God, but in man and his reason. From that moment on, learning was corrupted and the state was in decline. Driven by "false doctrine," people tried one system after another without ever finding solid ground. Referring to Goethe's *Faust*, Groen identifies disappointment and cynicism, materialism and self-conceit as the wages of the age's hubris. The evil fruits of the abandonment of principles, however, can be successfully combated by "recognizing God again as the center and source of truth. The Christian religion must be brought back to the fore."[133]

Groen then introduces four "means," not so much to prove this key idea as to "confirm" it. The means are revelation, philosophy, history, and universal consensus. Regarding revelation, Groen wants us to understand that truth in religion is not a "natural" phenomenon, but always depends on the revelation of God himself. As a natural being, man is hostile to God. If vestiges of truth can still be found in Islam or Greek mythology, they are there because of the memory of a once-revealed truth and a common origin. Thus, there are different "belief systems," all of which contain a "spark of truth," but there is only one religion "through which the severed link is reconnected." That bond is the Christian religion. Groen understands this in a Christocentric sense: "There is no other name under heaven given among men by which we must be saved but one Christ, outside of whom one lives without God in the world."[134] This Christocentric motif also allows him to speak relatively charitably about the Roman Catholic religion. It may differ from Protestantism in its view of biblical revelation, but Groen does not want to forget that there are Christians in the Roman Catholic church and that all stand on the foundation of the church of all ages. He deplores liberal theology in the Catholic church as well as modernism in the Protestant churches.

The second means of confirming the truth, according to Groen, is philosophy. Since he is "less familiar" with philosophical studies, "here even more than elsewhere," he asks the reader's indulgence.[135] It was certainly needed, for he buttresses his account with references to the three great philosophers of German Idealism: Schlegel, Schelling, and Hegel. What did Groen have in common with them? Immediately after the appearance of the essay, men more familiar with German philosophy expressed surprise at the connection Groen could make between his orthodox views and the views of these philosophers.[136] After all, Groen was a stranger to speculative thought, and the God of the philosophers was not the God he wanted to proclaim. Nevertheless, he believed that Hegel's philosophy differed from the others because it wanted to be "Christian."[137] Groen never read Hegel himself; he allowed himself to be led down the idealist path by the authors he did read: Friedrich Ancillon and again Victor Cousin, who had introduced Hegel to the French in the 1820s.[138] He also encountered idealist thinkers in the *Berlin Politisches Wochenblatt*. Be that as it may, Groen does not seem to have realized that these philosophers were working with very different concepts from his own. Once corrected by his critics, he never again invoked Schelling or Hegel.

The philosophical chapter focuses on the relationship between philosophy and religion.[139] Groen calls philosophy the "highest science," concerned with "the essence of things." This must necessarily lead to religion: "How could the philosopher not be led upward to the Supreme Being; how could philosophy not have descended, as it were, from the knowledge of that Being?"[140] True philosophy is bound to revealed Christian truth. When this bond is severed, the result is a deficient philosophy that engages in reasoning but gropes in vain for truth. This is why Greek philosophy is inferior to Christian philosophy. Modern anti-Christian philosophers, however, have fallen even lower than the Greeks. They break down without building up; all they do is introduce "uncertainty into science, anxiety and despair into the minds."[141] This last point is illustrated by noting that outside the cohesive force of religious faith, philosophy is beset by all sorts of "dualisms," such as the opposition between feeling and intellect, skepticism and science, the spiritual and the material. According to Groen, the Christian religion can resolve these oppositions in philosophy into a higher unity.[142] In this way, he presents a modified version of a basic theme in idealism, which also aimed at a "mediation" of opposites.

Near Death's Door and a Decision for Life

The third and fourth "means" subsequently demonstrate the validity of the first two. First, the course of history supports the view that what the Bible says about God and man is true. Second, there is a universal consensus among right-thinking people of all ages about what is true and good.[143] Groen rejects the Enlightenment view that history shows progress and that man and society will achieve ever greater perfection. According to Groen, history has long since given the lie to these "prejudices." Rather, it has become manifest that evil ideas produce evil results. And it is equally evident, Groen writes, that positive Christianity has been a "salutary force" in history.[144] This is a theme he will return to often. Our concern here is with the theoretical idea behind it. Groen does not leave us in the dark. He returns to what he has already discussed in connection with principles. Philosophy is concerned with the "essence" of things, which it discovers by conforming to revealed truth. By submitting itself to revelation, philosophy is enabled to formulate true theories, theories that are consistent with reality and find confirmation in history. False philosophy focuses arbitrarily on what must be called pseudo-essences, and thus fails the test of experience.

The question has often been debated whether we are dealing with a crypto-Platonist in Groen van Prinsterer as Christian thinker. The essay refers to Plato as a great philosopher, and the intellectual connection he makes between theory and practice seems Platonic. However, the question has never been asked, which the essay at least suggests: was Groen not a metaphysician or an idealist? The ascent of thought from an immanent "being" to a transcendent "being" recalls important themes in the philosophical tradition of metaphysics and idealism. The question that then arises is whether the distinction between faith and knowledge has been lost. Indeed, this remains an unresolved tension for Groen. Nevertheless, both interpretations, of Platonism and of idealism, ultimately miss the point. The connection that Groen assumes between supreme truths, principles, and the operation of both in history is ultimately not of a rational nature. These connections are grasped, so to speak, by faith. Groen presents them as proofs, whereas the critical thinker wants to see arguments. This is both the strength and the weakness of the book. Its strength is that it connects many phenomena and offers an interpretation of these connections. Its weakness is that the author makes connections and posits positions without providing compelling evidence. One critic told the author that he found the tone of the book "apodictic."[145]

Essay on Truth was published in the summer of 1834 and received an icy reception in Dutch intellectual circles. This was due not only to its "apodictic" style, but also to its patent orthodoxy. Groen was the talk of the Leyden academy. One result was a caustic exchange of letters between Groen and his old mentor, Professor Bake.[146] Bake wrote Groen that his "Bible exposition" was the reason "why men of experienced judgment disapprove of your book." If Groen had any credibility left in Leyden, this book destroyed it, especially among the theologians and classicists whose turf he had invaded. The essay received one or two critical reviews and was otherwise ignored. Few people who had received a complimentary copy from the author bothered to reply, and in The Hague hardly anyone spoke to him about it. Groen concluded that he had "offended most people."[147] Of course, he had expected opposition, but this level of response disappointed him. He was hurt by this academic excommunication. Van der Kemp was wrong: the book would not make history.

How different the reception of another Dutch work that appeared that year! This one was destined to be very influential. It is interesting to compare Groen's book with the magnum opus of the Utrecht professor Van Heusde, a work that would make history. Its title was a manifesto: *The Socratic School, or Philosophy for the Nineteenth Century*.[148] In this book, Van Heusde argued exactly the opposite of Groen. According to Van Heusde— who earned the name educator of Holland (*praeceptor Hollandiae*)—man is on his way to the good. Man possesses an organ that enables him to achieve moral improvement. This moral improvement goes hand in hand with the growth of knowledge and the availability of moral examples. Antiquity, the Socratic school, and the behavior of Jesus are useful in this regard. Van Heusde's Christian humanism coincided with the optimism of the nineteenth century man who believed in progress. It also resonated with the cultivation of virtue and the confidence in one's own moral superiority. Van Heusde was no outsider in the intellectual life of the nation, and for several decades his book would have considerable influence on the educational ideals of large groups of conservatives.[149] Below we will hear more about Van Heusde and, in particular, his admirers. Groen received a personal copy of the first volume of the book from the author, but he noted that the distance between him and his former teacher had become very great indeed.[150]

The circle in which Groen's book landed was small. Groen was now getting to know his real friends. Koenen, De Clercq, and Da Costa sent letters of praise from Amsterdam. The latter spoke of a book "according to the needs of our nation as well as our time."[151] Koenen thought the work was excellent and declared his solidarity with Groen's "Christian philosophy."[152] In The Hague, Van der Kemp read the book together with Dr. Abraham Capadose, and the young lawyer Jan Willem Gefken also sent a reply. These were voices from Groen's network of friends on which he could draw. They formed the early nucleus of the Réveil in the Netherlands. Warm relations with people outside these circles became rare. For a time, Groen feared that even his teacher Van Assen, with whom he exchanged news from the political and academic world, might break off their relationship because of the essay. Although Groen had repeatedly written to him about matters of faith, Van Assen could not follow him there. Despite their different religious views, however, they remained friends, and their correspondence continued until Van Assen's death in 1859. The relationship with Thorbecke, who had become professor of constitutional law in Leyden, also continued, although it became cooler. Thorbecke, who was a big hit with the students, reacted differently than the others, but his opinion of the essay was also cutting.[153]

After the discouraging reception of this first volume, Groen had little enthusiasm for writing a second volume, which he had planned to devote to constitutional and international law proper. "I don't have the slightest intention of doing so," he wrote to Van Assen in December. By that time he was completely absorbed in his work for the Royal Family Archives. As more often when having disappointments in the public world, Groen changed his focus to other work. After all, he was responsible for the Royal Archives. By 1834, the final arrangement for separating the various components of the archival collections had been completed. This arrangement would eventually form the basis for the establishment of the National Archives, which in the long run would become more important than the Royal Archives, although the latter would remain the most comprehensive family archive in the country. A second item on Groen's agenda was the publication of the letters of the early members of the House of Orange, as provided for in the Royal Decree of 1828. The king had approved a publishing program and provided the necessary funds. This undertaking, and especially the way it was carried out, shows that Groen was more of a historian than an archivist. He was not so much interested in the work of supervision as in opening up the sources for research into the history they represented.

The central figure in this history was William of Orange, also known as William the Silent. The entire first series of eight volumes, entitled

Unpublished Archives or Correspondence of the House of Orange-Nassau, covers the years 1552–84 and thus the life of William the Silent, who lived from 1533 to 1584.[154] What was new and surprising about Groen's editions was his inclusion not only of official letters relating to political affairs, but also of private correspondence between the prince and members of his family, correspondence that sheds much light on more intimate relationships. Groen did this deliberately, with a specific purpose in mind. He wanted to show that these were people of faith, people whose public behavior did not deviate from their private convictions. This harmony, which he also sought in his own life, was highly valued by Groen and many of his contemporaries. Those who value honesty and truth should demonstrate these virtues in their personal lives. Those who defend the faith should do so out of personal conviction. The members of the House of Orange had this conviction. Their character sheds light on their public conduct, which, Groen writes, was defined by "la cause Évangélique"— the evangelical cause, that is, "the rise, development, and defense of the Reformation."[155]

After some hesitation, Groen decided to write in French in order to make this publication of sources accessible to foreign scholars. In the fall of 1834, he was able to submit the texts for the king's approval, and in January 1835 the first volume was printed. William I was so pleased that he gave his archivist a free hand in compiling the subsequent volumes. The publication of the multi-volume archives became Groen's great project of the 1830s.

RELIGIOUS LIFE

The European world was a source of inspiration not only for Groen's historical studies but also for his spiritual life. Since their trip to Switzerland in the summer of 1833, he and Betsy had been oriented toward the international Christian community of the Réveil. What kind of movement was this, with no new theology, no ecclesiastical leadership, and no dominant personalities? To contemporaries, it was a diffuse movement that grew quietly and was noticeable among the upper classes. It was hard to tell where it began and where it ended. Those who were attracted to this awakening knew that the defining characteristic of the movement was an inner transformation. They recognized themselves in spiritual conversations, in the lively and direct use of biblical texts, in a lifestyle that excluded worldliness and reflected moral seriousness. Precisely because the Réveil focused on this

Near Death's Door and a Decision for Life

internal characteristic of Christian life, its "adherents" could continue to function within the conventional framework of national churches and received theologies. The free churches that had their cradle in the Réveil often arose unintentionally. Because the Réveil spread through the higher circles, it also had an international focus. The Groens, together with their friend Pieter Jacob Elout, Squire Van Soeterwoude, were the first people from the Netherlands to actively enter this international world of the Réveil.[156]

The Réveil originated in the French-speaking part of Switzerland. As early as 1820 or thereabouts, laymen and young pastors began to advocate a more vibrant faith life, an emphasis that soon contrasted with the prevailing moderate views. By the time Willem and Betsy came into contact with this awakening, it had already survived a number of clashes with the dominant class of preachers in the established church. The Swiss organization, known as the *Société Évangélique*, had not formally left the church but enjoyed the status of a free fellowship of believers. By 1830, the Réveil had expanded into Germany and France. In the Netherlands, Réveil piety was linked to the spiritual life that was developing in the circles of former students of the unconventional Bilderdijk. As early as 1826, a circle of people began to form around Da Costa in Amsterdam; they attended the Sunday evening religious meetings at his house and came at other times to listen to his Bible readings. A group in The Hague developed more slowly and was less concerned with forming circles of like-minded people, but here too the spirit of the Réveil would move a number of individuals and families. The Groens themselves did not convene a circle at their home, preferring to attend meetings at the homes of Secrétan and Elout van Soeterwoude.

Since their return to The Hague, Willem had become a conscientious churchgoer, carefully choosing from the variety of preachers to be heard in the city. He was allergic to pulpit orators who spouted the vague generalities of the *juste milieu*, the favored position of those who abhorred religious "extremism" and advocated the "golden mean" or middle ground. He also avoided the homiletic oratory of his old catechism teacher and friend of his parents, Rev. Dermout. Nor could he abide pastors who used the pulpit to preach scientific theology or flaunt scholarly learning. The Groens sought a service where Christ was central and the soul was nourished. They went to church twice a Sunday, once in their own Walloon congregation, where they enjoyed listening to Secrétan, and once in a service with the Reformed pastor Rev. Dirk Molenaar. The latter was known in the College of Pastors of The Hague as the champion of Reformed orthodoxy, a reputation he had earned by raising his voice in 1827 against the doctrinal freedom rampant in the Reformed church. His denunciation of the church's governing body had earned him a royal reprimand. Although Molenaar's preaching was not always engaging, the Groens went to hear him because of the seriousness of his message.

The Réveil in The Hague focused on the church. It was also prepared to defend the doctrines of the church and to uphold the three doctrinal standards of the Dutch church as established by the Synod of Dordt in 1618–19.[157] In 1830, Van der Kemp, another "follower" of Molenaar, took up the pen against the pastors Ypey and Dermout who, in his opinion, in their *History of the Dutch Reformed Church*[158] had spoken lightly of Reformed doctrine and rather positively of Arminianism. He produced a three-volume work entitled *The Honor of the Reformed Church Upheld*.[159] This work also found its way into the Groen home. We read about it in a letter from Betsy to De Clercq, where she writes, "I am busy reading the third volume of Van der Kemp. A solid book like this is really against my inclination, in fact it is quite distasteful; but it was lent to me in order to convince me that the Arminians are right and that the others have always misjudged and mistreated them. And behold, the opposite happens: the whole question, which was still obscure to me, becomes clearer to me with every page."[160]

The Groens would also take a firm stand in upholding the Reformed doctrine of the national church. However, they did not go along with the experientialism that also experienced a revival around 1830. This itch for religious experience, which resembled an element of strict pietism, was also a reaction against cold ritual and lukewarm spirituality. Its practice would be a harbinger of the Secession of 1834. Willem de Clercq reported from Amsterdam that books by the *"old writers"* of the seventeenth and eighteenth centuries[161] were fetching high prices. This was Willem and Betsy's first exposure to this kind of spirituality. And although they, like many in the Réveil, were attracted to the piety of ordinary men and women, the distinctions between the various stages of soul experience did not sit well with them. "We have very little of this kind of experiential religion here . . . but I honestly see nothing in God's Word about all these stages of experience," Betsy replied to De Clercq. "I read Bunyan's life with admiration; no doubt he describes it as it was; but I think one may question the usefulness of writing and publishing all those temptations, all those sometimes-strange sensations."[162] The Groens sought the simple Christian

Near Death's Door and a Decision for Life

life, one that indulged as little in theological speculation as in psychological introspection.

This simple Christian life, nourished by intense Bible study, touched also others. By the mid-1830s, there was a growing self-consciousness of Christian identity, a growth Groen called an "awakening." In what historians now call the Réveil, the French term was hardly ever used; it came into vogue only after the movement had passed its zenith. Note also that this was a revival without violent conversions, tent meetings, altar calls, or speaking in tongues. The "awakening" was to mean two things. First, Groen and his circle meant an increase in the number of people with a positive biblical faith who were not afraid to identify themselves as such. Second, "awakening" meant an attitude: the confidence to speak freely to others about the faith and to encourage them to take Christianity seriously. In fact, we see Groen doing just that in letters to friends and close acquaintants. The expectation was that this awakening, in both senses of the word, would bring healing and restoration to church and society. The term "Réveil" can then be reserved for the form of this awakening in the upper echelons of society, where the connection with the international Réveil movement was most easily made, although the upper-class Christians themselves thought in terms of an awakening that transcended the boundaries of different social classes.

As was to be expected, the Réveil did not stand by and watch the Secession of 1834. It sympathized with the struggle for biblical teaching and was scandalized by the reprisals against the pastors who supported that struggle. They shared the objections to the legal Church Regulations of 1816, which in effect imposed state government on the national church. They could also see certain parallels with the free churches that were beginning to emerge in Switzerland and Scotland. Nevertheless, the Réveil did not join the Secession. When one of their leaders, Rev. Hendrik Pieter Scholte, was allowed to attend one of Da Costa's Sunday evenings in the fall of 1834, where he proceeded to read a solemn statement urging Secession, Da Costa had replied directly that the struggle should be waged within the Reformed church, not outside it.[163] This was the position the Groens shared. They followed developments with great interest. Through correspondence with Betsy's mother in the North, they were well informed about the situation surrounding Rev. Hendrik de Cock. This uncompromising pastor in the Groningen village of Ulrum had advocated a return to strict Calvinism and had attacked milder pastors in the area as "wolves in sheep's clothing." When the regional church court suspended De Cock, and soon afterward defrocked him, his congregation formally seceded from the national church. Meanwhile, Rev. Scholte, after being rebuked by Da Costa, had visited Groen to consult with him on ways to uphold Reformed doctrine.[164] The Groens, however, could not approve of the Secession as such. They found its leaders too zealous and impulsive, and they also felt that this was not the way to give up the right to stand up for biblical doctrine in the Reformed church.

Although the Secession did not reach the Réveil, Willem and Betsy's spiritual orientation during these years became a source of tension with father Groen. He watched his children's spiritual development with increasing despair. Their choice of preachers and their association with orthodox people, their support of Van der Kemp against Dermout, their sympathy for Reformed pastors who came into conflict with the Synodical Council of the church—all this was too much for him. He did not hide his feelings from them, and gradually their conversations became more and more dominated by the growing gap between their religious views. Neither Groen's father nor Willem and Betsy were the kind of people to hide their feelings. Their conversations often created an uncomfortable atmosphere and were sometimes continued in writing to clarify arguments and positions. Groen's "Essay on Truth" and its cool reception was the last straw for old Dr. Groen. He saw his son taking positions that relegated him to the periphery of the social milieu where he should have been at the center.

In September 1834, the bomb exploded. What lit the fuse was Willem and Betsy's planned visit to Willem and Caroline de Clercq in Amsterdam. Father Groen knew De Clercq from his days in The Hague. De Clercq had become the editor of *Netherlandic Voices*, a weekly paper that had been published since May of that year by the Réveil circle in Amsterdam. This paper bore the unmistakable stamp of Da Costa and expressed the beliefs of orthodoxy in no uncertain terms. It caused quite a stir when it came out. Father Groen would have none of it and even called it "harmful"[165] because it showed too much sympathy for the group of Reformed pastors who had been stirring up controversy in the Reformed church for almost a year. When he heard of Willem and Betsy's visit, he erupted in a litany of accusations against De Clercq. Relations were so fragile that the visit could not take place. Betsy explained, "It takes a lot, after the accusations we heard recently, to say to a father: these are the people you disapprove of so much that we are going to visit now."[166] The whole affair disturbed

Willem terribly. He was "very depressed" at the time and hoped that relations would soon improve. Half a year later, the visit took place as planned, but the relationship with father Groen remained very sensitive and would never be entirely free of tension. The Groens rarely mentioned it to other people, but they suffered from it. Van der Kemp knew something of the problems when he wrote to Koenen that it was very unpleasant "for our friend Groen to be so hindered by his father in the free development of his views and sympathies."[167] Willem simply could not stand up to his father, and for the sake of peace, at the age of thirty-two, he still signed his letters, "Your obedient son."

THE HUNT FOR ARCHIVES

The reason for the rapprochement between father and son was probably Groen's appointment as an extraordinary member of the Council of State in March 1836. His old friend Van Rappard, who now worked in the king's cabinet, was able to tell him the good news. Father Groen had already been appointed in 1822 for his services to public health, so father and son were now united in this body. The councilors functioned as honorary advisors to the government, but this involved little additional work. There were plans to reform the council, just as the government wanted to restructure many other royal advisory and administrative bodies after the Secession of Belgium, but the king and his court often lacked the energy in those years to bring intentions to a successful conclusion.

Groen's appointment to the Council of State was also, and above all, a personal sign of appreciation on the part of King William I for Groen's work in the Royal Family Archives. This work was beginning to take on impressive proportions. By the spring of 1836, Groen had compiled three substantial volumes of the correspondence of the Prince of Orange and his Nassau brothers. His careful historical commentary on the letters met the exacting standards of the newly awakening historical scholarship and shed new light on the early years of the Eighty Years' War with Spain. Historical scholarship was undergoing a period of "going back to the sources." This "empirical turn," which also manifested itself in other sciences, meant for history that the intensive study of primary sources had to be the foundation of historical knowledge. Locating, making accessible, and interpreting old manuscripts became a core activity of historical scholarship. In Germany, scholars had begun publishing the *Monumenta Germaniae Historica*, a major project in which historians made available many of the key sources for writing German history. A similar project was being considered for the *Unpublished Archives or Correspondence of the House of Orange-Nassau.* The king was very pleased that the history of his august house was being made available in this way, and he discussed it with his guests with great appreciation.

As we have seen, the Royal Family Archives were located on Plein Square, so Groen did not have to walk far to get to his office. He also received historians from abroad who had read the published volumes of the archives and wished to discuss them with the editor. Given the origins of the Nassau dynasty, it is not surprising that this interest came mainly from Germany. Renowned historians such as Heinrich Leo and Leopold Ranke traveled to The Hague to consult with Groen. Groen, in turn, was familiar with their work and corrected their findings, when necessary, in his introductions to the sources.[168] As director, Groen supervised W. Häberling, who was charged with the care of the collections. Ongoing work included making inventories of existing archives and acquiring (sometimes purchasing) new archival collections. Next, documents that were no longer in good condition had to be repaired for preservation. The constant support that Groen enjoyed was, of course, important for the progress of the work. It was also important for his physical well-being. For half a year his eyes had been giving him trouble from all the peering and deciphering. His handwriting also showed signs of fatigue from time to time. From that time on, Betsy's handwriting appeared with increasing frequency in Groen's private correspondence. She relieved him by writing out letters and making copies of them.

In the spring and summer of 1836, in connection with Willem's work for the Royal Family Archives, the Groens went on a long tour visiting archives in France and Germany. Willem was looking for previously unknown letters and documents of the Oranges, but he was also doing historical research that might shed new light on the political history of the sixteenth century. He spent most of his time in Paris, where he met contemporary French historians such as Guizot, Mignet, and Michelet. However, his opinion of modern French historiography was not positive. He was particularly critical of Michelet's *History of France.* Groen's judgment gives us a good idea of his own view of historiography. Michelet, with his "wanton genius" and his "excitable imagination," had "run riot" in the field of history, as a result of which he "failed to see many things that were there" and "thought he saw many things that were not there." Groen attributed this historiographical defect to the itch to create a literary work. What characterized Michelet's history? "A pursuit of novelty, which too often crowds out the love of truth; a host of analogies, images, and pithy sayings, collected and amassed from everywhere, to keep the reader awake, and each time to captivate him with a new and ever stronger impression."[169] This was not the way he would write his own history of the Netherlands. More useful to him was his contact with Victor Cousin, whom he visited four times and with whom he discussed philosophy and public education. The latter topic provided ample material, since Groen, as secretary of the royal cabinet, had been busy with school legislation, and Cousin, who was to become France's minister of education in 1840, was preparing to travel to Holland to study the much-vaunted Dutch educational system (his report will be discussed below). When Cousin arrived in The Hague in September, however, Groen had not yet returned.[170]

In Paris, there was a very active Réveil circle centered around the young pastor Frédéric Monod. The Groens attended his church on Sundays. This compensated Betsy for the sacrifice she felt she was making by coming to Paris in the first place. In the milieu in which she moved in Holland, Paris had a bad reputation. After a few weeks she wrote to De Clercq, "Sometimes I can hardly imagine that I am in Paris, in that city and among those people against whom I have had such strong prejudices since early childhood."[171] But there were more good things to come. From Paris they went to Besançon, to the archives of Cardinal Granvelle, and then, in August, to the Merles in Geneva. There they attended the baptism of Willem Oswald, the son of Jean Henri and Marianne. Already during the pregnancy, the Merles had asked the Groens to be godparents of this child. The child was born in August, and now that it was a son, it was also named after Willem Groen van Prinsterer. Willem and Betsy were very touched by this sensitive gesture and in the years to come would show their warm interest in the child as he grew up.

After this interlude in Switzerland, they continued their journey to Stuttgart and Karlsruhe, near Kassel, where Groen discovered a dust-covered cupboard filled with letters and documents relating to Dutch war and religious matters. Back in Holland, he gave several public lectures in which he enthusiastically recounted these discoveries and other impressions of his journey. In the course of these lectures, he made no secret of what drove him to undertake this often dry and tedious work in dusty archives. Such remnants of the past, he explained, were useful "to refute errors and to dispel prejudices."[172] The "remnants" in question—the letters of the Nassaus and the Oranges—bore "the mark of simple Christian faith." Passing on that faith was an important motive for his work in the Royal Archives. It confirmed for him that the House of Orange had played a major role in establishing and maintaining the Reformed religion in the Low Countries.

The publication of the archives led the members of the Réveil to refresh and reinforce their interpretation of history, an interpretation that ascribed a providential role to the Oranges. Groen sent free copies to a wide circle of friends and acquaintances. With each volume, Da Costa and Koenen repeated their enthusiasm. Da Costa found the contents "instructive and comforting."[173] He himself gave several series of public lectures on sixteenth-century Dutch history during these years. The unfavorable impression created by the recent publication of Bilderdijk's *History of the Fatherland*[174] was corrected by the "learned lectures" of his chief disciple. If a Christian-historical worldview was to be credible, it had to rest on a solid foundation. Groen's work provided that foundation. The fact that Groen expressed his conviction that the Oranges were *"les hommes supérieurs,"* great men used by God to carry out his plans, won the approval of Da Costa and others of like mind.[175] It also led them to develop new expectations of the current members of the House of Orange. Looking beyond William I, they hoped that the crown prince, once king, would usher in a new era. The Réveil in Amsterdam in particular toyed with this idea. Those in The Hague did not allow themselves to be swept off their feet. The revival of the Orangist version of the nation's history did indeed support the prevailing sympathy for the monarchy, but at the same time it was becoming clear that the character and policies of the present Williams, now spread over as many as three generations, had different traits from those of the historical princes of the archives.

TO THE KORTE VIJVERBERG

Willem and Betsy were again confronted with death on March 3, 1837, when father Groen died after a short but serious illness. Within four years, Groen had lost his mother and now his father. Although his death was not entirely unexpected, Willem and Betsy were shocked. Betsy mentally drew a parallel between December 1832 and Willem's subsequent illness. Although his health was still fragile in the winter, this time "by God's goodness he weathered the storm."[176] Of course, the memory of the tensions and pent-up conflicts of recent years surfaced as they sorted through his many papers. It fell to Willem, as the eldest son, to divide the estate. In harmonious consultation with Keetje and Mimi, it was decided that Willem and Betsy should live in the house on the Korte Vijverberg. *Vreugd en Rust* became the country estate of Keetje and her husband Mari Hoffmann; the Hoffmanns had already made it their summer home during father Groen's last years. There was no property for Mimi, but she did receive her share of the large sum of money left by the parents. We do not know how much, but in any case, the fortune that Willem alone inherited was so large that he had to invest it. He did so in the *Dutch Trade Association* of his friend De Clercq, and in steamship lines and nascent railroad companies. Over the years, his portfolio performed well, and by the end of his life, forty years later, his estate was worth nearly two million guilders.[177] But the Groens also practiced the maxim *memento mori* when it came to their money: they always lived soberly and did not wallow in their wealth. Over time, they spent large sums on all sorts of Christian causes. The Groens, along with a few others, also provided a living for Da Costa, for whom the friends in Amsterdam had set up a special fund.

Willem now returned to the house where he had spent his youth. The houses in which Willem and Betsy had lived had not been very large, being designed for a modest household. By comparison, their new home was a palace. The house on the Korte Vijverberg had a high stoop, which added to its dignified appearance; it had three floors plus a basement and a separate floor for the servants' quarters. Its depth was also twice as great as its front. It did not have a garden, but it did have a backyard with a carriage house and stables, and an exit to another street. The size of the house gave Betsy a divided heart. "It is a beautiful house," she wrote to De Clercq. "Often I think: too beautiful for strangers and sojourners; then again, my vain heart takes great pleasure in it."[178] Beginning in the summer, she had to supervise the workmen, paperhangers, and painters who redecorated the house for her. When the project was finished, she wrote again to De Clercq, "The house on the Vijverberg is beautiful; may my heart not get attached to it."[179] On October 31, they moved out of their house on Plein Square and into the seventeenth-century mansion where they would live for the rest of their lives.[180]

What can we say about the layout of this house? In the first half of the eighteenth century, it was extensively enlarged and remodeled in the style of Louis XIV. It had lavishly plastered and painted ceilings, wide marble fireplaces with elaborate fireplace reliefs in twelve of the rooms, and rich ornamentation above the doors and windows.[181] Willem and Betsy refrained from putting their personal stamp on the architecture. Like Groen's parents, they left both the exterior and the interior untouched. They did, however, furnish the house according to their own tastes. Exact information about this is largely lacking. The Groens were not given to ostentatious frills. We never hear them talk about paintings or furniture. What little we do have suggests that they were, in their own way, comfortable with the Biedermeier style so characteristic of the period of Restoration. Biedermeier culture valued domesticity, intimacy, and personal character, and paid attention to beauty in history and nature. An emphasis on domestic bliss characterized Willem and Betsy's lives. Betsy had an eye for personal bric-a-brac. She was the one who regularly "surprised" Willem with a bust of a great historical figure as a birthday present for his study. A visitor would be greeted there by busts of Plato and Homer and, after 1837, the head of Bilderdijk in plaster. City life, however, offered little opportunity to enjoy nature. Betsy and Willem loved the Swiss mountains and enjoyed long walks in nature. Summers were often spent with mother-in-law Van der Hoop at the De Bult estate in Steenwijk. Here Groen would sometimes set off on horseback to explore the countryside. The Groens loved to travel during the summer. When they moved into their new home in 1837, they had no further plans to acquire a summer estate near The Hague. But in 1845, when their love of foreign travel had waned, they bought *Oud-Wassenaer*, a fine country house, though smaller than *Vreugd en Rust*. Here they spent the fair season, from the end of April to the end of September, as was the custom of their class.

Did their move to the stately house on the Korte Vijverberg raise their social status, as it had done for their parents? This circumstance, together with his birth into a respectable family of The Hague and his official connection with the court, probably enhanced the name of Groen van Prinsterer. His religious inclinations were well known, but the criticism of his essay had already been compensated by his outstanding work on the archives. That he had not been written off is shown by the fact that from the mid-1830s he was nominated several times by the provincial legislature of Holland for a seat in the Second Chamber, the lower house of Parliament. A candidate could remain quite passive in the face of such a nomination, and this is exactly what Groen did. He submitted to the nomination, was flattered by it, but gave no indication that he was angling for a seat in this rather powerless institution. He was never elected. The experience did, however, cause him to reflect on the role of Parliament in the political life of the nation. He detested the fact that the members of the Second Chamber could debate endlessly about sugar and coffee from the East Indies, but were silent on the great political issues. Although political power was heavily concentrated in the hands of the king, Groen believed that leading men should speak openly about the great issues of the day. He himself would now begin to do so more freely. Unlike his father, he made the most of his independence, no longer worrying about the approval or disapproval of society. His position had made him immune to that.

THE MEASURES AGAINST THE SECEDERS

Be frank and speak your mind! Groen put this into practice when he spoke out against the persecution of the Seceders. In the fall of 1835, he attended the trial of pastor Scholte in The Hague. At first the Secession could be seen as the action of a few orthodox pastors who rose up in revolt against the power that the Regulations of 1816 gave to less orthodox members of the church boards, but after some time it became clear that in the rural areas of the country many thousands of people were severing their ties with the national Reformed church and beginning to meet as free, independent congregations.[182] A preponderance of the lower classes in the movement, whose manners were not always very refined, created a distance between them and the upper classes.[183] But even there some had a heavy heart about the state of the national church. In Amsterdam, the young lawyer Maurits van Hall left the Reformed church. Van Hall had ties to the Réveil circle, which expressed understanding for this monumental step, though it deplored his action. Van Hall's "defection" caused his older brother, the future cabinet minister Floris van Hall, to remove him from the family law office. Maurits then moved to The Hague, where he ended up in a Secessionist church in the village of Scheveningen, among ordinary fishermen. Both Van Hall, who would die young in 1838, and Groen's friend Jan Willem Gefken acted as defense attorneys in court cases in which Seceders were prosecuted.

The fact that orthodox Reformed believers were being persecuted in the Netherlands was a thorn in the side of Groen and his Réveil friends. One did not necessarily have to identify with the Seceders to realize that the authorities were going rather far when they broke up their worship services as "unlawful meetings" and punished the offenders with heavy fines. Moreover, the law did not always prevent angry mobs from getting out of hand, resulting in personal injury and property damage to Seceders. As if that were not enough, soldiers were quartered in the homes of Seceders, who had to feed and house them. The government based its actions on the Constitution of 1815, which offered protection to "existing" religious denominations but implicitly withheld it from new ones. This, at least, was the official interpretation of the constitution. It was the aging minister Van Maanen who persuaded the government to take this hard line. Astonishingly, several articles of the Napoleonic penal code were applied to this most unusual situation, articles that allowed the police to disperse assemblies of more than twenty people. These legal provisions were so controversial that they were no longer taught at the Faculty of Law in Leyden. The government used them to show a stern face. The Belgian uprising was, of course, fresh in everyone's mind; the king even considered the possibility of renewed hostilities in the South. In view of this possibility, the unity of the Reformed church was seen as an important asset. But many, especially those in the cities, failed to see the effect of the reprisals and intimidation on the population at large. From his contacts at court, Groen surmised that the king did not see the effects either.

If the full effect of the persecutions did not penetrate to court circles, the king personally supported the hard line. In his eyes, the Seceders were "fanatics" whose adherence to the old confessions made them hostile to "the progress of ideas" and who "arrogated to themselves the infallibility of the papal see."[184] This was the language of a prince who has gone down in history as an "enlightened despot."[185] William I had no eye for questions of ecclesiastical polity. He regarded "those who adhere to the Canons of Dordt" as rebels against his government, and he would not spare them. In a conversation with a former minister, he revealed the articles of the penal code that were being used against them.[186] The fact that Groen was unaware of the king's hard line indicates the distance that existed between His Majesty and his family archivist. This distance was, of course, dictated by court protocol, but it was also reinforced by the deference Groen observed during audiences with the king. The subject of the religious persecutions had not come up between them since they began.

Nevertheless, in Groen's eyes, the "House of Orange" was still the protector of religious freedom in the Netherlands. Accordingly, he appealed to the king in writing, submitting a memorandum toward the end of March 1837, a few weeks after his father's death. In a covering letter, he expressed the hope that his memorandum might lead to a change in government policy.[187] Almost immediately, he began work on a more extensive pamphlet, which, when he received no response from the king, he published in early July. When he sent the king a copy of *The Measures Against the Seceders Tested Against Constitutional Law*,[188] he explained that "dutiful candor" had led him to this publication.[189] William I did not appreciate publications critical of his government, and Van Assen heard that he was "thoroughly annoyed."[190] The surprise blow would continue to annoy the monarch for some time; his relationship with Groen definitely cooled. Imagine a council of state, custodian of the royal family's archives, openly censuring the king's policies! The following week, Groen did not appear at the king's audience to personally deliver, as was his custom, a copy of the newly published fourth volume of the archives. Groen asked to be excused "on account of a hasty departure for Overijssel" to attend to some family business.[191] It seemed better to Groen that the king should not see him for a while. It is not hard to imagine how Groen's father would have reacted to all this. But Groen's publication of *The Measures* for the first time showed a confidence no longer burdened by the fear of patriarchal disapproval.

So Groen entered the lists in the name of the Seceders. This is clear from the beginning of his treatise:

> For some time now one has been hearing in the Netherlands of trials, of fines and imprisonments, of troop deployments, of harshly worded summonses; and all this is directed against a class of inhabitants—against Reformed Christians who have seceded from the church denomination established in 1816. It is natural that many people should ask sympathetically: What have they done that deserves punishment?[192]

Nothing, of course, in Groen's opinion; and he knew that many admitted as much in private conversation. But it was imperative that the persecution be stopped and that the Secession be given a fair hearing. To this end, Groen, in his usual approach, placed the events in a wider context: background motives in church and state had to be taken into account. The unrest in the church and the government's overly harsh measures stemmed from certain revolutionary ideas that, he argued, continued to guide the state after the Restoration of 1813. The constitution of that time applied these ideas to the church when it proclaimed the "equality of religions." This had led to religious indifference and decline, to a neglect of the power of the Christian faith. "The government of this Christian country scarcely mentioned Providence; the holy name of Christ was no longer mentioned at all."[193] The state no longer wanted to show its colors and invoked the separation of church and state.

At the same time, and this was the other side of the coin, the church was not granted any autonomy, but was seen as a social institution that was like "a servant to be held by the hand of the government."[194] With the Regulations of 1816, the church was "organized, centralized, bureaucratized." Directed by the Ministry of Worship, it became part of the "state machine." In the national church, political authority ruled over spiritual authority. The synod was given the task of protecting and maintaining this arrangement, not changing it. The changes that synods were empowered to make concerned by-laws and other ecclesiastical ordinances. These then became a source of disagreement between the synod and Reformed orthodoxy. The latter objected to a change made by the synod when it adopted an ambiguously worded *Form of Subscription* which had the effect of no longer requiring candidates for the ministry to declare that they agreed with the confessional standards of the church as being in harmony with Scripture, but only that they accepted these standards insofar as they were in conformity with Scripture. Groen was referring to what has gone down in history as the *quia-quatenus* question: should prospective office-bearers in the church be required to declare their agreement with the church's confessions as (*quia*) they conform to Scripture, or only insofar as (*quatenus*) they do so? The latter interpretation left much room for doctrinal freedom and thus undermined the unity of the church's faith. From that moment on, groups of ministers, "faithful pastors" as Groen calls them, pressured the synod to uphold Reformed doctrine. The synod, however, was unable and unwilling to comply with such requests. The opposition that resulted in Secession was therefore "natural and inevitable," according to Groen. The opposition had been provoked by both the synod and the government itself.[195]

When every protest had been waved aside and the opposition was still gaining strength, the synod had invoked the strong arm of the law, turning against Reformed people, members in good standing in the Reformed church, with whom it should have dealt sympathetically. While the government should have intervened to mediate, it chose sides and took excessive measures. The government and the synod treated the Seceders as if they were "runaway serfs." The Netherlands had become the scene of "religious persecution," Groen declared, a conclusion that must have sounded shocking and painful in the ears of his upright fellow citizens.[196] One may disagree with the Seceders, he suggested; one may call them narrow-minded, haughty, and uncharitable; but they should be treated justly and fairly.[197] Finally, in the last part of his pamphlet, Groen tested the measures against the existing public law—the rights and liberties enshrined in the country's constitution and statutes. His conclusions were as follows:

> The Seceders are residents of the Netherlands: therefore, no billeting.
> The Seceders are members of a religious persuasion that does not pose a threat to public order or security: therefore, freedom of worship.
> The Seceders are members of the Reformed persuasion, therefore they are entitled, no less than the members of the national church, to the same protection under the law as is accorded to all existing religious persuasions in the kingdom.[198]

Groen's pamphlet attracted considerable attention and debate. However, the issue was debated in a way that was typical of the immobile political culture of the time, where freedom of the press was more widely accepted than freedom of association and assembly. There were no conferences and no public discussions; the debate was conducted exclusively in writing. Groen's pamphlet did not go down well with people in the government, resulting in a shift of sympathies. His old friend Van Rappard, for example, rejected his position and would henceforth keep his distance. The main reaction from the government came in the form of a pamphlet written by Adriaan van Appeltere, a clerk in the Ministry of Justice, who took it upon himself to speak out against the "rank misjudgment of our respected government."[199] Van Appeltere had been the public prosecutor in the 1835 trial of Scholte in The Hague, and in that role had faced Gefken and Van Hall. So, he knew what he was talking about. Within a few months, his extensive pamphlet against Groen was ready, having been written in the Ministry with the personal help of Van Maanen.[200] The author fully identified himself with the government's policy and betrayed his irritation at Groen's reproach that the constitution contained the substance of "revolutionary" ideas and showed indifference to religions. The Justice official tried to deny this categorically in what he admitted was a "stylistically inferior" demonstration. He painted the Seceders as rebels and accused them of unseemly behavior. Van Appeltere was a political realist who sought workable solutions. Most of his pamphlet dealt with the role of government in relation to the various religious denominations. He argued at length that the government could not act any differently than it had, thus confirming the very thing that had stung Groen: the government had a political stake in the unity of the church and therefore no longer protected the freedom of believers.

It should have done so, Groen argued, on the basis of the historical rights of the Reformed church in the Netherlands. But how? It was Thorbecke who realized that Groen still had to struggle to find an answer to this question. He attacked Groen mercilessly on this point. In the month of September 1837, he published three articles in the local French newspaper *Journal of The Hague*, the sharp tone of which is surprising considering the friendship that existed between him and Groen. Thorbecke stated flatly that Groen's pamphlet was "the work of a party," a party that "seeks life among the dead," the orthodox Reformed party, for which the equality of religions is an "abomination." This party wants to have the field all to itself. Thorbecke even compared it to a "sick person" who wants to impose his "healthy" rules on others. The Leyden professor of constitutional law defended the government's right to regulate church life. This has always been the case in the past, at least from a European perspective. The church owes its rights to a grant from the state. During the Dutch Republic, he admitted, the Reformed church had always sought ecclesiastical autonomy, but it had never been entirely successful. In Thorbecke's view, this was a good thing. In his eyes, Groen clung to the old presumption of the "Calvinist clergy" and unfairly branded modern forms of public administration as despotic.

Thorbecke's response highlighted the fundamental contrast between the two positions. Groen responded to Thorbecke in several articles in the same newspaper.[201] He argued that Thorbecke's view amounted to "the absolute supremacy of the state over the church."[202] He believed that his opponent was mistaken about the nature of church law, which was not caesaropapist but biblical, "in submission to the Word of God."[203] The exchange of views was fruitless, however. Thorbecke rather haughtily replied that Groen wanted to joust but lacked the weapons, and he pitied his would-be opponent. Groen replied, "Strange! I debate without reason, yet he writes three articles to refute me."[204] Groen felt misjudged in his plea for the historical rights of the "Reformed persuasion," and he believed their old friendship was over. In the midst of their heated exchanges in the press, however, Thorbecke wrote Groen a friendly letter: "The subject we are discussing in public does not harm our special feelings for each other."[205] Groen thanked him for this note with what seems like naive indulgence: "I see from your letter with great satisfaction that you did not mean by some of your expressions what I think they imply."[206] In other words, Groen did not resent Thorbecke's sharp tone. After all, he himself had called for a "frank discussion" of public issues. And so, their friendship survived.

But did things improve for the beleaguered Seceders? Not at once, but gradually it did, in part because of the discussion that Groen sparked. But it was not in the interest of his opponents to dwell on the fate of the Seceders themselves. In their arguments, Thorbecke and Van Appeltere passed over the actual measures and prosecutions—the very points Groen was concerned with. He had gathered his information by subscribing to Pastor Scholte's monthly paper, *The Reformation*, a church paper that no one else in his circle read.[207] This interest in their plight was greatly appreciated in Secessionist circles; it goes without saying that Groen's pamphlet was received there with deep gratitude. In the years that followed, Groen continued to speak out against religious persecution, earning him a permanent place in the hearts of the Seceders. In 1876, at Groen's grave, his good reputation among the Seceders was once again underscored when Rev. A. Brummelkamp Jr. spontaneously stepped forward to honor the author of *The Measures Against the Seceders* on behalf of the Christian Reformed churches.

But this was forty years later. In the thirties, Groen wanted to see the Secession of his church as part of a broader revival movement. He saw it as a mirror image of the semi-ecclesiastical Société Évangélique in Switzerland, to which Merle belonged.[208] This also meant that what interested him about the Secession was always the future of the Reformed church. He never abandoned the idea that it was the Reformed church that needed to be restored. He was not an advocate of separatism, not an advocate of establishing new church structures through Secession, although he appreciated the Seceders in their function as gadflies. When Koenen once told him of rumors that Secessionist pastors were returning to the Reformed church and that, in his opinion, Secession had "had its day," Groen replied that he was sorry to hear it. "I wish we had had dissenters like those in Switzerland, capable of provoking the church to jealousy. Then the return of pastors could have been the result of the restoration of the church."[209] The Seceders were not on the same level as the free churches elsewhere, and Groen did not hide his disappointment with their dogmatic hair-splitting and petty bickering. But he was equally convinced that denominational divisions did not create walls between Reformed believers from different groups and social classes. He coined the term "Reformed persuasion" to describe this state of affairs.

CHOOSING WHERE TO STAND

With his declaration of his views on the church, Groen had completed his choice of where he would stand. The thirties had been the years in which he marked out his arena in the fields of politics, history, and the church. His religious maturity had led to a desire to bear witness to his deepest personal convictions. His position as director of the Royal Family Archives gave him the opportunity to broaden and deepen the vision he had acquired. Finally, these years had brought him financial and social independence. Only his fragile health was a constant source of worry. Since the serious illness of 1833, Betsy had lived with the idea that her husband might die young. She worried constantly about his health; in the winter of 1839, he was not well again. Willem had many coughing fits, felt a sharp pain in his side, and became so weak that he could hardly climb the stairs.[210] His "weak chest" was treated with bleeding and poultices, but again it took weeks for him to return to some semblance of normal. Betsy was not at ease until Willem was back upstairs working in his library. "Willem is well, very well, working while it is day," were her grateful words of contentment.[211]

The Groens were people of order and regularity. As early as seven o'clock in the morning, they had a short communal devotion with the servants, as was customary in Réveil circles. Even in winter they did not deviate from this hour. After the prayers, during which all knelt, everyone went to work. So Willem would be at his desk at a fairly early hour. This explains in part why, despite recurring bouts of illness, his output was considerable and a stream of publications came out of his "book room" or library. It began to dawn on Da Costa, Koenen, and De Clercq in Amsterdam that their friend and brother in The Hague was singularly responsible for carving out a certain position for the Réveil in church and society through his press activities. Groen's contributions were also more lucid than those that appeared in their periodical, *Netherlandic Voices*.[212] Attempts from Amsterdam to have Groen join the editorial staff of this journal, however, were unsuccessful. Groen did not want to be an editor at a distance, and he found little time to write for the journal in addition to his own work schedule. In addition, he felt more or less forced into someone else's shoes in such a collective enterprise. He preferred to be in control of his own work.

Groen's choice of where to stand, however, demanded a more precise definition, a further development, a broader unfolding. This theme recurs in contemporary reactions to his writings. After the publication of Groen's

Essay on Truth, the king sighed, "I wish Groen would make me a draft of a resolution which, according to his doctrine, I should include in the constitution." Van Assen, who reported this to Groen, added, only half in jest, "I support the motion."[213] After *The Measures Against the Seceders* appeared, the king no longer asked for drafts and sighed in a different tone. Nor did Groen offer any concrete proposals in connection with his criticism of ongoing developments in the church. However, he became the center of an informal opposition which, at least in The Hague, included Dirk van Hogendorp, Van der Kemp, Molenaar, Gefken, and Secrétan. But what were the positive results? Da Costa recognized that those who remained in the "historic Reformed church" were obliged to explain their position further. He expressed his desire "that the non-Secessionists do a little more to establish their position than merely protesting against the arrogations within and the persecutions without."[214] The men of the Réveil, united together, were about to enter a decade in which they would be occupied with the idea of presenting and elaborating their position. They would also be challenged by changing political and social circumstances. A period was dawning that would be marked by fresh ideas.

4

The Salt of Education, the Salt of the Earth

POLITICAL CHANGES

STRANGERS SOMETIMES SEE THINGS better. When Victor Cousin visited the Netherlands in the summer of 1836, he recorded his impressions of the political climate he encountered. His comments were disturbing. There was no vibrant political life, he noted, and the government quietly managed the country's affairs. Cousin found that the king, who was the axis around which the entire administration of the country revolved, enjoyed universal respect.[215] There was widespread appreciation in the country for Cousin's favorable report on the Dutch educational system, but the reading elite could hardly take his comment about a quiet administration as a well-meant compliment. "John Stick-in-the-Mud" symbolized the situation. Critics complained that the government was characterized by spineless ministers, a lack of openness, and decision-making behind closed doors. Thorbecke, like Groen, lamented the lack of public discussion and free debate, even in the Second Chamber, where the will of "His Majesty" made speakers timid.[216] Tholuck may have called the Dutch "sleepyheads," and Cousin found them "phlegmatic," but no sooner had the French visitor departed than opposition to the king's government began to grow. Shortly before 1840, it became clear that William I's system of government was coming to an end. The defiant policy toward Belgium had ended in a stubborn refusal to face facts. The return of the southern Netherlands to William's monarchical rule was out of the question, while the maintenance of the army on a war footing had burdened the national budget since 1831. The government had to take out loan after loan. The intransigent foreign policy not only deprived domestic politics of the energy needed to launch new initiatives but also drained the kingdom's finances.

The anti-autocratic movement that now gathered momentum was perhaps foreshadowed by the Secession of 1834, but it is more accurate to emphasize the desire of the educated middle class for greater political influence and the grave concerns of the financial community about the growing national debt. In 1839, the decision was finally made to accept the division of the kingdom. The king accepted the terms of separation proposed by the Great Powers in 1831. But this was only the beginning, not the end, of the problems facing William. It was time to clean up the political house. The division of the kingdom in any case required a revision of the constitution—the existing one was still that of the United Kingdom—and new constitutional views began to circulate. Thorbecke devoted a course of lectures at Leyden to the desirable changes and published the lectures under the title *Notes on the Constitution*.[217] A complete account of the financial problems was drawn up, which aroused great indignation when the extent of the chaos and waste became apparent. Even when foreign loans had to be taken out, the king's sons serving in the field were making exorbitant expenditures. Was it not unconscionable that the king's personal regime was ruining the country's finances? The call for ministerial accountability grew louder.

Growing opposition led to William's abdication in November 1840. There was another reason for his departure. After his wife's death in 1839, the king had become engaged to Henriëtte d'Oultremont—a Belgian countess, no less! Both her nationality and her Roman Catholic background led to strong disapproval of the proposed marriage, even from the moderate middle groups. William I now passed the throne to his son William II. As the latter began his reign, it was widely expected that the country would have a new beginning. The Belgian question was settled, and the youthful king showed signs of moving with the times. The new ruler gave greater freedom to Roman Catholics in the Netherlands and was more dynamic than his father. But much to the chagrin of the opposition, he made no changes, at least for the time being, to the autocratic form of government he had inherited. Nor did he change his father's conscientious bureaucratic approach to his job. The new king was a man of the army, known in the

Netherlands as the "Hero of Waterloo," and in the 1830s he had often been at the front in the South. The people of The Hague once saw their new king rush out of the palace to assist firemen at a blaze and then disappear from the scene when the fire was under control. He enjoyed the style of chivalry, but was not a man to preside over a roundtable of advisors. His father had sought the advice of prominent members of society, but William II felt no need for that. Still, he could be influenced, and so his policies could change. You never knew where he stood.

As a result of the succession, social and cultural life in the 1840s remained rather uneventful. The strong hand of William I was gone, and the leading elite no longer knew where things were going. These circumstances encouraged a ferment of ideas about the future of the country and finally gave rise to a proper public debate on the matter. There was doubt and uncertainty about the identity of the Netherlands. The rising liberals called for a revision of the constitution, while conservative forces saw their way clear to developing anti-papist agitation. Holland's merchant class wanted greater opportunities for trade and development, while the inland provinces struggled through years of poverty, disease, and hunger. The government had to try to overcome the threat of financial collapse, and society began to demand its share of power and leadership in the nation. The situation was complex, but also quite open. There was a soapbox for every opinion leader who could say what direction should be taken. These were the years when Thorbecke and Groen van Prinsterer took their message to the nation. Thorbecke did so earlier, more aggressively and more directly than Groen. Neither man had unquestioned authority over the public. These forty-year-olds were too young for that and had not yet established their reputations. But their voices were clear and carried far.

GROEN'S RELATION TO THE ROYAL FAMILY

The events in the royal family must have made a deep impression on anyone who was close to the court, who saw princes and princesses in church, and who had a deep respect for the House of Orange. In Groen's eyes, the events were dramatic. If they did not shake his fundamental attachment to the dynasty, they certainly lowered his expectations. His ties to William I were the strongest and most personal. Groen had served at the highest level of his government, and his relationship with the king was one of mutual respect. Although personal contacts were reduced to a minimum after the summer of 1837, Groen continued to feel a strong attachment to this king. Thus, the proposed second marriage was not only repugnant to him but also put him in a very gloomy mood. In his mind, the idea that a prince of the House of Orange, scion of a family that adhered to the Reformed religion, would marry a Roman Catholic princess was unthinkable. He applauded the fact that several ministers in The Hague, including Rev. Dermout, openly expressed their disapproval from the pulpit. At Groen's last audiences with the king, the atmosphere had not been very open, and the informal conversations hardly rose above the level of comments about the weather. Chatting about "the rain and a fine day" and other "unimportant things" while weighty issues hung in the balance caused Groen to return home in a melancholy mood.[218]

The abdication put an end to the shriveled relationship between William I and the director of the Royal Family Archives. A new relationship would have to be established with William II. Groen did not really know William II, in part because during the 1830s the crown prince was usually in the field with the troops. When William II took up residence in The Hague, Groen introduced himself at court, but their acquaintance did not go much further. A bond never developed between Groen and William II, such as had existed between him and William I, a situation that had given Groen the opportunity to bring his point of view to the attention of His Majesty.

In addition, the interest in the history of the Orange dynasty that had been so great with William I was largely absent with William II. The archives were published by a standing order of William I, but William II regarded them as the laurels of an earlier reign and showed little interest in them. All this did little to motivate the family archivist, who in previous years had felt that his work was a personal service to the king. Groen's work on the archives slowed down, and the volumes completed in 1841 and 1847 were not delivered personally, but in a parcel with a covering letter. He no longer visited the court, and when an equestrian statue of William the Silent was unveiled in November 1845, the publisher of his correspondence was not even invited.[219]

The slow pace of publication was also related to the poor housing of the Royal Family Archives. Once again, the court was to blame. In 1839, the palace on Plein Square was being prepared for the crown prince, the future William III, and Sophia von Württemberg, who were to live there after their wedding. The family archives had to move out. Groen had known about this in advance and had submitted plans for the purchase of a building as early as 1837. He wanted the archives to be housed in a spacious, modern building with fireproof rooms and controlled humidity. But his plans were deemed too costly, and with time pressing, a temporary solution was proposed. Pending a decision on a new building, the family archives were housed in a "hall" in the Binnenhof or inner courtyard of the parliament buildings. The room was located in the Cabinet of Japanese Rarities, a small collection of curiosities that Dutch administrators had shipped back to the mother country from the trading post on the island of Decima over the centuries. The curator was not exaggerating when he wrote to Groen that he could only offer "provisional accommodations."[220] There was not enough room for all the documents, and the safe containing the most valuable archival items was set up in the Noordeinde Palace. The whole situation soon proved to be less provisional than it had been made out to be. It was not until 1849 that new arrangements were made. For Groen, all this was far less than he had expected. From 1840 onward, he confined himself to overseeing the family archives and greatly reduced his involvement in day-to-day affairs.[221] By now, other priorities were on his agenda.

FIRST EXPERIENCE AS A PARLIAMENTARIAN

Naturally, Cousin's report on primary education in the Netherlands was soon on Groen's desk. He read it as soon as it came out, as he was wont to do with new books that everyone was talking about. He was already familiar with parts of it because they had appeared in the press before. That is why he was able to refer to Cousin in *The Measures Against the Seceders*. The context also explains this particular reference. Cousin had given a favorable assessment of the Dutch educational system, but not of its religious quality.[222] Positive religious instruction was not possible in the "mixed" or common schools of the Netherlands, and this had struck Cousin as a serious shortcoming that would weaken public morality. The Education Act of 1806 spoke of teaching children "all the civic and Christian virtues," but what, Cousin wondered, could that mean? An "abstract and philosophical" Christian morality?[223] Groen was taken aback by this passage and began a concentrated study of the practice of primary education in his country. It was a topic that also played a role in his circle of acquaintances—men of the Réveil, such as Elout, Capadose, Van der Kemp, and Aeneas baron Mackay—residents of The Hague who were looking for an acceptable school environment for their children. Groen wanted to know more about the situation in the world of education. Was it really true about Amsterdam, he asked his friend Koenen, that "the Bible is no longer read in the city's schools out of respect for the Roman Catholics?"[224] It was true. Groen soon became convinced that the common public school was incapable of providing the kind of religious education that was in keeping with the Christian character of the nation. Both Protestants and Catholics complained that the public school was too vague and unclear for all believers. Groen echoed this opposition against the current school system, relying on Cousin's recommendations for smaller classes, better teacher training, and above all, more intentional religious instruction.

Cousin's report and Groen's response to it both fit within the broader framework of the rising cultural aspirations of nation-states throughout Europe. Throughout the nineteenth century, education became a major focus of government attention. The formation of citizens in the spirit of the nation was emphatically taken in hand. In the modernizing states, education became the primary instrument for stimulating a national culture.[225] A "powerful lever," as Groen called it.[226] The question of the spirit in which education should be provided became a key issue for political struggle and social action. Such was the case in the Netherlands, where pedagogical ideals shaped public discussions of education. The Groningen School of Theology had in mind the moral elevation of man through acquaintance with the example of Jesus. The Socratic school of Van Heusde gave impetus to a kind of Christian humanism that aimed at the formation of a harmonious individual. And then there were the orthodox Protestants and Roman Catholics with their respective religious vision of education. The battle that broke out in the 1840s and would last for many decades was fought between, on the one hand, the proponents of the "mixed" school—a school free from instruction in the specific doctrines of any one denomination, and therefore a "nonsectarian" common school—and the representatives of Protestant and Catholic thought, who wished to educate children in their own religious atmosphere. For Groen, freedom of education was a natural extension of freedom of religion. Freedom of education, he said, is "freedom of religion with respect to one's children."[227] A country like the Netherlands, he explained, in which the Christian religion had left deep marks, should have a corresponding kind of primary education. In this way the spirit of the nation could be shaped by the gospel.

Education became a major issue in Groen's first term as a member of Parliament. In July 1840, he was delegated by the provincial government of Holland to the Double Chamber of the States-General, which was to deliberate and vote on proposals for a revision of the constitution. The Chamber was called "double" because the membership of the lower house was doubled for the occasion by the addition of "extraordinary members," of which Groen was one.

His election had a prelude. In March 1840, Groen had entered the battle for public opinion on constitutional revision by publishing his *Contribution Toward a Revision of the Constitution in a Netherlandic Spirit*.[228] The 150-page book was a position paper in the discussions on the desirability and extent of constitutional revision. A general revision was not Groen's goal, at least not all at once. He considered the existing constitution to be quite workable, provided it was understood and interpreted in a non-revolutionary and Christian-historical sense, with respect for the nation's heritage. He reproached the government and Parliament for not having done so. Only toward the end of *Contribution* did he make a few suggestions for revision that he considered "worthy of consideration."[229] This illustrated the difference between him and Thorbecke, who had just published a series of articles containing a complete draft of a new constitution. This went too far for Groen. In a letter to Van Assen, he called it a "forcing of decisions on questions which are not yet ripe for public discussion."[230] The difference was that Thorbecke's proposals were based on a general revision in the short term, whereas Groen believed that a transformation of the whole could only be achieved by gradual changes in the existing situation. It was his lifelong conviction that a constitution had to express what "lived" in the nation—what was in tune with the spirit of the people and resonated with them. Any revision had to be slow and gradual.

Groen and Thorbecke met in the Double Chamber. The extraordinary members were the newcomers who took an active and critical part in the deliberations with the sitting parliamentarians. The Chamber met during the month of August 1840. On several occasions Groen was supported by Thorbecke. The revision proposals that the government submitted to the Chamber were not very radical and disappointed most of the deputies. They concerned the addition of the province of Limburg to the Netherlands, the division of the old province of Holland into North Holland and South Holland, personal liability for ministers of the crown, and minor changes in the franchise. The proposals were so far from Thorbecke's ideal that he mostly kept silent. The same could not be said of Groen. He, too, considered the proposals "inadequate," but from his own point of view. He declared himself a member of the "opposition." In his first major speech, he reviewed the broad outlines of his published contribution: "a constitutional revision in and of itself will not benefit us; there will be no benefit except through a return to Christian, historical, Dutch principles."[231] According to Groen, the line that had been broken in 1795 and given no chance after 1813 had to be resumed. This meant overturning the rudder of the ship of state, not just revising the constitution.

> What do we desire? We desire to move from the realm of revolutionary institutions to the terrain of the historical rights of the people, from the realm of fictions to the sphere of reality; to a real government instead of a centralizing administration; to autonomous liberties and rights also for territories, municipalities, the Church, instead of a general destruction, at the pleasure of the State, of every organic entity. We want to move toward a House of Representatives that truly, and not only in name, represents not the people, but the Dutch people.[232]

Groen enjoyed his time in the Chamber, and he also had an attentive audience. Carel van der Kemp, who was present at the meetings, noticed that Groen's speeches caused a stir in the Chamber: "They all left their seats to crowd around him to hear him better. His voice was soft, but audible in the gallery. He improvised, and from that moment there seemed to be more spirit."[233] Apparently Groen's first attempts at parliamentary oratory were worth hearing: he was energetic, well-documented, witty in debate, and made effective use of titillating irony. He certainly needed these weapons, for his main ideas struck at the root of the basic outlook of many members. Vigorous debates ensued over Groen's views on the organization of the church, his repeated appeals for the Seceders, and especially his ideas on freedom of education. His assertion that education in the public schools was both unchristian and antichristian caused quite a stir. Such strong language had not been heard in the Chamber for a long time. But Groen refused to back down. The school was unchristian because the Bible was no longer read, and it was antichristian because God was presented as the "universal Father of mankind" without referring to Christ as mediator, thus preaching an idol, a "figment of human wisdom."[234] Bringing together the various religious beliefs turned "the salt of education" into an "impotent surrogate."[235] Groen's contributions touched a sensitive spot for the conservative supporters of the common public school. They defended the provision for "instruction in the virtues" on the basis of a vague "common morality," but Groen's response was sharp: "Look at the children, we have heard you say; look how they are together in sweet fellowship, without distinction of religious sect. But have you followed them in the rest of their lives? Have you seen much fruit of your so-called common Christian morality?"[236]

The Double Chamber had no authority to make decisions about education, but its debates raised education to a higher place on the political agenda. In November of that year, after the revised constitution came into effect, a state commission was set up to investigate religious grievances against the common school and make recommendations to the government. This move betrays the hand of William II, who was sensitive to Catholic grievances, as evidenced by the six appointees to the commission, two of whom were Catholics. Groen was also appointed—no doubt in recognition of his parliamentary merits, but certainly also with the intention of giving the commission the appearance of "impartiality." Each wing was now represented. It was a curious fact that Groen served on a commission with a Catholic bishop. Earlier that year, he had incurred the wrath of Catholics by stating in his contribution that the province of Limburg should be placed under a separate administration because of its religion, which differed from that of the rest of the Netherlands.[237] This was Groen's idea which Dutch Catholics took very badly and would long remember.[238]

The State Commission involved a great deal of work. This time Groen could not limit himself to "main ideas" but had to come up with a concrete solution. Groen dreaded the responsibility. Might it even be necessary to change the Education Act? An important question was whether, in addition to the public schools, there should be more room for the private schools that were springing up here and there, but which did not receive state funding. In the weeks before the state commission began its meetings, Groen received a flood of letters with alarms, suggestions, and requests from supporters, pastors, school inspectors, and teachers. It often made him feel "under a lot of pressure," Betsy reported from the home front.[239] Groen himself consulted his friends at home and abroad and also used his new correspondents to form his own opinions. He had become the nerve center of orthodox Protestant educational thought. Suddenly, the tranquility in which he had worked in recent years was rudely interrupted.

In other parts of the country, different ideas were expressed. For the first time, Groen received a message from the village of Hemmen in the center of the country. Here a young pastor, Ottho Gerhard Heldring, had worked hard to improve local educational opportunities. The existing common public school was not conducive to Christian education, Heldring told Groen: "The teachers are generally ignorant of the Bible stories and of the Bible in general."[240] In the city of Nymegen, according to lawyer Justinus J. L. van der Brugghen, whom we will meet again later, it was simply not possible to have a "Christian" education: if prayers were said by a Protestant teacher, Catholic parents would remove their children from school;[241] if it was possible to get a Catholic teacher to say a Protestant collect or set prayer, other parents would demand "that an Ave Maria and the sign of the cross be added."[242] The most vehement anti-Catholic voices came from the west and north of the country. The Netherlands would then be helping "the spirit of Catholicism and Jesuitism to break new ground in our dear fatherland."[243] And then there were the rural interests, that is, the interests of the village schoolmaster who drew his income from the local population. Competition from a private school would deprive him of his livelihood and leave him to teach the less gifted children. There were already some teachers, as one inspector told Groen in a veiled threat, who had resigned in anticipation of the disaster.[244]

The discussions in the Commission dragged on. The two Catholic members argued for the right to establish private schools. The three Protestant members argued that efforts should be made to improve the existing system of common schools, where children of all denominations were welcomed. The grievances could be addressed by admitting more Roman Catholic school inspectors and teachers.[245] Groen's view began to crystallize during the intensive meetings. He would favor a priori an extension of educational freedom. He saw the freedom to establish one's own schools as a right—"the right of parents and the Church; a right out of a duty to God. We claim it as a constitutional right."[246] While the state has a responsibility for public education, it has no right to place children under its supervision. The Act of 1806, a product of the Restoration, contained an element of coercion: like the church, the school was to be tied to the "leading strings of the government." Groen, on the other hand, recognized a role for parents and especially for the church, which had traditionally played an important role in primary education. In any case, there should be no division "between home, school and church." Thus, he appreciated the proposal of the Catholics, but at the same time felt that no time bomb should be placed under the existing system, which he called a "necessary evil." Possibilities for teaching Christian doctrine should be sought within the common school.[247]

The Antirevolutionary

What Groen had in mind he clarified in notes to himself as he prepared for the meetings. In a staccato style, he sketched out his ideal of a Christian school:

> No neglect of skills needed in society. No overloading and thus arousing dislike. No prying into mysteries. But the truths necessary for salvation are what we want to make the center of the child's intellectual and moral development. It is not necessary to teach the child many things, but what is useful; above all, what is necessary. This is our guideline. Let the teacher be a Christian; not only with the head, but also with the heart. Let the Bible be the book of books, the foundation of education and upbringing. The events, commandments, and promises of the Scriptures; Bible history, world history, and national history in relation to the truth of the gospel. Also, other parts of education. To relate, address, and exhort in a Christian manner. Warning against evil because it is sin, a transgression of God's law. Calling to duty out of gratitude for God's love for us. Thus, members of the church, useful citizens of the state.[248]

These notes take us to the heart of Christian schooling, Groen's salt of education.

The State Commission was unable to reach a solution. The three conservative members came up with a majority report that recommended improvements in the operation of the public school without changing the system. Groen, seeing no place for his own school in this system, came with a separate report advocating a drastic change in the system that would result in a division within according to religious persuasion. The public school would become a kind of hotel school; under the roof of public education there would be Protestant, Roman Catholic, and Jewish schools. In this way, the ideal of a Protestant Christian school would be guaranteed without curtailing the rights of other faiths. Groen did not work out this concept; he merely presented his idea. Finally, he recommended the extension of educational freedom to facilitate the establishment of private schools. This proposal was strongly opposed by the three Protestant signatories of the majority report, but supported by the two Catholic members. Both reports were presented to the king at the end of January 1841. The divided Commission, much to the chagrin of William II, had failed to suggest a politically viable course of action. Some adjustments were made in 1842, but these left the existing system largely intact. The increased ability to establish private schools proved to be merely cosmetic. As a result, the problems dragged on throughout the 1840s.

HISTORY FOR THE CHRISTIAN SCHOOL

After his work for the State Commission came to an end, Groen found it difficult to resume his normal activities. A new volume of the archives was awaiting final editing, but the public interest would not let him go. Van Assen wanted to nominate him as a full member of the Council of State. Groen, however, doubted that he could do much good there, given "my way of thinking"; he would much rather be elected to the Second Chamber, but he also realized that he did not stand much of a chance.[249] His pronounced political stance did not make him an attractive candidate for the provincial authorities, who would have to delegate him again. It was reminiscent of Bilderdijk when he wrote to Van Assen that his views did not fit in anywhere and that he had no choice but to continue as a private citizen.[250] Nevertheless, Groen had the public interest in mind at this time when he conceived a new plan. He began to write a book on the whole of Dutch history. Perhaps it was an old plan, since people in Protestant circles had been talking for some time about the need for such a history in order not to be dependent on the thirteen volumes of Bilderdijk that had begun to appear in those years.[251] Many felt that to appreciate this particular version one had to have heard Bilderdijk in person. In any case, Bilderdijk's lectures on history, when published, were very disappointing, certainly in the light of the many new facts that were increasingly being uncovered by the new historical science. Van der Kemp was invited in 1837 by the Amsterdam publisher Höveker to write "a popular history of the fatherland in two or three volumes, based on Christian Reformed principles," but he declined.[252] Da Costa had also toyed with the idea, but his work schedule was much more irregular than Groen's, and he was not quick to get a work ready for publication; moreover, he thought it only right that Groen, who was undoubtedly the best candidate in the field, should take up the task.[253]

If the idea of a Protestant history book had been around for some time, the occasion and the form of Groen's undertaking were new. With his publication, Groen wanted to be of service to the Christian school, the school he had in mind during his work for the State Commission. If the situation in the educational world was really so bad with regard to Bible knowledge and the application of Bible teaching, then good Christian literature should not be lacking. Groen's *Handbook of the History of the Fatherland*[254] was intended to fill a void.

It is clear from its form that Groen's *Handbook* promoted a particular view of education. The handbook became a history book in which biblical texts were interwoven at many points in the text. Again and again the author gives hints and suggestions to encourage Christian reflection on history. Unsympathetic readers later accused him of "piling Bible text upon Bible text" and "larding the whole thing with thick layers of theology."[255] In private letters to friends, Thorbecke spoke of the book with contempt, calling it a "delivery of texts from Mrs. Groen's sewing basket."[256] The emphatic use of the Bible was less a personal need on Groen's part to "speak the language of piety"[257] than it was an attempt on his part to meet the needs of Christian schools for educational materials. The Bible, as we have seen, had to be "the book of books" for Groen, also for the teaching of history. The biblical texts were the salt of Groen's Protestant version of history.

An open Bible in history class: this was also a polemical gesture in the direction of the Catholics. They were the ones who prevented the Bible from being read in public schools, at least where they had local influence. Groen wanted to bring the Bible back into the schools. He saw this as a more powerful weapon than the conservatives' attempt to prevent Catholics of having private schools. The "domination" of the "Roman Church" had been prepared "by setting aside the Word of God [and] sending the nation's most precious memories into oblivion."[258] This is how he formulated it for parents and teachers in the preface to his *Brief Survey of the History of the Fatherland*, which he completed in December 1841. This work of just over one hundred pages covered the entire history of the Netherlands and was intended as a guide for teaching history to children "from ten to twelve years of age." This little book delighted Betsy.[259] The following year, a small book of songs and poems was published to be used in conjunction with the history lessons. The texts for this collection were taken from Hieronymus van Alphen, Willem Bilderdijk, Isaac da Costa, Jacob van Lennep, Jacob Cats, and Joost van den Vondel. Meanwhile, Groen was working on the much more elaborate installments of the manual, the last of which would not be published until 1846. When Da Costa received a complimentary copy of the first installment, he wrote to Groen, "By reading a few passages aloud, I have already refreshed the heart of a promising young teacher, who immediately wanted to buy a copy."[260] This was exactly the effect Groen wanted. The manual would indeed find its way into the hands of many teachers and serve as a guide. They made indexes for it and popularized the historical vision articulated by Groen.[261]

Groen's interpretation of Dutch history would influence entire generations. He focused on the paramount importance of the sixteenth-century Reformation for the Netherlands. It was a time when the gospel was once again free to spread among the people of the Netherlands. The history that preceded it—Groen's narrative begins with the early Middle Ages—is characterized by the Christianization of Europe. The Protestant Reformation, however, brought a purer form of the faith, stripping it of "human accretions." Roman Catholic Christianity was replaced by Protestant Christianity. The new faith "rejuvenated, renewed, and ennobled" the Netherlands.[262] The confession of the Reformed church became the life principle of the Dutch Republic. But the people had to suffer for this confession, and they had to fight for it in a war that lasted eighty years. What was at stake in this war of independence was not a new political arrangement or a growing national identity, but the survival of the church. The republic had its origin in the political will to protect the Reformed church, with which the state had previously entered into a unity. The Dutch triumph over absolutism and the Inquisition was due to a strong faith in God, confirmed by extraordinary deliverances: "Faith was inseparable from divine blessings." The Dutch could always count on the House of Orange-Nassau. This house was called by God to a special mission, namely "to lead the Republic in guarding and upholding the Gospel, liberty, and justice."[263] The most telling examples were William of Orange, "the Silent" (1533–84), and his great-nephew William III (1650–1702). Groen repeatedly points to their Christian conviction and religious courage, even under the worst slanders and greatest disappointments.

Suffering for the faith and contending for its preservation were followed by a period of national greatness. Groen was convinced that faithfulness to the gospel had brought great blessings to the Netherlands. It gave strength to Christian institutions and made national virtues of "piety, industry, honesty, modesty, simplicity, and humility."[264] The greatness of the Republic in the seventeenth century was the result of taking the Bible seriously in its relevance to public life. Holland's gradual decline in the eighteenth century, by contrast, was the result of growing unbelief. Groen believed that the past "reveals God's omnipotence, wisdom, justice, and grace in the annals of a sinful humanity."[265] The handbook drew a close connection between "it is written"—that is, in the Bible—and "it has come to pass." Its quotations from Scripture make this clear. Nearly half of the Bible verses Groen quotes serve to emphasize a spiritual interpretation of events, whether negative or positive; another quarter deal with promises the Bible makes to those who honor God and threats of punishment and destruction to those who forsake God.[266] These things, Groen wanted to say, have happened; and the history of the Netherlands is a perfect illustration. Groen did not claim to have penetrated "the mysteries of the divine government of the world," but he did want to encourage people to return to the old religion that had once been "the soul of the state."[267]

Groen's *Handbook* with more than a thousand pages made him known to a broad section of the Dutch public. This was not due to any literary merit. Groen was no Michelet, nor did he attempt to write a bestseller. Rather, he presented an extensive factual account in short passages, sometimes in incomplete sentences.[268] Thus, the handbook was more of a textbook or manual than a narrative. It presented a responsible compendium of Dutch history according to the latest scholarship. As a factual account, it was a reliable guide that was welcomed by many. Of course, the thick volume was most welcomed in Protestant circles. There it was hailed as a monument to their particular version of history. What was remarkable, however, was that Groen, who had been so critical of Bilderdijk's method, presented an interpretation that was broadly similar to Bilderdijk's. The appreciation of the role of the House of Orange; the aversion to revolt and revolution against legitimate authority; the decline of the Republic as a result of unbelief and Francophilia; the rejection of the principle of popular sovereignty—all these themes had been present in Bilderdijk. Groen purified and softened them in the light of his own research, and he added a biblical interpretation that could be edifying. Thus was born the Protestant version of Dutch history on which generations were raised.

A CHILDLIKE FAITH

To nurture is more than to educate. Because the Réveil considered nothing more important than the human soul, it was concerned with the education of children. Its interest in the child was based on a high regard for the precious inner life of every human being. That is why it also cared for the poor, the sexually abused, and the elderly. But even more important than its social work in the slums was the care it gave to the spiritual development of the individual child.

In their private correspondence, members of the Réveil wrote about nurturing children in the faith. They looked forward with great interest to the moment when the children would make their personal decisions for Christ. Willem and Betsy, though they had no children of their own, shared in this interest, though in their own way. Groen directed his historical work toward children. On the title page of his brief survey, he had the publisher print the words from Deuteronomy 31:12, "Gather the children together, that they may hear, and learn, and fear the LORD your God." When the manual was finished, he chose a few phrases from Psalm 78:4–7 as its motto:

> We will not hide them from their children; we will tell to the coming generation the glorious deeds of the LORD, and his might, and the wonders that he has done . . . that the next generation might know them, so that they should set their hope in God, and not forget the works of God, but keep his commandments.[269]

Despite all this, Groen did not have the gift of speaking to children on their level. According to Koenen, the manual was too difficult for children. Groen was more effective in his efforts on behalf of Christian day schools.

By 1839, Groen was on the board of the Walloon church's orphanage, which included a school. The orphanage and school were partly populated by "problem youth." The regents had to deal with many "sins" and almost every month there was a child who had to "report to the office" to receive a stern rebuke from the solemn supervisors. Groen was involved in practical matters concerning the school, the children, and the teaching staff.[270] In addition, he spent several hours each Saturday evening at the orphanage talking with the older boys.[271] He may have given them catechism lessons; in any case, he was involved in preparing them to make public professions of faith.

As time went on, Groen's involvement in Christian education would only intensify. In the summer of 1842, he made an "excursion" to the Ruhr area to visit a number of Christian schools. He even sat in on a class taught by Mr. Zahn, an educator well known in Christian circles. Groen was pleased to see that the children "followed the lessons with rapt attention."[272] He had volunteered for this summer "internship" in connection with a private initiative in The Hague. Since 1842 he and a group of associates had taken steps to establish a Christian day school in that city. Such a venture had to follow the guidelines laid down in the royal decree of January 1842, with which Groen was of course very familiar as a former member of the State Commission. The new rules were intended to provide greater opportunities for private education. Groen and his friends were eager to find out if these rules were workable, so they applied to the city authorities for permission. The application process dragged on for years and was still pending in 1848. When the first application was denied, another was made, and then a series of appeals were made to the city, the province, and finally to the king, all to no avail. The request for a permit was, of course, in the nature of a demonstration against the existing situation. The men were airing a grievance and publicly requesting "the restoration of a former freedom in the weightiest of interests."[273] One suspects that the emphasis on this criticism of current educational policy was the reason that after a few years the petitioners received no further response. Their action for a Christian school in The Hague was smothered with silence.

While the men preferred public policy, the women turned to practical matters. Betsy kept in touch with the young Willem Oswald in Switzerland. The Groens were certainly not forgotten there. Merle wrote of Betsy's godson, "He is very fond of his name Willem."[274] At home, Betsy personally supervised the sewing school, was involved in the supervision of the Walloon church orphanage, and showed interest in the children of her friends by sending them gifts and Christian literature. Most importantly, Betsy wanted the children to know Jesus. The outspokenness with which the Groens promoted this idea created tension in the family. The already uneasy relationship with Keetje and her husband, Mari, took on an added dimension when friction arose over the raising of their only child, Jacqueline. The two couples even seem to have corresponded about it. Keetje defended herself against advice she ultimately found to be of little use: "It always pains me, dear Willem and Betsy, when I think how much you love the child and that you think we are not bringing her up right . . . but there is much that is good in books but hard to put into practice."[275] Apparently this was her impression of the educational concerns of her brother and sister-in-law; it was the voice of experience criticizing those who knew only theory. Willem and Betsy probably did not accept this criticism. All they wanted was for Jacqueline to become a Christian. So, on her birthday Betsy sent her somewhat spoiled niece some devotional books along with toys. Mother Keetje expressed her gratitude for the gift by writing back that the books looked "most interesting."[276] A phrase like that usually means little interest. In their relationship with Keetje and Mari, Willem and Betsy felt the same distance they had felt toward father Groen.

The friends of the Réveil had respect for the child and could see through its eyes. For them, the child's world, childhood in general, was a guarantee of sincerity of faith. A child's simple trust in God was the model for adults. A childlike acceptance of the truths of the gospel was sufficient. Groen repeatedly warned against the desire to "enter into the mysteries."[277] Believers were not to seek the "hidden counsel" of God, but to adhere to the "Scriptures." Groen's difficulty with the doctrine of election is rooted in his aversion to anything that might stand in the way of a childlike faith. When Groen's *Handbook* comes to this doctrine in connection with the Arminian controversy of the early seventeenth century, he remarks that the eye of faith must be fixed on Christ and not on "what is closed to us."[278] The life of faith in the Réveil was anti-intellectual and preferably non-theological, and it was reflected in the trusting faith of the child. The man who best exemplified this in his life was Willem de Clercq. The friends of Réveil were shocked by the news of his sudden death on February 4, 1844, leaving behind a wife and seven children. Groen walked around for days "as if in a daze,"[279] then fell ill again, complaining of nerves. Da Costa, for his part, could hardly find the words to express his grief. He had recovered by the time he spoke at the graveside. Groen later thanked him from the bottom of his heart for what he said there: "Willem de Clercq was a child. That was the dominant trait of his heart and his life, toward people and toward God."[280] The Réveil opened its soul at this grave. It too wanted to be childlike in faith, as Willem de Clercq had been.

This was also true of Groen. From the first time he met him, Willem de Clercq had been an "example" to him, he confessed.[281] Groen, too, had a childlike quality, and according to those around him, he was a model of quiet confidence. In social interactions, Willem was "so mild and childlike," Betsy once wrote to a friend.[282] He showed an interest in people's lives, including those in the working-class neighborhoods, whose homes he visited several winters in the company of his friend Elout. He was grateful for small things and rejoiced in every sign of affection and solidarity. He exuded a degree of benevolence that seemed naive and sometimes turned out to be based on false expectations of sympathy and affinity. But he also had another trait that was particularly evident in his public behavior. He did not always feel safe there and could attack with biting sarcasm and defend himself with caustic retorts. Certainly, Groen did not give himself away easily in social circles: his face could suddenly freeze and he would abruptly end a conversation by falling silent. In this he very much resembled his father's stiffness and inflexibility. The circle of real friends around him remained small. It was with a small group that he later entered the Second

Chamber, and he rarely made new friends there. They were afraid of his intellect and annoyed by the contentious tone of his speeches. In their eyes, his stubbornness in holding to his personal views made him useless for dealing with practical matters. As he became more of a public figure, he began to take on the appearance of "the general." Willem de Clercq could have foreseen this: he knew that Groen's childishness was in tension with his personality. It had been a prominent theme in their conversations and correspondence over the years.

THE CHRISTIAN FRIENDS

In the first half of the 1840s, Groen seems to have reconciled himself to a role on the fringes of society. He worked steadily on his historical publications, served several terms on the consistory of the Walloon church, corresponded and consulted with friends and acquaintances, but lived the life of a private citizen, isolated from the larger world. He was seen as a man who lived for a life of scholarship, but was barred from a university post because of his peculiar views. In the meantime, he founded his own academy on the second floor of his large house on the Korte Vijverberg. In number of publications, he surpassed many an academic of his time.

From the second half of the forties, the public role he would later play began to take shape. The first step was not taken by Groen himself, but by Heldring, the Reformed pastor of Hemmen, a village in the backwoods of the Veluwe. Heldring was involved in all kinds of church and social work: fighting alcoholism, digging wells, promoting literacy programs, organizing poor relief. At the same time, he wanted to strengthen Reformed doctrine in the church and had been excluded from the Classical Council because of his "orthodoxy." His fellow pastors also did not go along with him in his social activities. Since 1840 he had corresponded with prominent figures in the Réveil. In May 1845, after an extended conversation with Groen, he sent a long letter to the brethren in Amsterdam and The Hague, urging mutual consultation and joint ventures, especially in the area of social action.[283] The letter unleashed latent energies. It was in the spirit of the hoped-for revival. The brothers in Amsterdam were ready to organize something, and Groen made sure that the circle of brothers in The Hague responded positively to the proposal. The two fronts were soon united and a first meeting was held in Amsterdam at the end of August. This was the first of the meetings of the "Christian Friends" who were to meet in Amsterdam for several days twice

The Salt of Education, the Salt of the Earth

a year under Groen's leadership. Groen's election to chair the meetings underscored his prominent position in the Réveil.

The meetings were highlights for the chairman, who had found his spiritual home in the Réveil. But Groen did not put his stamp on the meetings. The Christian Friends were a loose association of brothers from different denominations and places. Most participants did not want a "society," a formal association with a mission statement; they felt that an association would be too "activist" and too binding. Groen himself was in favor of a "closer union," but he could not persuade a majority to support this idea.[284] In the beginning they thought of the Société Évangélique in Switzerland as a kind of model, and this idea also came from Groen. But they could not make up their minds, and in the end, they preferred a loose structure. This meant that the nature of their meetings, apart from their orthodoxy, remained somewhat vague. Because Lutheran, Episcopalian, and a few Secessionist pastors participated, the Christian Friends were seen by some kindred spirits abroad as "a step toward independence."[285] Reformed pastors would have found little appeal in this notion. Half a dozen of them, including the new star on the Réveil horizon, Dr. Nicolaas Beets, attended the first few meetings. The lay element dominated, however, and pushed the theological discussions to the background. According to Groen, this was a good thing: Christian friends should be able to rise above theological differences by meeting and deliberating together as brothers.

Thus, while the participants in the meetings were not really committed to any particular action, they were all convinced that some form of coordination of their activities could do more to advance Christian interests in the country. Groen had long been convinced that they could not confine themselves to criticizing the apathy of others or protesting against the encroachment of liberal theology in the church. In several places, Christian Friends energized people. The number of attendees grew from about forty to two hundred in a few years. This fact alone made their meetings an event of considerable weight in church and society. At the semi-annual meetings, reports were read on activities in the church, education, missions, and social work, and new initiatives were proposed and discussed. Beets referred to this as "sprinkling the world with the salt of the earth."[286] In fact, brothers from all parts of the world came to Amsterdam to report on their travels or visits to foreign mission fields. At the very first meeting it was decided to start a magazine, of which Koenen, who declined, and then Heldring were invited to become editors. The first issue of *Christian Voices* appeared in late 1846 on a monthly basis, and the journal would continue to appear until 1875.[287]

From a broader perspective, the organization of regular contact among these brethren can be seen as a reaction to the growing influence of liberalism and modernism. A new era was dawning in which the upper middle class would become increasingly involved in church and social affairs. This could only mean that the spirit of theological modernism would gain ground, since the upper classes were more liberal than orthodox. The Christian Friends were a counter-movement coming from the same upper classes, but in a different direction. A considerable portion of the articles published in the early volumes of *Christian Voices* were directed against the views of the Groningen School of Hofstede de Groot. This circle would always react vehemently against any new expression of liberal theology. The extent to which the interests of religion took precedence among them can be seen from the fact that *Christian Voices* paid little attention to the fight against liberalism in politics. Groen was about the only one who used its pages for political reflection. From 1850, Mackay began to contribute a monthly political column. This characterizes a situation in which few members of the Réveil were explicitly engaged in the study of politics.

After 1845, the spirit of revival sailed before the wind. New initiatives saw the light of day, and Christian activity visibly intensified. This stimulated Groen to reformulate his political and constitutional views. During the winter of 1845–46 he organized a series of Saturday evening lectures in the library of his home. He regarded them as a more or less final attempt to present the full range of his beliefs, this time orally. The central thesis of the lectures was that "the history of the last half-century is the peculiar development of revolutionary ideas."[288] In the final stages of completing his *Handbook*, he was forced to confront that half-century, and he puzzled over the proper way to analyze the period. Yet this analysis was crucial to his response to the spirit of the times. The literary and cultural journal *The Guide* (*De Gids*), founded in 1837 and now growing in influence as a battering ram of the spirit of liberalism, had begun to publish essays and articles on the French Revolution that Groen felt needed refuting.

It was a select company that gathered at Groen's house on Saturday evening. The host usually worked quietly on his publications, but this time he had been so quiet about his plan that Capadose, who lived in the same city, did not even know about it at first. The friends in Amsterdam were very surprised and even a little annoyed by Groen's lack of communication.

For a while, Koenen even considered traveling to The Hague to attend some of the lectures. Groen did not exactly please the Amsterdam brothers with this affair, and in the years that followed it would lead to some estrangement between them. They compared his series to Da Costa's public lectures, which were announced well in advance and attracted large audiences, sometimes as many as two hundred people. Groen himself faithfully attended Da Costa's readings in The Hague, but for his own lecture series he limited the audience to about twenty people by personal invitation. These included his two brothers-in-law, Hoffmann and Philipse, then a circle of like-minded men such as Elout, Gefken, Van der Kemp, Mackay, and Singendonck, and finally a group of politically interested gentlemen of The Hague.[289] Most of them worked in the judiciary or held positions in government agencies. Curiously, there were no clergymen in the audience. In 1847, the lectures were published under the title *Unbelief and Revolution*.[290] This publication contains the most mature formulation of Groen's political, historical, and philosophical views, and it was to gain considerable importance among Groen's spiritual descendants.[291] It is translated in several languages—as did not occur with his other publications—and is still read today. Let us look at the reasons for this reputation.

UNBELIEF AND REVOLUTION

What Groen presented in his lectures was not entirely new. It was the subject of "the revolution" that he had already discussed in his *Netherlandic Reflections* and in the latest installment of his *Handbook*. One member of the audience, Gefken, thought he had heard it all before.[292] Indeed, the question arises as to why, after all he had said about the revolution, Groen kept coming back to it. The preparatory studies preserved in manuscript in his archives suggest that the subject had become almost an obsession for him. Around 1840, he began taking notes again. He would not have done so had he not felt that he was on the verge of discovering the key to the political and social problems of his time. The revolution became for him the key to understand the world-historical changes he observed in his time. Groen belonged to those thinkers of the late eighteenth and early nineteenth centuries—Edmund Burke, Friedrich Julius Stahl, François Guizot (in his later period), and Jacob Burckhardt—who were convinced that the phenomena of the French Revolution and the Napoleonic Wars, the constant revolutions in politics and the world of learning, the marginalization of the church, and the decline of religious convictions were all interrelated, and that these phenomena represented a colossal break in the history of European civilization. What had taken place was an "inversion of the general spirit and mode of thought" of world-historical proportions; state, society, and the world of learning had each contributed to this catastrophic upheaval, which was "manifest in all Christendom."[293] For Groen, the revolution was the dissemination of the religion of mankind, the introduction of a new style of thinking and acting that he saw as a threat to everything he held dear as a Christian. The burning passion that pervades his lectures suggests how grave the situation really was in his eyes.

The negative part of his argument—showing what had *not* caused the revolution—was vehement, so vehement that he barely had time to get to the positive part of proving his thesis. This negative part does not deviate in the main from what he had written earlier, but this time he provided a broader argumentation. The great political revolutions, he argued, were ideologically prepared by revolutionary ideas: liberty and equality, popular sovereignty, the social contract, society as a human construct. These ideas imply a view of man as an agent and mover of history, and so they could only have become operational after a "complete skepticism" had taken hold of men's minds, rendering them incapable of believing in a living God who guides history. A spiritual vacuum was created that could be filled with human concepts. Government and state institutions were stripped of their divine origin and were seen as purely human creations. They could easily be removed to make the desired changes. Thus, man-made theories and concepts replaced the general spirit and mindset of European civilization. But this was only the beginning. The effect was not long in coming. According to Groen, there was a necessary and inevitable connection between unbelief and revolution in all areas of life, a connection so close that it could be captured in the image of the tree and its fruit.

However, in implementing this new approach to state and society, the revolution came into conflict with history. So it had to get rid of history as well. "The abolition of revelation and history is the life principle of the revolution."[294] The revolution was "a-historical," it was up against the testimony of the ages, Groen noted. The rule for the great thinkers of antiquity was "to begin with the Godhead and to consult experience," and thinkers of later times did the same. To silence this testimony, history had to be falsified. The revolution does this as easily as it reconstructs states. It creates a revolutionary interpretation of the past that is as absurd as it is grotesque.

The Salt of Education, the Salt of the Earth

Everything in antiquity and the Renaissance that was republican, or passed for republican, was now interpreted in a revolutionary sense. But republican thought and republican institutions of the past still recognized a divine right of government, whereas the revolutionary constitutions did not. This was the cardinal difference. The revolutionary mind, however, has no regard for historical "realities," but only for its own concepts. In this way it subjects history to its dictates.[295]

Part of the fame of Groen's critical analysis rests on the fact that he showed something of the effect of ideology in the age that began with the Enlightenment. People's minds were intoxicated with a new worldview that was rationalistic and dogmatic. Groen explored the "irresistible superiority" of this new view of reality and traced its course through the successive phases of the French Revolution. History, after all, is "the flaming script of the holy God."[296] Groen sought to demonstrate the necessary course of the Revolution in the historical events of France. The practical implementation of radical ideas led to the Reign of Terror with its outbreaks of excessive violence. Common sense was blinded and the conscience of the people was "seared with the hot iron of revolutionary sophisms."[297] Even leaders like Robespierre, who caused much bloodshed, were but instruments of an idea that controlled them. Liberty, equality, and fraternity became their very opposites. Men lacked a sense of responsibility, a minority terrorized the majority in the name of all, and no one was sure of his security or his life in a society that had once been presented as a utopia.

This political masquerade is a hallmark of the ideology. Even when peace seemed to prevail, the fires of war were being stoked across the borders. People were usually unaware of this masquerade; they allowed themselves to be deceived and swept along. This insight remained crucial for Groen. Liberals in every country were playing with fire, even when they embraced moderate forms of ideas derived from the Revolution. They proposed changes that appeared to be improvements on existing practices. Who could be against that? But under this guise, ideas were admitted that turned everything upside down. Today's liberals, says Groen, want to change the forms, but not the root of the evil:

> I gladly acknowledge their good intentions. I dare say that in some respects their proposals are preferable to the present arrangement. However, I am convinced that after changing the forms, they will not have changed the essence of things. Retaining the root of the evil precludes a restoration that is truly radical, that is, that comes

from a different root. With the best of intentions, there will be a change of violent men while maintaining violence; the same despotism of the revolutionary state; the same atheism of the law; the same neglect of the supreme lawgiver and king; the same subjection of the church to the state; the same centralization, at once sword and shield of the regime; the same arbitrary disregard of historical rights and nonstate spheres.[298]

Among the liberals who could expect such fruits of their labor was Thorbecke, the intellectual author of a number of constitutional "drafts and sketches."[299] Against him, too, Groen prophesied these words.

So, what was Groen's alternative to all this? First of all, a choice must be made in the hearts of men. Two principles are opposed to each other and cannot both be accepted. Just as revolution is the fruit of disbelief, so the desired development must begin with faith, with Christian faith. Only the bond with "heaven" can prevent humanity from falling into the abyss.[300] These are principles that, because of their religious nature, require radical acceptance or total rejection. The fight against the revolution begins with submission to the truth of the gospel.[301] "Against the Revolution, the Gospel!" Here is the origin of the slogan that Groen would later adopt, indicating the gravity of the choice to be made. Any confessor of the gospel who takes this seriously will automatically end up in the realm of antirevolutionary principles. But what exactly are they? The antirevolutionary principles have a broad application, says Groen. Is this perhaps the reason why the reader looking for precise formulations has to do with notes and hints scattered throughout the book? The positive part of his argument is not clear, and even in the few chapters that seem to deal with it directly, he allows himself to be carried away by polemics.

Groen's goal, of course, is to develop the foundations of a "Christian constitutional law." In the process of formulating it, he wrestles with the views of authors whom he considers authorities on the subject and arrives at two or three lines of thought, which he does not always attempt to harmonize. The first of these lines of thought is biblical. Governments are instituted by God to meet the needs of "a fallen humanity."[302] The phrase reveals that Groen was not a theologian. Theologians would wrestle with the question whether government was given with creation or added after the fall. Groen does not address this question, but he does note that "the essence of a state, in the fullness of its requirements," was already present on earth "in the first family."[303] It is also in this light that he reads the text of Romans 13:1, "the powers that be are ordained of God." He takes a broad view of these words. "The powers are not merely permitted; they are willed, instituted, sanctified by God Himself."[304] Groen will not easily find himself in rebellion against an authority that seeks to do evil but is legitimate. The duty to obey the government is strongly emphasized by him, more strongly than any possible right of rebellion—with only one qualification: he was not willing to subscribe to an interpretation that would oblige one to "hail today as a power ordained by God the crowned robber who yesterday banished our legitimate prince."[305]

Then there is a second line of thought in Groen's Christian political theory, which is based more on natural law. It has given rise to much debate in later times. According to Groen, the state belongs to the fixed structures of the created cosmos. It is based on principles that are eternal; it belongs to the very constitution of the universe. If anything, it is here that the Platonic feature of Groen's thought comes to the fore again. He echoes the formulations of his *Essay on Truth* when he writes that there are "immutable ideas based on God's will and nature."[306] They contain "standards" for this world. These standards are fixed in an order of creation and also in a sacred order of law, which at the same time constitute restraining forces that limit the course of the revolution. The revolution can never have a free course, because it is in conflict with "nature and law." All the theorizing about state and society cannot undo the fact that there are fixed givens that must always be taken into account, such as the "true needs" of man, the human conscience, the particular nature of institutions.[307] A state is not a human invention, but an institution of all times. Thus, Groen appeals here to given structures that are simply there.

This appeal to "nature"—a hobbyhorse of many conservatives—is not strongly articulated by Groen, however. More important for him is the appeal to history. This brought him to a terrain where he felt most at home. Groen loved to invoke historical rights and historical developments, realities that must be respected. It was a weapon he often used in his struggles in church and state. To nineteenth-century eyes, it could indeed look like a powerful weapon. For was it not true that history forged the character of a nation? Were not the sources of national life to be found in the past? Then it was not strange to insist that the distinctive character of a nation's political institutions, its constitutional forms and customs, and certainly the rights and liberties of its people, had to be in harmony with specific historical developments. These were different for the Netherlands than for

France or England. In the case of the Netherlands, the special role of the Protestant religion and the leading role of the Orange dynasty had to be taken into account.

In Europe, Groen argued, constitutional law had undergone an organic historical development; the "nature" of the institutions had enjoyed the beneficial effect of historical growth.[308] In this way, all the elements of a nation's social and political life had evolved into a differentiated society. This development had to be honored, and here Groen showed his debt to the historical school. History is a divine dispensation that must be respected. When revolutionists, in their passion for rapid reconstruction, attack this dispensation and ignore the relationships that have grown over time, they disrupt the work of centuries. In many ways they had already done this, including in the Netherlands. It had led to "omnipotent government," to "despotic authority," to a kind of "revolutionary monarchy." The situation cried out for "Christian politics." This would have to be a type of politics that avoided the political style born of the Revolution. An antirevolutionary politics would have to consist of a gradual return to structures and forms rooted in the nation's past. Groen concluded that "the real need of our time is the application of the Christian constitutional law, modified according to our circumstances."[309] This was a constitutional law defined by rights and freedoms acquired in the past. The Netherlands was a country in which ethnic groups, cities, regions, and provinces, as well as the Reformed church, had each acquired a distinctive place. These rights and liberties were dear to the nation. Not that they could never be changed, but any further development had to be in keeping with what had already been established. This patchwork of rights and liberties guaranteed the Netherlands that state authority could never grow into a form of "omnipotent government." To be sure, the Orange dynasty had always had monarchical traits, even in the days of the Dutch Republic, but it was a "tempered monarchy," tempered by the powers of the people. Nevertheless, the prince was the center of the state. More than that, he was the nucleus of the state, the legitimate bearer of sovereignty. He had acquired this sovereignty in the course of history, but it had been given to him by God. The state developed from the sovereign rights of the prince. In agreement with Von Haller, Groen simply says that the state is "the highest development of private law." The origin of the state lies in the personal domain of the prince. Around it, in the course of time, at least in the Netherlands, grew a body of privileges, of which the people are the bearers. The people exercise legitimate influence in matters of public interest, albeit within the orbit of their determinate competence. The theory later developed by Abraham Kuyper as "sphere sovereignty" finds here its first tentative formulation.

Groen's audience at the evening lectures was generally quite impressed with what he had to offer. Johan Anne Squire Singendonck, a clerk in the First Chamber, had enjoyed both the content and the style, and had heard "higher poetry" in them. Elout and Mackay also approved of the lectures. With this series of lectures, Groen had gained a small group of political disciples. In Mackay it brought about a kind of conversion. He declared that he had been freed from "misconceptions" and that his basic convictions had been given a decisive "push."[310] His political writings during these years bear the stamp of Groen's spirit. The notes he jotted down in Groen's study were shown to Van der Kemp, who had a secretary copy them into legible longhand in a hardbound notebook that began to circulate among friends.[311] Groen had filed his lectures in a drawer, feeling that he would have to revise them before submitting them to print. He did release one of them for publication in *Christian Voices* to help launch its first issue in June 1846.[312] But first Groen turned back to the handbook to finish its final installment and to the archives to complete the last volume in the series. He found no opportunity to revise the lectures. The following year, political tension began to grow in Europe. Unrest in Switzerland and Germany heralded what would become the European year of revolution, 1848. Groen saw this as "ample confirmation of my views." In light of current events, he decided to publish his lectures without delay and without alteration. He now wanted to reach as many people as possible. An arrangement with his publisher was quickly made, and in the summer of 1847 Groen sent nearly a hundred free copies of his new book to friends and acquaintances.

Unlike thirteen years earlier, when he had circulated his *Essay on Truth*, he now received a flood of responses from all quarters. *Unbelief and Revolution* was immediately recognized by friend and foe alike as an important publication. Kindred spirits regarded it as a profound book with a great vision, a masterpiece in bringing religious questions into close relationship with political problems. It helped them discern the political trends of the day. At least that was the experience of an Amsterdam bailiff, Johan Adam Wormser. A member of the Secession church, Wormser had corresponded with Groen for several years. He attended Christian Friends meetings and was instrumental in the attempt to establish a private Christian school in Amsterdam. In reading *Unbelief and Revolution*, he came to realize that "many of my own ideas about history and constitutional law are mixed with revolutionary ingredients."[313] He saw the book as a "testimony against unbelief" that he would read and reread. That was also done by Groen's followers since then. Many editions and reprints would be published in the next two centuries.[314]

The many pastors who received a copy also responded positively to the work. For example, the pastor-poet Johannes Petrus Hasebroek wrote to the author that the book had given him "firm ground" under his feet. A very special letter of thanks came from another pastor-poet, none other than Beets, who wrote, "Reading your work was so gripping that I could not finish until I had read everything and prayerfully closed the book yesterday afternoon." He saw the work as "a service to the country" and expressed the hope that Groen would "publish many more works of this kind."[315] Such encouragement was hardly needed. Groen began to publish work after work, and in the years 1846–48 he reached the height of his career as a scholar and publicist. The full-length version of *Handbook* was now complete, and the first series of *Archives* was completed with an eighth volume and an index volume prepared by the publisher. Meanwhile, Groen obtained the king's permission to plan a second series, which would publish the letters and papers of the Princes Maurice, Frederick Henry, William II, and William III.[316]

Following the publication of *Unbelief and Revolution*,[317] Groen published a series of articles on the church question in *Christian Voices*. The eight installments, begun in the fall of 1847, were published in book form the following spring under the collective title *The Rights of the Reformed Persuasion*.[318] While this work was in print, the revolutionary fever of that year gripped the Netherlands, and the decision was made to revise the constitution. With this in mind, Groen composed a popularized version of the message of *Unbelief and Revolution* and published it under a title that echoed the slogan of the revolution: *Liberty, Equality, Fraternity*.[319] As if that were not enough, in the fall of 1848 he began writing his *Constitutional Revision and Unity*.[320] This massive production was, of course, written in longhand. It is no wonder that during these years Groen developed a nagging muscle spasm in his right hand, a condition we now know as repetitive stress injury (RSI). The condition caused tremors that can still be seen in his handwriting and that would recur during long periods of writing. It made Betsy's secretarial assistance more necessary than ever.

Despite this handicap, Groen exerted a growing influence through the written word during these years, and that influence was only enhanced by an increasing volume of correspondence in many directions. He was a beacon of light and became a prominent figure in the broader Protestant community. He received requests for advice and recommendations, even in matters beyond his competence. When asked to serve on a committee to improve church music, he politely declined, citing his total ignorance in the field of music; his letter of reply is filled with jocular irony: "Not that I would refuse to reflect on all that is beautiful and pleasing, not that I would regard as indifferent the way in which the halls of Sion resound with praise; not that I would be willing, out of puritanical zeal, to do without the uplifting tones of a well-played organ; not that I would not rejoice at the improvement of congregational singing over the singing of the days of my youth, when, in order to touch the hearts, our ear-drums were shattered!"[321] Nevertheless, he concluded, he had to decline consultations with music experts. There must have been a moment of levity at the meeting of the experts when Groen's letter was read. He did, however, devote himself with great enthusiasm to the fields in which he was proficient. If the constitutional revision of 1848 had not led to drastic political changes, he would have continued to be an effective publicist for many years. We would know him today as a historian and a churchman, not as a politician.

EFFORTS AT CHURCH REFORM

We cannot close this chapter without saying something about Groen's position in the church. Renewed efforts at church reform, to which the friends of the Réveil increasingly urged one another, were part of this episode in his life. In the 1840s, the Réveil became a movement that sought to purify the Reformed church. Its struggle was directed against heterodoxy, which was becoming more and more evident in a society that was slowly modernizing and which, thanks to the support of the upper middle classes, was also finding new platforms to preach its message.

The story begins in 1842, when the synod received a petition signed by "seven gentlemen from The Hague." They were Dirk van Hogendorp, Marinus Gevers, Abraham Capadose, Guillaume Groen van Prinsterer, Pieter Elout van Soeterwoude, Johan Singendonck, and Carel van der Kemp. The address was written by Groen and urged the synod to uphold the confessional standards of the Reformed church. The document grew out of a strong sense of indignation felt by many that since 1834 pastors of local congregations and professors of theology had been free to propagate the most far-reaching theological modernism, while orthodox believers who upheld the historic confession of the church were thwarted in many ways. To restore the church to health, the synod would have to uphold pure doctrine in a generous yet faithful manner. The church holds to a body of doctrine, the address argued; that is its raison d'être. The least the synod could do was to uphold that doctrine "in substance and in essence," as the synod itself put it.

The petition received wide publicity throughout the country, but it fell on deaf ears in the synod. Nor did it help that some leaders stood on the sidelines. Da Costa would not sign the address because he did not see much point in insisting on confessional standards. The result was that the 1842 address remained an event confined to The Hague.

When the Christian Friends meetings began, it proved difficult to get the church question on the agenda. The subject was avoided at the first meeting in order to avoid internal divisions. Groen, who always pushed for "openness," did not like this evasion, and as chairman he kept pushing to get the question of church reform on the agenda. Surely, he wrote to Mackay, faith should unite hearts and believers should work in fellowship.[322] This was also the view of country pastor Heldring, who in his unpolished form continued to call for reformatory action. Groen's extensive series of articles on the church question in *Christian Voices* was also intended to force a breakthrough in his circles. His position on the church had three themes: the relationship of the confessional standards to the integrity of the Reformed church, the relationship to the Seceders, and the relationship between church and state.

Groen's view of the maintenance of the confessional standards immediately makes clear why he felt that a discussion of the church need not sow the seeds of disruption in the circles of the Réveil. He was not afraid that a document of human origin would ever take precedence over Scripture, as Da Costa feared, but neither did he agree with the radical Seceders who spoke of faith only in the language of the confessions. For Groen, the confessions had ecclesiastical, not theological, authority. His line of argument proceeded from a formal ecclesiastical as well as historical starting point—from what later came to be known as the "juridical-confessional" standpoint. Already in his 1834 "Essay on Truth," he had pointed to the ecclesial function of confessional statements: without confessional standards there is really no church.[323] Confessional standards constitute a common statement of opinion regarding the essential truths of Scripture. If people do not adhere to them, individualism and modernism are given free rein, and in the long run there is no church fellowship. At the same time, a church is not constituted by its creeds, but by the power of the Word of God. The formulations in confessional standards, including those of the Dutch Reformed church, are meant to reflect that life-giving Word itself. This particular church is united to the holy Catholic church, the church of the apostles and church fathers and reformers, whose foundation is the work of Christ.

Thus, confessional standards are the expression of the faith of the church as a communion. They are not so much the "life principle" of the church as they are its "autobiography."[324] They show what errors have been combated and what doctrines have been upheld. This has been done in harmony with the church of all ages. The content of their creeds binds a particular church to the confessions of the universal church. Once accepted, the confessional standards are a touchstone for the further development of the church. If they are set aside, the church loses its connection to the universal church. Then it loses its position and becomes a sect. This is what happens when revolutionary thinking takes hold of the church; then it turns into a society that binds itself by means of a social contract. The connection to the past is then lost. Groen's efforts were aimed at the proper maintenance of the confessional standards of the Dutch Reformed church. Those who defended this cause against the synod were right to call on the denomination to uphold its historic confessions. With regard to the church, Groen used the same Christian-historical argument as in political matters. There were rights, freedoms, and positions that demanded respect. With this argument Groen also parried a blow from Hofstede de Groot, who had accused those who argued for preservation of being "formalists" or "slaves to mere forms." Even in this particular polemic, Groen was able to take an intermediate position: the question was not whether the confessions had to be binding in every detail, but whether one was willing to recognize that the confessions contained truths that the church must consider precious and indispensable.[325]

Those who defended the legitimate rights of the historic confessions of the Reformed church also had to decide what to make of the Seceders who had left the Reformed church in 1834 for the sake of those confessions. By 1849 there were more than 150 congregations with nearly a hundred pastors and a rapidly growing membership of nearly ten thousand souls.[326]

Groen wanted to explain his position to this group as well. He made it clear that they had his warm sympathy and that he regarded their zeal and devotion to the faith as an example to himself and other Reformed men. But he did not spare them his criticism. The Seceders had abandoned their "appointed station" and avoided the "obligatory struggle."[327] He criticized the spirit of hair-splitting, division, and schism that had begun to manifest itself among them. Secession had "broken the force of the religious awakening in the Netherlands."[328] His greatest complaint, however, was that after 1839 the Seceders had applied to the civil authorities for permission to form independent congregations. In doing so, they not only became a church alongside the Reformed church, but they also bartered away the main issue of 1834. At that time, they had judged that the Reformed church had become a "false" church and they had denied that the government had any authority over the church. Now they even agreed not to use the word "Reformed." Groen felt that by applying for a license they had forfeited their independence and surrendered the right of the church (*jus in sacra*). In principle, this was a great loss.

Groen blamed Rev. Hendrik Pieter Scholte in particular. In his first article in *Christian Voices*, Groen attacked him by name. In his *Rights of the Reformed Persuasion*, he would drop this personal passage. Of all the Secession pastors, Scholte was the best known in Réveil circles. But they had an unfavorable impression of him: he had an inflated ego and was ultimately a fanatic. Groen clearly had a bone to pick with him when he began his polemics. Scholte's activity in church affairs had borne only "bitter" fruit. In addition to Secession and application for recognition, there was Scholte's encouragement of emigration. Indeed, in the 1840s many Seceders decided to emigrate to America. Scholte himself, together with the Rev. Albertus Christiaan van Raalte, would cross the ocean to settle in "the land of the free." Given the persecutions, this was understandable. Nevertheless, Groen lamented the fact that the exodus "deprives the fatherland of a large portion of its best inhabitants, [deprives] the Christians of ardent supporters, and in some regions paves the way for the advance of the popery."[329]

A discussion with a number of Secessionist pastors about his critical articles did not change Groen's mind. Although he sometimes attended Secessionist services, his ecclesiastical viewpoint was far removed from theirs. Another issue contributed to this. While Scholte, in his monthly journal *The Reformation*, spoke of the diabolical nature of states, and while many Seceders favored the greatest possible separation of church and state, Groen consciously spoke of a "union of church and state" during these years. Scholte's statement that states were of the devil was refuted by Groen in *Unbelief and Revolution*.[330] His view was diametrically opposed to Scholte's. According to Groen, the state must be called Christian because of its connection to the Christian church. At least it should be so in the Netherlands, whose statehood arose for the sake of the church. Groen had already argued this in *Handbook*, noting that the Reformed church had been the "dominant church" in the Netherlands. The church had exercised great influence on the morals and laws of the republic. Groen believed that such a mutual connection between faith and politics was beneficial to society, and he would like to see this connection restored in nineteenth-century Holland. It was revolutionary thinking that desired and promoted the separation of church and state. Even the Swiss theologian Alexandre Vinet, who was widely read in Réveil circles, advocated an absolute separation of church and state. Vinet's argument would gain influence among some Réveil friends: how could the peace of the gospel ever be reconciled with state coercion? Groen judged that Vinet was infected with the revolutionary virus and, in contrast to this kind of thinking, consciously spoke of a "union" of church and state, while maintaining the distinction and independence of the two institutions. However, misunderstandings about Groen's intentions on this point have been common. Immediately after the publication of *Unbelief and Revolution*, Koenen wrote to Groen that he was asking for the impossible by trying to make the Reformed church the "dominant church" again; for how could that be possible given the "equality of all religions in our country since 1795"?[331] Groen replied as if stung by a wasp, writing in a disappointed tone that Koenen, who had read everything Groen had ever written, understood nothing of his "antirevolutionary and therefore also anti-reactionary" views.[332] He meant a union of church and state "in the abstract." He did not want to deprive anyone of acquired rights; he also always spoke of "Christian tolerance"; but he believed that the "Reformed persuasion" had the historical right to demand for its faith, which was the faith of the nation, a certain influence in the public sphere. So he wasn't talking about any formal relationship between institutions; he was talking about the Reformed religion, which for historical reasons could be called the national religion. The state, which of itself must come to recognize the highest truths, should adopt the creed of this religion as its own. In this way the government of the Netherlands could be a Christian government.

The Antirevolutionary

Groen used his work *The Rights of the Reformed Persuasion*, once it was published in book form, as a polemical pamphlet. His purpose was to reiterate and this time to strengthen the demand that the confessions be maintained in the church. What he had begun in 1842 remained his goal. Throughout 1847, as he worked on his series of articles, he continued to approach his Réveil friends on the subject. He asked for their reaction and eventually for their cooperation in taking action. Since the prayerful response to *Unbelief and Revolution* that he had received from Beets, he tried to involve this pastor in an initiative to get pastors and lay people to sign a joint statement. Groen had a strong desire for the lay element to be clearly visible in the struggle for the "healing" of the church, but he needed the pastors to gain credibility with the church authorities. Otherwise, it would look again like a "mutiny of the gentlemen from The Hague," which the synod could simply ignore. That is why he has now rejected an initiative by a number of pastors for a joint consultation that could also include some lay people. Such an arrangement would only confirm the prejudiced view of the pastors that lay people could not really judge these matters. Groen desperately wanted Beets to participate because of his prominent position and his involvement in the brotherhood of the Réveil. But Beets had no desire to play a leading role on the ecclesiastical front. He did not like Groen's polemics. He spoke to Groen of "armor in which I cannot fight" and refused in letter after letter.[333]

In the spring of 1848, Groen and several friends organized a large meeting for pastors and church members to discuss the state of the church. The Christian Friends had decided to issue a statement on the administration and organization of the Reformed church at their May meeting.[334] The background to this decision was the debate in the church about a revision of the 1816 regulations, which was on the agenda of the synod. The ideal of the Réveil was a return to Presbyterian polity, that is, to the autonomy of the local congregation. In addition to Groen, the organizing committee consisted of Heldring, Secrétan, Van Toorenbergen, Mackay, Da Costa, and Capadose. Invitations were sent out to all the congregations and pastors in the country to come to Amsterdam on August 18 for a joint discussion. Groen urged Beets to serve as chairman. His urging was in vain. Three weeks before the Amsterdam meeting, it became clear that Beets would not accept a leadership role. Groen now chaired the meeting himself. The meeting was held in the Odeon and was attended by 33 pastors and 208 Reformed church members.[335] The meeting thus remained a lay affair. To the great disappointment of many, Beets had not even made the trip to Amsterdam. Capadose loudly denounced this, calling it clerical pride that would not tolerate lay influence in church affairs. When communication was later resumed to clarify this painful episode, it became clear where the shoe pinched. Beets saw the meeting as an expression of opposition and rebellion in the church. He himself did not want to promote change in the church through concrete steps. He was a man of pedagogical ideals who preferred to educate the church through teaching and writing rather than forcing decisions in a public setting.

The Amsterdam meeting produced a statement addressed to the king and the synod, calling for a change in the governmental structure of the church. The local congregation should become autonomous again and the Reformed church should be revived as an independent body, free from government regulation. A plea was also made for the maintenance of the central tenets of Reformed doctrine. A few weeks later, the synod filed the statement away as "received for information." It is hard to say whether the statement had any influence on the 1852 Amendment to the Rules, which did in fact give the local congregation a little more autonomy. The meeting at Odeon would mark Groen's last activity on the ecclesiastical front for the time being. He had been unable to translate the cause of 1842 into a widespread movement. Nevertheless, he realized that the time had come for the ideals he cherished to take concrete form in society. The arena in which he would attempt this for the next eight years was politics.

5

Public Trials

THE REVOLUTION OF 1848

IN 1850, THREE HUGE steam-driven pumping stations, the *Leeghwater*, the *Cruquius*, and the *Lijnden*, began a gigantic task: draining the Haarlemmermeer. It would take them three years to turn this mass of water into thousands of acres of agricultural land.[336] The reclamation plan was a long time in the making: the steam engines were named after hydraulic engineers from three centuries ago.[337] The final steps were taken under King William I. The preparations took a long time, but when the day finally came, it was interpreted as an unmistakable sign of progress and modernization.

Around 1850, a similar sign, trailed by enormous clouds of smoke, moved along twin iron rails on a path just north of the Haarlemmermeer. The speed of the locomotive, which pulled colored carriages for three different classes of passengers, was not very high: about forty kilometers per hour. The total length of the country's railroads at that time was barely over two hundred kilometers. There was no complex network; there were only two lines: one from Amsterdam to Rotterdam, with stops at Haarlem, Leyden, and The Hague, and another from Arnhem via Utrecht to Amsterdam. Utrecht and Rotterdam were connected by rail in 1855. There was no international connection yet, and it would take another two decades before railroads began to open up the country in earnest. The railroads of the 1850s offered a limited increase in mobility to a limited number of people. The lucky few were those who could afford to travel this way. Most

Dutch people continued to rely on horse-drawn carriages or barges, or to travel on horseback or on foot.[338]

Contrasting with the modest modernization was a conspicuous stagnation. The economy had not flourished since independence was gained at the start of the Kingdom in 1813. Hardly any new jobs were being created in the cities of the Netherlands. There were no new initiatives to offset the decline in the urban population and the swelling ranks of the urban poor. In the countryside, crop failures, unemployment, and abject poverty struck the lowest classes. Thousands of people left for America to try their luck. Among them were a relatively large number of Seceders, who left the country with bitter complaints on their lips. As if all this were not bad enough, in the fall of 1848, another cholera epidemic, the "poor man's disease," broke out, once again claiming thousands of victims. At the end of the great epidemic of 1833, it was hoped that the disease had finally been conquered, but its return was just as much a sign of the times: for large sections of the population, conditions had not improved. The cynicism is palpable in the report of the Utrecht physician H. J. Broers after his visit to the carnival festivities in the center of the city: the city fathers had not wanted to cancel this form of popular entertainment, and the good doctor saw one dead person after another being carried away on a stretcher, while others shouted to each other, "Sing and dance! Sing and dance!"[339]

According to Dr. Broers, the leaders of his country's three million people had not awakened from their slumber until the revolutions that swept Europe in 1848. February and March of that year brought a rude awakening. On February 22, a popular uprising broke out in Paris that not only cost the government leader Guizot his career but also put an end to the reign of Louis Philippe. The revolution then spread to the German territories. Everywhere, the princes made concessions, installed liberal ministers, and promised written constitutions. On March 13, demonstrations by students and artisans in Vienna forced Metternich, the European symbol of post-Napoleonic reconstruction, to resign. At the news, King William II in The Hague turned liberal overnight. Until recently unwilling to agree to any constitutional revision, he now appointed a committee composed entirely of liberals to prepare a comprehensive revision of the constitution. As the volatility of the Amsterdam stock exchange showed, this did not end the general nervousness and sense of panic. Business failures were common, and in the early spring of 1848 many a private fortune went up in smoke. There was unrest throughout the spring, with street riots in The Hague and

Amsterdam. In France, Paris resembled a war zone that June. In Holland, great navigational skill was required to stabilize the ship of state.

The Dutch liberals had their long-awaited constitutional revision dropped into their laps. Thorbecke declared that he would have preferred the decision to be made "out of wisdom and not out of compulsion," but he naturally did not hesitate when he was given a leading role in the revision committee. He had been expressing his views on a new constitution since 1839. After the "national disillusionment" following the revision of 1840, the Leyden professor had moved in a decidedly liberal direction. In 1844, he had argued for direct elections to the Second Chamber (instead of indirect elections by the provincial legislatures). After all the preparatory work, the work of 1848 did not take long. By April, the committee was able to present a draft revision that included some drastic changes: ministerial responsibility, direct elections; freedom of education, religion, association, and assembly. Thorbecke wanted to narrow the gap between the upper middle classes and the instruments of government. All "citizens" were to have access to the public sphere. From May to October, the proposals for revision were debated in the Second Chamber and again in a Double Chamber. Although the liberals were in the minority, Parliament, urged on by circumstances and actively encouraged by the king, approved the revision in a "sacrificial orgy of political convictions," as Groen put it in less than flattering terms.[340]

In fact, the approval was given with great reluctance. The members of Parliament felt that they had to accept the inevitable—not a unique scene in Dutch history.[341] Against this background, the constitution of 1848 was far from being embraced wholeheartedly. In the years that followed, strong opposition to the new constitutional framework would occasionally flare up, as it did during the no-popery movement of April 1853. But in 1848 the maxim was "United we stand." If one wanted to preserve the throne and avert revolutionary unrest, one had to swallow objections and accept the inevitable. The poet Jan Wap even considered the political turn of 1848 a masterstroke of the king:

> The hurricane arrived, coercing kings to flight.
> But he on Holland's throne, impervious to fright,
> Faced down the storm and, holding fast his rule,
> Threw Hydra overboard into the deepest pool.[342]

In the fall of 1848, the call for unity and concord around the king and the constitution was loud. On November 3, the new constitution was solemnly proclaimed from town halls throughout the country, followed by the ringing of church bells. At the entrance gates of the Noordeinde Palace, a banner was hung that read in large letters "God with us." It was one of the few things that filled Groen with gratitude as he surveyed the course of events.

However one viewed the new constitution, it was a sign of modernization. Just as the railroads opened up the space of the Netherlands, the revised Constitution of 1848 opened up the public square. It provided a new infrastructure for political life, albeit a limited one at first. It placed the franchise on a new footing, although its extension was not spectacular: only a limited number of people benefited from it. Thorbecke's "citizenship" was limited to the wealthy. The promise of new constitutional freedoms still had to be fulfilled by ordinary legislation. The new political infrastructure could only be used gradually, and the pace at which it was introduced was for a long time determined by conservative administrators. Nevertheless, the new constitution was a monument to renewal, a sign of a society slowly opening up. Perhaps it was less drastic than it was sometimes made out to be, but it established a new direction for thought and action. Things were shaken up, and it would take years for everyone to find their footing. New legal issues and new distributions of power understandably played a role in all of this. And so, the million-dollar question would soon be, who would benefit from this modernization?

OUTSIDE THE POLITICAL ARENA

Groen van Prinsterer did not take part in the political events of 1848. In fact, he spent most of the revolutionary year in *Oud-Wassenaer*, far from the political turmoil. For the fourth time, Willem and Betsy spent the summer season on their country estate, which they had purchased in 1845. Tired of "traveling in foreign lands," they sought peace and relaxation close to home. Betsy, in particular, seems to have been increasingly plagued by headaches and fatigue from all her activities. Willem's health was better, although he was careful to avoid the harsh winter weather. Toward the end of April, accompanied by servants, they retired to the village of Wassenaar, to return to the city sometime in September to reoccupy what they jokingly called their "winter quarters." Once installed in their country home, they would go out less and receive fewer visitors than in the city. This was the intention, as the increasing number of visitors to the house on the Korte Vijverberg sometimes made life in the city too hectic. Still, The Hague was not far—a short hour by carriage—and from time to time, Willem and Betsy found themselves back in the city. *Oud-Wassenaer* was not far from the railroad. The connection between Leyden and The Hague, passing through the village of Wassenaar, was completed in 1845. The Groens became grateful users of the railroad. From 1845 we see Willem making regular visits to Amsterdam. Groen often advised his guests to take the train to *Oud-Wassenaar*. He would then have his servant pick up the guest by carriage from Wassenaar or The Hague.

During the months of March and April, Groen was a close observer of the movements at the Binnenhof, but then he left the city. The tranquility of his country home was not to be used for further studies, however; his historical work had already come to a standstill for some time. Beginning in the summer of 1847, he was busy writing articles and pamphlets in which he expressed his views on issues of ecclesiastical and political life. The urge to somehow have a voice in the public affairs of his country was translated into a flood of pamphlets that appeared month after month. They compensated somewhat for his absence from the political stage. For the time being, politics occupied him more intensely than the ecclesiastical question of the Odeon meeting in Amsterdam. Immediately after that meeting, he had resumed his series of writings on the political situation. Strangely enough, the provincial legislature of South Holland did not delegate him to the Double Chamber to debate the constitutional revision; despite all his published political commentaries, he was not considered this time. But Groen knew it could be worse: not even Thorbecke, the intellectual father of the revision, was delegated. This made Groen's forced passivity less strange: the moderate center did not want any trouble from the wings, given the political tensions. How different, for both men, from the situation of 1840!

Still, Thorbecke's expulsion was in line with the pattern of hostility that had become palpable at the University of Leyden, where he was known as arrogant and stiff, pedantic toward his colleagues, to whom he often felt superior. Even Van Assen no longer spoke to his former student and protégé. Thorbecke created a legion of followers for his doctrinaire liberalism, especially among former students, but he also provoked his own conservative counter-movement wherever he went. The atmosphere at Leyden University around 1848 was extremely tense, and after his work for the constitutional committee, Thorbecke longed to be called back to The Hague. Here, however, influential men had decided to bypass him for as long as possible. Groen followed everything from *Oud-Wassenaer*.

He raised his voice outside the political arena like a caged animal unable to reach its prey. By the fall of 1848, Groen felt gloomy and discouraged, "more discouraged than befits a Christian," he confided to Mackay.[343] Yet he continued to write as much as his "weak hand" would allow. Warning and informing had become his daily occupation. He was eager to apply the antirevolutionary principles outlined in *Unbelief and Revolution* to the political issues of the day. Even among his Christian friends, he had much to explain. The moderate shock of the bloodless revolution had stirred up new ideas among them as well.

GROEN AND THE CONSTITUTION OF 1848

The men of the Réveil were divided over the revised constitution. In The Hague, Mackay, Van der Kemp, Singendonck, Elout, and Groen were extremely concerned about the events they had witnessed in March. They thought it risky that the king, in the face of news of the overthrown governments abroad, had said he was ready to make great concessions. Such fickleness was hardly a sound basis for embarking on the long-awaited constitutional revision. It would be a "wretched piece of bungling," thought Mackay, who had personally tried to persuade the king to change his mind.[344] Groen argued that the revision of so important a state document as the constitution should be done under the motto *festina lente*, "Make haste slowly," and in any case should not be undertaken by a "coterie which a month before had scarcely been of any importance."[345] He identified the liberals of 1848 as the Dutch revolutionaries who got their chance when "panic terror" became the mainspring of politics in The Hague. It is characteristic of revolutionary times that a small minority, masquerading as the general will, succeeds in seizing the reins of government. The public approves because it always leans toward the "rising sun." This was Groen's view of the whole episode, and he wrote it down in a hundred variations.

The mood in Amsterdam was different. Da Costa saw the revision of the constitution as the dawn of a new era for the Netherlands. He saw the world-shaking events of that year as divine dispensations. According to Da Costa, it was unique that while elsewhere in Europe princes and peoples were at odds, in the Netherlands they were working together to create a new political and social order. He hailed the increased freedoms in education, religion, and commerce as a welcome correction of the recent past. In late May 1848, Da Costa published a pamphlet, *The Moment*, in which he warmly endorsed the revision. According to him, Europe had entered the stage of popular liberties, and the revolution of 1848 could serve God's plan for humanity: it brought greater opportunities for missions, evangelism, and Christian education.[346] Koenen also thought in these terms, and in May he sent a petition to the Second Chamber declaring his support for the liberal proposals; although he still had some objections, he was willing to sacrifice them on the "altar of the fatherland."[347]

Groen was now paying the price for not allowing his Amsterdam friends to attend the lectures on *Unbelief and Revolution*. His friends in The Hague embraced his political vision, but the Amsterdam friends did not, or did so with reservations. Da Costa had once written to Mackay that God was "not quite so antirevolutionary" in ruling the nations and the church.[348] In 1848 it became clear for the first time that there were at least two approaches to politics in the Réveil—a legal-historical approach and an approach that emphasized spiritual-religious factors.[349] According to Groen, Da Costa was mistaken about the nature of revolution. In his response to *The Moment*, Groen wrote that he was not afraid of the new forms, but that he believed these new forms were already animated by the "spirit of the age." Anyone who did not see this was chasing an "illusion." Because they were friends, Groen was able to remind Da Costa of his 1844 statement, "They shall not have us, the gods of this age," and now added, in reference to the poet of those words, "And behold, they already have us."[350] In the July issue of *Christian Voices*, Singendonck reviewed Da Costa's pamphlet in the spirit of Groen. Groen applied a generous dose of goodwill when he remarked a few weeks later that Da Costa and he, for all their differences, were nevertheless in substantial agreement.[351] But Da Costa would not close his spiritual eye to the "evangelical" element he saw in the great political events of the day, and though he remained a warmly sympathetic antirevolutionary, he was an antirevolutionary of a personal vintage.

While Da Costa did not want to limit himself to a "mere protest" against the revolution and wanted to express his appreciation for the developments of his time, Groen was not at all inclined to do so. He hardly ever expressed the positive elements, which he certainly noticed, in public. For Groen, too, the new constitution had generally brought what he felt his country needed. First and foremost, he appreciated the freedoms of education and religion. The repeated failure to obtain permission to establish private schools would be a thing of the past. And freedom of religion would mean an end to the church oppression of the Seceders. It was also a great gain in Groen's eyes that ministers of the crown would henceforth be answerable to Parliament for their actions; had he not, since 1830, advocated greater ministerial responsibility and cabinets formed independently of the crown? He also favored increasing the influence of the people through direct elections to the Second Chamber. Groen was definitely not one of the conservatives who wanted to restore the pre-1848 order. In the Double Chamber, there were three men who shared Groen's views: Willem baron van Lynden, Johan Frederik baron Reede van Oudtshoorn, and Groen's friend, Mackay. The latter conferred with Groen about his contributions to the debates in the Chamber. But Mackay also accepted the proposed revisions, albeit with a protest of principle.

The most important thing, according to Groen, was to make a sharp protest based on fundamental principles, since the constitutional revision was "connected with the whole revolutionary course of the age." This was his assessment, as expressed in a pamphlet entitled *Constitutional Revision and Unity*, which he sat down to write in the fall of 1848, but which grew into a series of pamphlets that ran until the fall of 1849.[352] As the Double Chamber met, Groen took a gloomy view of things, fearing "a society subverted by unbelief."[353] Groen was convinced that the "fallacies" of the Revolution, now that liberalism was doing so well, would find application in the Netherlands. The political reversal would be felt in virtually every question of law and legislation. This problem would preoccupy Groen for the rest of his political career. He believed that politics should be about the recognition of acquired rights, and thus about the recognition of a deeper kind of justice. With the help of the writings of Stahl, with which he became familiar at this time, he would describe this type of justice as *Gottes fügung*—divine guidance.

Liberalism was far from such a conception of law and justice. The liberal mind can see rights only as the representation of certain interests, which must either be recognized or not. Thus, in their view, the recognition of a given right depends on human choice. When right is equated with interest, authority can degenerate into an omnipotent power that takes care of interests according to its own insight. Right, conceived as interest, can then easily become the plaything of political circumstances. Law can be bent by political compulsion or political whim. The revolutionary mind thinks in these terms, Groen argued, and Thorbecke's constitution incorporates them. Everything it promises can turn into its opposite. Groen doubted, for example, to what extent Christian education would be truly free under a liberal regime. For Groen, therefore, the new constitution was not "promising good" but "pregnant with disaster."[354] The spirit of the revolution has unsettled the whole structure of the state. "I am convinced that we are heading for hard times," he wrote to Da Costa from *Oud-Wassenaer* in September 1848.[355]

Groen's criticism of the spirit of the constitution came to a head on two points that differed most from his own views. The first point concerned the position of the king. In Groen's view, the Netherlands was a "moderate monarchy" and the king was the bearer of Dutch sovereignty. Thorbecke was not so sure. In his view, the Netherlands had been a "constitutional monarchy" since 1813. It was the constitution that determined who was the bearer of sovereignty, and therefore the question went back to the people. This was also the view expressed in the draft constitution. Groen, on the other hand, insisted that sovereignty belonged to the House of Orange. By bowing to the principle of popular sovereignty, the Netherlands had become a "republic plus a king." Groen saw this as a blatant failure to appreciate the special history of the Netherlands, which had been able to develop into an independent state under the providential leadership of the Princes of Orange. In Thorbecke's view, it was of no political consequence to place the sovereignty of God behind the sovereignty of the crown, but according to Groen this was precisely the issue at stake, an issue of the greatest moment in a Christian view of the state. Otherwise, the crown would become a mere convention and the king a "puppet on a swing." The debate that Groen provoked on this question in 1848 and 1849, a debate in which professors from Utrecht and Leyden also participated, was significant for all later Protestant views of the state, which saw the sovereignty of the Netherlands as entrusted to the House of Orange-Nassau.

Groen also detected the principle of popular sovereignty in the new electoral law. This was his second major theme during these years. Thorbecke had opted for a census franchise, which was quite common in neighboring states. This meant that only those citizens who paid the highest taxes had the right to vote. Based on this criterion, about eighty thousand men would be eligible to vote after 1848. Groen did not oppose the extension of the franchise as such—in fact, he thought it could go a little further—but the material criterion was repugnant to him. Census suffrage turned the electorate into an amorphous mass. It failed to consider the nation in its historical ranks and rights. To illustrate what he meant, Groen liked to hold up to his countrymen the British parliamentary system, which at least left room for the influence of different social orders. There were other people who had just as much right to have a say in the interests of the nation. For this reason, Groen deliberately appealed to "the people behind the voters," as he often put it. Later, under the influence of Da Costa and Stahl, and after "the people behind the voters" had become more and more involved in antirevolutionary politics, Groen would considerably soften his initial criticism of the electoral system. These people belonged to his "party" as much as those who had the vote.

In 1848, Groen's voice was one of dissent. It was the dissent of a man who had been left out. The establishment clamored for unanimous support of the new constitution, but Groen deliberately disrupted the desired national concord. He considered it irresponsible to "remain silent while our institutions are being changed" and to feign unanimity. The example of Bilderdijk came to his mind again at this crucial juncture in Dutch history. "Where there is pernicious concord, there it is desirable to end the concord; there it is a duty to break up the collusion."[356] Had not Bilderdijk done the same in his day, when he disrupted the general concord by attacking ideas so dear to the majority? Like Bilderdijk, Groen reaped angry wrath. The president of the Second Chamber, Willem Boreel van Hogelanden, who had witnessed everything since March 1848, let him know that he was deeply offended by the term "reprehensible indulgence" that Groen had used in his *Constitutional Revision and Unity*.[357] Boreel, who had attended Groen's "lectures on unbelief and revolution" in the winter of 1845, thought it was easy enough for Groen to vent his criticism while sitting in his study; he had no idea how difficult it had been in the first months after March to prevent a popular revolt from breaking out in the streets and to save at least "a few good principles" from the hands of the "ultra-reformers."

Of course, Groen did not want to limit the range of his dissenting voice to his study. However, it was only after the electoral system had been revised that he had a chance to be heard in Parliament. Beginning in 1849, members of the Second Chamber were elected by district. About sixty-eight districts with about forty-five thousand inhabitants each were represented by sixty-eight seats. Every year, elections were held in part of the districts to replace the "personnel" of the Chamber. The new system meant that Groen was no longer dependent on the provincial legislature of South Holland to be delegated to Parliament; at election time, political friends anywhere in the country could nominate Groen as a candidate for their district. As a rule, election campaigns were conducted by the candidates' partisans; the candidates themselves did not participate in a campaign.

In December 1848, Groen was elected by a district far from Holland: he would represent the district of Harderwijk in the province of Gelderland. This result came after a hard-fought campaign in which local liberals accused Groen of wanting to restrict religious freedom because of his "religious sentiments."[358] These very sentiments, however, won him the support of the region's pastors, and the mayor of the village of Barneveld, Nairac, informed Groen in advance that he was the "preferred candidate" of the voters in his community.[359] With this measure of support, Groen won his seat in the Chamber.

The government of the day was led by a weak ministry headed by Donker Curtius and De Kempenaer—weak because it was struggling to implement the provisions of the new constitution while trying to keep its intellectual father out of the government. Groen saw this exclusion of the "master" at the hands of bungling disciples as grossly unfair. Apparently, they wanted Thorbecke's principles but not his person. But Thorbecke came. He was elected to the Second Chamber at the same time as Groen.

WILLIAM III

Shortly after Groen and Thorbecke took their seats in Parliament, King William II died suddenly. After suffering a severe fall during a visit to a Rotterdam shipyard, an old heart problem kicked in and he died in his beloved city of Tilburg on March 17, 1849. Groen had seen him for the last time on February 13 during the Speech from the Throne. William's son, the thirty-two-year-old crown prince, would now ascend the throne. If William II was a man without policy or program, William III had a reputation for being unpredictable, moody and crotchety, a lover of hunting and country life, given to coarse language and prone to vulgar amusements—not a man of keen political insight or administrative zeal, but mindful of his royal prerogative when it suited him. In everything he was the opposite of his grandfather William I. His marriage to Sophia of Württemberg was a failure from the start. The terribly unhappy queen bore three sons, none of whom would ever succeed their father. She was frankly relieved when a legal separation was agreed upon in 1851. On May 12, 1849, the new king was sworn in at the Nieuwe Kerk in Amsterdam. Groen was present ex officio, both as a member of Parliament and as a member of the Council of State. William III swore allegiance to the new constitution, which he declared must now be put into effect. We do not have Groen's impressions of the ceremony or of the new king, with whom he had spoken on a few occasions but whom he hardly knew.

The relationship between the family archivist and the new monarch was no more intimate than that with the late king. Groen and William III did not like each other. Groen respected the king for his office and would never lack respect for the monarch's authority. But the differences in lifestyle and character between the two men were irreconcilable. As family archivist, Groen continued to communicate with the court through the royal cabinet, now headed by his former bosom friend Van Rappard. But William III had no interest in Groen's work as family archivist; he took only a cursory note of it. While the new king's daughter Wilhelmina[360] would one day think so highly of Groen's manual that she would carry it with her wherever she went,[361] her father was not taken with it. "Mr. Groen has described the House of Orange as he sees it, but not as it was and is. He is in favor of a dominant Church, and that is wrong."[362] This was said to Mackay, who tried to explain Groen's more nuanced views, but the king would not be moved. Under William III, the family archives were treated stingily, even though the king recognized that Groen was a capable and dedicated director whom he would hate to lose.

A much warmer relationship existed between Queen Sophia and Betsy. It dated from the time when the two ladies lived within a stone's throw of each other, the queen on Plein Square and Betsy on the Korte Vijverberg. The queen seems to have enjoyed walking with Betsy along the Buitenhof and the Lange Voorhout. William III's wife was talented and intelligent, but she was defeated by the marital quarrels and domestic troubles she experienced. She was, however, a strong and independent woman who tried to make her own way and created her own circle of friends. Among them was Betsy, though more on the periphery than in the center of the circle. Their conversations were often of a religious nature. Their relationship remained fairly constant over the years. Two letters survive in the royal archives, one from 1859 and one from 1877, in which the queen always refers to Betsy as *ma chère amie*. Naturally, Betsy learned a great deal about daily life at court from these conversations. They probably did not give the Groens a positive impression of William III's sense of vocation and of his role as prince of Orange. The Réveil, and the Groens in particular, always paid close attention to the correlation between inner devotion and outer fidelity. In this case, they saw both the tree and its fruit, and drew a veil over what they knew of it, out of their not inconsiderable love for the House of Orange.

IN THE POLITICAL ARENA

During his first year in Parliament, Groen was unable to make his mark. The Donker Curtius-De Kempenaer Ministry was struggling with eroding support in the Chamber and was not going to get much into the law books. Now that it was time to translate the new constitution into ordinary legislation, Groen wanted nothing more than to talk about the fundamentals of public policy. But he found little occasion to do so. His most conspicuous political works were his pamphlets, in which he was free to express himself. These political commentaries, distributed outside the Chamber, immediately marked him as a strong-minded politician. Groen saw his pamphleteering as an attempt to awaken the public spirit, which he felt was still asleep as it had been in 1829 when he published his first pamphlet. The "nation" needed to know what was at stake in its name. When the ministry fell in September 1849 and Thorbecke was finally called in, Groen published an analysis of the political situation. He felt that Thorbecke's merits were finally being recognized, and he looked forward to a more direct exchange of views in the Chamber on the principles of 1848.[363] Thus, his pamphlet dealt with the impending struggle against the doctrinaire liberal and his ideas, ideas that Groen condemned. At the University of Leyden, his pamphlet was read with enthusiasm. For a short time Groen became the hero of the anti-Thorebekians among the faculty. Even the critical Bake returned to Groen's camp.

With Thorbecke at the head of the government, Groen came to life in the Chamber. The first time Thorbecke's ministry faced the Chamber, Groen asked about the cabinet's guiding principles. "Just watch us," was Thorbecke's firm reply. In December, Groen attacked the cabinet for the lack of unity among the various ministers. In his view, a cabinet should be "homogeneous," that is, it should have a uniform policy. Only then could it have strength in the Chamber and get things done. This would remain one of Groen's basic principles, which he would remind every future cabinet of. The liberals in the Chamber were very angry with Groen for trying to play one minister off against another. But their anger was no proof that Groen was wrong. While Thorbecke would concentrate in the coming years on the administrative laws that were needed—an electoral law, a municipal law, and a provincial law—these were really the individual achievements of the minister of the interior, namely Thorbecke himself. The cabinet as a whole was less successful and less united. Thorbecke's first ministry was a liberal one, thanks to Thorbecke, but not thanks to the other ministers.

Meanwhile, the old friendship between Groen and Thorbecke had cooled to a more or less civil relationship between parliamentarians. Both men were fully aware of the ideological difference that separated them. Sitting in the Chamber behind the government table, Thorbecke was driven to distraction by Groen's speeches and interpellations. As early as 1840, Groen's published speeches in the Chamber had infuriated Thorbecke. "For the life of me I can't read these things. All these arguments about practical matters of state—it is as if one wanted to replace the sun with Chinese fireworks."[364] In the Chamber, he could not stand Groen's pyrotechnics either. He complained of a "general war" against his ministry that was obstructing the work that had to be done "in accordance with the requirements of the Constitution." Thorbecke's liberalism, however, inspired Groen to mount a kind of opposition in grand style. He never tired of pointing out, in his quiet voice, the great clash of fundamental principles caused by the government's policies. This clash was all too real. Thorbecke described Groen's appeal to the history of the nation and to acquired rights as "looking for the living among the dead." In Groen's talk about faith and politics, he saw nothing but "pious smoke and mirrors" and regularly dismissed it as "out of order." As for Groen's claim to speak on behalf of a "party" and to offer "systematic" or "principled" opposition, Thorbecke condemned it as inconsistent with the unity and concord that should exist between citizens, Parliament, and government, at least if all were willing to act rationally.

In order to understand the different political styles and attitudes that shaped Dutch parliamentary democracy, it is necessary to study the struggle between Groen van Prinsterer and Thorbecke. Dutch parliamentary traditions were not yet established so soon after the revision of the constitution. Groen made a significant contribution to the way members of the Dutch Parliament conduct debate and opposition to this day. Groen was convinced that liberals such as Donker Curtius and Thorbecke looked with admiration at the French and Belgian political models, which were considered "modern." There, the government was given a great deal of leeway in policymaking, and the Chamber basically went along with it. By contrast, Groen deliberately promoted the English model. The British Parliament had room for a loyal opposition, was familiar with the phenomenon of party formation, initiated more independent inquiries into government measures, and, in short, was much more conscious of its role as the representative of the nation. Thus, Groen championed the rights of the Second Chamber at a time when the Dutch Parliament was still discovering the political role it could play.

The Dutch polder of the 1850s was allergic to parties. Parties were associated with the discord and division of the past. The political factions of the eighteenth century were still seen as horrible examples. The strife between Orangists and patriots had torn the country apart, and after 1795 the hopeless division in the National Assembly had paved the way for French domination.[365] Such was the general consensus. Thorbecke tried to deny the existence of parties in the Chamber. Floris Adriaan van Hall, leader of the Conservatives, believed that Groen was doing the country a "disservice" by talking about "parties."[366] Groen, however, believed that parties should be represented in the Chamber to represent the different principles present in the nation. If "a few Englishmen" could be invited to come over, they would hear that it was not at all strange to have parties in a "constitutional government."[367] And so Groen consistently spoke of his "party," including not only his allies in the Chamber, Mackay and Van Lynden, but also that part of the nation that identified with the antirevolutionary banner raised at The Hague.

At the meeting of the Christian Friends on April 10, 1850, Groen introduced the subject of party formation to what he hoped would be a sympathetic audience. He read a paper in which he was able to refer to a question by Professor Stahl that had been sent to him by friends in Berlin: What did the Dutch brethren think about the formation of political parties?[368] That would mean, Groen explained, voters' clubs or riding associations,[369] manifests about principles, political programs, and propaganda. "Active support" for parliamentary work was essential, he added, including press coverage. The time had come for antirevolutionaries to unite locally and consult with each other.

A discussion followed, but without clear conclusions. Gefken, who was very much in favor, noted in his autobiography that most of those present did not seem to understand the issue.[370] There was also opposition. Van der Brugghen, a judge from Nymegen, wrote a memo to himself in response to Groen's plea, in which he formulated his objections to the formation of a Christian party. He feared that it would be a straitjacket binding people's conscience. The antirevolutionaries, if they formed a party, would thus be using an "unevangelical procedure" in their fight against unchristian politics.³⁷¹ Van der Brugghen, under the influence of Pastor Vinet of the Swiss Réveil, had come to a different view: Christian outreach must be strictly separated from any institutional form, because such forms are law, not gospel. But what are the Dutch antirevolutionaries doing? Instead of touching hearts, they come with external forms like a program, a newspaper, a separate faction in the Chamber. And so, with Christian arguments, Van der Brugghen arrived at the liberal position. The liberals called the voters' clubs a bad institution, one that "prevents the voters from sending to the National Assembly the man of their choice, honest and competent, of fixed political principles, free and independent." The purpose of elections could not be to delegate someone who would exchange his independence for slavish obedience to a program drawn up by the voters.³⁷²

This was an individualistic view of political representation that appealed to many in the upper circles, but soon seemed far too romantic for everyday politics. The antirevolutionaries sought something else very early on. A year after the Christian Friends' discussion, the first local antirevolutionary voters' club was organized. Da Costa had taken the hint, and in the spring of 1851 *Netherlands and Orange* was founded in Amsterdam. It was to be the mother of all antirevolutionary voters' clubs. In a brief statement, the founders declared, "All power is of God, the sovereignty of the people is in conflict with the Word of God; the Constitution has accepted and affirmed the sovereignty of the House of Orange from this time forward."³⁷³ Thus the spirit was Groenian, down to the last detail, for Netherlands and Orange sought to oppose not only popular sovereignty but also "state omnipotence."

The formation of the antirevolutionary voters' club provoked many accusations of discord and dissension in the days that followed. One liberal commentator found the statement "so barbarous, so intolerant, so medieval, so inflammatory, so unconstitutional, in a word, so pernicious and so ridiculous, that one might think the product was sent into the world by people who have an interest in sowing discord and dissension."³⁷⁴ Given this hostile atmosphere, it was not surprising that the number of antirevolutionary voters' clubs did not grow very quickly in the years that followed. Another club was founded in Utrecht, thanks to the efforts of Professor Barthold de Geer van Jutphaas. The voter club in Zwolle would soon follow. Groen encouraged people here and there to emulate these examples, but as a member of Parliament he was not allowed to get involved. He was happy to leave the organizational details of his party to the spontaneous initiative of others.

An antirevolutionary newspaper was born under better circumstances. It was more or less thrown into Groen's lap shortly after the April 1850 meeting. The conservative daily *The Netherlander* was in financial trouble, and Beets mentioned Groen to the Utrecht publisher Kemink. Groen was willing to guarantee the publication financially and could take over as editor-in-chief. He wanted to run everything himself anyway, so as not to be obliged to consult others. Being editor-in-chief meant that Groen would be responsible for the daily editorials and the overall direction of the paper; it would not be his job to manage the day-to-day affairs of the paper, which was just what he wanted. *The Netherlander* was laid out and printed in Utrecht, and Groen would send in his contributions from The Hague. From time to time, he would contact Kemink. Thus, from the summer of 1850, Groen had a paper that could serve as his mouthpiece, the "organ" of the antirevolutionary party. The range of this modern medium, however, was not wide. Apart from books and pamphlets, little use had yet been made of freedom of the press. Dailies were expensive because they were heavily taxed under the Stamp Act, and subscriptions to *The Netherlander* ranged from five hundred to a thousand. It was a big job for Groen every day, but in Singendonck and especially Wormser he had some reliable collaborators.

THE WALLOON ORPHANAGE

The busy career of a politician brought great changes to Willem and Betsy's lives. Willem experienced what many a parliamentarian has discovered: there is little time left for anything but politics. He had to work his way through piles of paperwork, all while working for the newspaper. The only way to cope was to make the most of every hour of the day and to avoid all non-essential social engagements. Immediately after his election to the Chamber, he asked to be released from his eldership in the Walloon church, where he had served for six years. In addition to serving as an elder, he was a board member of the church's orphanage. One of the recent issues the board had to deal with was taking precautionary measures to protect the children of the orphanage from a resurgence of cholera. But Groen also resigned from this board after serving for ten years. The latter decision was perhaps even more difficult than the first. Willem and Betsy had been closely involved with the orphanage and the day school run by the deacons of the church. Since 1845, Betsy had served the orphanage as one of the regents and was a member of the ladies' auxiliary, which ran the day-to-day operations of the home and school. The home had a resident "father" and "mother," but Betsy knew the children personally and was no less a mother among them.

Thus, Willem and Betsy had a difficult time when the consistory of the Walloon church had to make a decision in 1852 after a scandal at the school. Unruly behavior, curfew violations, petty theft, and even drunkenness were occasional problems, but a teacher who had abused one of the girls was a problem of a different order, for which there could be no tolerance. A number of girls at the orphanage informed the authorities of the teacher's sin. At first, the teacher pretended that his victim had a faulty memory, but after persistent accusations and some bad scenes, he no longer denied that he had taken the girl in question "on his knees and kissed her."[375] Of course, everyone realized that the teacher had to be removed immediately. However, the consistory took matters into their own hands and fired the principal and the board of directors, who were thus made to share the blame for the whole affair. Willem and Betsy disagreed with this decision and felt that the consistory's actions were authoritarian and reckless. It meant an abrupt end to Betsy's involvement with the children, whom she loved dearly.[376] She retired in a huff. Relations between the Groens and the Walloon consistory were never the same.

IN THE OPPOSITION

Groen did not have much time to deal with these church problems. He did write about them in *The Netherlander* but that was the end of the matter. The antirevolutionary "party" was beginning to take shape, and Groen's focus was on his struggle in the Second Chamber. His central question was this: What will the Netherlands look like once the revised constitution comes into effect? What role can Christian principles play in it? These were the "higher interests" that he always put first. These interests were not at stake in the debates over the postal bill or the deliberations over colonial profits. But they were at stake whenever general political principles were discussed, or the question of education, or developments in foreign policy.

The Netherlander devoted a great deal of space to foreign affairs. For Groen, events abroad showed that the principles of the Revolution were at work everywhere. For him, foreign policy always acted as a catalyst for great political ideas. In Groen's eyes, France continued to pose a grave threat to the rest of Europe—as it had in 1789, as it did in 1830 and 1848. When Napoleon's nephew, Louis Napoleon, the president of France, staged a coup in December 1851, Groen was horrified. He believed that history would repeat itself and soon bring a "second Napoleonic intermezzo" with the spread of war throughout Europe.[377] Groen and Mackay, the latter in his column in *Christian Voices*, believed that Belgium could quickly fall prey to this new Bonapartism. And after Belgium, the Netherlands would be next. This was an axiom of European politics. As events unfolded, peace prevailed, but so did Groen's suspicions. He used foreign events in his polemics with the liberals to rub their noses in the fact that they shared the same potentially violent principles.

Meanwhile, in the Chamber, he fought those liberal principles with fire and sword. His former friend and now opponent, Thorbecke, introduced a large number of bills in Parliament, notably an electoral bill and a provincial bill in 1850 and a municipal bill in 1851. Groen pulled out all the stops, especially during the debates on the municipal bill. He felt that the bill was imbued with an alien notion of centralization that left little room for local autonomy. The liberties and rights of the municipalities would be nullified by "general laws" that would bring legal equality; "municipal bondage," Groen called it. The municipal bill failed to reckon with the specific nature and history of cities, towns, and villages and served only to complete the "political regimentation of the nation."[378] The bill demonstrated that the freedom promised by the liberals ended in state coercion. All this was said in sharp tones, and Thorbecke's response was equally unsympathetic. Groen's accusation that the bill showed "systematic centralization" was met by Thorbecke with a grin. "Let us assume that the bill can be accused of 'centralization,' then the accusation is mitigated by the modifier 'systematic.' The honorable member, I am sure, prefers systematic to non-systematic centralization, and to that extent I shall be glad to regard the modifier as half compensation for the reproach directed at me."[379]

The immediate effect of Groen's opposition in the Chamber was negligible. The same was true of education legislation. It was clear that the freedom of education, now guaranteed by the constitution, had to be regulated by legislation. The objections to the public school were as strong as ever. Year after year, Groen inquired whether any progress had been made on an education bill, but Thorbecke was in no hurry. Groen therefore argued for interim measures. He believed that a start could be made with the separation of Catholic and Protestant pupils, "a separation desired by both sides." But even for such "transitional measures" he did not get the support of the Chamber. Conservatives and liberals alike saw Groen's ideal of facultative splitting ("optional separation") as a breach of national unity, which, after 1848, needed to be strengthened. The slogan "In unity lies strength" found a corollary in the field of education in the slogan "National strength through public education."[380] Groen, however, saw this unity in mixed common schools as the very corruption of the nation. On this point, the liberal Van Dam van Isselt launched a fierce attack against Groen in the Chamber of Deputies. Referring to the "rebellious" Odeon meeting in Amsterdam, he concluded his speech by saying, "The time has come to tell Mr. Groen and his followers that many people are saddened by the fact that they approve of creating unrest in church and state."[381] The speaker received "warm handshakes" from members of the Chamber, indicating their agreement with his tirade against Groen.

There was no room in the Chamber for both "ordinary Christianity" and the "antirevolution." Men who professed a "colorless Protestantism" distanced themselves from Groen.[382] People throughout the country were rather shocked to hear of these clashes in the Chamber, unaccustomed as they were to sharp political debate. The Christian Friends gave Groen well-meaning but useless advice.[383] After his first clashes with Thorbecke, they expressed the wish that he would tone down the "ironic element" in his speeches and become the mild and tolerant parliamentarian he had been in 1840.[384] At the same time, they appreciated the efforts to raise an antirevolutionary banner in the Chamber. Many sympathizers considered opposition to Thorbecke to be imperative, and many wished for his downfall. Van Rappard, the director of the royal cabinet, attended cabinet meetings to take minutes, and as early as 1851 he wished "that the sun would set on this ministry."[385] The high noon of Thorbecke's first ministry, however, would be long and stormy. Thorbecke did not risk introducing an education bill, but he would succeed in antagonizing almost every Protestant in the country. His Poor Law, which proposed to take some of the poor relief away from the church and give it to the state, had already provoked much protest. Things went from bad to worse when, in early 1853, it was revealed that he intended to implement a permanent agreement with the pope to grant Dutch Catholics the right to have bishoprics restored in the Netherlands.

The Antirevolutionary

THE NO-POPERY MOVEMENT OF APRIL 1853 AND THE YEAR OF DISASTER

The Thorbecke ministry went down under full sail in a storm of anti-papism in the country. This anti-papism had developed during the forties as a phenomenon accompanying the beginning of Catholic emancipation in the Netherlands. If the Catholics exercised their freedom, they could outnumber the Protestants in the west and south. Numerous societies and associations were formed to stem the tide. Protestant farmers with fertile wives were to be given land in the Catholic province of Brabant, and evangelization efforts were to be intensified in order to free the pope's subjects from their "superstitious beliefs." In the fall of 1852, rumors began to circulate that the government was negotiating with the pope for the restoration of bishoprics. Catholics and Protestants alike were aware of the historical significance of this act, though with different emotions. For the first time since 1579, the pope of Rome would have a say again in the Netherlands. The restoration of his authority was based on the liberal freedoms guaranteed by the Constitution of 1848. The March 7 papal allocution announcing the measure spoke of the restoration of the church in the lands of "Calvinistic heresy"—a phrase that went like a shock wave through the country. Protestants of all stripes exploded in furious anger. Church-going people took to the streets, forming a nationwide "Great Protestant" movement. Their manifestations in March and April 1853 would change the political map of the Netherlands.

Utrecht was the center of the resistance. Remarkably, it was Van Heusde's students, along with a number of pastors, who were seen in the front lines against Thorbecke. Utrecht chemistry professor Gerrit Jan Mulder was the soul of the resistance, which included part of the academic community. Mulder was an avowed enemy of Thorbecke's liberalism and disapproved of the Constitution of 1848. He considered the new parliamentary culture a fiasco and direct elections an absurdity. Inspired by the Socratic school of Van Heusde, Mulder believed that the leadership of state, church, and society should be in the hands of strong men, well-versed in knowledge and virtue. Such men should not be exposed to all kinds of criticism all the time. He advocated the return of power to the king, who should not be "fenced in" by endlessly deliberating assemblies. No authority could come from paper constitutions and agreements. Authority had to be embodied in powerful figures ripe for leadership. Mulder made himself the mouthpiece of a conservative group that would prefer to turn back the clock to before 1848. In 1853, the new order of things revealed to all how dangerous it really was: it extended rights to the pope, the head of an "intolerant" church, in a country attached to its traditions of freedom and Protestantism.

Supported by the vast majority of the clergy, the protest movement grew rapidly. Emotional petitions against "ultramontane domination" were widely circulated and signed by many people. On April 15, no fewer than fifty-one thousand signatures were presented to King William III in Amsterdam. In the previous years, the king had clashed several times with his first minister, Thorbecke, and he feared that his position as monarch would become weaker and weaker under a liberal regime. At the great meeting in Amsterdam, he dropped his prepared speech and let it be known that the cabinet had caused him "many painful moments" and that "the bond between the House of Orange and the Netherlands has become even more intimate and precious" as a result of the events of that day.[386]

These words could be interpreted as the king's wish to see the end of the liberal cabinet and perhaps even the Constitutional Order of 1848. In any case, the king's words sealed the fate of the government, which resigned collectively the next day. This reaction did not surprise the king: even before his visit to Amsterdam, he had been consulting advisors about a new government with a greater political role for the monarch. To Mulder and his conservative followers, it seemed that the king was now asserting his political authority. The elections of June 1853 were anti-Thorebekian and anti-Catholic and resulted in a decisive shift to the right.

On that fateful April 15, Da Costa was in the palace on Dam Square for an audience with the king and witnessed the presentation of the petition. Those present speculated about the fall of the cabinet and the political aftermath. In the midst of a group of onlookers, Da Costa had voiced his opinion: "What else but a Groen Ministry?"[387] Some raised their eyebrows, others shrugged their shoulders. But even if doubts were expressed, it was clear that the no-popery agitation had at a stroke brought the antirevolutionaries into the camp of the victors. Groen's fundamental criticism of Thorbecke now seemed to pay off. But his position differed fundamentally from that of Mulder and the conservatives. Groen did not believe that the restoration of the Roman Catholic episcopate was unconstitutional. The "public rights of religious beliefs" that he had defended on behalf of the Seceders applied no less to Catholics. The Dutch Catholics got what they were entitled to, and the pope's statement about Calvinist heresy was only an "incident." The peculiar position of the antirevolutionaries among the parties was the very reason why Da Costa wanted Groen to form a new government. Groen, too, believed that the antirevolutionaries, not the conservatives, stood for the policies that could bring about national reconciliation. However, no matter how much the no-popery storm filled the sails of the antirevolutionaries, their ability to maneuver did not become any easier.

Groen was neither a rabid anti-papist nor a member of an anti-papist club. Nevertheless, he welcomed the demonstrations of the churchmen, interpreting them as a sign of the "not yet extinguished principles of religion and nationality," as he wrote to Professor Vreede of Utrecht.[388] But he condemned the fact that these demonstrations and actions were often directed against the person of Thorbecke. A serious defect of the no-popery movement was that all the agitation did not defeat liberal principles. Political success could not be built on mass agitation.

While Protestants marched in "orange parades," Groen stayed at home and did not show his face in the crowds. Nevertheless, the politicization of church people did not leave the antirevolutionaries unaffected. Their organizational activities met with both encouragement and competition at the local level. Beginning in April 1853, Mulder and his followers established voter clubs called *King and Country* in Utrecht, Gouda, Leyden, Rotterdam, and The Hague. These conservative clubs soon outnumbered those of the antirevolutionaries. The situation often led to alliances at election time or encouraged Groen supporters to accept membership on the boards of conservative clubs, as was the case with De Geer in Utrecht. Groen warned his supporters to maintain their independence, but at the same time it was clear that the antirevolutionaries were profiting from this revival of public interest in politics.

From the perspective of Catholics as well as liberals, the adjustment on the political front looked grim and threatening. The Catholic press was very negative about Groen. His handbook was portrayed as an example of anti-Catholic historiography, and his stance on primary education was interpreted as motivated by anti-Catholicism. Nor had people forgotten that he had once recommended that the predominantly Roman Catholic provinces of Brabant and Limburg be placed under a separate political administration. The Catholics in the Chamber therefore supported Thorbecke. After all, his liberal principles had made him a champion of Catholic liberties. These Catholic supporters of Thorbecke saw Groen as the main instigator of the no-popery movement. And if they did not see it, the liberals helped them to see it. The liberal journal *The Guide* considered Groen van Prinsterer to be Thorbecke's main opponent, and in the fall of 1853 one of its contributors, the young liberal historian Robert Fruin, opened the attack on Groen with a pamphlet entitled *The Antirevolutionary Constitutional Law of Groen van Prinsterer Explained and Evaluated*.[389] The pamphlet, which was published in the fall of 1853, was a response to Thorbecke's attack on Groen. Fruin stated that Groen's opposition in recent years, "with all its fine oratorical talents, its humor, its irony," had produced nothing more than "tempests in a teapot" in an attempt to bring down the government. Moreover, Groen had sown discord in church and state by dividing citizens into revolutionaries and antirevolutionaries and then setting them against each other. Fruin's contribution showed that the hatred of the liberals was directed not so much against the moderate center or the colorless Protestants, but against the antirevolutionaries, and above all against Groen.[390]

The increase in antirevolutionary votes in the June 1853 elections was due to the anti-liberal mood in the country and the conservative agitation of the moment. The conservatives won a large majority of seats in the Chamber of Deputies. In addition to Groen, Mackay, and Van Lynden, Elout, Hubert van Asch van Wijck, and Van Reede van Oudtshoorn, who had all run as antirevolutionaries, were elected. The same could not be said of Van der Brugghen, the Réveil man, who was elected in the district of Zutphen with the support of moderate liberals, conservatives, and antirevolutionaries.[391] Van Lynden, who had known Van der Brugghen as a colleague on the bench of the Nymegen District Court, was not happy with this new member of the Chamber: he was easily influenced and would bring more grief than gain as an ally. In any case, he was not an "antirevolutionary."[392] Van der Brugghen, for his part, wished to maintain his independence and did not join the antirevolutionary faction formed in June in *Oud-Wassenaer* under the leadership of Groen. True to his convictions, he did not want to be a member of a "party." Nevertheless, he proved to be a valued supporter of the six antirevolutionaries. When he lost his seat a year later in the by-elections for part of the Second Chamber, he wrote to Groen that he was sorry he could no longer "share in the honor as well as the abuse and defeats of the antirevolutionaries."[393]

Indeed, abuses and defeats had been plentiful. The 1853-54 session was a "year of disaster" for the antirevolutionaries. The atmosphere between the antirevolutionaries and the conservatives quickly turned sour. Was it Groen's fault that he criticized the cabinet from the beginning? The cabinet expressed its displeasure with the pope's remarks, but said nothing about the public rights of Catholics, and thus, Groen complained, were not promoters of national reconciliation but merely "liberal conservatives." This was the beginning of a disastrous chain of events. The conservatives, after all, saw themselves as reconcilers of the nation. The alliance at the polls now ended in enmity in Parliament. The antirevolutionaries were in an isolated position, but according to Groen, their "isolation"—standing out as an independent and distinct group with a consistent set of principles—was their strength. A low point in relations was reached during the debates on the Poor Law in the spring of 1854, which in the eyes of the antirevolutionaries still curtailed the rights of the church in this area. None of their amendments passed. As the June 1854 election approached, the personal attacks on Groen became more vehement; rumors even circulated that he was bribing voters out of his vast fortune. Groen had held the seat for the district of Zwolle since 1850, and had been re-elected in 1852 and 1853. In 1854 he fell out of favor with the voters. His seat for Zwolle went to a liberal, and Groen disappeared from the Chamber at the same time as Van der Brugghen. Thus, the hopes of the antirevolutionaries were disappointed, despite the political support of the no-popery movement. Groen was exhausted and disillusioned and thought his political career was over. His spirits were lifted, however, by the open letter to Groen van Prinsterer published by Da Costa that summer. "You will always be an example," Da Costa said, referring to Groen's parliamentary struggle and the Christian witness it had given.[394] What he said about a "Groen Ministry" was not very realistic, but Da Costa's moral support of the antirevolutionary caucus was most welcome to its weary members.

THE END OF THE CHRISTIAN FRIENDS

During Groen's years in Parliament, the pace of social life had visibly quickened. People traveled more, the distance between friends and like-minded acquaintances shrank, and meetings and gatherings became easier to organize. The biennial meetings of Christian Friends in Amsterdam had become a less unique phenomenon than when they began. People's agendas filled up more quickly and many resorted to meeting in organizations. Associations multiplied. In 1852, the pastors who belonged to the Réveil had formed a closed society, which the following year took the name *Ernst en Vrede* (Earnest and Peace), after the magazine it published.[395] *Ernst en Vrede* counted the influential Walloon pastor Daniel Chantepie de la Saussaye among its leading members, and the society took a critical stance toward the lay meetings of Christian Friends. The Réveil—it was Chantepie who first consistently referred to the movement by that name—had one major flaw: it lacked any connection with the theological scholarship of the day. This theological deficiency was addressed in *Ernst en Vrede*. The meetings of these educated clergymen were not open to "laymen." Even Da Costa, celebrated for his Bible lectures, was not welcome. It was clear evidence, Groen noted with regret, of an "esprit de corps" that did not take the laity seriously in the church. What would become of the Christian Friends' ideal of joint action by church members and ordained ministers?

Groen himself attended Christian Friends meetings only sporadically after he entered Parliament. Preparing for the Chamber and writing for *The Netherlander* took up all his time. As a result, he lost contact with a wider circle of people. "I'm talking to you in print, aren't I?" was his annoyed reply to former correspondents who complained about their empty mailboxes. He reserved handwriting for when it was absolutely necessary, given the poor condition of his hand. Of course, reading Groen's published speeches in Parliament or his daily newspaper was no substitute for the lack of personal contact. Another source of frustration for his supporters was that Groen did not get around to personally discussing the criticisms of his positions as presented in *The Netherlander*. It so happened that most of the pastors of *Ernst en Vrede* were not satisfied with Groen's position regarding the church. They saw no advantage in insisting on maintaining the denominational standards in the church. "Not maintenance, but development" was their motto. The church was to be "medically" delivered from modernism. They took offense at the "juridical standpoint" of what they called "The Hague School." This group had become a party that resorted to polemics within the church. Beets took exception to the "provocative, defiant, bitter, and embittered" tone of *The Netherlander*.[396] On the other hand, the laymen in The Hague felt that the prescriptions of the church doctors were neither very clear nor very effective. A kind of resentment and alienation developed between the laymen and the orthodox pastors. "We really can't do anything with our pastors," was Van der Kemp's succinct conclusion.

After the launch of *Ernst en Vrede*, Groen seems to have realized that he, too, had contributed to the estrangement. In any case, he no longer missed the semi-annual meetings of Christian Friends. Ever faithful to his ideals, he saw this contact between brothers as a platform for overcoming differences. In the summer of 1853, he threw the cat among the pigeons: "What will be done at last, or will nothing ever be done, especially by our faithful pastors, to maintain, or at least to proclaim—for that too is first of all to maintain—the rights of the church to its own confessions and church doctrine?"[397] This question was later discussed at the fall meeting of Christian Friends. The men of *Ernst en Vrede*, however, were conspicuous by their absence. Chantepie had responded in writing but still refused to come to the meeting. Beets had not been seen in Amsterdam for some time. The meeting was little more than an exchange of views as the key players were absent.

Groen used the year of respite after the "year of disaster" in Parliament to sort things out. He hoped to breathe new life into the meetings of Christian Friends, and he began to wonder how to go on with *The Netherlander*. The murderous rhythm of editing a daily was beginning to weigh on him, and he longed to write more substantial works again. If people were offended by his journalistic polemics, then perhaps a change of genre would be a good thing. At the same time, he realized that the antirevolutionary party needed an organ for influencing public opinion. The situation on the political and ecclesiastical fronts was complicated, and it would be a dereliction of duty to quit the paper without further justification. His confidant at the time, whom he consulted regularly, was Wormser, the decisive bailiff who worked for the court in Amsterdam. Wormser had written articles for *The Netherlander* from the beginning and was very active in all kinds of Christian work. Groen trusted this simple believer from the common people more than he trusted the ordained ministers. Wormser was to become Groen's "privy councilor."

Wormser had educated himself by reading the writings of Groen. He had borrowed these works from F. A. van Hall when he was still working in his law office.[398] Wormser firmly believed that the Reformed persuasion, which in Groen's view included both the Seceders and the orthodox members of the national church, needed to flex its muscles and develop a public presence. As early as 1850, he had written to Groen, "In spite of all the present optimism, we still have nothing ecclesiastical: no school, no magazine, no association, nothing that identifies itself with the Reformed persuasion . . . that is why I am seriously considering making an attempt to start something that would manifest itself as a Reformed institution."[399] This marked the beginning of his efforts to try to get a Reformed seminary off the ground in Amsterdam. Seceders and others were to work together for this purpose. The seminary would be an alternative to the theological training offered at the state universities in Utrecht, Groningen, and Leyden, which were either "colorless" or "modernist." Groen supported the initiative, but it met with little sympathy and much suspicion from the pastors. The plan had to endure much ridicule from these quarters.[400] Wormser's initiative failed when the Seceders withdrew at the last minute, but this sad ending did not change his unwavering zeal. On many occasions Groen was encouraged by Wormser's perseverance.

In the summer of 1854, Wormser learned of Groen's "ambivalence." Groen wanted to reduce his work for *The Netherlander* and publish collections of old essays and articles to show how unfair the slander against him in the Chamber had been. The number of subscribers to the paper simply would not increase, and apart from the *Handbook*, there was not much interest in his books. Müller, Groen's publisher, could hardly recoup his costs, as he showed with some very discouraging figures: of the speeches in Parliament of 1849, 337 copies were unsold, and of the speeches of 1850, 291 copies remained in stock; also, in stock were 253 copies of *The Rights of the Reformed Persuasion*, and 174 copies of *Constitutional Revision and Unity*. What to do, Groen wondered? Wormser's answer was simple and surprising: "Your readership does not go to Müller to buy books. We should appeal not to the upper classes, but to the middle and lower classes. The common people understand your writings quite well: only yesterday an office clerk volunteered that he was very much in sympathy with your *Unbelief and Revolution*, while a doctor who recently borrowed my copy told me that he couldn't make head or tail of it."[401] Wormser had been an unofficial agent for Groen's publications for some years, making sure that workers in the docks and factories could read them in their free time. On one occasion he told of a cigar factory where one of the men on the shop floor was reading Groen's *Liberty, Equality, Fraternity* to his colleagues, while the other cigar rollers, hungry for knowledge, pitched in to make up his wages.[402]

Still, Wormser was taken aback by the publisher's figures. Nevertheless, he urged Groen not to give up on *The Netherlander*. He submitted plans to continue publishing, but according to a new formula. Unfortunately, the publisher did not consider the proposal feasible. Groen himself, however, saw the need to continue, and he now felt doubly supported by Wormser, who had been very productive that summer in terms of articles for the paper. It was these very articles, however, that once again angered the pastors. Wormser did not mince words when he accused the theological faculties of being unfaithful or indifferent to the doctrine they were instituted to teach, thus clearly identifying himself with "The Hague School," albeit in his case as a voice from Amsterdam. Professor Van Toorenenbergen, one of the few ministers whose position was close to Groen's, expressed his fear that *The Netherlander* would further strain relations among the faithful. Wormser's "legalistic" writings should be reeled in, he wrote. "It seems to me rather precarious to combine the struggle in the church and the political struggle in one and the same paper. The circle of supporters in the latter field is much larger than in the former. Hence those constant clashes . . . which only spoil and paralyze our relations with one another."[403] Van Toorenenbergen put into words what the men of *Ernst en Vrede* were thinking: antirevolutionary politics was fine, but it had to be based on a broader ecclesiastical standpoint than Wormser's. Groen, on the other hand, stood four-square behind Wormser. The editor-in-chief and his associate editor believed that the political course to be followed was determined precisely by convictions rooted in the confessions. Politics, according to Wormser, was supported by the church.[404] As for Groen, he saw no difference between the "confessional party" in the church and the "antirevolutionary party" in politics.[405]

Groen made every effort to resolve the differences with the self-proclaimed "ethical-irenic" ministers of *Ernst en Vrede*. At the fall meeting of Christian Friends in 1854, Chantepie was invited to read a paper on the nature of the church. Heldring would be another speaker. The meeting was presided over by Groen, as before, and was attended by more than two hundred people. Many pastors made an appearance. However, Groen's plan to remove misunderstandings by having discussions in a brotherly atmosphere failed. Chantepie spoke about the "confessional" way of the church, seemingly reaching out to Groen, but at the same time condemning "exclusivism" and "subjectivism." His message was a warning against any form of party formation—the great concern of the pastors' society.[406] Heldring, too, had come under the influence of an irenic approach and now preached gentleness and tolerance. After the papers were presented, a Baptist evangelist from the slums of Amsterdam, Jan de Liefde, rose from his chair and delivered a fiery speech against the Reformed church and the pastors who preached meekness but would never be martyrs for the truth. The pastors were deeply offended and insisted on a motion of censure. The motion was carried and De Liefde left the room. The atmosphere was now poisoned and nothing more could be accomplished. The meeting broke up, and Groen himself, who still had a two-hour trip ahead of him, immediately left for the train station. The remaining brothers met that same evening to clear the air, but what had gone wrong in public could not be repaired in private.

The tumultuous meeting in the fall of 1854 was to be the last meeting of Christian Friends. The following spring, Groen proposed that no new meeting be called. It had become "mere routine," he wrote to Da Costa, and he had little interest in "artificially prolonging what is old and worn out."[407] Da Costa agreed, now that "clerical sensibility on the one hand and demagogic openness on the other" had dealt the meeting a "mighty blow."[408] The Friends all received a letter and would never meet again. The group of ministers gave their commentary by ignoring it. "The more prominent ministers are abandoning us," Wormser observed during the days when a meeting would normally have been held.[409] These were also the days when the decision was made to cease publication of *The Netherlander*. Groen had been unable to find anyone to take over, and the publisher was unwilling to make the paper a weekly unless Groen stayed on as editor. In 1855, Wormser was suffering from severe rheumatism and would never regain his full health after that year. Although the editor reported to Groen that a number of friends had been "moved to tears" by the news that the paper would be discontinued,[410] Groen lamented the lack of allies. "The pen has slipped from my hand," he admitted in one of the last issues. He had been editor-in-chief for more than fifteen hundred issues. After completing a series of concluding articles, which he had reprinted in a separate volume under the title *Epilogue to a Five-Year Struggle*,[411] he longed only for rest. For the first time in many years, Betsy and Willem took another long trip that summer, this time to the British Isles. After five weeks of vacation, they returned to The Hague in early September, refreshed and in good spirits.

BACK IN PARLIAMENT

The democratic system in nineteenth-century Holland required potential members of Parliament to allow their election to "happen" to them while remaining personally inactive. Passive suffrage was never as passive as it was in the first years after 1848. The fate of the candidates was in the hands of the voters in the districts. They nominated those to be elected by a plurality of votes. Of course, there was lively consultation between the electoral committees and prominent men in the country who could advise on the suitability and political inclinations of certain candidates, but this only confirmed the rule that candidates needed a recommendation to be elected. The creation of local antirevolutionary, conservative, and liberal voters' clubs meant that the system of prior consultation was streamlined and intensified. The formation of national parties, however, was undesirable under this system, since it could limit the freedom of local voters. When Groen spoke of his "party," he was repeatedly accused of curtailing this freedom. The most serious accusation was that he interfered in his own election, but the clearest proof that this accusation was undeserved came in September 1855: he was nominated in his hometown by the conservative voters' club *King and Country* and promptly elected by a small margin. A surprising result! Groen quickly learned that his nomination had been supported by the private recommendation of Gerrit Jan Mulder, the man behind the no-popery movement.

What Mulder was doing behind the scenes was looking for an alternative to the incumbent cabinet.[412] He knew he had the tacit support of the king, who was dissatisfied with the Van Hall ministry. The Poor Law of 1854 and especially the new education bill proposed by Minister Van Reenen were not in keeping with the policy of reconciliation that the cabinet was supposed to pursue on behalf of the king. In January 1854, Van Rappard had even resigned from the royal cabinet and joined the Ministry. Mulder was in contact with a number of prominent conservatives and tried, through confidential consultations, to bring about a change in government policy. He also engaged the new director of the royal cabinet, F. L. W. de Kock, which was not difficult for him since Mulder was a member of the board of the "Kings' School" in Apeldoorn, where the royal princes received their education. Beginning in the summer of 1855, influential conservatives also tried to bring the antirevolutionaries into their networks. The recommendation of Groen's nomination for the district of The Hague had been given "in the hope of a return favor"—so De Geer had found out.[413]

Shortly after his election, Groen received a letter of congratulations from Mulder, who asked if he could come over and consult with Groen. Other antirevolutionaries were also approached. A central figure in all this was De Geer, who had resigned from the board of the Utrecht club *King and Country*, but who continued to meet Mulder regularly at the university. So it was that the men met in Utrecht in October of that year, when Mulder laid out his strategy. After the fall of the Van Hall ministry, conservatives and antirevolutionaries would have to pull together in the ensuing elections, just like in the days of 1853. A "Christian Conservative Ministry" could then take office, with three posts reserved for men of the antirevolutionary school. In order to achieve this, it was imperative to work together behind the scenes without delay.[414] What did Professor De Geer think of this? De Geer was not sure and wanted to write to Groen in confidence. He had also inquired as to which antirevolutionaries were to be invited into the cabinet. Well, they had thought of a man like Van der Brugghen. In fact, he was the next name on their list. That fall he received a conservative nomination in a by-election in the district of Sneek. But although Van der Brugghen was eager to return to the Second Chamber, he did not get enough votes this time.

How did Groen react to these attempts by conservatives to make common cause with the antirevolutionaries? Coolly and rather stoically. He did not consider himself bound to the conservatives by his own election in The Hague, he did not trust Mulder and his clique, and he had a distaste for their methods. Groen had always been an advocate of open debate and did not want a change of government without a real change in governing principles. Was this rapprochement perhaps another example of a lack of knowledge and a real misunderstanding of his political ideals? And how could this backroom politics compensate for the weak role the conservatives had played in Parliament in opposition to the liberals? His experience in the "year of disaster" had taught him that antirevolutionaries did not gain strength through "combinations." He shared these thoughts with De Geer when he wrote his final reply. "To be sure, we must be polite and friendly; not aloof; eager to emphasize the commonality of wishes and sentiments where they exist. But nothing could be more harmful to us, I think, than to become, if only in appearance, a fraction of a party which, because it is on the slippery slope, will repeatedly be swayed, even against its will, by its liberal fellow believers."[415]

The conservatives thus failed to lure Groen into their camp. In one respect, however, they were not deceived. Groen's return to the Chamber strengthened the forces of opposition to the ruling government. Thanks to his unexpected return, Groen enjoyed a stronger position in the Chamber than in previous years. In addition, he now had Elout, Mackay, Van Lynden, and Van Reede on his side. And his brother-in-law Hoffmann, although not a member of the antirevolutionary council, often voted with the antirevolutionaries. Groen's activities now intensified the political struggle against Minister Van Reenen's education bill. The bill had been introduced in 1854, six years after the constitutional revision, but its readings in the Chamber were still protracted. In 1853, the king had requested a solution to the education question, and the royal wish was high on the Van Hall Ministry's education agenda.

However, the education issue had become a thorny political problem. Nothing had been done for too long, and the wishes coming from different directions were difficult to reconcile. The idea of dividing or separating the public school as a local option, depending on the religious composition of the local population, had gradually gained political weight. It also began to gain sympathizers in Roman Catholic circles, although it remained a proposal from the Protestant side. Many liberals and conservatives of the moderate center were more attached to the public school, because it could educate the nation from school days upward in mutual understanding and national concord. Conservatives wanted the public school to provide "non-sectarian" instruction in the Christian religion; liberals preferred a public school that was religiously neutral. Private education was still out of the question, although such schools were growing. In 1849, the country counted 2,448 public schools and 789 private schools; in 1854, there were 2,480 public schools and 909 private schools.[416] Thus, in five years, the public system had grown by 1.4 percent and the private schools by 15 percent. The latter category was co-financed by parents or founded and fully financed by churches. Secessionist church members were particularly active in establishing private schools.

Minister Van Reenen's education bill was particularly concerned with public education. The minister wanted to keep the public school, but it had to be "non-religious" so as not to offend anyone. He also offered the possibility, depending on local conditions, of establishing a separate school if people wanted one with a specific religious stamp. The package was inadequate in the eyes of the conservatives; it was totally unacceptable to the antirevolutionaries. The conservatives felt that such a public school was too colorless: if they were to cash in on the turn of 1853, the public school should not be allowed to deny the Protestant character of the Netherlands. The antirevolutionaries considered the public school to be based on a false principle, which would serve unbelief by spreading a diluted faith, and they opposed it with the principle of separate public schools; what was a special clause in the Van Reenen bill was to become the central idea of the law. Van der Brugghen, meanwhile, writing from Nymegen, let the antirevolutionary committee know that he did not agree with the creation of separate schools. He complained that the bill was silent on the establishment of private schools. He rejected the idea that the state should facilitate the establishment and operation of Protestant Christian schools: in his view, this would amount to state coercion. Nevertheless, he wrote to Groen shortly after the bill was introduced in the Chamber that he thought the bill was acceptable.[417] It was another of those moments when doubts about Van der Brugghen grew stronger. But his friends and acquaintances, if puzzled, still looked at him through the magnifying glass of obliging goodwill.

Van Reenen yielded to the opposition in the Chamber. In December 1855, he returned with an amended bill in which he showed that he had listened to a section of the conservatives. The public school could not be "non-religious" but had to promote morality and respect for religion. Of course, nothing could be taught that might offend Protestants, Catholics, or Jews. The idea of separation as a local option—the safety valve in his earlier proposal—was now discarded. For Groen and his allies, the bill was a step backward. The ideal of a Christian public school, desired by at least part of the nation, was further away than ever. If this bill were to pass, it would mean that many years of struggle had been lost. All forces had to be mobilized to prevent this. This time Groen had the support of the pastors. As early as their December 1855 meeting, *Ernst en Vrede* passed a resolution supporting Groen's long-standing efforts to make "separate (Protestant and Catholic) schools the rule."[418] Groen persuaded the pastors to launch a petition against the bill. He even provided them with the wording. By early February 1856, the petition was ready, and Heldring, Chantepie, and six other pastors presented it to the Chamber. It asked that the public school not be deprived of the Christian religion and that the nation not be deprived of its Christian character. It advocated the Groenian ideal of separate public schools as a local option to allow for the "unfettered" use of the Bible. The action was taken up by church councils, teachers' associations, schools, and periodicals, and in April the Chamber was flooded with letters and documents containing tens of thousands of signatures. In this way, a widespread movement against Van Reenen's education bill stirred up the country. Petitions to this effect also arrived from Nymegen, one of which was signed by Van der Brugghen, who could not stand aside, although he did not sign it wholeheartedly either.[419] In Utrecht, De Geer even managed to get Mulder and his group to sign a petition.[420] Groen tried to increase the pressure on public opinion by approaching Victor Cousin again with the request that, "in a time of crisis," he might once again raise his voice in the Dutch press.[421] Cousin did not reply.

On the floor of the House, Groen urged that the petitions not only be received for information but that they be seriously considered. He called them "a cry of distress" from the nation, an awakening of the "political conscience of a largely Christian population."[422] This stance made him the leader of the opposition to the cabinet and the head of the national movement for Christian schools. Groen attempted to use the petition movement as a fulcrum for demanding an amended education bill, and later he would repeatedly invoke it. According to him, a significant portion of the nation had now spoken out against what was proposed. The House, however, chose to ignore this. The debate on the bill would not be completed before the summer recess, and it became clear that the cabinet was on its last legs. Groen, however, was not waiting for a cabinet crisis. He hoped that the debate on the education bill would take its normal course through Parliament.

THE YEAR OF CRISIS

The prime minister's office in The Hague was a stone's throw from Groen's. He had seen Thorbecke working there, and later Van Hall. In May 1856 it looked for a moment as if Groen himself would be the next occupant of that office. King William III had decided to dismiss Van Hall's cabinet. He was dissatisfied with the performance of the ministry, which had achieved little since 1853 and had failed to resolve the education question, instead turning it into a cause of national agitation. While the cabinet wanted to ignore the petition movement, the king saw it as a cry from the people that he wanted to satisfy.[423] He did not wait for the June elections, but began looking for new leaders in May. In this way he hoped to avert a conservative defeat at the polls and a renewed call for Thorbecke. Two people were asked to give their opinion on the political situation that had arisen: the old colonial administrator Jean Chrétien Baud and Groen van Prinsterer. They received a letter from royal secretary De Kock asking them to answer a series of questions. The questions made it clear that His Majesty was not satisfied with the political order established in 1848. He wondered whether direct elections and freedom of the press had not had a negative effect and whether preparations should not be made for a more conservative revision of the constitution.

Naturally, Groen was honored by the request, especially since it included the question of whether he personally would be willing to serve in a new cabinet. Clearly, the time had come when he could no longer be ignored. By May 23, his detailed reply to the king was ready. Groen's answer to the constitutional question was firm: direct elections had not had a negative effect. On the contrary, it was a good thing that the nation was involved in political affairs. Any constitutional revision or other "startling changes" were unwise. What he wanted was for the existing constitution to be interpreted in the sense he had always advocated. The government's policy should find its support in the "Protestant faith," which saw in the "constitutional king" the descendant of the illustrious princes of Orange. Blessings were to be expected if their rights in church and school were recognized and a "confession of the Savior" and the "use of the Word of God" were considered normal.[424] Groen focused on his own views, tried to call on the Protestant nation within the order of 1848. The political signal he gave at that time was of great importance. Had he sided with the court's constitutional second thoughts, a serious constitutional crisis would have been imminent. As for his own possible role, he was cautious. He was not particularly in favor of a change of cabinet to begin with, and he was not personally inclined, except after "mature deliberation," to give up his "free position" in the Chamber—a position, he added, "which perhaps accounts for any strength I possess." He feared the opposition he usually encountered "whenever people feared I might gain some influence." Nevertheless, he ended his reply with the reassuring words that he would not refuse to serve His Majesty if there was a chance of success in bringing about the changes he proposed.[425]

Groen's reply of May 23 was interpreted as a conditional refusal. Baud also declined. At this point, the king felt that he was at a dead end with these two men and began to look for another way out. But this was a more negative interpretation than Groen himself had intended. Groen had a particular view of the role of a constitutional monarch. Thus, he believed that the king had the perfect right to form a new cabinet. His letter set out certain conditions for such a move, and he offered his services if the king would support him in doing so. Although he was aware of the practical difficulties, he hoped that the king would call upon him for a very specific task, in this case the regulation of primary education. If a new government came in with a "royal and national program," as in 1853, Groen was ready to take on the task. The polite language at the end of his letter suggests that he felt it was up to the king to cut the knot and simply call his servant.[426]

After submitting his letter of advice, Groen received no response for some time, so he focused on his reelection in The Hague on June 10. One way or another, he wanted to be back in the Chamber to take part in the debate on the education bill. It was also important to get as many antirevolutionaries in the Chamber as possible, now that the electorate was likely to move in a more liberal direction. The absence of a newspaper of their own was now felt as a great deficiency by the antirevolutionaries. Day after day, Groen wrote pamphlets and distributed them throughout the country. On the first of June he learned from Singendonck that Van der Brugghen had been offered the post of minister of justice. Singendonck was Van der Brugghen's brother-in-law, and he played a behind-the-scenes mediating role in the formation of the new cabinet. Singendonck had also heard that the king wanted the education issue resolved in accordance with Groen's views.[427] To avoid being sidelined, Groen requested a conference with De Kock. They discussed Groen becoming minister of foreign affairs, but Groen felt that things were moving too fast and hesitated. He shied away from a cabinet position and only wanted to be part of it to resolve the education issue. He also felt that the timing was very unfortunate, just before an election while the education bill was still before Parliament. It would look like royal interference in the normal political and parliamentary process. However, he did not refuse outright, but asked for wider consultation, preferably with the king and several ministerial candidates. Groen did not want to be part of a cabinet that would be internally divided—an assessment of the political situation among the conservatives that turned out to be quite accurate. Much was going on behind the scenes. Obviously, both De Kock and Van der Brugghen were not very keen on having Groen in the cabinet. Singendonck gradually came to share this feeling, although he had initially urged Groen not to be "too difficult."[428] In the end, the king himself, who seems to have clung to Groen's candidacy the longest, followed suit.

Meanwhile, June 10, the day of the election, had come and gone. Groen did not win a majority in his hometown in the first round; a run-off was necessary. In addition to The Hague, there was still a chance to be elected in Zwolle, and then in Leyden, where Groen had also registered as a candidate. While waiting for the results, Van Hall resigned. On June 11, Groen had another conference with De Kock, learned of the hesitations regarding his person, and was also informed that there would be a meeting between Van der Brugghen and the king on June 14. "Would I be willing to attend? Oh, yes, if I am told that His Majesty wishes it; I do not want to be in the way."[429] Groen hoped for a clear decision on the part of the king in favor of a program and a team of ministers who could be of one mind, at least on the issue of education. On June 12, he took the initiative to send a letter of advice to De Kock. It was not to his advantage that he stuck to his original goal and strongly advised against the formation of a new ministry. A different ministry, but of the same conservative color, would be a failure, he said; it would be worn out the moment it started. It would be better to repair the present ministry and allow the education bill to be completed. If the ministry was to go, there were only two options: either a Thorbecke ministry or a ministry that, through several members, had a bond with that part of the nation that "is attached to the faith and history of the nation and the national dynasty."[430] That would be a ministry, in other words, with Groen at its center. From this letter, too, it is clear that Groen did not want to recommend himself, but that he wanted to be called. But his candidacy was no longer in the picture. His objections, difficulties, and conditions made him a difficult man to do business with. "You are too strictly honest," Van Assen admonished him.[431] At the court, the decision had been made: Groen would be dropped.

On Saturday, June 14, Groen received a note at *Oud-Wassenaer* from Van der Brugghen asking if he could come by the next day. Van der Brugghen was staying with his brother-in-law Singendonck for a few days. Groen already knew that he would consult with the king. When Van der Brugghen got out of the carriage that Sunday afternoon, a surprised Groen realized that the new ministry would have room for only one antirevolutionary. Van der Brugghen had been summoned from Nymegen, had accepted the mandate to form a cabinet, and would be the head of the new ministry. "I, not you, am the man of the hour," were his opening words, and he rubbed salt in the wound by declaring that "a Groen ministry would have become a Polignac Ministry." This obvious reference to the weakest and shortest cabinet in French history was not misunderstood by Groen; he was all too familiar with the less than complimentary label for this strange French cabinet, *un effet sans cause*.[432] Of course, he could have seen that he would have had only modest support in the Chamber. But why had he not been considered alongside Van der Brugghen? If the king wanted an education bill along the lines of Groen's, why had he not intervened on Groen's behalf? These questions went through his mind as Van der Brugghen sat across from him, but he could not put them to his visitor.

The choice of Van der Brugghen was a slap in the face for Groen. He was piqued, he later admitted, "in view of my political career."[433] At the same time, he was worried, for he did not see Van der Brugghen as a man of independent thought. The man had allowed himself to be co-opted, Groen concluded, to serve as the figurehead of a cabinet that would be as weak as its predecessor. The conversation at *Oud-Wassenaer*, which lasted an hour and a half, was stiff and awkward. Van der Brugghen talked a lot and not much to the point. Groen, painfully affected, confined himself to the bare essentials. Van der Brugghen's goal was to get Groen's assurance of his support in the Chamber. The "Christian-conservative" ministry that Mulder had already predicted in the fall of 1855 was about to become a reality, and it would generally be seen as a rapprochement with the antirevolutionaries. Nothing could damage such a cabinet more than Groen's opposition. The prime minister–designate paid him this visit on Sunday afternoon to guard against this. Groen could make no promises, especially since Van der Brugghen had no concrete plans. Groen referred to his views on the public school and his support for the idea of separate schools as a local option, a position that was by now well known, and he assumed that Van der Brugghen, for his part, would stick to his old objections to the public school. The latter left *Oud-Wassenaer* on the vague assumption that he had secured Groen's support. Or so he told his fellow ministers, who joined him two weeks later when the new cabinet was sworn in. Almost to a man, they were Mulder's kindred spirits. According to Mackay, who usually mirrored Groen's opinion, it was a "mishmash."[434]

This was not the opinion of many friends. They were delighted with the appearance of Van der Brugghen. Was it not, as in 1853, the decision of the king himself to change course and try this approach? The turn of April 1853 could finally begin to bear fruit for the cause of Protestantism. Koenen hoped for an "energetic program."[435] Chantepie, Heldring, and Beets openly declared their support for this cabinet. Chantepie did so in a lengthy article in *Ernst en Vrede*, declaring that the "antirevolutionary element" had now moved from the "ecclesiastical-confessional to the evangelical-spiritual terrain."[436] Van der Brugghen was indeed the man of the hour, and the pastors counted their blessings. Support from this side did not wane when the government announced in its opening statement in the Chamber that it would not "depart from the principle of the common school to which the nation has been attached since 1806." Groen had received the text of the government's statement from Van der Brugghen four days earlier; at that time, it did not contain the sentence about the common school.[437] Now that it was there, everything became clear to him: Van der Brugghen had no backbone. In Groen's eyes, this passage was tantamount to treason. It was the ultimate concession to the conservatives, in total disregard of the purpose of the petition movement. He has since referred to it as the "fatal clause." "Our defeat was complete before the battle began," he later wrote.[438] He shared his great alarm with a limited group: De Geer, Elout, Mackay, Van Lynden, Gefken. Outside this small circle he kept his counsel, for he could not expect to make any headway against the general euphoria. Even Da Costa supported the cabinet because, as he said, it was "monarchical and Protestant in direction and inclination."[439]

Meanwhile, Groen had yet to win a seat. He lost the runoff in The Hague. In Zwolle, he did not even make it past the first round. It looked like it would be difficult to get Groen into the Chamber. In early August, however, after a run-off election in Leyden ended in a tie, a new election in that district secured him a seat thanks to a comfortable lead in the polls.[440]

Among the congratulatory letters is one from Van der Brugghen. "Immediate assimilation" reads Groen's grim pencil scrawl at the top. The letter is friendly enough, but Groen could see nothing in it but another attempt to entrap him.

> Will 1853 finally be vindicated in 1856–57? Only time will tell. This much is certain: we have a different and better administration, and the mutual sympathy of those who do not belong to the ultramontane-Thorbeckian alliance is of a better quality. Your election in Leyden was the fruit of this. If ever the slogan of sincerity and peace is indispensable today, especially in the political field. I am very pleased with La Saussaye's [Chantepie's] article on the new ministry, and I am sure that it recommends principles that can lead not to isolation, but to the moral assimilation of much good that is still to be found among our people.[441]

The hard-edged, inflexible politics of Groen van Prinsterer had been replaced by a more irenic approach to politics that Protestants of various stripes could shake hands on. Van der Brugghen had become the alternative to Groen, who, sidelined by the king, had, in the eyes of many, run his course.

THE DEFEAT

The ministry was monarchical, but it was also extra-parliamentary: its head was not even elected to the Chamber, as were several other ministers. The cabinet had to prepare itself for a fierce confrontation with the Chamber. Van der Brugghen got exactly what he had feared: both Thorbecke and Groen were his determined opponents. However, he felt supported by encouraging letters from Chantepie and Beets. What did Beets write? "Thorbecke is as little a typical Netherlander as Groen, even though their partisans would like to make them out to be. But you are. Count on it!"[442] The moderate center, which still saw so much good in the public school, could no more tolerate Groen than it could the doctrinaire Thorbecke. Through the networks of pastors, the parole was circulated further in an attempt to get rid of the now unpopular antirevolutionaries. In October 1856, Mackay, as editor of the political column in the journal *Christian Voices*, was informed by editor-in-chief Heldring that he no longer believed in the "juridical-confessional" standpoint. They wanted to be done with Groen's party, which was too exclusive to have any lasting effect.

The big clash between Groen and Van der Brugghen came in November. The debate in the Chamber would clarify Groen's position with respect to the cabinet. Groen questioned the extent to which this cabinet could be considered an antirevolutionary cabinet, arguing that the reason for its formation was the petition movement, which had so clearly expressed itself in favor of separate state schools. In his reply, Van der Brugghen put as much distance as possible between himself and the antirevolutionaries. He was not personally an antirevolutionary, he declared, nor was he an opponent of the common school. The atmosphere became electric when he expressed the hope that in the future "the antirevolutionary school of my friend, and especially of him personally, will not again prove to be so exclusive, so obstinate, as to be incapable of seeing, appreciating, and supporting any good except that which comes directly under its own auspices."[443] From this point on, Groen hammered home to his readers that Van der Brugghen had now repudiated the very principles he had recently professed. Had he not, half a year earlier, co-signed a petition against the Van Reenen bill? Groen accused him of "mystification," whereupon Van der Brugghen in turn accused Groen of practicing a "policy of antecedents." After these skirmishes, the two bruised warriors still wrote letters to each other with the salutation, "Dear Friend and Brother." Van der Brugghen's heart bled at the thought of personal estrangement. He believed he could do no other than what he was doing. Groen wrote that he had never before had such a painful experience in the Chamber, but he persisted in his view that Van der Brugghen was inconsistent and had denied his past as a champion of Christian public education.[444] Meanwhile, an exchange of letters also took place between Chantepie and Groen.[445] Chantepie was a straight shooter and, unlike Beets, did not shy away from direct confrontation with Groen.

He declared himself of one mind with Van der Brugghen and called Groen's program outdated and coercive.[446] Groen replied that he wanted to give an important part of the population what it was entitled to and deplored the role the ministers had played. "I cannot gloss over the fact that the direction you and Beets have given to the magazine and the Pastors' Association [of *Ernst en Vrede*] has made impossible what might have been possible in a good cause, and that it has opened a source of discord and confusion, the outcome of which I await with great concern."[447]

When the education bill was introduced in the House in February 1857, it was awaited with great anticipation. The bill, it turned out, was a new compromise, but it differed little from the objectionable Van Reenen bill. The common public school would serve in a general sense to promote "Christian and civic virtues"; there would be no provision for separate schools, and private schools would be eligible for state subsidies. This last clause was Van der Brugghen's personal contribution. When the bill was published, it caused a rift in the clergy. Rev. Van Toorenenbergen and Rev. Van Rhijn were unimpressed and called Van der Brugghen a "psychological enigma." Chantepie, quite disillusioned, turned his back on the minister. Heldring and Beets, however, defended the bill because at least there was a place for the Christian religion in the public school. Groen pointed out that Heldring had been the first signer of the pastors' petition to the Second Chamber the year before. But Heldring now explained that he did not want to sow discord. Singendonck came to his brother-in-law's defense, claiming that the "Christian principle" in the bill was more than a name or a slogan.[448] Given this division within their own circle, a new petition was out of the question. A few signatures were still collected, and Da Costa composed a piece, but the mood was lackluster and a petition was hardly worth the effort.

That spring, Groen wrote pamphlet after pamphlet opposing the education bill. By early June, the bill was before the House. Naturally, the proposed nature of the common school received the most attention. Van der Brugghen agreed with a formulation offered by Thorbecke that the teaching of Christian virtues should be interpreted as "religious instruction transcending sectarian differences." This gave a liberal interpretation to the relative neutrality of the public school. In Van der Brugghen's view, specifically Christian education had its place in private schools. However, the clause regarding subsidies for private schools did not survive the debates. As a result, the new law did not allow any compensation for private education. The minister had moved further away from his original position and closer to that of the liberals. The bill could now count on a majority, given the combined votes of conservatives and liberals. The antirevolutionaries, who had fought so hard for the Christian public school for years, were left empty-handed. The disappointment was immense. Immediately after the vote in the Chamber, Groen wrote a note while still in his seat, and when he got up and left, he had someone deliver it to the president. He ended his public trial by resigning his seat on the spot. Wormser and Da Costa were personally informed by Groen before his resignation became public. Relations between Groen and Van der Brugghen never healed, although the latter wrote to Groen in a conciliatory gesture with "words of peace." In a stiffly formal letter, Groen replied that a "real rapprochement" was not possible at this time and that he could only withhold the hand of fellowship.[449]

The passage of the Education Act of 1857 marked a break in Groen's life. It put an end to an ideal in which he had believed for seventeen years. This ideal was closely related to his conception of the "Christian state," rooted in Dutch history. A government of the Netherlands, of all places, should stand up for the rights of Reformed Christians. Their freedom of religion and education should not be marginalized but should be officially and publicly recognized and protected in the public school system. Such a policy of recognition would signal that the government took seriously God's providential guidance of the Netherlands and thus God's sovereignty. Last but not least, Groen's ideal concerned the children themselves. They should be reached at school with the Bible and biblical teaching. A common Christianity without the Bible could never foster the power of true faith and could not be an alternative to the kind of Christian education Groen had in mind. The fact that a brother from the Réveil circles had allied himself with the conservatives and made Groen's ideal impossible was experienced by him as a betrayal. One of his correspondents drew a parallel with the classical drama of Caesar, with Van der Brugghen in the role of Brutus: "Et tu, Brute!"[450]

If the comparison with Brutus went a bit too far, Van der Brugghen was no closer to Cicero. He lacked the unity of personal character and political conduct that Groen had always admired in the Roman statesman and that he took as a normative for his own public activity. Therefore, by the end of the drama, Van der Brugghen's very character was called into question. The criticism of Van der Brugghen's fickle character was one of the most serious accusations of that year. Groen stood his ground, but at times he felt that he was politically alone. Only Elout, Mackay, and Van Lynden stood by him, while Wormser and Da Costa supported him from afar. But where were the pastors? Groen could not understand why leading clergymen would not support the principle at stake in the school legislation.[451] Their irenic attitude made them averse to what they regarded as the greatest evil of the antirevolutionaries, namely, that they operated in a closed rank, ending in the formation of a party. To use the jargon of the antirevolutionaries, the pastors were as "politico-phobic" as they were "orthodoxo-phobic." The majority of them switched to support Van der Brugghen. They were even willing to change their program. Some followed Beets, who believed that a common school with "Christian virtues" would best serve society and national unity. This was also the opinion of the Groningen theologians, who, together with their standard-bearer Hofstede de Groot, welcomed the law of 1857. Throughout that year, Groen remained undaunted and continued to look for points of attack. Gradually, however, those around him began to see him in a different light, and this paralyzed his activity. In the dramatic parliamentary year of 1856–57, the critics who said that Groen was always against everything and that it was impossible to work with him seemed to be right.

6

Martyr and Popular Tribune

THE END OF THE RÉVEIL

THE STROKE OF 1857 was a knockout blow for the Réveil. The movement resembled a defeated army: small groups of wounded men, with shoulders slumped, limped off the battlefield. They formed small islands in Amsterdam, Nymegen, and The Hague, where they carried on as best they could. But as a nationwide movement, as a public current, the Réveil was over. It had never sought its strength in organization, but rather in mutual friendship and personal bonds. The "awakening" that resulted from this approach had spurred public action. But when the phase of struggle and battle arrived, the mutual trust on which everything depended disappeared. The leaders of *Ernst en Vrede* felt that the pastors had to lead the awakening into theological channels. They wanted to fight theological liberalism. They refused to join forces with the laity who were moving toward orthodoxy. The laity, on the other hand, had nothing to do with terms like "ethical" and "irenic" and felt that the battle lines were becoming too vague. Once moved into the political realm, the battle was fought almost exclusively by the losers. With the exception of Beets, Van der Brugghen, and a few others, none of the former circle of friends embraced the common school that was enshrined in the law of 1857.

The time had come to mourn, to lick one's wounds, and to reassess the situation. Groen had a brief period of flickering fire shortly after his departure from the Chamber. He corresponded with Wormser about starting another political paper as well as a church paper, and with De Geer about starting an association to promote the interests of private education. The advocates of biblical education had begun to realize, even before the Primary Education Act was passed, that the private school would have to become their focus. Both plans, however, would soon be off the table. Wormser was eager to come forward with a clear Reformed identity. The people who do not unequivocally embrace the Reformed confession, he argued with Groen, have always proved to be harmful to the cause.[452] Wormser thought of starting a weekly or monthly magazine, with Groen at the helm and himself as second in command. But as the fall set in, Groen wavered and didn't push through. His energy was spent. He complained of being tired, and for a whole month he battled a bout of the flu. Finally, he let Wormser know that he would no longer engage in the polemics of the day. He felt it was "time to be silent."[453] Nor did an association for private education get off the ground. The men were really unfamiliar with the terrain and unprepared for the task. They held a conference on the subject in the fall, but without concrete results. At a meeting in Utrecht that December, they talked about setting up a permanent committee. Groen, already discouraged by the prospect of confused discussions, was not present. They talked about it among themselves, but that was all.

After 1857, political life would never be the same for Groen and his co-religionists. "Internal division has rendered us powerless, at least for the time being," was Groen's assessment.[454] Indeed, according to public opinion, the antirevolutionaries were finished. The *Arnhem Courant* described Mackay, Elout, and Van Lynden as the last of a dying breed. The press reviewed the final results of Groen van Prinsterer's political career. The liberal monthly *The Guide* poked fun at the antirevolutionaries and their thwarted leader: "Mr. Groen's role as the champion of a political trend had long since fizzled out"; the Chamber of Deputies had "quietly" let his party fight itself to death, and "no national day of mourning accompanied Mr. Groen's departure."[455] The upper class, to which Groen belonged and whose ear he coveted, also regarded Groen as a washout. Groen himself seemed resigned to this tragic role. Bruised, if not broken, he decided to retire from public life. "The events of recent years," he wrote to Pastor Heldring, "have destroyed any power I might have developed in the ecclesiastical and political spheres."[456] Groen now embarked on the project for which he had received the king's permission ten years earlier: the publication of a second series of archives.[457] The culmination of this series would be the letters of

Prince Maurice in his struggle with the political leader of the Republic, Johan van Oldenbarnevelt, during the Twelve Years' Truce with Spain. There, Groen would again find himself face to face with adversaries: men who were known to be theological liberals. At the age of fifty-six, he may have considered himself an "emeritus" in the struggle between church and state, but he was not ready to retire from the battlefield of historiography.

THE ROYAL FAMILY ARCHIVES

And so we see Groen return to his old job at the Royal Family Archives. His position there was not quite the same. In 1849, the rooms in the Cabinet of Japanese Rarities in the Binnenhof had been vacated and all the archival documents had been moved to Noordeinde Palace. This is also where Häberling worked, the civil servant who, on Groen's instructions, blew the dust off the documents, deciphered them, and then copied them. During Groen's years in Parliament, Häberling prepared the pieces that would be included in future volumes of the archives. However, he became ill, struggling with mental problems, and died after almost twenty-five years in office. At that time, Groen made it known that he wanted a change in his job description. He wanted to be relieved of the actual care of the collection. The family archive was far from the ideal he had once envisioned for it. Placing the priceless collection in the attic of the palace had not only made oversight impossible, but had also made the archives "almost inaccessible."[458] This cry of alarm led to some action. An attempt was made to deposit the collection in a building in the Buitenhof. But this plan also failed. Groen accepted only limited responsibility for the situation and concentrated on the part of his task that he was determined to retain: the publication of the archival documents relating to the House of Orange-Nassau.

The first volume of the second series was published in 1857. It covered the period 1584–99 and included the documents that had been copied by Häberling. At this point Groen needed a copyist and received permission to hire one.[459] Four more volumes followed in rapid succession. In 1858 the important second volume was completed, covering the period 1600–1625, with Maurice and the Synod of Dordt. The final volume would appear three years later, covering the princes Frederick Henry, William II, and William III, and ending with the year 1688. Thus, Groen stopped at the Glorious Revolution, the successful counter-movement of the Stadtholder/King William III against Catholic absolutism in Europe. He still had a vague plan to extend the second series to 1702, the year of William III's death. At this point, however, the politician in Groen once again ruled out the life of the historian.

The five volumes of the second series were again highly acclaimed by professional historians. In the meantime, Groen's liberal opponent, Robert Fruin, had been appointed the first professor of Dutch history in Leyden. Fruin, as we have seen, did not share Groen's political ideas, but he agreed with his ideas as a historian. He called him "the pioneer of our modern historiography."[460] Long gone were the days when Groen had to defend his project against attackers who regarded it as a kind of juvenile voyeurism (as one critic had done when the first series of the archives appeared[461]). For his part, Groen admired Fruin's monograph on a critical decade in the Eighty Years' War[462] and once again demonstrated that he knew how to appreciate talent in his political opponents.

With the same nobility of spirit, in his second volume Groen judged a black sheep of Protestant historiography, Johan van Oldenbarnevelt (1547–1619). For the first time, the stirring letters written shortly before and after the dramatic beheading of the advocate of Holland were published. In a lengthy 148-page introduction, Groen presented his interpretation of the great conflict between Maurice and Oldenbarnevelt, an episode so controversial in Dutch history.[463] New light was shed on the event by the letters exchanged between Maurice and his cousin Willem Lodewijk, stadtholder of Friesland. The harsh verdict—Oldenbarnevelt was found guilty of treason, which carried the death sentence—was not unjust, according to Groen, but the lawyer's life should have been spared because of his great services to the country.[464] In the words of the contemporary poet Vondel, they should not have "fed him to the crows and ravens." When Da Costa received this volume on his vacation, he immediately responded that the correspondence largely confirmed the Calvinist interpretation of the conflict between Oldenbarnevelt and Maurice: the prince's triumph over the stubborn lawyer meant the salvation of the Reformed church. But Da Costa could not understand Groen's "high esteem for the abilities of statesmen in the enemy camp."[465] Oldenbarnevelt had an "aversion" to the divinely named Orange and was possessed of a stubborn pride and a cruel character to boot. In his political-historical essays, Da Costa seems to have regarded this as a hereditary trait in hostile statesmen of all ages. Take Thorbecke: the only thing missing was that he "has not yet had the opportunity to prove it." The ultimate punishment Oldenbarnevelt received was therefore just. Da Costa would not have hesitated to personally sign Oldenbarnevelt's death warrant.[466]

It was not long before Catholic writers entered the historiographical fray over the interpretation of Dutch history. Liberals, Catholics, and Protestants, the three schools of interpretation that had long dominated Dutch historiography, began their intense debates in the 1860s over the proper reading of the nation's history and the nature of Netherlandic nationality. The time was approaching for the three-hundred-year commemoration of the high points of the struggle against Spain, and Groen saw it as his duty to intervene, a duty made all the more difficult by the fact that the faculties of the Dutch universities did not include a single representative of the Calvinist and Orangist version of history that he espoused. The academic study of history was in the hands of liberals, and there was no sign of that changing. Groen admired their empirical qualities and exacting scholarly criticism, but he found them lacking in sensitivity to the spiritual dimensions of history. What bothered him about liberal historians was the pride of place given to short-term and purely mundane explanations. Their histories did not show the clash of principles, but of personal ambitions and material interests. They overlooked the strength of religious faith and courage that Groen admired so much in the Oranges. What was lacking was a scholarly treatment of history from the perspective he had demonstrated in his *Handbook*.

Groen felt somewhat compensated by the American historian and diplomat John Lothrop Motley, whose book *The Rise of the Dutch Republic* was published in 1856. The archives Groen edited had been Motley's "constant guide through the labyrinth" of sixteenth-century Dutch politics.[467] Groen regarded Motley's work as a "magnificent tableau" of the birth of the republic, and he was particularly pleased with what Motley said about William of Orange: "His inmost soul is revealed in his confidential letters."[468] In 1858 Motley had returned to The Hague to continue research in the National Archives and the Royal Family Archives for his work on *The History of the United Netherlands*. Groen had regular conversations with him and provided him with documents. The first volume of Motley's work appeared in 1860 and was soon strongly contested by Catholics because of its portrayal of the Dutch Revolt. On several occasions in the 1860s, Groen, for his part, fought Catholic versions of Dutch history. When Jan Willem Brouwers, at the commemoration of the Battle of Heiligerlee, called Louis of Nassau a religious "dissembler" and a military "bungler," Groen took up the defense of this national hero and wrote a scathing 128-page tract in three parts entitled *Heiligerlee and Ultramontane Criticism*[469] published in 1863.

It was in 1863 that Groen first attempted to sever his ties with the Royal Family Archives. There was no improvement in the accommodation situation, and Groen foresaw that he would not be able to do any new scholarly work. He was not satisfied with the copyists he had to hire, and his polemical spirit constantly drew him into debates with his contemporaries. In 1863, he took exception to the way the commemoration of 1813 was being discussed. A national committee had been set up to raise funds for a national monument. Groen had reason to fear that it would become a celebration of entrepreneurs, for a circular that was distributed stated that the "core of the nation" consisted of men who were active in trade, shipping, and industry. The text reflected satisfaction with the burgeoning Netherlands economy. King William I was hailed as the founder of the new prosperity. According to Groen, however, a commemoration of 1813 should not focus primarily on commerce and industry, but on throwing off the French yoke, regaining freedom and independence, and remembering Orange. To shed a broader light on the blessing of 1813, he published *Commemorating 1813 in the Light of National History*.[470] To commemorate 1813 merely as the restoration of material prosperity amounted to "murdering the national soul." With this polemic, he was once again far from the tranquility of archival research. But his offer of resignation was not accepted. In 1863, an assistant was appointed in the person of J. W. Sijpesteijn, whom Groen had nominated. The court wished to keep the name of Groen van Prinsterer attached to the Royal Family Archives.

SEMPER IDEM: EVER THE SAME

Obviously, it was not easy for Groen to rest on his laurels. In the end, his self-imposed period of silence would be brief. He did return to work that he could do on his own, but the silence of study drove him back into public life. He felt the need to express his views on current events and to hear what his friends thought of them. The small Réveil circle that remained in The Hague was a suitable milieu for discussing public affairs. During the winter season, social life continued as usual. Every week there was an evening at someone's house where the old and trusted friends met: Elout, Mackay—both still members of the Second Chamber—Capadose, Van der Kemp. Relations with Singendonck, who now called himself an ethicist, had cooled, as had relations with Pastor Secrétan (who, as it happened, had left the country in 1860). Gefken was also no longer part of their company; he had gone to Surinam in 1856 to serve as attorney general. The friends had great respect for the thirty-year-old pastor of the German church, Rev. R. Th. J. Kögel, who was soon invited to join them. The circle now took on a more German flavor, as Kögel brought with him a number of his friends, such as K. I. B. von Hodenberg, Hanover's ambassador to The Hague. Another newcomer was the diplomat J. P. J. A. Count van Zuylen van Nijevelt, a convert to the faith who was introduced by Elout. However, he was in active service and was abroad for long periods at a time, so he did not show his face very often.

What sparked discussion in this circle was foreign policy. After 1848, Europe had entered a period of international tension. The status quo among the five European powers, in place since the Congress of Vienna in 1815, had been destabilized in the decade following the year of revolution. In 1853, the Crimean War demonstrated that Britain and Russia had no qualms about going to war with each other. It was the first serious clash between the Great Powers that had been united in the Grand Coalition against Napoleon in 1815. The fact that France sided with Britain in this conflict was ominous in the eyes of the friends in The Hague. In 1852, Louis Napoleon had proclaimed himself emperor of France, accompanied by the ringing declaration that "the Empire is peace." This declaration alarmed the smaller powers in particular, who feared France's historic tendency toward expansionism. The Netherlanders watched Napoleon III's maneuvers with suspicion. When Willem and Betsy visited Paris in the summer of 1858, on their way home from Switzerland, they were acutely aware that they were in the "Babel of our days."[471] Standing at the Dome des Invalides, where Napoleon I rests in his magnificent tomb, they were convinced that he had come back to life in his nephew Napoleon III.[472] This conviction became concrete in the fall of 1858, when France supported the movement for Italian unification, the *Risorgimento*, which took up arms against Austria. Austria controlled much of northern Italy after 1815 and was the most important power in the region next to the pope and the papal states. By supporting the *Risorgimento*, France was able to expand its influence in Italy.

The new fear was that the involvement of the Great Powers might lead to a general war on European soil. Austria was allied with Prussia, together they dominated the German Confederation, and France had cooperated with Britain in the Crimea. In the fall of 1858, the Dutch Parliament anxiously debated whether the country might be drawn into a European conflict. The Netherlands had obligations to the German Confederation, which included the southern Dutch province of Limburg. The antirevolutionaries pointed out that France's involvement in the conflict meant that it would not be a war of "local interest." Behind France's action lurked a revolutionary ambition, "the scope and subject of which is incalculable," as Van Lynden put it in the Second Chamber.[473] The Great Powers should force France to respect international law and support Austria against the warring Italians; the international community would only remain sound if it upheld international law. This was the theme that Groen defended among his friends in The Hague when war broke out in the spring of 1859. The international conflict was the topic of their evening meetings. Groen was vehemently opposed by Capadose, who saw it as a "supreme act of justice" that Napoleon III was being used by God to teach a lesson to repressive Austria and at the same time to Roman Catholic Italy.[474] In Amsterdam, Da Costa also saw the war primarily as a divine nemesis against "papist and perfidious Austria." He hoped for new opportunities to spread the gospel after the war. Had not Catholic Italy recently imprisoned Protestant evangelists? "Let God's justice take its course," he wrote Groen.[475] It irritated Groen that his friends did not fear the spirit of the revolution as he did. Why did they not see the ideological deception by which treaty rights suddenly became scraps of paper and violence was invoked to achieve illusory ends? Could such a policy ever lead to peace and stability? These questions were on his mind in June of that year as he traveled to Bad Ems, Germany, for a cure the doctor had prescribed for Betsy. It was at Ems that the startling news arrived that France and Austria had signed an armistice and made peace at Villafranca. Italian independence had thus not been achieved. From Ems, Groen wrote to Mackay, "Our friends, who had expected so much good for liberty and Protestantism from the Italian expedition, can learn from this war that it is not Christian to base one's hopes on actions that begin with the disregard of sacred rights."[476] In the following years, Italian nationalists would fight Austria on their own. In this nationalism, Groen saw the revolution at work, breaching the dikes of the European order. If this revolutionary spirit took hold of the minds, the European world could be overturned again, as it had been in 1789–1813. Groen's grand vision of revolution was often misunderstood outside his immediate circle of friends. Time and again he seemed to be defending the ultra-conservative Austrian Empire.

When the word "ultra-conservative" was used for the first time to characterize his political thought, Groen could no longer remain silent and had to come out of "retirement" once again. The word had flown from the pen of Rev. Chantepie de la Saussaye in his retrospective on the dissolution of the ministerial association *Ernst en Vrede*: "We ministers," Chantepie had written, "had to resist the 'ultra-confessional' and 'ultra-conservative' tendencies of the antirevolutionary school." At the time, Groen was busy editing and publishing his *Selected Writings*.[477] In the preface to the first volume, he protested against the "bizarre description of my principles."[478] According to Chantepie, the kingdom of God was developing in the "storms of history," even in revolutions, while the forces of conservatism in church and state only wanted to hold on to historical forms. Groen reacted with barely concealed anger. "I have never been an advocate of such nonsense," he retorted. Historical development is good and desirable, but he was antirevolutionary for the reason that "where the revolution rules, there is no chance of development and progress, no choice but between systematic levelling or preservation at all costs."[479] Had Chantepie not read his writings? Had the struggle in the Chamber not been directed against the conservatives who wanted only the status quo? One might say that the antirevolutionary party had failed, but one must not pass a faulty sentence.

Now that Groen had ventured into apologetics, a second publication followed. This time he took issue with an article published in a Swiss daily by J. P. Trottet, a pastor in Groen's own Walloon congregation in The Hague.[480] Rev. Trottet informed Swiss readers about the religious situation in the Netherlands and distanced himself from the "ultra-orthodox" group in his own congregation. Once again, Groen was portrayed as a stubborn man opposed to all progress. Groen's extensive treatise *The Antirevolutionary and Confessional Party in the Reformed Church of the Netherlands*[481] was intended to correct something in this portrait. "We are accused of preaching a conservatism that goes too far. We believe that we have simply been faithful to the Gospel."[482] In this work Groen gave an initial analysis of the crisis of 1856–57. The cause lay in the entrance of Van der Brugghen: "at the very moment when everything seemed to point to imminent success, we were deserted by several of those who had previously made common cause with us."[483] The opposition of friends brought about a complete reversal: from defeat in the Chamber to a sudden and general flight, "during which the party seemed to have been quite annihilated."[484] Groen had already summoned up enough courage to speak of a party that had been "temporarily" put out of action. Its recovery, however, depended, among other things, on restoring the health of the church and reminding confessional pastors that "in a church based on doctrines of faith, the aim must not be to argue about its doctrines, but to build one another up on the basis of these doctrines."[485]

Groen wanted to be a martyr for his beliefs, not the tragic figure people thought he was. The difference between the two depends on one's point of view. A tragic person is a sad figure who inspires pity; a martyr is a hero of faith who inspires the admiration of his co-religionists. To believe that a martyr grows from his defeats is to fear nothing. Groen had this firm belief after the defeat of 1857. A spirit of stubbornness came over him that made him decide to stand alone if necessary. He would not hear of giving up, even though the world he had lived in was slowly disappearing.

His world was indeed changing. In 1855, Merle d'Aubigné's wife, Marianne, died. In 1858 their friend would remarry in Dublin to an Irish woman, a circumstance that put some distance between them. In the fall of 1858, Groen's sister Keetje died at the age of sixty. She lived to see her daughter Jacqueline married to Otto Baron van Wassenaer van Catwijck. Groen's old mentor Van Assen died in 1859. Four times in 1859 Willem and Betsy traveled to Groningen due to the failing health of Betsy's mother. She died that fall. In early 1860, Groen's dear friend Da Costa died. Stahl died in Berlin the following year. In 1862 Van der Kemp and Wormser died. A few days before his death, Groen visited Wormser on his deathbed to honor their friendship. This friendship, Groen told him, was "one of the most precious privileges that God's providence has granted me in my life's journey."[486] He had also visited Da Costa shortly before he died; it had been an "unforgettable farewell."[487] Beets spoke at the graveside, and then Groen. Where people are attacked for their principles, martyrs are born, he said, referring to Da Costa—and to himself.[488] After the funerals of all these departed friends, the indefatigable Groen went on. A new era was dawning, with new faces.

CHRISTIAN NATIONAL PRIMARY EDUCATION

New people brought new dynamics. In 1860, others succeeded in what had been unsuccessful in 1857: the organization of an association to support private Christian education. The men who took the initiative in Amsterdam were Jozua van Eik, Jacobus de Neufville, and Nicolaas Feringa, while in the rest of the country plans were circulating on paper. M. D. van Otterloo, headmaster of a public school in a rural village, had already drawn up a constitution for such an association. Feringa, a teacher in a "ragged school" in Amsterdam, felt that there should be some broader coordination, partly to prevent well-meaning people from starting a school without consulting others. In consultation with others, he drew up a constitution, after which Groen van Prinsterer was approached. They very much wanted Groen to become president of the association. He was the national symbol of the school struggle. Groen, as he always did when he had to commit himself to something, had many objections and reservations, but in the end, he agreed to serve. His objections concerned the way in which the foundation of the association should be formulated. He wanted to include ethical-irenic pastors, but at the same time he wanted to have an unambiguous formulation of the basis of the association. The solution adopted was that the association, "founded on the immutable truths" of the Reformation, would have as its purpose "the promotion of Christian education."[489] According to Groen, these immutable truths were to be understood as referring not to the "letter of the confessional standards" but to the "confession of the martyrs."[490]

In the fall of 1860 and spring of 1861, Groen presided over the meetings that gave birth to the Christian National Primary School Education. He was able to get only a few of the pastors to join. Heldring had come around since 1857 and was eager to cooperate. Beets declined. A new leading spokesman for the ethicists, Dr. J. H. Gunning Jr. wrote that he did not know any "immutable truths" but that he would become a member anyway. Rev. van Rhijn, Groen's own pastor in Wassenaar, withdrew because he felt that the base's language was too orthodox and that Groen's presence would give the association too much of a party stamp. Others also expressed their fear of "dogmatism and formalism," and so the old divisions remained. The more individualistic upper classes were more cautious than the emerging middle classes, who wanted to see action. Groen himself did not want to take on executive and practical tasks, preferring to be involved only at arm's length. The association operated out of Amsterdam and maintained a busy correspondence with local schools and church councils. The work was carried out by acting president De Neufville and forty-year-old secretary Feringa, while honorary president Groen van Prinsterer was the figurehead of the association.

After 1857, there were several possibilities for starting a private Christian school. Such a school could be a private initiative. A few individuals would raise money, hire teachers, and supervise the operation of the school. Such an "association school" was favored by dissenters such as Van der Brugghen and De Liefde. A private school could also be the enterprise of a teacher who saw it as an investment to generate personal income. In this case, the school would take on the color of the teacher. Finally, there was a type of school that was the result of a church initiative. Then it took the color of that church. It was the philosophy to promote and support these church-run schools. Now that the state had failed to allow "Christian National" education in the state schools, the church as a public institution had to take its responsibility and actively promote this type of education. The new foundation wanted to play an advisory role and, if necessary, provide financial support. While the Seceders had also established a number of private schools, Christian National School Education was primarily an effort by members of the national church. From the beginning, the Seceders felt that they were being ignored and would never feel completely at home in this "shelter" of the Reformed. In 1868 the Seceders formed their own Association for Reformed Primary Education.

Christian National School Education played a stimulating role in the opening of "Bible schools," as they came to be called. The rise of these schools was partly related to the way in which the 1857 law was applied to the public school. In most places, the practice favored restraint; the term invented for this unofficial policy was "neutrality."[491] People of other religious beliefs were not to be offended, and teachers and boards tried not to do so. This mandate had become more difficult since 1857, when Jewish children began attending public schools, where any mention of Christ was forbidden. The word "Christian" proved to be an empty formula. At the same time, in other places there was little change, because the population was so homogeneous that the public school could easily be orthodox Protestant. This was the case, for example, in an area like the Veluwe in the center of the country. As a result, many pastors in this region were not at all in favor of private Christian schools. Religious instruction had not disappeared from the public schools either, although it had to be scheduled after school hours. There were still many ways for creative laymen and ministers to get around the strict application of the 1857 law. In Groen's eyes, it was all too sneaky and covert. He spent large sums of his personal fortune at this time to help establish Christian schools throughout the country.

The Antirevolutionary

HOLLAND'S STAHL

Groen had agreed to serve only as honorary president of Christian National School Education in order to devote the energies he had left at his "advanced age" to the publication of the archives. In 1861 he had reached the halfway point in the life of prince Willem III. In the fall of that year, however, he allowed himself to be interrupted in his work and tempted to write an occasional piece. A leading Dutch legal journal needed an obituary of Friedrich Julius Stahl. Groen's friend from Utrecht, De Geer, himself a professor of Roman law, had suggested that Groen should write it. Stahl had been the last representative of the historical school of jurisprudence, and it was well known that Groen had been influenced by it. The opportunity was too tempting to pass up. Admittedly, Groen had never met Stahl,[492] but the acquaintance with his writings in 1847 and 1848 had brought about a change in his views. Freed from his "private law" definition of sovereignty, he now thought of it in "public law" terms. That is, he recognized the rights of distinct social spheres within the state. In this he went even further than Stahl. In the Netherlands, Groen was considered a kindred spirit of Stahl. In a French article, one had disparagingly referred to him as "*le Stahl de la Hollande.*"

The purpose of an obituary is, of course, to describe the life and work of the deceased. But those who expected a treatise on Stahl's scientific achievements were disappointed. In his *In Memoriam Stahl*, Groen himself is present from beginning to end.[493] The obituary became a fourfold essay: a commentary on antirevolutionary politics in Germany and the Netherlands; a polemic with opponents who liked to call themselves evangelical or irenic; an act of homage to a Christian martyr; and, finally, an appeal to contemporaries not to drink the poisonous cup of unbelief and revolution. The parallels with Groen's own life were too many to ignore. In addition to being a scholar of constitutional law, Stahl had been a member of the Prussian Parliament for many years, where he shone as a great orator despite his weak voice and delicate frame. Stahl had also been active in the Lutheran church. The contrasts were equally striking: Stahl had penetrated to prominent positions in the academic, political, and ecclesiastical worlds; Groen had not. The contrast was no less striking in the political results. While the Christian principle had been banned from public institutions in the Netherlands, Prussia had received a different constitutional rule: "freedom for the individual and preservation of the Christian national principle for the public institutions."[494] That Prussia had what the Netherlands lacked was due in part to the "success" of Stahl and his political friends.

The context of Groen's obituary was the failure of Dutch Christians to appreciate antirevolutionary thought. Groen knew that part of the reason for this failure was lack of interest. The hunger of educated Christians for devotional works of every kind was insatiable, but they were poorly informed about politics and the school struggle. Groen often lamented the general lack of familiarity with the things for which he used so much printer's ink. He was genuinely surprised, as late as 1861, when Rev. Schwartz, editor-in-chief of the religious weekly *The Herald*—virtually the only Christian opinion paper left since the disappearance of *The Netherlander*—asked him if Groen "condemn[ed] all revolutions."[495] The ignorance behind such a question was still on his mind when he composed *In Memoriam Stahl*. This question haunted him from 1829 to 1862, he wrote. "No, I am not against every revolution, not against the Glorious Revolution of 1688, for example, but I am against the Revolution." What this meant could be gleaned from Stahl's writings: "The revolution is the systematic overthrow of ideas, whereby human self-conceit and arbitrariness are substituted for the ordinances of God as the foundations of state and society, of truth and justice."[496] To illustrate this, Groen and Stahl had turned to history. History has shown that where faith no longer connects with heaven, people are dragged into the abyss of pantheism and materialism. France was and remains the most telling example. Because French political thought was directed against the Christian religion, it was unable to establish political freedom on a stable public order.

Knowledge of history protects against speculative and illusory politics. But according to Groen, this was not even the core of Stahl's convictions. That was to be found in the "simplicity of his Christian faith." Stahl had been called "ultra-confessional," but that was to misjudge him. What was Groen's answer to his Dutch readers? "In today's atmosphere of unbelief, any measure of leniency could so easily lead to the danger of a general religiosity which, under the slogan of love, disregards its own origin, its Christian faith, and which, out of a dislike of dogma, attaches no importance to any kind of revealed truth." This was the attitude of the confessor who stood in the breach for truths. For himself, however, Stahl had been "content with what is hidden from the wise and prudent and revealed to babes." This is how Groen saw Stahl; this is how he wanted to see himself, not as a scholar or a statesman, but as a confessor of the gospel. That this entailed the position of a martyr was inevitable. As with Stahl, so with Groen. Consolation could be found in the words of other martyrs, such as those of William of Orange to Marnix of Saint Aldegonde: "Let them trample you and me, if it be granted us to suffer for the Church of God."[497]

Predictably, this was too much the language of piety to be suitable for a legal journal. Groen's obituary did not sit well with legal scholars. Within months of its publication, Professor Tellegen criticized Groen's views in a lecture to students in Groningen. He felt that Groen had praised Stahl too much and portrayed the Revolution as the source of all evil. Once again, Groen found that he was poorly understood, even by the country's legal scholars. Were they such bad readers? "Our learned men shrug off a work that is based on Christian beliefs," De Geer wrote to Groen from Utrecht.[498] He would know, for he saw it every day around him at the university. "They swear by a few authors," he observed. "They take a look at this or that book and then run off to make a name or a fortune." Groen had long hoped that a kindred spirit would be appointed to a university chair to practice and propagate antirevolutionary law. Groen had wanted to see the Groningen professor Cornelius Star Numan, who had first drawn his attention to Stahl, appointed in Leyden, but Numan had died an untimely death. His son now sent Groen a letter of thanks for Stahl's obituary.[499] But that obituary could not replace a university chair, nor was it a calm exposition of antirevolutionary constitutional law. Groen was too polemical to do what he should have done to ensure a proper understanding of his views: namely, to set forth once again, in a systematic fashion, the full range of his antirevolutionary thought.

BACK IN PARLIAMENT

If Groen was under fire among the social elite, his reputation among the middle and lower classes continued to grow. His name was widely known, not least because of the *Handbook*, a cheaper edition of which was published by Höveker in 1852. By 1862, more than twenty-two hundred copies had been sold, and Groen was able to sit down and prepare a revised edition.[500] Christian teachers were very grateful to him, and he experienced the sympathy of many Protestants in the country. Groen was, as Van Lynden once put it, the political leader of a few in the Chamber and of "thousands" outside the Chamber.[501] Basking in so much sympathy throughout the country, he could not remain outside the Chamber for long. What Van Lynden had said to Groen in 1857 when the latter resigned his seat came true in 1862: "Someday we shall fight together again from these green benches."[502] Van Lynden himself had to do very little to fulfill this prophecy. If it had been difficult to get Groen elected in the 1850s, it became much easier in the next decade. He was a candidate in three districts in the summer of 1862. He was elected in Arnhem and took his seat in the Chamber. Here he did indeed find Van Lynden at his side. Mackay and Elout both resigned their seats. Mackay was appointed vice president of the Council of State, and Elout would soon follow him in that august council of government. Groen had also been approached for this council, but he had long known that he was not suited for it.

As it was, the antirevolutionary squadron in the Chamber was not exactly imposing. The liberals continued to view Groen as a tragic figure whose mind was stuck in the past. In the Chamber, the liberals soon said openly that the party of which he so often spoke "consisted of little more than the honorable member himself."[503] But Groen was in his element. Once he had the floor, no one could really ignore what he was saying. Those who debated him had a hard time; those who did not want to take that risk kept their mouths shut and let him talk. This happened quite often during this second parliamentary period of Groen's career. Only the ministers answered, and only because they were obliged to. In 1862, after a period of conservative-liberal cabinets, Thorbecke finally returned to lead another government. Initially, Groen approached his ministry in a spirit of cooperation. At the outset he declared that he accepted the "secular state," the liberal axiom, as a practical situation. But then Groen had to insist that the word "Christian" be removed from the Education Act of 1857 and that everything be done to give private schools an equal place with public schools. Public subsidies were not yet on the agenda; only years later, in 1889, would a start be made on financial equality. Groen's goal, pure and simple, was to gain public recognition for Christian education, which would serve its own function alongside neutral public schools. His program took into account the defeat of 1857, and his new strategy could be a support for the association of Christian National School Education.

The fact that Groen's politics were not generally understood during these years was, of course, related to such political swings. Did antirevolutionary politics really accept the neutral state? Thorbecke, too, could not believe that Groen had changed; he would ignore "the position that my esteemed friend says he wants to take at this moment" because he was "convinced that he is the same man he was years ago."[504] For the rest, Thorbecke was happy about Groen's return to Parliament and was willing to engage in lengthy debates with him. Not for a moment, however, did Thorbecke consider amending the school act. He denied that the school act was prejudicial to private education and advised Groen to form an association to promote the interests of private education. (He seems not to have known that such an association already existed.) Thorbecke believed that the word "Christian" in the school act was appropriate for a country with a Christian tradition. The "religion that transcends denominational differences" was not the same as neutrality, as Groen claimed. No, Christianity was the "common root" of society and therefore had to have a place in the public school. All he had wanted to achieve in 1857 was a clear separation of church and state, and he had succeeded.

Both Thorbecke and Groen, masters of debate with completely opposing visions, could have gone on like this for years, but it looked as if Groen could not keep up. In January and February of 1863, he suffered a long illness in which his lungs and bronchial tubes again caused serious problems. He was unable to attend parliamentary sessions and was very weak throughout the spring. Confined to his study, he wrote historical memorials around 1813. His political friends throughout the country encouraged him to continue as a politician. By this time, it was clear that he was no ordinary parliamentarian: he was the people's tribune of the orthodox Protestant people, their icon in the Chamber.

When the people's tribune returned to the Chamber, it was immediately clear that he would face a difficult and painful period. Groen was eager to debate principles, but he encountered increasing irritation from his colleagues. "They are bulldogs barking at you," Van Lynden said of his colleagues.[505] Not everyone was waiting for a high-level debate, and Thorbecke did not always have the time or patience for a parliamentary "joust" with the antirevolutionary "leader without an army." Sometimes Groen was snubbed; most of the time his motions were rejected by a large majority. Now that he was getting no cooperation from the liberals, Groen decided to fight back. By tabling a private member's memorandum in the fall of 1863, he succeeded in sparking a broad debate on education that involved the entire House.[506] Once again, however, it became clear that a majority of liberals and conservatives were willing to rally around the 1857 law, but there was also cautious support from a few Catholics and other conservatives. No one supported Groen's motion to censure the word "Christian" in the act, but

Groen's effort did not fail to have an effect on public opinion. This debate was, for the time being, the highlight of his second parliamentary term.

The fact that Groen was perceived as a nuisance in the Chamber had to do with the fact that he wanted to reopen a debate that, according to most members, was not on the agenda. The government had come with an ambitious program. Thorbecke's second ministry went to the lists armed with shovels: on the order paper were bills for the construction of canals and railroads and for the regulation of the drainage of the river Meuse. Another issue was whether to abolish the system of forced labor in the Dutch East Indies. Groen was only peripherally involved in many of these issues. Just as he had groaned over the details of the postal act and the hunting act in an earlier term, he now groaned over the details of water management and the colonial question, subjects in which he was not at home. The minister of colonial affairs, Isaac Fransen van de Putte, had little sympathy for Groen's reflections, and in March 1864 he lashed out at him. But a martyr who feels the heat at his feet does not complain. Neither did Groen.

During the elections of 1864, he was again the target of the liberals. This time Fruin added his two cents by accusing Groen of "political immorality." The occasion was Groen's announcement that antirevolutionary candidates in every district must adopt as a common campaign slogan "opposition to the common school"—the beginning of the formulation of a national program. Fruin thought this was disrespectful to the voters, whose input was thus nullified. Groen thought this was nonsense: the voters still had the last word.

Fruin could write as much as he liked, Groen only grew through liberal criticism. Nothing is more beautiful than to rise as a moral force, Thorbecke once reminded himself in a comparable situation.[507] Groen now experienced the same. His power, however, did not grow within the Chamber but outside of it. He was reelected, but in the Chamber he found virtually no opportunity to reopen the educational debate. Henceforth, the Chamber turned a deaf ear to his pleas on behalf of Christian schools, secretly hoping that he would one day cease and desist.[508]

In October 1864 Groen fell ill again and was in poor health all winter. In early 1865 he resigned his seat. It was a forced resignation, and he explicitly left open the option of returning to Parliament. "At least there I speak to the galleries," he wrote to Mackay, "and those galleries reinforce my message throughout the country."[509] "Groen van Prinsterer," said one supporter, is able to draw "electric sparks" from the "Christian-historical nation."[510] While speaking in the Chamber, Groen retained his influence in the country. Even as a nonmember, he continued to write about the Chamber and the issues it debated. Van Lynden complained, however, that Groen increasingly followed his own example by "never recommending anybody."[511] In other words, he no longer recommended any candidates and simply referred to "the antirevolutionary principle" as embodied in himself. In doing so, he alienated his fellow antirevolutionaries and made himself vulnerable to the charge that he did not tolerate any other opinions than his own.[512] After publishing his advice in broadsides during the spring 1865 elections,[513] he continued his political commentary that fall in *Parliamentary Studies and Sketches*, a small periodical that appeared regularly—at his own expense, of course.[514] The core of these reflections and observations concerned the school question as it had figured in Groen's own political career. These publications were not widely distributed, reaching only the upper classes. But these journalistic salvos, vociferous reminders of Groen's political personality, were an effective means of countering the many attempts to declare him politically dead.

THE CHURCH QUESTION

It was of course out of the question that Groen, with his strong need to express himself publicly, could leave the church question in peace. Here, too, he broke his silence. After the Odeon meeting of 1848, he had not spoken directly on church matters. Meanwhile, the orthodox middle class had awakened, and this giant without influence began to stir mightily in the church. This was the social milieu of a man like Wormser, whose spiritual legacy Groen championed. When he began to do so after sixteen years, it was because of great unrest in the Reformed church of The Hague. Beginning in 1854, the pastor of that church was Rev. J. C. Zaalberg, an outspoken representative of theological modernism. At a time when modernism was becoming more and more entrenched in the pulpits of the country and had persuaded ministers such as Conrad Busken Huet to renounce their ordination, Zaalberg openly and aggressively denied the facts of salvation history through the spoken and written word. He apparently took his cue from the Amsterdam preacher Ph. R. Hugenholtz, who in his 1864 Easter sermon proclaimed that he did not believe that Christ had risen. This led to much murmuring among the congregation and a riot outside the church. Groen responded to this event by publishing a word of protest. The church should say an unequivocal No! to "boundless doctrinal freedom" and "godlessness." What was needed was a strong sense that what makes the church the church is first and foremost the unity of faith. The church should be mindful of its historical position and proceed from its "unchanging foundation."[515]

Groen wanted the consistory to intervene and bar Zaalberg from the pulpit, but he did not get the support of his own pastor, Rev. J. H. Gunning Jr. The latter wrote a letter to the members of his congregation admonishing them to remain calm.[516] Although he set against modernism, he believed that the only way to combat theological liberalism was to rely on spiritual means. Gunning would make a name for himself in the Reformed church and eventually become a professor. When he came to The Hague in 1861, he wrote that he wanted to act as a peacemaker between the ethical-irenicists (to which he himself belonged) and the confessionalists. Gunning believed that the ethical-irenicist position was a development of the "theology of the revelation." Like Chantepie, he distanced himself from the confessional standpoint, which he called "conservative." According to Groen, the disagreement was not theological. He saw the disagreement between ethicists and confessionals as an ecclesiastical and moral problem. He saw the ethicist position as lacking in character, and therefore lax. He was stung by the fact that the ethicists were irenic toward the modernists but became polemical the moment they caught sight of the orthodox. There was a sizable group of orthodox churchgoers in The Hague, and this group was also very particular. When Chantepie came to The Hague to preach, the "confessional and antirevolutionary party" stayed away. Chantepie complained about this demonstrable absence and suspected that Groen was behind it.[517] In 1864 Groen exchanged polemical tracts with Gunning. He asked him what exactly the ethical-irenicists had accomplished in the cause of restoring the historic Reformed church. Was not the result the opposite of what was intended? They branded the confessional school as old-fashioned and disparaged them with the epithet "obscurantists." The ethicists encouraged clericalism by refusing to consult with the laity. And by doing nothing, they ran away from what they should have done. They left the modernists alone out of respect for theological scholarship. Meanwhile, the historic church for which Wormser and Da Costa had fought so hard was allowed to die a slow death. It was imperative to defend the confession of the church and to back up that defense with concrete action. So Groen argued in pamphlet after pamphlet. But Gunning, too, could produce polemical pamphlets, and he did so in abundance. He believed there was more than one way to achieve the desired end, and he stuck to his guns. On a personal level, however, Gunning and Groen maintained a good relationship. Willem and Betsy enjoyed his preaching.

According to Groen, however, a turning point was reached in 1864. It was time for something to be done in the Reformed church now that modernism was flexing its muscles through the pulpits. This whole matter touched Groen to the depths of his soul. On one occasion, during a visit to Gunning, he became very emotional.[518] At that time he wrote a pamphlet entitled *Suffering and Contending for the Faith*,[519] which he did not publish because its tone was too sharp. It asserted that so far it had been the laity who had suffered and struggled. He recalled the memory of Van der Kemp, Van Hogendorp, Da Costa, Wormser: these men had fought for years to restore the church, but the clergy had given them "more opposition than leadership or example or support."[520] Groen's urgent appeal in 1864 for immediate consultation between pastors and laymen led to the founding of the Confessional Association in the Hervormde Kerk. This Confessional Association in the Reformed church was an organization without an explicit theology, but with an explicit confessional and ecclesiastical standpoint. Heldring was to give it leadership. Groen was involved in the preparatory phase, but was ultimately unhappy with the outcome. From the outset, he feared that "systemic laxity" would undermine the nature of the association and that it would therefore not insist strongly enough on the removal of modernism from the church.[521] The piece he composed for this occasion was also never published. The galleys are in his archives with the note, "Set aside as too polemical."[522]

Groen's appreciation of the laity led him to resist social class distinctions in the church. Many ministers were attached to these distinctions, which gave them a social position among the upper classes. When Rev. Gunning wrote his pamphlet in 1864, he intended it only "for the cultured of the parishioners."[523] The clergy preferred to deal with the educated part of the church. Thus, it took fifteen years before congregations were given what the new Church Order of 1852 had promised: the right to elect elders and deacons. Conservative ministers, wedded to the system of co-optation, tried to delay as long as possible, but they could not hold back the tide. Nor could the modernists refuse: it would be inconsistent to enfranchise citizens in the state but deny them seats in the ecclesiastical colleges. In 1867, the day finally came when the middle classes were given a voice in the church. This meant that the sleeping giant of orthodoxy had been awakened. Groen, of course, welcomed this development. The Odeon Assembly of 1848 had already voted to return to the Presbyterian model of self-governing congregations. It was therefore a joy for Groen to find among the many pamphlets that came out at that time one written by a young preacher named Abraham Kuyper. There had been brief contacts between the two men since 1864 regarding Kuyper's research on church history.[524] Now that Kuyper had spoken so clearly in favor of democratization in the church, it was Groen who resumed correspondence with him. Groen's letter was read in the vicarage of the rural village of Beesd as "an encouraging word that gives a man self-confidence."[525] Shortly thereafter, the postman in Beesd delivered a copy of *Unbelief and Revolution* as well as Groen's photograph.[526] From this time on, Groen and Kuyper would be allies in the struggle against conservatism, first in the church and later in politics.

FAREWELL TO POLITICS ONCE MORE

That conservatism was entering a new phase in politics had become clear since the summer of 1866. After Thorbecke's resignation at the beginning of that year and a brief liberal cabinet interlude of a few months, the conservatives were back in office. A new generation had emerged around J. Heemskerk Azn,[527] and they seemed to be doing well. These conservatives had no particular ideas, as Mulder had once done, but were pragmatists and defenders of the status quo. What united them was a strong anti-liberal sentiment. By the summer of 1866, after four years of liberal rule, the political winds were once again in the conservatives' favor. King William III rejoiced at this turnaround, which freed him from Thorbecke. As in 1856, the conservatives looked to the antirevolutionaries for support. The antirevolutionaries, in turn, hoped that the conservatives would be willing to put the school issue back on the political agenda. As early as 1865, Count van Zuylen van Nijevelt, a former ambassador to Berlin, had been elected to the Chamber as an antirevolutionary. He regularly consulted Groen on political and educational matters. Van Zuylen took part in the negotiations for a new cabinet. He was to be offered the portfolio of foreign affairs. He told Groen that he would try to get education on the new government's agenda, but he could not get the conservatives to agree. Van Zuylen acquiesced, judging that reopening the school debate was out of the question.

This was exactly the attitude Groen had feared. He saw it as an exact repeat of the drama of 1856, and he told Van Zuylen that he no longer cared to meet for joint consultation. "Grief would probably cause me to utter expressions that would hurt you as well as me."[528] Here was once again a friend, a member of Christian National School Education, author of a pamphlet on the educational question with the word "duty" in the title,[529] who proved spineless at the crucial moment. At the time, Groen had been nominated in several constituencies, but he feared having to serve another term in the Second Chamber. At the age of sixty-five, he would be crushed between the cabinet and the opposition. One encouraging fact was that for the first time in years, the antirevolutionaries were poised to make gains at the polls. And indeed, new antirevolutionary faces entered the Chamber: Theodoor Baron van Lynden van Sandenburg, Alexander Baron Schimmelpenninck van der Oye, Groen's nephew-in-law Otto Baron van Wassenaer van Catwijck, and Levinus W. C. Keuchenius. The latter was a civil servant in the Dutch East Indies and had been recommended by Groen as a specialist in colonial affairs. Groen was also elected but resigned his seat shortly thereafter. The prospect of having to oppose a conservative, antirevolutionary cabinet on education was too painful for him. In his parliamentary studies and sketches, he was highly critical of the new ministry.

Groen was not a man who insisted on discipline and order among his followers; he relied on his personal reputation. As a result of his early departure from the Chamber, he was unable to put his stamp on a new group of antirevolutionary members. As it was, his early criticism of the ministry was too harsh for their liking. Groen may have been the national "leader" of the party, enjoying much moral authority and respect, but in the Chamber each member wanted to decide for himself what positions to take. Keuchenius was really the only one who followed Groen's line. The former high-ranking civil servant from Batavia was the kind of principled man Groen admired. He also shared Groen's position in the church. In the Confessional Association he urged that clear steps be taken to deal with modernism. It was not long before Groen and Keuchenius were on good terms; their relationship quickly became warm and cordial.

In September, Keuchenius became the instigator of a conflict between the government and Parliament that would have significant political consequences. In early September it was announced that the king had appointed the minister of Colonial Affairs, Pieter Mijer, governor-general of the Dutch East Indies. The Chamber was not pleased. It had expected this leading conservative to initiate a new colonial policy. After all, the conservatives had formed the government with a mandate to work out their views on colonial affairs, on which the Chamber was deadlocked. The new appointment seemed to ignore the government's mandate and thus to snub Parliament. It was Keuchenius who introduced a motion of censure, which passed with the support of the liberals. The cabinet, however, argued that such appointments were the prerogative of the king and that Parliament had no right to pass judgment on them. The king supported this view by retaining the cabinet and dissolving the Chamber. New elections would have to produce a more compliant Parliament.

The ministry was playing for high stakes. Every conservative force had to be rallied to win the contest in the Chamber. The government made it a constitutional issue: did the king, the government, have (or not have) its own political leeway, over which the Chamber had no say? The question divided the antirevolutionary caucus. Most so-called antirevolutionary members of Parliament had voted against Keuchenius's motion and supported the cabinet. But what did the master himself think? Groen left no doubt. He believed that the Chamber had a perfect right to censure the government's conduct. He included a detailed explanation of his view in his *Parliamentary Studies and Sketches*. It was the government that had acted unconstitutionally, not the Chamber. According to Groen, the Keuchenius motion had not attacked a single right of the king, but had censured an act of the sitting government. He knew that the conservative nobles who were angry with Keuchenius would now be angry with him. This was indeed the case. Count van Zuylen had already been lost to Groen, Van Wassenaer was struggling to keep the bond with "uncle," and Schimmelpenninck admitted afterward that he had mistaken the motion for unconstitutional and had therefore foolishly voted against it.[530]

Prominent antirevolutionaries were divided on the issue. Groen received the avowed support of De Geer, but his appeal to Van Lynden to sacrifice his "individual opinion" for the sake of party unity was in vain.[531] Elout and Mackay, in particular, were "saddened" by the affair. They were also saddened by the division that had arisen among antirevolutionaries throughout the country. Rev. S. H. Buijtendijk was well aware of this when he wrote, "Keuchenius's motion and Mr. Groen's support of it have caused a rift in the ranks of Groen's friends, which, I believe, will not heal quickly."[532] In a number of voters' clubs, tensions arose between Groenians and conservatives who supported the cabinet.[533] Conservative spokesmen wrote to the press to express their astonishment at what they saw as the antirevolutionary leader's political pirouette. But the liberal constitutional expert, Professor J. T. Buys, came to Groen's rescue, praising him as a consistent defender of the rights of Parliament. In the circles of The Hague's administrative and political elite, however, Groen was more isolated than ever. As for himself, he felt that as a result of the ministry's actions, "a complete Babel reigns in the political sphere."[534] In this situation, there was little point in further comment. After the November 1866 elections, he stopped publishing his parliamentary studies and sketches and for a time resumed his voluntary silence on national politics.

The Van Zuylen-Heemskerk ministry continued to struggle with a Chamber whose majority opposed its policies. Twice the Chamber was dissolved, but the balance never tipped in favor of the cabinet. In 1868, the government threw in the towel. The last conservative attempt to bend the Constitutional Order of 1848 in a more monarchical direction had failed. After 1868, the conservatives never regained a comparable position of power. During the two years when the cabinet was exhausted fighting the parliamentary majority, Groen kept a low profile. A cartoon from this period shows a slowly drowning Mr. Heemskerk, while Mr. Groen walks by on the other side, deaf to the cries for help. A ministry that did not provide the opportunity to reopen the question of education could expect this treatment from him. The antirevolutionaries in the Chamber, hardly distinguishable from the conservatives, preferred to keep Groen out of their parliamentary deliberations. His advice would only hinder them in the Chamber. Meanwhile, the country's best-known antirevolutionary was turning his attention to other horizons. He would continue to write as long as he had the energy. But it was clear that his parliamentary career was over. His gray years had come, he remarked in the autumn of 1866. Groen now joined the ranks of elder statesmen. But he had not yet finished speaking his mind.

REVOLUTION IN BERLIN

Groen usually found his way to the Royal Family Archives when he was looking for a quiet place to work. This place was no longer available to him. At the beginning of 1866, Groen's assistant Van Sijpesteijn died unexpectedly. Groen was once again alone in his work. He could not possibly take over the management of the archives himself, so he was allowed to appoint a successor, which he did at the beginning of July. By the end of August, however, he had heard nothing. He concluded that William III did not have the same confidence in him as William I or William II. He asked the king directly whether this was an invitation to resign.[535] Only that fall was he informed that he had to make a new nomination. Groen was annoyed and submitted his own resignation, which was again not accepted. The matter dragged on, and the priceless collection was placed under the supervision of a court aide who knew nothing about archives. The great German historian Leopold von Ranke, on a visit to The Hague, found this more than a pity. The way things had gone was hardly in accordance with Groen's wishes, but this had been the case for a long time. He now considered his work on the published archives complete.[536]

Meanwhile, Groen's study at his homes on the Korte Vijverberg and at *Oud-Wassenaer* resembled the kind of offices that elder statesmen are wont to set up. Groen van Prinsterer had become a political institute, a one-man think tank. He expressed his views on political problems, took care to distribute his writings far and wide, and tried to encourage new political talent to walk the thorny path of antirevolutionary politics. If there was a trace of more than superficial interest, he would send such talented young men an autographed photograph of himself. These photos were too expensive to send as fan mail, as football players or pop stars do today. Only true friends received one. But Groen hoped they would become more than just sympathizers with his political universe.

Betsy was indispensable to the running of this political institute. She handled the incoming and outgoing mail, independently answered letters addressed to her husband, kept address lists and supervised mailings, did many practical things for him, and talked things through with him. And she did it with love. This was not only Willem's world; it was also hers. In addition to this work at her husband's side, she also had her own affairs to attend to, such as overseeing several schools and running a number of almshouses for the elderly. In 1864, Betsy was one of the founding members of a society that established a hospital and nurses' training school, named after the honorable Miss De Bronovo.[537] The hospital's first location was a building on the Kazernestraat owned by the Groens and opened by Queen Sophie in January 1865. (Subsequent queens continued to show interest in the hospital well into the twentieth century.)

Because of all this practical work, the doorbell of their mansion rang more often for Betsy than for Willem. They tried to keep the mornings free of interruptions for the sake of Willem's work, which required Betsy's assistance. This was easier in *Oud-Wassenaer* than in the city. Willem's right hand remained problematic, and he preferred to dictate the longer letters. Letters written by hand were written on small sheets of paper and were always short. We get a glimpse of life in Groen's "political institute" from a reply letter written by Betsy herself. "'Shall I answer the letter from our dear friend Singendonck?' I asked. 'Yes, please,' he replied, and again his gray head bent over the table covered with books, newspapers, letters, galleys."[538] This was written in 1864, when Groen was still a member of the Chamber, but it does not look as if the appearance of his workroom a few years later was much different. He was always surrounded by newspapers and books, of which he received a large number. He had subscriptions to the major daily newspapers and church bulletins. Also impressive was the number of periodicals he ordered from abroad. There was the journal of his political friends in Berlin, the *New Prussian Newspaper*, often called the *Cross Newspaper* because of the iron cross on its masthead. There was also the French *Christian Review*, and the English *Pall Mall Gazette*. No one in Groen's circle read as many foreign newspapers as he did. They were his sources for independently following European politics and staying informed about the political movements of his fellow antirevolutionaries abroad.

Well-informed about European politics, Groen had already begun to express his alarm about Prussia's foreign policy in his parliamentary studies and sketches. In 1862, Bismarck had become chancellor and foreign minister. This sympathizer of Stahl soon proved to be a champion of German unification. In 1864, he defeated Denmark in the war and annexed Schleswig. Was the annexation of other small states only a matter of time? Groen kept himself informed by letters from Hanover from the former envoy Von Hodenberg, who had returned. In 1866, Bismarck incited Austria to declare war on Prussia in a dispute over the territory of Holstein. The "fraternal" contest did not last long: in a matter of seven weeks, Prussia defeated Austria, once a leading military power on the European continent. Many Protestants in Germany and the Netherlands rejoiced at the humiliation of Catholic Austria.

Groen rose in protest. Bismarck's Realpolitik was pure power politics based on naked force, in defiance of the foundations of the European order. To praise this kind of politics was to pay homage to the spirit of the Revolution. Did people not notice that the war against Austria had been accompanied by the annexation of Saxony, Hanover, Weimar, Hesse-Kassel, Nassau? Could the Netherlands be next, as a so-called component of

Greater Germany? Groen was not alone in thinking so. Fear of annexation gripped The Hague in those years. When the *Cross Newspaper*, in its issue of February 14, 1867, suggested that a closer union with Prussia would be the obvious way for the Netherlands to preserve its "distinctive character," Groen issued a public protest. Toward the end of March, he published *Prussia and the Netherlands*, a thirty-page pamphlet written in French and addressed "to my friends in Berlin."[539] By the latter he meant Stahl's party, which he believed was now supporting Bismarck's "Napoleonic policy." He reminded them of Stahl's statements and appealed to them to distance themselves from this type of statecraft.[540]

When the *Cross Newspaper* responded that there was no question of annexing the Netherlands and that Groen was wrongly painting apocalyptic visions, Groen wrote a second pamphlet, this one more than seventy pages long entitled *The Prussian Empire and the Apocalypse*.[541] It sounded an even stronger warning. The friends in Berlin had been blinded by success and had created an ideology of modern nationalism. Groen developed two theses: (1) The law of God is obligatory, national interest is a false god, an idol; (2) The antichrist of our time is the glorification of the ego, raised to a system by rationalism and revolution.[542] He hoped that his Christian friends would come to see that the politics of Bismarck were nothing but the Napoleonic politics that the French had learned to abhor years before. Groen saw the emerging nationalism and imperialism of his day as political self-deification, and he fought both ideologies as fresh manifestations of the spirit of the Revolution. He prophesied that if modern nationalism ever triumphed, "we shall see the atrocities of a new barbarism amidst the most exquisite refinements of civilization."[543]

He was still concerned about developments in Germany in August 1867, when the Fifth General Assembly of the Evangelical Alliance met in Amsterdam. Groen had attended the fourth assembly in Geneva in 1861, but it did not meet with his unqualified approval. The division between ethicists and confessionalists that existed in his own country was also evident in the Alliance. Leaders of the free churches were dominating, and they were pushing positions that troubled Groen. At first, Groen did not plan to go to Amsterdam. Mackay, Elout, and Groen wanted to stay away together. In the end, Elout and Groen decided to go anyway. The meeting was a manifestation that lasted a whole week. Once there, Groen asked permission to speak, even though he was not on the agenda. The reaction of the presiding committee gives an indication of Groen's great reputation in these circles. He was an *éminence grise* of the international Réveil, and it would probably be the last time he spoke in that company, so they were more than happy to grant his request. As Groen stepped up to the podium, he was greeted with loud applause. His voice was weak, so the audience crowded forward to hear him. Addressing them in French, he spoke of "the religious nationality," a nationality sanctified by the Christian religion. The Netherlands was a unique example of this, founded in the sixteenth century for no other reason than for the sake of the gospel. The founding of the Dutch Republic was the work of martyrs. The Dutch nation was not a nation that prided itself on its blood, but rather offered space to religious refugees in order to create with them a center of Protestantism. This glorious past, he said, still filled him with hope. He called on those present to pray for the Netherlands—"Priez, priez pour la Hollande!"—and asked them to work for a truly Christian nationality when they returned home.[544] Groen had difficulty finishing his partly improvised speech. Unbroken in spirit, but with a visibly weakened frame, he made a deep impression. As he descended from the platform, the audience sang a psalm of blessing.

A month after this impressive moment, we find Groen in Berlin. His pamphlets denouncing German nationalism had struck a chord with an old friend, Ludwig von Gerlach, who had invited him to Berlin. Von Gerlach's politics were similar to Groen's. He had gone against the prevailing opinion in his circles by condemning Bismarck's "policy of facts." Suddenly it was "as if God's holy commandments no longer extended to the fields of politics, diplomacy, and war, and as if these fields had no higher law than patriotic egoism."[545] These words, written in the *Cross Newspaper*, had Groen's wholehearted approval. They had led to a break between Von Gerlach and Bismarck. Of course, Von Gerlach could not introduce Groen to the Iron Chancellor. Groen saw Bismarck from the gallery of the Prussian Parliament. This was the Bismarck who solemnly assured a member of his party that he had fought "on his knees" to preserve peace with Austria.[546] Groen was shocked by this mixture of religiosity and violent politics and found it most repugnant. How could godly piety lead to such results?

INCREASING ISOLATION

The year 1868 brought no more uplifting experiences. Groen's political involvement did not diminish, on the contrary, but his behavior became unpredictable in the eyes of his supporters. When a new dissolution of the

Chamber in January 1868 made elections necessary, Groen presented himself as a willing candidate in all districts. The message was that he invited all antirevolutionary voters' clubs to nominate only the party leader with his well-known program regarding the education act. This was Groen's protest against the antirevolutionary incumbents who were doing nothing to reopen the education debate and who were demonstrating mealy mouthed politics. In Groen's estimation, the antirevolutionary party had been absorbed by the dominant conservatives since 1866. According to him, the antirevolutionary campaign should not make the continuation of the conservative cabinet the election issue, but the question of education. The only credible way to do this was to nominate Groen. In this way, he wanted to lift the education question "out of the quagmire of combinations and speculations" and raise it again as "an issue of conscience for the people of the Netherlands."[547] Groen saw his candidacy as an uncompromising choice of principle, and he hoped for personal approval, a signal of "national resonance."[548]

Groen's action provoked two kinds of reactions. Of course, people had deep respect for the old man who had continued to believe in his ideal at great personal sacrifice. He had proudly resisted pressure from those around him not to damage the Christian conservative camp. But in the meantime, his actions had become extremely impractical, and people pitied him for his poor performance. Groen had hoped for a miracle that never came. As for the antirevolutionary camp, people began to wonder how to proceed. Groen's action essentially meant that he had crossed the work of others. Some districts had already come to terms with antirevolutionary candidates. During this period, De Geer became the man who communicated with the voters' clubs about their nominations. Unlike Groen, De Geer recommended names. For him, the 1868 campaign was a clear indication of the need for some central coordination and direction in the future. Groen himself could not be overlooked, given his reputation, but he lacked "tact and supervision."[549] Thus there were two perspectives on the approach to be taken. As far as Groen was concerned, he saw himself as the hub of the party and suffered from the defect that afflicts more elder statesmen: he was no longer open to the advice of others.

Groen had become something of a last Mohican in his own milieu—even within his own extended family. This became clear in June when his sister Mimi died at the age of sixty-two. Though she and her husband had always lived near Willem and Betsy and often sat at family dinners, she was rarely a topic of conversation. She demanded little attention for herself, Groen said on the day of her funeral.[550] While Keetje, like her mother, loved high society, Mimi led a primarily domestic life. She gave birth to eight children, four of whom died young. Her family must have kept her busy. She herself had to deal with illness and other health problems. Willem and Betsy held her in high esteem for her calm acceptance of whatever came her way. When she died, they mourned her deeply.[551] Willem was now the only surviving member of the Groen van Prinsterer family. His two sisters had not reached old age: he lost them at sixty and sixty-two. Willem himself was now sixty-seven years old, and the thought of his own death preoccupied his mind.

At the celebration of Groen's sixty-seventh birthday at *Oud-Wassenaer*, Pastor Van Rhijn, as usual at special family gatherings, pulled a piece of paper out of his pocket. It was a poem about Groen that he had written for the occasion. It ran as follows:

> I sing a man, God-fearing sage,
> Who's lived his life till ripe old age,
> A war for church and state to wage.
> Throughout the land he gained much fame
> No one will e'er forget his name
> That man, now growing weak and grey,
> Defender of our Heiligerlee,
> Is full of spirit still today.
> For his long life we thank our Lord.
> The Lord himself be his reward.[552]

The well-intentioned doggerel, written under the impression of Groen's recent polemic with the Catholic Abbot Brouwer over the Battle of Heiligerlee, was certainly not intended as an epitaph. Nevertheless, it looked very much like an epilogue to Groen's career. As an epilogue, however, it was to prove premature. Groen would still have enough energy for new battles with conservative politicians and preachers.

A PARTING OF THE WAYS

In the fall of 1867, Rev. Dr. Abraham Kuyper left the small village of Beesd for the big city of Utrecht. It was a dream come true for an ambitious pastor who did not want to stay in the provinces. Beets, the pastor in the Utrecht church, had recommended him, and Kuyper was welcomed as an orthodox minister. It soon became apparent, however, that he was not of Beets's orthodoxy. In Beesd, Kuyper had become a Calvinist under the influence of his studies in the history of the Reformation and through contact with ordinary parishioners. He had become aware that there was a form of Reformed religiosity that had been kept alive in certain strata of the population and passed on to new generations for centuries. Kuyper was a forceful and energetic personality who could dominate from the pulpit but certainly did not want to limit himself to that. He also favored a firm approach to the ecclesiastical issues that were being publicly discussed in those years. According to Gunning, the Reformed church was being governed by pamphlets.[553] Kuyper participated fully from his base in Utrecht. He advocated a return to Reformed polity in the church. If the ordinances and the synod hindered this goal, the church should be freed from these straitjackets.

Kuyper was fascinated by the maneuvers Groen was making in both the ecclesiastical and political realms. He followed Groen through his publications and developed into a follower. In Utrecht, Kuyper championed orthodoxy and fought against the "half-heartedness" of the conservative majority. It was here that he first met De Geer, who acquainted him with the antirevolutionary program of the education act. With the elections of 1869 in sight, the question of how the antirevolutionaries should conduct the campaign arose again. Given Groen's age and physical condition, it was inconceivable that he would again run in every district. A common line, however, would be of the utmost importance. That would be the gain from Groen's solo effort in 1868. In May 1869 a meeting of Christian National School Education in the consistory room of the Cathedral church of Utrecht discussed a common strategy. Kuyper had been invited to give the opening address. It was at this meeting that Groen and Kuyper first met and shook hands. The opening address that Kuyper gave was after Groen's heart: *The Appeal to the National Conscience*.[554] As Groen had always done, Kuyper placed his trust in a Christian national spirit that lived in the minds and hearts of many Dutch people and that could be a point of support for a new direction in politics.

A crucial political question arose during the discussions. It was proposed that Christian National School Education go on record in favor of removing the word "Christian" from the Education Act of 1857 and to seek a revision of the constitution to achieve equal treatment for private and public schools. This proposal was in the spirit of Groen. It was "satanic" to keep the word "Christian," Kuyper declared: "Under the fine cloak of this word the nation is being educated in an unchristian manner." This was not the language one had ever heard from a pastor! Beets and Chantepie were also present at the meeting and showed great indignation. Beets stood up and said that it was "demonic" to try to impose religious neutrality on the common school, where so many "Christian things" were still going on. This time the ethicists got the worst of it. The meeting rallied around Kuyper, backed by chairman Groen. Beets and Chantepie left the meeting in a huff. Groen did not regret the break for a moment. It was the public consequence of different points of view that had tried to coexist peacefully for too long. For the moment, Groen could not get enough of this clearing of the air. He saw it as a preparation for a "victory" that would one day be theirs, though a day he did not expect to live long enough to see for himself.[555]

7

The Old General

MODERNIZATION

IF, IN YOUR OLD age, you still remember a loose remark that one of your professors threw out in a lecture, you must have been fascinated by it all your life. When Groen's teacher Borger once disapproved of the word "vacation" (*vacantie*), he spoke of the "vocabulary of youth."[556] Apparently "vacation" became a fashionable term around 1829. Borger himself seemed to have no use for it. Groen, too, gave the impression that he could do without it. When he was at home, he worked at a steady pace. August was usually the month when the Groens took a short trip abroad or within the Netherlands. Now that they had advanced in years, however, they no longer traveled and rarely left The Hague or Wassenaar. Nor did Groen attend large gatherings. The 1869 meeting of Christian National School Education in Utrecht was the last one he attended. Large gatherings were too tiring and they upset him. So, he stayed at home and worked in his study. Meanwhile, society around him was changing at a rapid pace. There were more meetings than ever, and travel increased accordingly. However, Groen's followers always wanted to hear what the "general" thought about whatever they were doing in church or politics. It was fine with Groen if a small committee met in his house. The house on the Korte Vijverberg could easily accommodate that. Kuyper, who loved to travel, regularly took the train to The Hague, especially after 1870, when a direct railroad connection from Utrecht via Gouda to The Hague was completed. "The new railroad is to our advantage," Groen concluded.[557]

The Antirevolutionary

The opening up of the country was proceeding apace. A network of railroads would soon cover the last remnants of the geographic space of the Netherlands. In 1870, for the first time, it was possible to travel from the northeastern town of Winschoten to The Hague on the southwestern coast. The entire country could be covered in a single day. This also meant that newspapers and mail could be delivered throughout the country in one day. Not surprisingly, the tax on newspapers was abolished in 1869. The expensive seal that had to be affixed to the paper at the post office became a thing of the past. Cheaper paper and faster distribution made it possible to expand circulation and reach new groups of readers. While Holland's infrastructure had been in place since 1850, the 1870s saw an acceleration in the spread of information. Telegraphic communication also grew in popularity. In 1860, the system handled two hundred thousand domestic telegrams; by 1880, that number had risen to two million.[558] Before the advent of the telephone, of course, this was the fastest medium available, although sending a telegram remained expensive. The reduction in travel time and the acceleration of the exchange of information helped to shape a new society. From 1870, Dutch cities began to expand, commerce and industry received a powerful boost, and a middle class emerged that wanted to participate in political and cultural life. If all this social ferment were to be well-channeled, men with organizational talent would be socially indispensable.

Such a talent could no longer be expected to blossom in a man like Groen. He belonged to a bygone era when a limited number of men dominated public life. These men influenced each other by exchanging ideas and agreeing on certain rules, but each of them valued his individual freedom. Political success was measured by the triumph of one's ideas over those of others. This had always been Groen's strategy. He had an aversion to organizing things and was happy to leave that burden to others. Nor did he want to be bound by agreements that might limit his independence. He preferred to work alone rather than in a forced combination with others. It was not his job to give the antirevolutionary party an organized public presence. As a member of Parliament, of course, he was not supposed to be involved in setting up voters' clubs, but even in times when he did not hold a seat, Groen contributed little to the National Association of Voters' Clubs. He was happy to see them established, but his interest usually ended there. Groen was a trailblazer, not an organizer. A voters' club should be organized, he believed, whenever there were vibrant antirevolutionary politics. If there was no such life, there was no need for a voters' club to prolong

The Old General

its existence. When the Amsterdam club *Netherlands and Orange*, which had been the party's very first voters' club, was dissolved, Groen agreed. He relied on his published word to set the voters in motion.

In the age of modernization, however, this was not an attitude that would get you very far. It presupposed familiarity with specific individuals, a form of trust that could no longer be relied upon in an emerging mass society. In 1869, the conservatives moved to create a General Voters' Association that could supervise and coordinate election campaigns in the country's electoral districts. The antirevolutionaries also tried to improve the coordination of their electoral strategy that year. Utrecht was the center of these activities. Under the leadership of De Geer, a number of gentlemen held several meetings to decide whether they could form a central committee and adopt a common electoral platform.[559] On April 16, they invited representatives of the antirevolutionary voters' clubs to meet in Utrecht. And they came, from all parts of the country, from the far northeast to the deep southwest. Kuyper was also present at this meeting. Groen was invited but excused himself. It is doubtful that De Geer regretted this: Groen might pose a risk to achieving a united front, and besides, he had not been involved in planning the meeting. The meeting decided to form a central committee and to focus on a single issue, the struggle for Christian education. The resolution was loosely worded, and when it was reported to Groen, he found it inadequate. In fact, he refused to endorse it. Had his own antirevolutionary colleagues forgotten his program for school legislation? Groen and Kuyper consulted, and soon they came forward with a sharper wording in order to revise the constitution and remove the term "Christian" from the education act.

In May and June 1869, Groen waged his own campaign, independent of the central committee in Utrecht. In a series of pamphlets entitled *At the Ballot Box*,[560] he hammered home the message he had been proclaiming since 1866: the antirevolutionaries must organize as an independent group alongside the conservatives. They should run their own candidates in every district, even if they had little chance of winning. Only in runoff elections could one consider voting for a conservative.

The 1869 election brought no change. The same names returned: Van Wassenaer, Saaymans Vader, Schimmelpenninck, Bichon van IJsselmonde—all Christian conservatives of aristocratic stock. Groen quickly realized that little could be expected of these men. During the debates in response to the speech from the throne, not one of them said a word about education. Groen openly expressed his deep disappointment at this missed opportunity.

The pre-election discussions of 1869 had been not only about fielding candidates, but also about launching an antirevolutionary daily. Now that the tax on newspapers had been abolished, an antirevolutionary daily might again be feasible. There was, of course, *The Herald*. When Groen's *The Netherlander* ceased publication in 1855, this weekly, under the editorship of Rev. Carl Schwartz, reported church and school news, but few people were really satisfied with it. For ten years Groen had refused to publish in *The Herald* because Schwartz did not hold the antirevolutionary viewpoint. In the spring of 1869, a new initiative was born. Subscriptions were opened for a daily newspaper that would bear a familiar name, *Netherland and Orange*. But the response was too meager, and the plan was dropped. What did change was that Kuyper was added to the editorial board of *The Herald*, and this would be the beginning of his impressive journalistic career.[561]

Groen also responded to the impulse of 1869. Beginning in August of that year, he started a new periodical, a more permanent form for his pamphlet series. The name was already forty years old, *Netherlandic Reflections*.[562] As he declared in the first issue, the name was a program, just as it had been in 1829. "Today, as then, only our Dutch identity, rooted in the history and religion of our country, can be a sufficient guarantee of national strength and prosperity."[563] Had Groen remained the same over the years? In the core of his convictions, yes; but not in the way he would now elaborate and apply them. He insisted, however, that for all the radical steps he had taken in the past, he had never changed in essence. And he simply assumed that it was self-evident that he was the standard for what should be considered antirevolutionary politics. In this way, he was able to decide which political currents went in his direction and which went in the opposite direction. He liked to remind his readers of the saying *Saevis tranquillus in undis*, "Calm in the midst of raging waves." By 1869, it seemed that the tide was once again in his favor. The liberals appreciated his ceaseless opposition to the conservatives in the cabinet and the Chamber. Was his own circle finally beginning to understand this opposition? He hoped so. "Perhaps now, more than before, I can be the de facto leader of the antirevolutionary party."[564] He knew that his advancing years would not allow him to play an active role. But the *Netherlandic Reflections* could pass on "suggestions" to his followers. And so, it became a periodical in which the old general could express himself freely. The way he did so was touching:

sometimes commenting on the politics of the day, sometimes reminiscing about his own parliamentary battles. At first, the *Netherlandic Reflections* appeared once a week or once every two weeks; later, the intervals were sometimes so long that the series would go dormant for months.

It was striking that the old man felt the need to publish his thoughts. The appearance of Groen's journal prompted the renowned literary critic Conrad Busken Huet to write a sympathetic essay in the journal *The Java Messenger*.[565] According to Busken Huet, Groen's public life was "one of the most beautiful phenomena in recent Dutch history." The *Netherlandic Reflections* read like pages from a diary. "For years, Mr. Groen has not sent a page to print in which he does not speak of himself in the first-person singular or plural, not one in which his 'I' is not the center of attention. All of his writings could, in a sense, be called 'memoirs.'" This characteristic did not bother Busken Huet. He recognized that Groen had gained a unique position as a voice of the people: "His 'I' and 'we' are not the revelations of a private life, much less the expressions of an intruding vanity, but the organs of a school or trend, of a power in the state, of a larger or smaller fraction of the people." He thought it was very special that Groen always managed to remain civil in his polemics, that "when something coarse was addressed to him, he always answered with something delicate." The former pastor realized that such self-control must be based on great inner strength. What was so admirable about Groen was that however hurt he must have felt at times, he never showed it in his writings. "His writings are a model of polemics, partly because they are a model of self-control." Busken Huet saw in Groen "a passionate man, a man of anger," who suppressed this tendency with "an iron will, only to reveal it later in the tempered form of criticism and satire."

No doubt Groen saw these fine characterizations of himself. Sure, words like "devotion to duty" and "responsibility" were his stock in trade; he still had his old work habits and rarely went on vacation. But personally, he would have emphasized some other aspects. He would have emphasized higher principles that did not allow him to shirk his duty, principles to which he wanted to remain true above all else, steadfastly, without wavering, without fear or favor, without compromise. He saw the publication of the *Netherlandic Reflections* as an imposed task. His quarrel in the evening of his life was with inconsistent and half-hearted men who confessed the antirevolutionary principle with their mouths, but were so pliable in practice that their persons were in the limelight, not their principle. This kind of struggle demanded the example and energy of the whole man, and that was the kind of man Groen showed in his *Netherlandic Reflections*. The political issues of the day provided him with material to test against his principles. If necessary, he was prepared to fight man to man to defend the results of such tests. Great tests of strength were to follow, in the assessment of both international and domestic affairs.

BISMARCK, GROEN, AND KUYPER

In 1870, an event that had long been feared took place. On July 19, the emperor of France declared war on Prussia. The trigger was a diplomatic conflict over the succession to the Spanish throne, but the real issue was hegemony over Europe. Hostilities began immediately. The war, fought with the most modern weapons, soon proved that Prussia was more than a match for the invincible France. On September 2, the French army under Napoleon III, completely surrounded by the enemy near Sedan, surrendered. Two days later, the Republic was proclaimed in Paris. The republican government refused to accept German peace terms (which included the cession of Alsace and Lorraine), whereupon Bismarck resumed the war. In early 1871, he brought besieged Paris to its knees and imposed his peace in the famous Hall of Mirrors at Versailles.

Naturally, the Dutch watched this unusually bloody war with bated breath. Prussia had become the unrivaled superpower in Europe. Many people were impressed by the German display of power. This was certainly true in Protestant circles, which also saw a spiritual dimension in the outcome of the war. Finally, they said, France had received the punishment it deserved. Gefken believed that it had been "God's will" to humiliate France.[566] Chantepie provided a further argument for his theory of revolution, speaking of Prussia's "cultural vocation for the world."[567] But anyone who thought that Groen would rejoice that the ever-revolutionary France had been subdued was deceived. France had declared war, it was true, but Bismarck had instigated it. Bismarck practiced "Napoleonic politics," using the war to promote German unity. The powerful chancellor should have used his influence for peace, but instead he had used the diplomatic incident to wage war. Neither the German nor the French nation, Groen argued, had anything to do with it.[568] The extent to which Bismarck's policy was revolutionary was evident in the annexation of Alsace and Lorraine. The year 1870 proved to be in direct line with 1830 and 1848, when power had also trumped justice.

Groen's judgment of Prussian politics once again placed him in an isolated position within his own circle. In *The Herald*, Schwartz applauded Prussia's victory. Groen's compatriots could no longer understand their friend, who had always warned so strongly of the French danger. Groen replied that his purpose was "to provoke a profitable exchange of ideas with Christian friends, here and elsewhere, especially in Berlin, as to the attitude we ought to adopt in the face of the disregard of the evangelical touchstone of constitutional and international law."[569]

This exchange of ideas was not very fruitful. From Berlin he received a letter from a young Dutch diplomat, Frederik van Bylandt, who wrote to him, "I am fully convinced that in the field of international politics you are on the wrong track."[570] Friends at home were appalled by his frank opinion. In early 1871, Elout told Groen in no uncertain terms that his attacks on Bismarck's policies were making him very unpopular and that "his influence was detrimental to Dutch interests." Groen should stop seeing everything through the lens of 1866. Elout urged his friend to be much milder in his judgment of Bismarck.[571] Was Groen shocked by this warning from a friend? We know him too well by now to realize that such soothing words had no effect on him once he was convinced that he was arguing for a principle.

Groen could not be persuaded to change his mind, not even when Kuyper did not share his view. Kuyper had become editor-in-chief of *The Herald* in 1871 and expressed his views on the Franco-Prussian war. Kuyper was pleased with the outcome and hoped that the German victory would mean a definitive end to the influence of French principles in Europe.[572] He praised the Protestant principles of Prussia. It is noteworthy, however, that he also advocated the principles of law in international relations. Kuyper demanded that "relations between nations be ordered and judged according to the rule of law, in a word, that a 'law of nations' be recognized, resting on a sound moral foundation."[573] This was a recognition of Groen's basic premise, but the conclusion was still different. Kuyper believed that Prussia had a right to claim Alsace and Lorraine; Groen did not, but he assured Kuyper that their difference need not cause alienation between them. "In foreign policy we may differ," he wrote to the chairman of the Voters' Club in Kampen, where he had dedicated followers at the Theological School of the Seceders, "but Dr. Kuyper is our first-class ally."[574] Kuyper, however, would be converted to Groen's point of view. When Bismarck proved to be a domestic chancellor who curtailed the freedom of socialists and Catholics, Kuyper joined Groen in judging the despotic, Napoleonic nature of Bismarck's regime. Thanks to his unwavering stance, Groen had made at least one important disciple. Henceforth, Kuyper would approach foreign policy in terms of strict international law, an approach that would remain a hallmark of later antirevolutionaries.[575]

THE ELECTIONS OF 1871

Another feat of unwavering steadfastness was performed by Groen in the election year of 1871. The central committee of 1869 had been dissolved, and something had to be set up again. Early in 1871 Kuyper contacted De Geer. He wanted to see a broader program, "not only on the educational question, but in a more general sense." The press could be helpful in spreading it. But De Geer had little enthusiasm left after his experience in 1869, and so Kuyper was left with the task all alone. He also received no encouragement from Groen. The "leader" was not able to give a general program and considered it "unnecessary and dangerous." The antirevolutionary principle was well enough known, and those elected should not be too restricted in their freedom of movement.[576] This was the voice of an old-style parliamentarian who favored a large measure of individual liberty. Kuyper was irritated. He had expected more responsiveness. "If we pastors are to do anything in journalism, our venerable statesmen must prepare the material for us." Was that all Groen had to offer? "A life like yours must lead to a political testament. You have never been able to realize your ideas in time, and therefore you have never fully expressed them with an eye to the future. Can they not be shared?"[577] Indeed, Groen had nothing more to offer. His political legacy was his person, not a program.

On April 18, 1871, Kuyper chaired a meeting with the editors of some five Christian periodicals. Now that a general program seemed unattainable, they adopted a platform consisting of three planks: (1) a declaration that the Christian-historical school represented an independent party; (2) the demand that the free school become the rule, the state school a supplement; and (3) the demand that the electoral system be reformed and the voter qualification lowered.[578] The Christian journals would make propaganda for this "editors' program." Three days later Kuyper came to The Hague to give a public lecture on "Modernism." In the afternoon he visited Groen and reported on the meeting of the editors and its results. Groen was pleased with the clear statement about the independence of the Christian-historical school. But the thorniest issue Kuyper had come to discuss was the election of candidates. Groen had very little confidence in the antirevolutionary incumbents. Earlier he had hinted in his paper, "It has been rather openly intimated that we should not re-elect those who are considered representatives of the Christian-historical school."[579] Kuyper hoped that things would not go further than this veiled threat. He was able to convince Groen that the incumbents were still needed. The editorial board had already decided to put them on the list of recommended candidates.

When Kuyper left Groen's house, he felt greatly relieved. Toward the end of April, the Christian press would announce the program and the candidates, and once that was taken care of, Kuyper would be able to take a vacation abroad to recover from his total exhaustion. But in May of that year the Chamber dealt with the budget of the Ministry of the Interior. The graying Thorbecke had just formed his third ministry. As usual, Groen followed the debates in the Chamber. He found the behavior of the antirevolutionary members so weak that his old unease returned. Although they should have entered the lists in the name of Christian education, they did not take a single initiative and allowed themselves to be intimidated by Thorbecke. Groen was now convinced that the party could not go on with such people. If a program was to be credible at all, should it not be embodied by people who showed that they were serious about it? Groen was unable to reach Kuyper. He later admitted that he felt completely caught between a rock and a hard place.[580] Nevertheless, he made up his mind and wrote off everyone who had proved to be half-hearted and pliable. Only three names remained on his list: Kuyper, Van Otterloo, and Keuchenius (who had returned to the East Indies). This trio would guarantee "a concrete program and a clear protest." Groen published his shortlist in *Netherlandic Reflections*. Van Wassenaer, the leading figure in the parliamentary faction and tipped as a candidate for Leyden, realized what was happening and tried to have a conference with his uncle, which was refused. The members had never asked him for a conference and were certainly not going to get one now.

When Kuyper returned home from his travels abroad, he was completely surprised and disoriented. He let Groen know that he was at the end of his tether. The campaign had begun; there could be no retreat. The nomination of candidates was in full swing: "This cannot be reversed in two weeks." Kuyper realized that Groen was desperate, but he felt that Groen's intervention was ill-timed. In desperation he wrote to the old man, "Surely one must take reality into account."[581] De Geer was less perplexed: the whole turn of events had only confirmed his view of Groen's practical shortcomings. Others also shook their heads at Groen's maneuver, like Gefken, who was a candidate in Zwolle. "Our dear friend Groen has lately . . . fallen into a great deal of eccentricity." Gefken also knew the cause. "It is the result of Groen's disappointment and being ignored. Nevertheless, our friend, as a leader, is treading a slippery path. . . . A lack of practical sense is an undeniable trait in our worthy Groen. But no wonder. No children and no public office."[582] But Groen stuck to his guns. His advice to nominate only his chosen three stood. He wanted the elections to be a "national demonstration," as in 1868. Once again, the motto was "In our isolation lies our strength."

Kuyper was able to come to an agreement with Groen. Both strategies would be followed: the program of the editors and the advice of the old leader. Of course, it was a recipe for disaster.

The five Christian papers made their recommendations, and Groen made his in *Netherlandic Reflections*. These two separate actions caused considerable confusion in the electoral districts. Some voters' associations followed Groen's advice; a larger number probably did not.[583] The voters were confused as well. Van Otterloo was sure that many "in the confusion of the moment" did not know what to make of the "watchword of the general" and did not vote for the recommended candidates.[584] The result was that Van Wassenaer and Saaymans Vader were re-elected, but Gefken and Bichon van IJsselmonde were not. The three recommended candidates also failed. Of the sixty thousand votes cast nationwide, Kuyper, Keuchenius, and Van Otterloo had received only three thousand, or 5 percent. These figures convinced Groen that there was a part of the population that would vote antirevolutionary if the choice was between a conservative and an antirevolutionary. This opinion was shared by a number of pastors. "Our constituency is again staked out," wrote the Christian Reformed professor Anthony Brummelkamp from Kampen; a purely antirevolutionary support group had become visible.[585] Groen carefully and gratefully reported such comments in his *Netherlandic Reflections*. Kuyper grumbled for a while about his thwarted plan, but he soon regained his courage. In addition to a newspaper, the antirevolutionaries needed to establish a national voters' league—as he put it, "so that the next elections will not find us unprepared again."[586] Voter organization needed to become more professional.

While many from the emerging middle class sympathized with Groen's break with the conservatives, many of Groen's old friends from the upper class were quite upset. Shortly before the elections, Van Wassenaer had written an open letter from Marienbad, where he was "taking the waters." He was very hurt "that you [Groen] call on all Christians in the Netherlands to register their protest against our position in the Second Chamber." The offended nephew continued, such an act, at election time, must be "an act of desperation, regardless of the wounds you inflict." Could he, Van Wassenaer, be responsible for the fact that "the holy cause" for which Groen was fighting "has a low standing in the eyes of the world"?[587] Van Wassenaer voiced what was the talk of his social circle. Another victim, Gefken, noted in his diary that Groen no longer had both feet on the ground and, moreover, had fallen into a "solistic style." "Today his old friends, Mackay, Elout, and we, as well as Singendonck and de La Saussaye, cannot follow him in his domestic and foreign policy."[588] Nor did the friends appreciate Groen's justification of his actions in *Netherlandic Reflections*. Once again, Elout was the messenger of what was troubling them, although he did it in writing: "Again and again I hear the remark that you too often quote not only yourself, but also everything favorable or flattering that appears elsewhere."[589] This man-to-man struggle was not fruitless, however. Groen's action had not brought about a change in the antirevolutionary faction, but it had sent a strong signal: the antirevolutionaries did not belong with the conservatives. This was the message Kuyper could take into the future. But first they had to talk. On August 31, a reconciliation meeting was held at the home of Van Wassenaer, who had privately invited the most prominent antirevolutionaries. The whole affair had greatly disturbed Van Wassenaer, partly because it affected his relations with his "esteemed" uncle and aunt. Groen was among those who attended, although he felt the invitation came five years too late. The meeting was cordial and conciliatory, and brotherly relations were restored. Kuyper delivered a speech that made a deep impression. He spoke of the need for mutual consultation and of the special importance of Groen's views on school legislation. The men agreed to uphold the slogan "The private school the rule, the public school the supplement" and to consult regularly with Groen.

Little came of the good intentions. The members of Parliament fell back into their old roles and stayed away from Groen as much as possible. Groen would not repeat the action of 1871. Shortly after this last specimen of steadfastness, he let Kuyper know that it was all becoming too much for him and that he wanted to retire from politics for good.

The Antirevolutionary

DYING A LITTLE

Ten days after the reconciliation meeting at Van Wassenaer's, Groen celebrated his seventieth birthday. The gratitude of the Reformed people was expressed in a gift from the Christian teachers. In this circle Groen enjoyed almost boundless authority as a champion of Christian education and as the author of the widely used manual on the history of the Netherlands. A delegation from the teachers' organization came and presented Groen with an album containing 238 photographs of its members. For the Grand Old Man, it was "the most touching token of affection" of the day.[590] The farewells had begun. Betsy and Willem had to say goodbye to the flowers and birds of *Oud-Wassenaer*. The house had become too big and required too much work, even for the butler who had grown old with the Groens. After twenty-five years, they sold the house, which was demolished shortly thereafter. Betsy seems to have saved one of its bricks. The small castle that the new owner built on the site still stands today. In 1871, the Groens bought the Elout estate of Blankenburg, not far from *Oud-Wassenaer* and closer to the dunes.

In the same year, the Groen's connection with the Royal Family Archives came to an end. A letter from King William III, dated February 4, 1871, brought the final release. Groen had been looking forward to this for a long time. On several occasions since 1866 he had expressed his wish to be released from his post. The manner in which the supervision of the collection had been arranged was irresponsible in his eyes, and he felt frustrated by the feeble efforts at court to find a proper solution. Under these circumstances, he did not want to take on any more duties in the archives. He did not even want to receive mail addressed to the archivist, and he returned such mail unopened. This signal was finally understood, and Groen was finally relieved of the post he had held for forty years. He did not say a word about it. He had considered it his vocation to shed light on the religious beliefs of the members of the House of Orange for the benefit of modern Holland. He had been disappointed that this aspect had found little echo at court. There was not even a vision to study the past from the point of view of the Orange dynasty. Now Groen let it fall from his shoulders. There was enough work to be done for an old man who found himself overwhelmed by newspapers, books, and magazines that cried out to be read.

Groen van Prinsterer still saw publishing as a task assigned to him, but after completing number 150 of *Netherlandic Reflections*, he had to stop. He caught his usual winter flu and became very weak. By February, however, he was sufficiently recovered to resume writing. As he told his readers, "Looking to Him who lifts up and strengthens the weak, and grateful for the many kind inquiries, even from non-subscribers, I am reluctant to withdraw entirely from reviewing the affairs of the country."[591] He would, however, refrain from engaging in jousting that might sap his energies. In subsequent issues, he wrote repeatedly that he had sought too much to fight for his principles in the events of the day. On April 1, 1872, he was relieved. On that day, the first issue of the daily newspaper *The Standard* appeared under the editorship of Abraham Kuyper. This was the antirevolutionary paper that people had been talking about for several years, and Kuyper was very pleased with it. Groen had little to add to the journalism of *The Standard*. He declared himself "homogenous" with Kuyper's commentaries, although he did not forget to add that while he was of one mind with Kuyper, he, Groen, reserved his independence. The issues of *Netherlandic Reflections* now became more and more the background noise of the retired antirevolutionary leader. Its issues were valuable as moral support for the people at the front; they are less interesting as a source of information about the events of the time.

In the last volumes of his journal, Groen was preoccupied with pet themes and personal reminiscences. He was still capable of trenchant formulations, but a lifelong idiosyncrasy as a writer became more visible: weakness of composition. Loose thoughts, commentaries, and memories followed one another without any apparent connection. Especially after Thorbecke's death in June 1872, *Netherlandic Reflections* was devoted more and more to private reminiscences and explanations of his own life and career. Thorbecke's death left a deep impression on him. He shared in the universal mourning and remained silent for several days. Thorbecke's death, he let Kuyper know, "has affected me terribly."[592] Memories began to flow again. Thorbecke was, in Groen's eyes, the most important figure in Dutch politics since William I. He set the tone and was favored by the spirit of the age. But to Thorbecke's attitude of "It should be otherwise," Groen had posed, "I may not do otherwise." He declared, "In what I considered desirable for the Netherlands and for Orange, Thorbecke always opposed me and defeated me. Nevertheless, there remained a sweet glow of the friendship of our youth."[593] From this point on, the paper alternated between melancholy reminiscence and political commentary. Groen remembered Da Costa, Wormser, Merle d'Aubigné, who died in the fall of 1872, and Chantepie de la Saussaye, who died in 1874. Current events did not disappear completely, but they became more and more distant.

Meanwhile, developments in antirevolutionary circles gained momentum. After the publication of *The Standard*, an Anti-School Law League was founded, a movement that defended the private school. It was a movement with strong grassroots support, a populist movement to which the Seceders also contributed.[594] After an uncertain start, the Anti-School Law League would mushroom into a national organization with local chapters and tens of thousands of supporters. Kuyper and De Geer were members of the executive committee and sought to align the movement with the position of the antirevolutionaries in Parliament. The slogan "The free school the rule, the state school the supplement" became the slogan of the League, and in 1873 the board became the central steering committee in the national election campaign. Groen followed the rise of this new movement with great interest, but relied on Kuyper, De Geer, and Van Otterloo for information. He became a member, hoping that something good would come of it. Kuyper realized that Groen's prestige was still so great that the old leader's blessing would carry considerable weight. Kuyper regularly approached Groen with requests to include brief comments in *Netherlandic Reflections* in support of his views and undertakings. The correspondence of these years between the old Groen and the young Kuyper is one of the most fascinating reads in the history of the antirevolutionaries.[595] The two men were also in constant contact on the church question. Kuyper's fight against the ethicists had Groen's full support, and he also warmly agreed with Kuyper's campaign for the "liberation of the church." The Réveil had led to free churches in Switzerland, France, and Scotland; it had not done so in the Netherlands. Would it happen yet?

It was Groen's view of the Reformation in the Netherlands, as well as his conception of the relationship between church and state, that prevented him from welcoming Secession and the establishment of free churches. In his view, the Dutch Reformed church was the link to the life of the historic nation. He continued to hold this view in his old age. On the other hand, he was willing to consider radical steps because of what he called the "boundless doctrinal freedom" in the Reformed church. He felt a kinship with the Seceders in their resolute decision of faith and their Christian zeal. Their church life, however, confirmed his fear that believers can often make things too difficult for themselves by excluding others for petty reasons and by insisting on doctrinal precision. Groen had always called himself Reformed and a Calvinist, but he kept his reservations. As a child of the Réveil, he was afraid of any theological system. Building on Christ alone was enough. Kuyper, on the other hand, felt that the Réveil fell short theologically. When Kuyper converted to Calvinism as a new worldview, including the doctrine of election, Groen expressed reservations. He was a "Calvinist" but also a "child of the Réveil." He saw election as a topic for theologians to debate; believers should live by "free grace" and not wrestle with the wrong questions. He was more enthusiastic about Kuyper's plan for a new organization of the church. Based on the autonomy of the local congregation, a league of church councils was to be formed, which would automatically replace the denomination created by the regulations of 1816 (revised in 1852). The Seceders were then also to join this new church. This particular plan of Kuyper's was never carried out. If it had been, Groen would undoubtedly have joined it.

Groen's admiration for Kuyper was great; he was always willing to make time to consult with him, although he confessed that he found these discussions both "exciting" and "exhausting."[596] In July 1872, Kuyper also discussed with him the sensitive question of who should succeed the old leader. Groen gave him a vote of confidence, but also felt that Kuyper needed to gain a position of authority of his own.[597] From that moment on, Groen decided that he could go out as "leader."[598] He spoke of retiring after "forty years of service." Kuyper, after taking his seat in the Chamber in 1874, regularly visited the Korte Vijverberg. He needed support in his attempt to get the sitting antirevolutionary members to accept a program. The 1873 elections had strengthened the antirevolutionary phalanx. In a by-election the following year, Kuyper joined this group and tried to persuade them to close ranks. He discussed the broad program with Groen, who gave his approval. To Kuyper's great disappointment, in the fall of 1874 his attempt would run aground on the individualism of the members who did not want to commit themselves, much less to the radical ideas of Kuyper. As a result, Kuyper became quite isolated from his antirevolutionary colleagues. In this difficult situation, however, he was encouraged by Groen, who remained his great example. Kuyper deliberately spoke to Groen about certain episodes in the latter's parliamentary career, and Groen told him the story of 1856 and 1857. These conversations did both men a great deal of good. Their friendship was a source of strength for them in their very different circumstances.

THE ANTIREVOLUTIONARY

MAURICE AND OLDENBARNEVELT

The old general was not yet finished. A new front suddenly opened up in the field of history. In 1874 he felt it his duty to take up the cudgels against his old acquaintance, the American historian John Lothrop Motley. With pain and difficulty, he managed to put together *Maurice and Barnevelt*.[599] The book was a response to Motley's recent biography of Johan van Oldenbarnevelt.[600] Groen had kept in touch with Motley and had a long conversation with him during his visit to the Netherlands in 1867. The picture that Motley now painted of Prince Maurice was in stark contrast to the judgment that Dutch historians had formed of the prince since the publication of the archives. Fruin and Bakhuizen van den Brink, for example, leaders in the field, did not see Maurice as an ambitious schemer who used religion merely to achieve his personal goals and to get rid of Oldenbarnevelt. This caricature reappeared in Motley's book. The biography was written in a lively style, but also with a personal coloring and with literary effect in mind. Groen summed up its tenor in these words: "Motley misinterprets Maurice's character as well as the life principle of the Dutch Republic. He portrays Maurice . . . as a hypocrite who, out of long-cherished ambition and resentment, used theological quarrels to avenge his frustrated ambition on the 70-year-old statesman [Oldenbarnevelt] and to brand as narrow-minded fanaticism the tenacity with which the Calvinists clung to the core of the martyr faith that had provided the cement of the state [i.e., the doctrine of election]."[601]

Groen contacted Motley in the spring of 1874 to ask whether he had really read all the sources; in particular, Motley did not seem to have consulted the volumes of the archives that had been published since 1857, collections that Groen had prepared at great speed, partly for Motley's benefit. Had Motley not read the letter of remorse that Maurice had written to his cousin William Louis, count of Nassau and landowner of Friesland, after the beheading of Oldenbarnevelt?[602] In his reply to Groen, however, Motley declared that he had indeed done his homework.[603] Shortly thereafter, Groen informed him that the biography had left him no choice but to defend Maurice personally.

The book Groen wrote in the fall of 1874 is undoubtedly the most remarkable of his entire corpus. French, German, English, and Dutch passages are interspersed throughout its four hundred pages. Whole sections are quoted from Groen's *Introductions to the Archives*, and the private correspondence between Maurice and William Louis is reproduced in its entirety.[604] The most important part is the historical overview, in which Groen gives his view of Maurice and Oldenbarnevelt and the role of religion in each of their lives. Another part of the book contains personal recollections and interpretations related to Groen's contacts with Motley and the progress of Dutch historiography.[605] Busken Huet, always an admirer of Groen, called the book "masterful," though "disjointed." "A novice who dared to write such a book would be sent home by the critics. But not to worry. A novice cannot produce such a work."[606] Groen had put the full weight of his talents into defending the integrity of both Maurice and Oldenbarnevelt and exposing the distorted picture Motley had painted of Reformed Christianity in the Netherlands. The latter was precisely the "lifeblood" of Dutch history, as Kuyper noted in *The Standard*. Reactions in the country to Groen's latest book were generally positive. The work was strange, it was choppy, but the fact that an old pioneer of historical scholarship had defended the honor of the fatherland was greeted with much sympathy. One thing had become clear once again: an attack on the reputation of the first Oranges was an attack on Groen van Prinsterer.

THE SECRET OF GROEN'S LIFE

The writing of *Maurice and Barnevelt* was only an intermezzo in the work that Groen had set himself in the last years of his life. It seemed to him, especially after he had handed over the leadership to Kuyper, that he should shed light on his personal life. He had already been approached from several sides with the request to write his memoirs. At first he would not hear of it. He admitted where the problem lay: he was still being drawn into the debates of the day. But gradually he began to feel that perhaps the best he could contribute was to provide information about his own career. Despite his openness, despite all the writings he had published, Groen was still an enigma to many of his contemporaries. "After a long career, I am a stranger in my own country," he admitted.[607] His views were not understood or taken in the opposite sense he intended. Personally, he blamed it on the fact that his ideas were diametrically opposed to the dominant spirit of the age. But his personality was also an issue. The liberals saw him as a "Protestant Jesuit," a sectarian zealot; the ethical-irenicists saw him as an un-Dutch type because he did not conform to the moderate center. What was considered "nebulous" and "obscure" about Groen also had to do with his style of writing and his paradoxical statements. His slogans were almost never understood at first. This was especially true of his assertion that isolation is strength. But also, his statement about the conservatives as "the inconsistent wing of the liberal party" and his distinction between the "historical nation" and the "constitutional nation" required intellectual effort beyond the comprehension of the average reader.

In his twilight years, Groen gave glimpses of the deeper motivation of his life. He did not want to write a memoir, as he was no longer capable of lengthy works. He did something else: he painted a portrait of himself in his letters. Not that the idea of publishing his correspondence was entirely his own. In 1870, his Amsterdam friend Jozua van Eik, who was president of an association for the promotion of Christian literature, suggested that he publish his correspondence with Da Costa. Groen took his time. The first volume of the approximately 150 letters between him and Da Costa appeared two years later.[608] Thanks in part to the positive reactions from his immediate circle, Groen began to realize how important the publication of his correspondence would be for the elucidation of his own life's work. After Thorbecke's death, he decided to publish his correspondence with the great liberal leader as well.[609] The liberal press responded positively. The second volume of Da Costa's letters appeared in 1873. All this made for fascinating literature for Groen's close followers. Kuyper read the letters with great eagerness and inquired about many points in his conversations with Groen.

By now Groen had acquired a taste for the genre. The series devoted to the Da Costa letters was not finished when he published the first volume of his correspondence with Wormser in 1874.[610] The two old friends now flanked each other. Groen felt that the correspondence with Wormser was important for the reader to get a more balanced view of his own ecclesiastical standpoint, a standpoint closer to Wormser's Reformed position than to that of Da Costa, who always tended to paint somewhat outside the ecclesiastical lines. It was, of course, very interesting to note that Groen, always so assertive and self-confident in his publications, appeared in his private correspondence to be a much milder judge of persons and opinions. The man of painful decisions and unshakable principles turned out to be a sensitive man and a tender soul who reached out to the hearts of his friends. Of course, critics wondered what criteria Groen had used to make his selections. Were any letters left out, for example? Groen replied that he had followed the same method as with the correspondence of the princes of Orange: he had included everything of historical significance, including the less flattering. For those with an eye for connections, it was a remarkable sight: the historian who had always worked hard to publish the correspondence of others was now publishing his own in the same way.

The connection, however, is not far-fetched. In fact, there is a deeper reason for it. Did Motley not say that one does not really know the Oranges until one has read their personal letters? It was the same with Groen's letters. In his published letters he revealed the deeper motive of his life. That motive was his belief in the born-again personality who trusts in God and is aware of his Christian calling, and who is therefore not discouraged by defeats or setbacks. He had seen this kind of personality in William the Silent, whose character, personal convictions, and outward behavior were all of a piece. That was the kind of person he wanted to be: staying the course, if necessary, against everyone and everything, in the firm determination to defend the rights of Christians. Groen believed that every Christian, if he had a backbone and spoke out, could be the beginning of new developments. This was the deeper motive, the secret of Groen's antirevolutionary life. He had seen this trait in other personalities who were his models: Willem Bilderdijk, Willem de Clercq, Isaac da Costa, Johan Adam Wormser. He surrounded himself with their portraits. The motto of the House of Orange[611] was engraved in his mind: "You don't have to succeed to persevere, you have to prevail to keep up the fight." This explains why, after many a lost battle, he could write, "In defeat lies the germ of victory." Thus, in the evening of his life, we do not meet a man who looked back on his life with bitterness. For hours he would lose himself in the many letters he had so carefully saved. It produced in him a mood he described as "grateful and melancholic."

In his very last year, he completed the publication of his correspondence. In addition to the Da Costa and Wormser letters, a smaller collection of letters saw the light of day, *How the Education Act of 1857 Came to Be*.[612] He would also turn the spotlight back on this great conflict, a critical juncture in Groen's political biography. He had been struck by a comment in a government announcement in the spring of 1875. The wording was similar to that of the summer of 1856: there would be no new education law, since the nation had been "attached" to the common school since 1806. Groen wanted to refute this claim by publishing the letters from 1856 and 1857 that were kept in his personal archives. The collection, when published, included a large number of correspondents, especially pastors: Heldring, Chantepie, Beets, but also Van der Brugghen himself and Singendonck. The letters showed that many of the writers initially supported the ideal of separate state schools, but that after the summer of 1856 they had become more like Van der Brugghen. In the end, they were deceived by a man who, at the crucial moment, broke faith and went back on his word. Groen attributed this to a lack of personal integrity.

Recognizing an active role for Christian faith in public life, Groen's thinking became increasingly concerned with the question of the Christian personality. This is a personality that knows that it must be willing to witness, to struggle, and to suffer.[613] The life of a Christian in public affairs will be marked by difficult choices and painful consequences. This conviction became an integral part of Groen's *idées intimes*, a conviction that he had a hard time convincing his own circle, the circle of the upper classes. He saw the flip side of this conviction in the behavior of the ethicist pastors, who placed personal faith at the center, but who did not turn the confession of the mouth into a confession of the deed. Groen did not want to be like that. He wanted to set an example for others by having the courage of his convictions and openly witnessing to the truth that filled his heart. This inevitably led to clashes with those who did not see religious convictions as providing solutions to the great questions of church and state. It speaks volumes that the personal bond that Groen was almost always able to maintain with opponents broke down in the case of the spokesmen of this school: Van der Brugghen, Beets, and Chantepie. Of this trio, Beets was still alive when Groen died; he was in the habit of delivering a eulogy at the graveside of many a prominent Christian, but he remained silent at Groen's funeral.

SURSUM CORDA (LIFT UP YOUR HEARTS)

The end was not unexpected. For several years, Willem had been increasingly bothered by deafness and stiffness, the infirmities of old age. He often complained of being exhausted and feeling very weak. Some of the short letters he still managed to write consisted of only a few lines written in a staccato style. Putting the finishing touches on the volumes of correspondence became such a chore that he asked the publisher for help. Almost all of his old friends preceded him in death. Mackay died in March 1876; Groen was able to say goodbye to him, and Mackay again told him how much he owed him for giving form to his convictions. Kuyper had collapsed in February 1876 and left for the south of France, suffering from a severe breakdown. Groen was now in frequent contact with Alexander de Savornin Lohman, who was filling in for Kuyper as editor of *The Standard*.

On April 26, he was still able to walk on Betsy's arm. The next day they were about to do the same when Willem told her he'd rather go to bed. The doctor was called and said that he could not diagnose any particular ailment. Betsy relayed this to everyone who sent notes inquiring about his health: "My husband is very weak at the moment without being really sick."[614] The work stopped. Friends watched the last phase of this life from afar. Betsy corresponded almost daily with Lohman, as she had with the De Clercqs during Willem's life-threatening illness in 1833. For the next two weeks, the patient remained lucid. There were days when Groen hoped he would recover. There were also restless nights when he faced the terror of death. Early on the morning of May 3, he had Betsy record that he had received a vision of light in his dying agony, which he considered "a very present help" that gave him "inexpressible peace." Two days later the vision was repeated, this time more powerful: "Last night I made Bunyan's journey—all resurrection and glory. I have never had such clarity." His whole life had passed before him. He could only give thanks. "Every point since my childhood has been a gracious preparation for what was to come next."[615] After this, he went through several more difficult days filled with inner struggles that finally resulted in total submission. When Betsy reminded him of the visions of light he had been allowed to see, he replied, "Don't talk too much about it, as if I looked to anything else . . . found rest in anything else . . . than in the Lord Christ alone, His righteousness alone." Betsy prayed with him and read from the Bible. Willem's mind remained clear. From time to time, he spoke audibly, "To have defended the truths that now give me such comfort . . . ." And, "Predestination has been much abused—a great and wonderful truth: from God and to God are all things." And finally, "Now I can go in peace. Lord, to whom shall we go? To Thee alone!"[616] After May 15, his condition worsened and he was no longer fully conscious.[617] Betsy told friends that he no longer spoke coherently. It was difficult for her to witness: "For myself, I cannot recall a greater trial—this mouth that had uttered such clear, excellent thoughts." The days were also trying for the maids; they remained on duty day and night and would not hear of hiring "outside help." By May 16, the patient was barely eating. Two days later, Betsy told friends that Willem was dying "very peacefully—without pain or fear." He lay quietly in bed, his eyes closed, his hands folded. A Bible beside him was open to a passage he had underlined, Revelation 7:13–17. The text spoke of martyrs for the faith who would come out of the Great Tribulation and be led by Christ himself to the "springs of the water of life," where God would wipe away every tear from their eyes.[618] Groen had still managed to scribble in the margin, "Amen, Jesus Christ, Amen."[619] In the morning of May 19 breathing suddenly stopped and Guillaume Groen van Prinsterer passed away.

The announcement came from Betsy's hand:

> Passed away today, with unwavering faith in his Lord and Savior,
> to Whom he had dedicated his life, my beloved husband
> Guillaume Groen van Prinsterer.
> The separation after a marriage of 48 years with such a man
> fills my soul with deep mourning. The comfort of the Gospel alone,
> and the hope of a blessed reunion alleviate my sorrow.[620]

The funeral took place on May 23. A large cortege drove from the Korte Vijverberg to the cemetery, *Ter Navolging*. Among the mourners were many members of Parliament from various parties, several ministers of the crown, members of the Council of State, the mayor of The Hague, teachers, pastors, and even a group of students. Two wreaths adorned the coffin, one from Queen Sophie, as this unhappy member of the royal family honored the deceased.[621] At the graveside, Elout spoke from personal memory, portraying Groen as a knight without fear or reproach. He was followed by a number of speakers. Donald Mackay spoke on behalf of his family, Rev. Brummelkamp Jr. on behalf of the Seceders. In the midst of all these distinguished men stood a humble schoolteacher, Abraham Meijer, from Rotterdam. "So here I am," he began, somewhat intimidated. He wanted to speak on behalf of six hundred teachers representing "tens of thousands of children." He spoke of the great treasure they had lost in this "confessor of the Gospel," but he was convinced that Groen's struggles for Christian education would still bear much fruit. For this reason, Meijer said, it was wrong to consider Groen impractical. "Strange self-deception! He attracted so much opposition because he was so practical."[622] According to this schoolmaster, the word of the childless Groen would do its work for generations to come.

The funeral was a public event that few could miss. Newspapers carried obituaries. *The Standard* published an "In Memoriam" under the title *Sursum corda: Lift up your hearts!* Did this farewell mark the end of an era in Dutch politics? The day before Groen's death, a statue of Thorbecke had been unveiled in Amsterdam. What about Groen? Two images remained:

that of a martyr and that of a tragic figure. Pastor van Rhijn had called him a martyr in his eulogy. Those who did not share his faith saw him as a tragic failure. On the day of the funeral, the liberal Willem Hendrik de Beaufort wrote an entry in his diary about Groen, calling him a great stylist and an astute historian, but also an ineffectual statesman. "If the merits of a statesman can be measured by his achievements, his were few. Adhering to a conviction shared by few, he was never able to exert any real influence on the course of events."[623] If Groen were a tragic figure, no statue would ever honor him; posterity does not usually erect statues for tragic figures. And it is true that Groen has been honored far more modestly than Thorbecke: a bust of Groen in the Second Chamber is the lasting public tribute that posterity has paid to him. As the Catholic leader Herman Schaepman put it at the time, "Thorbecke stood above the people; Groen van Prinsterer lives on in the hearts of the people."[624] If Thorbecke was honored for the civil constitution he achieved, Groen was honored for who he was, the fighter and confessor.

BETSY'S FINAL YEARS

Betsy lived long enough to see the various assessments of her husband's life, but too short to see what Groen's spiritual descendants would accomplish. The year 1876 was a low point in the history of the antirevolutionary party. Kuyper was traveling abroad, and it was an open question whether he would be able to resume an active life. In the eyes of the public, the antirevolutionaries were as good as finished. As early as 1877, the first biography appeared in the well-known series *Men of Consequence in Our Time*.[625] It was written from a liberal perspective. The "relative fruitlessness" of Groen's efforts made a "tragic impression" on the author. The antirevolutionary policy, if it could ever be put into practice, would set humanity back two centuries and condemn it to a fatal standstill. It was not surprising that more than one speaker at the graveside sighed, "What might this gifted friend of King and Country not have been to us if he had not sought his strength in such absolute isolation from the current of our modern ideas?"[626]

Betsy probably cared little for such judgments. Her existence had become empty, and she now lived on all the memories of her years with Willem. She took care of the many things that still needed to be done: the library, the houses, the staff. When a delegation of antirevolutionaries visited her a few months before her death, she said what she had heard Willem

The Antirevolutionary

say so often: I live in the past now. The world in which the antirevolutionaries continued to fight was becoming more and more distant. So, Betsy saw a little of the first fruits of her husband's life. In the summer of 1878, the antirevolutionaries finally closed ranks in Parliament and across the country. They were driven together by a new education law sponsored by the liberal ministry of Kappeyne van de Coppello, a law that continued to discriminate heavily against private Christian schools. In the face of this overwhelming liberal onslaught, all conservative sentiments melted away, and only antirevolutionaries remained. Seceders and Reformers, rich and poor, upper and lower classes, all now stood shoulder to shoulder in the breach. We do not know if Betsy signed the People's Petition that circulated throughout the country in the summer of 1878, but she probably did. Three hundred thousand signatures on a petition did not stop the law from going into effect. But the indirect result was that it created a critical mass to support the organization of an official antirevolutionary party with an articulated program.[627] Betsy did not live to see it. She died a few weeks before, on March 14, 1879. At the founding meeting of the Antirevolutionary Party (ARP) on April 3, 1879, Kuyper gave a speech in which he recalled the lifelong struggle of Groen van Prinsterer and the recent death of his widow. And so, the names of these two people appear at the beginning of a new page in the continuing history of Dutch Protestantism.

Endnotes

1. Archives Groen van Prinsterer, Algemeen Rijksarchief, The Hague, nr. 4. Hereafter cited as Groen Archive.
2. Dr. Groen derived the name Van Prinsterer from his great-great-grandmother. It belonged to a noble family with its own coat of arms. The Van Prinsterers originally hailed from Germany, settled in the Low Countries around 1500, and had since risen on the social ladder. Groen Archive, nr. 2.
3. Cf. Simon Schama, *Patriots and Liberators: Revolution in the Netherlands, 1780-1813* (London: Collins, 1977). E. H. Kossmann, *The Low Countries, 1780-940* (Oxford: Clarendon, 1978), 96-100.
4. The purchase price was 20,000 guilders. The building today houses the Royal Cabinet or clearing house of all state papers; cf. N. Cramer et al., *Het kabinet der koningin. Geschiedenis van het Instituut en het huis aan de Korte Vijverberg* (The Hague: Monumentenzorg, 1991), 80.
5. Earlier stadholder-less periods, which lasted from 1650-72 and 1702-47, were greatly deplored by those in the Dutch Republic who were loyal supporters of the House of Orange and who resented the ascendancy of the regent class which was largely composed of the wealthy urban gentry.
6. P. J. Groen to Cornelia and Willem Groen, undated [ca. 1808]; Groen, *Briefwisseling*, 1:1. For complete bibliographical details, consult the bibliography.
7. Especially C. Tazelaar has done so in his *De jeugd van Groen, 1801-1827* [*Groen's Youth*] (Amsterdam: Uitgeversmaatschappij Holland, 1925), 24.
8. The Dutch name was Maatschappij tot Nut van 't Algemeen, founded in 1784 and dedicated to the promotion of education among the lower classes and the improvement of schooling in general.
9. Maatschappij tot Nut van 't Algemeen [Society for the Common Good].
10. Cf. Peter Baggen, *Vorming door wetenschap; universitair onderwijs in Nederland, 1815-1960* [*Education Through Scholarship: University Education in the Netherlands*] (Delft: Eburon, 1998), 58ff.

Endnotes

11. G. Groen van Prinsterer, *1813 in het licht der Volkshistorie herdacht* (The Hague: Gerretsen, 1863), iv.
12. Letters of 18 May and 16 October 1816; Groen Archive, nr. 124A1. These letters were not included in the published *Briefwisseling*.
13. A. H. Groen to Willem Groen, 20 January 1816; Groen, *Briefwisseling*, 1:7.
14. There are still some letters of a personal nature in the (as yet restricted) collection of the family De Hoop van Slochteren in the Provincial Archives of Groningen.
15. Statistics in Baggen, *Vorming door wetenschap*, 66.
16. See G. Groen van Prinsterer, *Autobiographie* (1872), in *Bescheiden*, 2:502.
17. Groen, *Autobiographie*, 502.
18. H. van Alphen, *De gronden mijner geloofsbelijdenis, opengelegd voor mijne kinderen* (Utrecht, 1786).
19. It was not uncommon among the upper classes to read published sermons of renowned preachers; cf. David Bos, *In dienst van het Koninkrijk; beroepsontwikkeling van hervormde predikanten in het negentiende-eeuwse Nederland* (Amsterdam: Bert Bakker, 1999), 301–3.
20. Groen, "Dagboek" (1822), in *Bescheiden*, 1:9–32.
21. The Pieterskerk, i.e., the Church of St. Peter where the Mayflower pilgrims worshiped during their years in Holland, 1609–20.
22. Groen to P. J. and A. H. Groen, 20 October 1822; Groen, *Briefwisseling*, 1:32.
23. Cf. Harry Van Dyke, "Groen van Prinsterer's Appreciation of Classical Antiquity," in *In the Phrygian Mode: Neo-Calvinism, Antiquity and the Lamentations of Reformed Philosophy*, ed. Robert Sweetman (Lanham, MD: University Press of America, 2007), 13–39.
24. Groen, *Bescheiden*, 2:503.
25. Groen, *Bescheiden*, 2:502.
26. Cf. J. L. van Essen, *Een ziel van vuur; opstellen over Groen van Prinsterer en zijn omgeving* [*A Soul of Fire: Essays on Groen van Prinsterer and His World*] (Leiden: J. J. Groen en Zoon, 1992), 17.
27. Groen, "Dagboek," in *Bescheiden*, 1:14.
28. Groen Archive, nr. 124A.
29. Groen, *Autobiographie*, in *Bescheiden*, 2:503.
30. P. J. Groen to Willem Groen [December 1823]; Groen, *Briefwisseling*, 1:37–38.
31. Groen, *Briefwisseling*, 1:44.
32. Groen, *Briefwisseling*, 1:53.
33. Groen, *Briefwisseling*, 1:733–34. J. Mulder, *Groen van Prinsterer. Staatsman en profeet* (Franeker: Wever, 1973), 32. Also G. J. Schutte, *Mr. G. Groen van Prinsterer* (Goes: Oosterbaan & Le Cointre, 1977), 20.
34. Groen, *Verspreide Geschriften* (Amsterdam: Höveker, 1859), 1:41.
35. Groen, *Verspreide Geschriften*, 1:40.
36. Groen, *Verspreide Geschriften*, 1:79.
37. Groen, *Verspreide Geschriften*, 1:86–87. In the copy of this letter that father Groen sent to Willem the same day, he left these two points unmentioned.

Endnotes

38. Groen, *Verspreide Geschriften*, 1:92.
39. Groen himself speaks of alderman, *Briefwisseling*, 1:89. Gewin mentions that the father of Betsy was "mayor of Groningen," *In den Reveilkring* (Baarn, 1920), 32.
40. Groen, *Briefwisseling*, 1:151.
41. Groen, *Briefwisseling*, 1:34.
42. M. E. Kluit, *Het protestantse reveil in Nederland en daarbuiten, 1815–1865* (Amsterdam: H. J. Paris, 1970), 204.
43. Groen, *Briefwisseling*, 1:82.
44. Groen, *Briefwisseling*, 1:81.
45. J. Dermout to Groen, 31 August 1827, Groen Archive, 124A1.
46. Remieg Aerts, *Land van kleine gebaren. Een politieke geschiedenis van Nederland 1780–1990* (Nijmegen: Sun, 1999), 69.
47. J. Steur, "Staatssecretarie en Kabinet des Konings onder Willem I," *Bijdragen en Mededelingen Betreffende de Geschiedenis der Nederlanden* 84 (1969) 88–138.
48. Groen, *Briefwisseling*, 1:140.
49. Groen, *Briefwisseling*, 1:138.
50. Von Haller's work will not have been unknown to Groen. He used it as early as 1826. Cf. J. L. P. Brants, *Groen's geestelijke groei. Onderzoek naar Groen van Prinsterer's theorieën tot 1834* (Amsterdam: Van Soest, 1951), 41. Was Merle able to arouse renewed interest in Groen for this work? In any case, Groen was now reading Von Haller in a French translation.
51. The phrase appears in a letter to his father dated 1 March 1829, Groen, *Briefwisseling*, 1:140.
52. H. M. Belien, D. Van der Horst, G. J. van Setten (red.), *Nederlanders van het eerste uur. Het ontstaan van het moderne Nederland 1780–1830* (Amsterdam: Uitgeverij Bert Bakker, 1996), 241–42.
53. Cited in: K. H. Roessingh, *Het modernisme in Nederland* (Haarlem: Bohn, 1922), 42.
54. Groen, *Briefwisseling*, 1:141.
55. Groen, *Briefwisseling*, 1:143.
56. Groen, *Verspreide Geschriften*, 1:42.
57. Groen, *Verspreide Geschriften*, 1:55.
58. Groen, *Verspreide Geschriften*, 1:55.
59. Groen, *Verspreide Geschriften*, 1:62.
60. Groen, *Verspreide Geschriften*, 1:65.
61. Groen, *Verspreide Geschriften*, 1:66–67.
62. Groen, *Verspreide Geschriften*, 1:58.
63. De taal der overheid die van d 'onderzaat
Zal weer dezelfde zijn, tot welzijn van de staat
Men zal de dorpeling die de last van 't rijk helpt dragen
Niet langer meer in' t Frans een dure penning vragen. Jan Frans Willems, *Aen de Belgen*, (J. S. Schoesetters, 1818).
64. Belien, Van der Horst, and van Setten, *Nederlanders van het eerste uur*, 241.

Endnotes

65. Curiously, then, it was apparently not distributed at all among the opposition press in the South. Groen, *Briefwisseling*, 1:159.
66. This was the impression Sophie of Wurtemberg received when she first arrived in the Netherlands. Cf. C. A. Tamse, *Queen Sophie 1818-1877* (Zutphen: Walburg, 1984), 62.
67. Quoted in P. A. Diepenhorst, *Groen van Prinsterer*, 2nd ed. (Kampen, 1941), 38–39.
68. Kluit, *Het protestantse Reveil*, 193.
69. Willem Groen van Prinsterer wrote 211 more letters in the period 1830-44. This data is taken from the catalog of the Réveil Archives in Amsterdam. Willem de Clercq made the statement in his diary. Cf. A. Pierson, *Willem de Clercq naar zijn dagboek* (Haarlem: N.p., 1888), 2:138.
70. Groen, *Briefwisseling*, 1:694.
71. Pierson, *Willem de Clercq naar zijn dagboek*, 2:111–12.
72. G. Groen van Prinsterer, ed., *Brieven van Mr. Isaac da Costa* (Amsterdam: Höveker & Zoon, 1872), 1:1. Groen notes that his first meeting with Da Costa took place in the spring of 1830. However, we follow the dating of De Clercq, who described this meeting in his diary of 17 November 1829. Groen probably erred (forty years later) in reproducing the date.
73. Groen, *Verspreide Geschriften*, 1:75.
74. Quoted in H. T. Colenbrander, *Willem I. Koning der Nederlanden* (Amsterdam: Meulenhoff, 1935), 304.
75. Groen, *Briefwisseling*, 1:236.
76. Groen, *Briefwisseling*, 1:155.
77. Groen, *Briefwisseling*, 1:191.
78. Groen, *Briefwisseling*, 1:230.
79. Cf. for example, his opinion of November 1829, included in Groen, *Verspreide Geschriften*, 1:70–81.
80. Groen, *Verspreide Geschriften*, 1:81.
81. A. Smits, *1830 Scheuring in de Nederlanden*, deel 3 (1999), 99.
82. Groen, *Briefwisseling*, 1:252.
83. *Nederlandsche Gedachten*, I, 27 February 1830.
84. *Nederlandsche Gedachten*, II, 24 April 1830.
85. Groen, *Brieven Da Costa*, 1:1–4.
86. Pierson, *Willem de Clercq naar zijn dagboek*, 2:138. The Dutch envoy J. G. Verstolk van Soelen wrote to the king on May 8 that *the Nederlandsche Gedachten* was too much set on the position of the "old republic" and needed to rise to a "broader position." Groen, *Briefwisseling* 5:785.
87. *Nederlandsche Gedachten* II, 8 September 1830.
88. Groen, *Briefwisseling*, 1:339.
89. Groen, *Briefwisseling*, 1:340.
90. *Nederlandsche Gedachten* II, 30 September 1830.
91. *Nederlandsche Gedachte*n II, 3 November 1830.
92. Groen, *Briefwisseling*, 1:503.

Endnotes

93. *Nederlandsche Gedachten* II, 19 February 1831.
94. Groen, *Briefwisseling*, 1:490–91.
95. Groen, *Verspreide Geschriften*, 1:121–54.
96. *Nederlandsche Gedachten*, III, 27 September 1831.
97. *Nederlandsche Gedachten*, III, 26 March 1831.
98. J. C. H. de Pater, "Burke en Groen van Prinsterer," in *Stemmen des Tijds* 14 (Utrecht, 1925), 99.
99. Cf. B. Woelderink, "Groen van Prinsterer's First Years at the Royal Archives (1831–1841)," *Jaarboek Oranje-Nassau Museum* (1993), 93–101.
100. Groen, *Briefwisseling*, 1:501.
101. Groen to Van Assen, 20 December 1831; Groen, *Briefwisseling*, 1:518.
102. *Is het goed niet bevreesd voor de cholera te zijn?* (The Hague: Roering, 1832); reprinted in Groen, *Verspreide Geschriften*, 2:136–39. Offprints appeared in Amsterdam and Rotterdam. Ms. in Groen Archive, nr. 23. Cf. Groen, *Briefwisseling*, 1:583.
103. Groen, *Verspreide Geschriften*, 2:136.
104. John 11:25–26.
105. Groen, *Verspreide Geschriften*, 2:139.
106. Betsy Groen to Willem de Clercq, 28 December 1832; Groen, *Briefwisseling*, 1:647.
107. Betsy Groen to Willem de Clercq, 27 June 1832; Groen, *Briefwisseling*, 1:578.
108. Betsy Groen to Willem de Clercq, 17 January 1833; Collection De Clercq, Réveil Archives.
109. Betsy Groen to Willem de Clercq, 19 January 1833; Collection De Clercq.
110. Betsy Groen to Willem de Clercq, 12 February 1833; Collection De Clercq.
111. Betsy Groen to Willem de Clercq, 27 January 1833; Groen, *Briefwisseling*, 1:648.
112. Betsy Groen to Willem de Clercq, 10, 11, 15, 19, and 23 January 1833; Collection De Clercq.
113. Betsy Groen to Willem de Clercq, 18 February 1833; Collection De Clercq.
114. Groen to Willem de Clercq, 8 March 1833; Collection De Clercq.
115. Groen to Willem de Clercq, 14 April 1833; Collection De Clercq.
116. G. Groen van Prinsterer, *Al dan niet volharden?* [*Persist, or not?*]; response to a memorandum of the minister of Foreign Affairs, 25 September 1833; in Groen, *Verspreide Geschriften*, 2:106–20, at 114.
117. Groen, *Verspreide Geschriften*, 2:116, 118.
118. Groen, *Verspreide Geschriften*, 2:119.
119. Van Assen to Groen, 10 November 1833; Groen, *Briefwisseling*, 2:711.
120. Groen to De Clercq, 6 December 1833; Collection De Clercq.
121. De Mey van Streefkerk to Groen, 8 December 1833; Groen, *Briefwisseling*, 1:721.
122. G. Groen van Prinsterer, *Proeve over de middelen waardoor de waarheid wordt gekend en gestaafd* [*Essay on the Means by Which Truth Is Known and Confirmed*], (Leiden: Luchtmans, 1834), xii, 217, at xi.
123. *Proeve over de middelen waardoor de waarheid wordt gekend en gestaafd*, xi.
124. *Proeve over de middelen waardoor de waarheid wordt gekend en gestaafd*, vi.

125. Hereafter cited as *Essay on Truth*. For ease of reading, citations throughout the present work will use English equivalents of the titles of Groen's works, even though no published English translations exist (except for *Unbelief and Revolution*).
126. Quoted in M. E. Kluit, "Uit de briefwisseling van C. M. van der Kemp (1799-1861) en H. J. Koenen (1809-1874)," *Bijdragen en Mededelingen van het Historisch Genootschap* 63 (1942) 1-290, at 60. Hereafter cited as "Briefwisseling Van der Kemp-Koenen."
127. G. Groen van Prinsterer, *Proeve over de middelen waardoor de waarheid wordt gekend en gestaafd*, 2nd ed. (Amsterdam: Höveker, 1858), xii, 96.
128. Groen, *Essay on Truth*, 97-98, note.
129. G. Groen van Prinsterer, *Ongeloof en Revolutie; eene reeks van historische voorlezingen* [*Unbelief and Revolution: A Series of Historical Lectures*] (Leiden: Luchtmans, 1847), 35.
130. Reference to the "Overzigt" [Overview], in Groen, *Verspreide Geschriften*, 1:147.
131. Groen, *Essay on Truth*, 5.
132. Groen, *Essay on Truth*, 6.
133. Groen, *Essay on Truth*, 26.
134. Groen, *Essay on Truth*, 43.
135. Groen, *Essay on Truth*, 74.
136. It was the Leyden professor of theology Joannes Clarisse who expressed his surprise in a conversation with H. J. Koenen; see Koenen to Groen, mid September 1834; Groen, *Briefwisseling*, 2:86.
137. Groen, *Essay on Truth*, 92n2.
138. Groen quotes Hegel in French, using Victor Cousin's *Fragments philosophiques pour servir à l'histoire de la philosophie* (Paris, 1829); see Groen, *Essay on Truth*, 77.
139. Cf. Jacob Klapwijk, "Calvin and Neo-Calvinism on Non-Christian Philosophy," *Philosophia Reformata* 38 (1973) 43-61, at 49-51.
140. Groen, *Essay on Truth*, 76.
141. Groen, *Essay on Truth*, 84.
142. Groen, *Essay on Truth*, 85-91.
143. Groen, *Essay on Truth*, 172-75.
144. Groen, *Essay on Truth*, 108-23, 138-42.
145. Prof. Jan Bake to Groen, 16 March 1835; Groen, *Briefwisseling*, 2:113.
146. See Groen, *Briefwisseling*, 2:81-82, 112-14, 115-16, 125-27.
147. Groen to Koenen, 25 August 1834; Groen, *Briefwisseling*, 2:83.
148. Ph. W. van Heusde, *De Socratische school, of wijsbegeerte voor de negentiende eeuw* [*The Socratic School, or Philosophy for the Nineteenth Century*], 4 vols. (Utrecht: Altheer, 1834-39).
149. Cf. Ronald van Raak, *In naam van het volmaakte; conservatisme in Nederland in de 19de eeuw: van Gerrit Jan Mulder tot Jan Heemskerk Azn* [*On Behalf of Perfection: Conservatism in the Netherlands in the 19th century from Gerrit Jan Mulder to Jan Heemskerk Azn*], diss., City University of Amsterdam (Amsterdam: Wereldbibliotheek, 2001), 29 ff.
150. Groen to Van Assen, 8 December 1834; Groen, *Briefwisseling*, 2:101-2.

Endnotes

151. Da Costa to Groen, 24 July 1834; in Groen, *Brieven van Da Costa*, 1:11.
152. Koenen to Groen, 30 July 1834; Groen, *Briefwisseling*, 2:79.
153. This would become apparent in 1837 when he attacked Groen's public defense of the Secession from the national church; cf. P. A. Diepenhorst, *Groen van Prinsterer*, 1st ed. (Kampen: Kok, 1932), 235.
154. G. Groen van Prinsterer, ed., *Archives ou Correspondance inédite de la Maison d'Orange-Nassau*, 9 vols. (Leiden: Luchtmans, 1835–47).
155. Groen *Archives ou Correspondance inédite de la Maison d'Orange-Nassau*, 1:viii.
156. Elout visited Switzerland as early as 1827 and in 1835 would marry the Swiss lady Elisabeth Henriëtte, comtesse de St. George; cf. B. de Gaay Fortman, "Jhr. Mr. Pieter Jacob Elout van Soeterwoude (1805–1893)," *Antirevolutionaire Staatkunde* 11 (1938) 46–103, reprinted in Fortman, *Figuren uit het Réveil* (Kampen: Kok, 1980), 315–88, at 320.
157. Namely, the Belgic Confession (1561), the Heidelberg Catechism (1564), and the Canons of Dordt (1619).
158. A. Ypey and I. J. Dermout, *Geschiedenis der Nederlandsche Hervormde Kerk*, 4 vols. (Breda: Van Bergen, 1819–27).
159. C. M. van der Kemp, *De eere der Nederlandsche Hervormde Kerk gehandhaafd tegen Ypey en Dermout*, 3 vols. (Rotterdam: Van der Meer & Verbruggen, 1830–33).
160. Betsy Groen to De Clercq, 23 December 1833; Collection De Clercq.
161. Reference to collections of sermons and devotional works written by Theodorus and Wilhelmus B. Brakel (father and son), Bernardus Smytegelt, Theodorus van der Groe, Abraham Hellenbroek, Jacob Koelman, Jodocus van Lodensteyn, Willem Teellinck, and others, and also translations of the writings of Scottish and English divines such as the Erskine brothers and John Bunyan.
162. Betsy Groen to De Clercq, 18 December 1833; Collection De Clercq.
163. Koenen to Groen, 22 October 1834; Groen, *Briefwisseling*, 2:89–90.
164. Cf. Groen to Koenen, 14 November 1834; Groen, *Briefwisseling*, 2:96. See also the exchange of letters between Groen and Scholte in Groen, *Briefwisseling*, 6:715–19 [1844–46].
165. Kluit, *Het protestantse Réveil*, 401. See also Groen to P. J. Groen, 31 March 1834; Groen, *Briefwisseling*, 2:49–53, at 52; Groen to P. J. Groen, 5 May 1835; Groen, *Briefwisseling*, 2:116.
166. Betsy Groen to De Clercq, 21 September 1834; Collection De Clercq.
167. Van der Kemp to Koenen, quoted in Kluit, "Briefwisseling Van der Kemp–Koenen," 62–63.
168. He corrected many details found particularly in Leo's *Zwölf Bücher Niederländischer Geschichte*, 2 vols. (Halle: Anton, 1832, 1835).
169. G. Groen van Prinsterer, "Reis in Frankrijk en Duitschland, voor het Huisarchief des Konings" ["Journey in France and Germany in Behalf of the King's Family Archive"], in *Verspreide Geschriften*, 2:263–80, at 269. See also W. H. de Savornin Lohman, ed., *Groen's reis naar Parijs en Besançon in 1836 ten behoeve der Archieven* [*Groen's Journey to Paris and Besancon in 1836 for the Sake of the Archives*], *Bijdragen en Mededelingen van het Historisch Genootschap* 42 (1921) 1–106, at 37–38 and 48–49.

170. Cousin's report of his journey is contained in his *De l'instruction publique en Holland* (Paris, 1837).
171. Betsy Groen to De Clercq, 14 June 1836. Reveilarchief Amsterdam.
172. Betsy Groen to De Clercq, 14 June 1836; Collection De Clercq.
173. Da Costa to Groen, 20 February 1835; Groen, *Brieven van Da Costa*, 1:13.
174. Willem Bilderdijk, *Geschiedenis des Vaderlands*, ed. H. W. Tydeman, 13 vols. (Leiden: Warnars, 1832–53). Defying historical consensus, the work suffered from hyperbole and unsubstantiated verdicts.
175. See Da Costa to Groen, 1 August 1835; Groen, *Brieven van Da Costa*, 1:15.
176. Betsy Groen to De Clercq, March 1837; Collection De Clercq.
177. See J. Steur, "De geldelijke nalatenschap van Groen van Prinsterer" ["The Financial Estate of Groen van Prinsterer"], *Tot Vrijheid Geroepen* 22 (1976) 78–87, at 83.
178. Betsy Groen to De Clercq, 29 August 1837; Collection De Clercq.
179. Betsy Groen to De Clercq, 29 October 1837; Collection De Clercq.
180. The commemorative stone that was attached to it in 1884 and is still visible today has the wrong date: not 1838 but 1837 was the year that launched this new phase in the life of the Groens.
181. A description is found in N. Cramer et al., *Het Kabinet der Koningin; geschiedenis van het instituut en het huis aan de Korte Vijverberg* [*The Queen's Cabinet: History of the Institution and the House Along the Korte Vijverberg*] (The Hague: Monumentenzorg Gemeente's-Gravenhage, 1991), 102–10.
182. About the Secession, see Gerrit J. Schutte, *Het Calvinistisch Nederland; mythe en werkelijkheid* (Hilversum: Verloren, 2000), 105–24; Gerrit J. TenZythoff, *Sources of Secession: The Netherlands Hervormde Kerk on the Eve of the Dutch Immigration to the American Midwest* (Grand Rapids: Eerdmans, 1987).
183. Cf. Janet Sjaarda Sheeres, *Son of Secession: Douwe J. Vander Werp* (Grand Rapids: Eerdmans, 2006).
184. Expressions used by King William in a conversation with a retired diplomat; see *Gedenkschriften van A. R. Falck* [*Memoirs of A. R. Falck*], ed. H. T. Colenbrander (The Hague: Nijhoff, 1913), 657.
185. See chapter 2.
186. *Gedenkschriften van A. R. Falck* (n[X-REF] above).
187. Groen to King William, 23 March 1837; Groen, *Briefwisseling*, 2:192.
188. G. Groen van Prinsterer, *De Maatregelen tegen de Afgescheidenen aan het Staatsregt getoetst* (Leiden: Luchtmans, 1837). The pamphlet saw two reprints that same year and was favorably reviewed by Heinrich Leo in the Berliner Politisches Wochenblatt of 3 February, 1838. I refer to this work as *Measures Against the Seceders*.
189. Groen to King William, 13 July 1837; Groen, *Briefwisseling*, 2:199.
190. Van Assen to Thorbecke, 9 August 1837; in G. J. Hooijkaas, ed., *De Briefwisseling van J. R. Thorbecke*, 7 vols. (The Hague: Nijhoff, 1975–2002), 3:61. Hereafter cited as *Briefwisseling van Thorbecke*.
191. Groen to King William, 17 July 1837; Groen, *Briefwisseling*, 5:85.
192. G. Groen van Prinsterer, *De Maatregelen tegen de Afgescheidenen*; reprinted in Groen, *Verspreide Geschriften*, 2:1–48, at 1–2.

Endnotes

193. Groen, *Verspreide Geschriften*, 2:5.
194. Groen, *Verspreide Geschriften*, 2:10.
195. Groen, *Verspreide Geschriften*, 2:19.
196. Groen, *Verspreide Geschriften*, 2:43.
197. Groen, *Verspreide Geschriften*, 2:31.
198. Groen, *Verspreide Geschriften*, 2:31–32.
199. A. W. van Appeltere, *Het Staatsregt in Nederland, vooral met betrekking tot de kerk, en de handelingen der regeering ten opzigte der Afgescheidenen, nader toegelicht* [*Elucidation of Dutch constitutional law in particular with regard to the church, and the government measures with respect to the Seceders*] (The Hague and Amsterdam: Van Cleef, 1837), ii.
200. Van Appeltere was allowed to make use of the notes of Minister Van Maanen; cf. *Briefwisseling van Thorbecke*, 3:85.
201. G. Groen van Prinsterer, "Droit publique ecclésiastique; réponse aux articles communiqués, insérés dans le Journal de la Haye du 9, 10 et 11–12 Septembre," *Journal de La Haye*, 23 September 1837; the exchange continued in the *Journal* of 27 and 28 September and 1 October (Thorbecke) and 7 October (Groen). Groen reprinted his responses under the title "Antikritiek" in *Verspreide Geschriften*, 2:49–77.
202. Groen, *Verspreide Geschriften*, 2:52.
203. Groen, *Verspreide Geschriften*, 2:53.
204. Groen, *Verspreide Geschriften*, 2:60.
205. Thorbecke to Groen, 7 October 1837; Groen, *Briefwisseling*, 2:218.
206. Groen to Thorbecke, 8 October 1837; Groen, *Briefwisseling*, 2:219.
207. *De Reformatie; tijdschrift ter bevordering van Gods Koningrijk in Nederland* [*The Reformation: Journal for the Promotion of God's Kingdom in the Netherlands*], Amsterdam, 1841–47.
208. Groen to Koenen, 23 November 1837; Groen, *Briefwisseling*, 2:223.
209. Koenen to Groen, 23 April 1840; Groen to Koenen, 26 April 1840; Groen, *Briefwisseling*, 2:313–15.
210. Betsy Groen to De Clercq, January 1839; Collection De Clercq.
211. Betsy Groen to De Clercq, 21 November 1843; Collection De Clercq.
212. *Nederlandsche Stemmen over godsdienst, staat-, geschied- en letterkunde* [*Netherlandic voices on religion, politics, history and literature*] (1834–38), a weekly, later a monthly, successively edited by Da Costa, Koenen, Van Hall, and De Clercq.
213. Van Assen to Groen, ca. 10 March 1835; Groen, *Briefwisseling*, 2:110.
214. Da Costa to Groen, 26 September 1837; Groen, *Brieven van Da Costa*, 1:36.
215. Cousin, *De l'Instruction publique en Hollande*, 9.
216. Quoted in I. J. Brugmans, *Thorbecke*, 2nd rev. ed. (Haarlem: Bohn, 1948), 55.
217. J. R. Thorbecke, *Aanteekeningen op de grondwet* (Amsterdam: Müller, 1839).
218. Groen to De Clercq, 5 December 1839; Groen, *Briefwisseling*, 2:284.
219. Groen to Van Assen, 23 December 1845; Groen, *Briefwisseling*, 2:717. This was extra painful in view of the fact that in a public lecture in 1842 Groen had spoken extensively about the plans for such a statue; cf. G. Groen van Prinsterer, *Willem*

Endnotes

1, gelijk hij uit zijne briefwisseling nader gekend wordt [*William 1 upon Closer Acquaintance Through His Correspondence*] (Amsterdam: Müller, 1843), 27; reprinted in Groen, *Verspreide Geschriften*, 2:298–318.

220. J. J. van Straalen to Groen, 9 December 1838; Pieces regarding the Royal Archive, Koninklijk Huisarchief, 35 xxii–94.

221. This is also apparent from the correspondence file of the Koninklijk Huisarchief, which deals with only the most important matters. The years in the Binnenhof were the most inactive ones for the Family Archives.

222. Groen, *Verspreide Geschriften*, 2:8.

223. Cousin, *De l'Instruction publique en Hollande*, 223.

224. Groen to Koenen, 29 January 1837; Groen, *Briefwisseling*, 2:185–84.

225. Cf. Charles L. Glenn, Jr., *The Myth of the Common School* (Amherst: University of Massachusetts Press, 1988).

226. G. Groen van Prinsterer, "Nota" [minority report education, dated 24 December. 1840]; *Verspreide Geschriften*, 2:157–80, at 162.

227. G. Groen van Prinsterer, *Bijdrage tot herziening der Grondwet in Nederlandschen zin* [*Contribution Toward a Constitutional Revision in a Netherlandic Spirit*] (Leiden: Luchtmans, 1840), 89. Reprinted, with slight revisions, in *Verspreide Geschriften*, 1:155–253, at 212.

228. See previous note.

229. Groen, *Verspreide Geschriften*, 1:224.

230. Groen to Van Assen, 1 April 1840; Groen, *Briefwisseling*, 2:312.

231. G. Groen van Prinsterer, *Adviezen in de Tweede Kamer der Staten-Generaal, in dubbelen getale* [*Parliamentary Speeches in the Double Chamber*] (Leiden: Luchtmans, 1840), 45.

232. Groen, *Adviezen in de Tweede Kamer der Staten-Generaal, in dubbelen getale*, 46.

233. Van der Kemp to Koenen, August 1840; in Kluit, "Briefwisseling Van der Kemp–Koenen," 214.

234. Groen, *Adviezen* (1840), 80–81.

235. Groen, *Adviezen* (1840), 57.

236. Groen, *Adviezen* (1840), 81.

237. Groen, *Verspreide Geschriften*, 1:218–19.

238. Groen, *Briefwisseling*, 3:559. The theme came up again as late as 1860 in correspondence with the Catholic poet and editor Thijm; see Joseph Albert Alberdingk Thijm to Groen, 7 December 1860; Groen, *Briefwisseling*, 3:455. Cf. J. H. J. M. Witlox, "Groen van Prinsterer," in *Varia Historica* (Hertogenbosch: Teulings, 1936), 114.

239. Betsy Groen to De Clercq, 26 December 1840; Collection De Clercq.

240. Heldring to Groen, 14 November 1840; Groen, *Briefwisseling*, 2:336.

241. There was no compulsory school attendance at this time.

242. Van der Brugghen to Groen, 6 December 1840; Groen, *Briefwisseling*, 2:353.

243. W. H. Warnsinck Bzn. to Groen, 4 December 1840; Groen, *Briefwisseling*, 2:351.

244. Theodorus van Swinderen to Groen, 16 December 1840; Groen, *Briefwisseling*, 2:357.

Endnotes

245. G. Groen van Prinsterer, "Discussiën in de staatscommissie" (1840–41), in *Bescheiden*, 1:598–661, at 622–28, 658–59.
246. Groen, *Bescheiden*, 1:648.
247. Groen, "Nota," in *Verspreide Geschriften*, 2:162–68.
248. Groen, *Bescheiden*, 1:648.
249. Groen to Van Assen, 15 February 1841; Groen, *Briefwisseling*, 2:375–76.
250. Groen, *Briefwisseling*, 2:376.
251. W. Bilderdijk, *Geschiedenis des Vaderlands*, 12 vols.
252. Kluit, "Briefwisseling Van der Kemp–Koenen," 153–54.
253. Da Costa to Groen, n.d. [ca. August 1841]; Groen, *Brieven van Da Costa*, 1:71.
254. G. Groen van Prinsterer, *Handboek der Geschiedenis van het Vaderland*, in 5 installments (Leiden: Luchtmans, 1841–46). Reprinted 1852; rev. ed. 1872; repr. 1875, 1876, 1895, 1928; last reprint, in 2 vols., by Uitgeverij Kool, Veenendaal, 1978.
255. Thus C. W. Opzoomer, *Onze godsdienst [Our Religion]* (Amsterdam: n.p., 1874), 113.
256. *Briefwisseling van Thorbecke*, 4:58.
257. Thus H. Smitskamp, *Groen van Prinsterer als historicus [Groen van Prinsterer as an Historian]* (Amsterdam: H. J. Paris, 1940), 88, who similarly overlooks Groen's educational objective.
258. G. Groen van Prinsterer, *Kort Overzigt van de Geschiedenis des Vaderlands [Compendium of the History of the Fatherland]* (Leiden: Luchtmans, 1841), iii–iv.
259. Betsy Groen to De Clercq, 23 December 1841; Collection De Clercq.
260. Da Costa to Groen, n.d. [ca. August 1841]; Groen, *Brieven van Da Costa*, 1:71.
261. A. J. van Lummel, *Register op het Handboek der Geschiedenis van het Vaderland van Mr. G. Groen van Prinsterer* (Utrecht: Kemink, 1877).
262. Groen, *Handboek*, §84.
263. Groen, *Handboek*, §104.
264. Groen, *Handboek*, §106.
265. Groen, *Handboek*, §1.
266. See M. te Velde, "Het Schriftgebruik in Groens Handboek der geschiedenis van het vaderland" ["The Use of Scripture in Groen's Handboek"], in G. Harinck en R. Kuiper, eds., *Groen van Prinsterer en de geschiedenis* (Kampen: Kok, 1994), 39–59, at 42.
267. Groen, *Handboek*, preface and §86.
268. The sentence fragment became one of his stylistic traits in later years; cf. Herbert Donald Morton, "'A Christian Heroism': Elements of the Style of Guillaume Groen van Prinsterer," in J. L. van Essen and H. Donald Morton, *Guillaume Groen van Prinsterer: Selected Studies* (Jordan Station, ON: Wedge, 1990), 101–9. This collection contains "Guillaume Groen van Prinsterer and His Conception of History" plus three other essays on Groen's struggle for Christian education as well as a special essay on Groen's prose style.
269. Ps 78:7.
270. Cf. minutes of the Weeshuis [directors of the orphanage], Archives of Waals-Hervormde Gemeente, The Hague.

Endnotes

271. Betsy Groen to De Clercq, 18 April 1840; Collection De Clercq.
272. Ms. notes, Groen Archive, nr. 44.
273. See the appellants' petition of 1846 to the king, reprinted in Groen, *Verspreide Geschriften*, 2:181–89.
274. Merle d'Aubigné to Groen van Prinsterer, 4 February 1840; Groen Archive, nr. 124A6.
275. C. A. Hoffmann née Groen van Prinsterer to Groen, 13 December 1839; Groen Archive, nr. 124A1.
276. C. A. Hoffmann née Groen van Prinsterer to Groen, 13 December 1839; Groen Archive, nr. 124A1.
277. Groen, *Bescheiden*, 1:648. He uses this formulation several times as he sketches his ideal of the Christian school.
278. Groen, *Handboek*, §239.
279. Groen to Da Costa, 5 February 1844; Groen, *Brieven van Da Costa*, 1:147.
280. Groen to Da Costa, 18 February 1844; Groen, *Brieven van Da Costa*, 1:150.
281. Groen to J. Hora Siccama, 28 February 1844; Groen Archive, nr. 124A7.
282. Betsy Groen to De Clercq, 23 December 1841; Collection De Clercq.
283. See Groen, *Briefwisseling*, 5:141–44.
284. Groen to Bodel Nijenhuis, 6 February 1846; Groen, *Briefwisseling*, 2:727. Groen relates that the second meeting of the Christian Friends, held the week before, had been attended by forty-two persons.
285. Koenen to Groen, 10 March 1846; Groen, *Briefwisseling*, 2:731. Koenen reports having read this in the British journal *The Witness* of 28 February 1846.
286. Beets to Groen, 19 November 1847; Groen, *Briefwisseling*, 2:843–44.
287. *De Vereeniging: Christelijke Stemmen*, Amsterdam, 1846–75. We will translate the name of this journal as *Christian Voices*.
288. Groen to Bodel Nijenhuis, 4 December 1845; Groen, *Briefwisseling*, 2:715.
289. Regarding the audience, see Harry Van Dyke, *Groen van Prinsterer's Lectures on Unbelief and Revolution* (Jordan Station, ON: Wedge), 139–50.
290. G. Groen van Prinsterer, *Ongeloof en Revolutie; eene reeks van historische voorlezingen* [*Unbelief and Revolution: A Series of Historical Lectures*] (Leiden: Luchtmans, 1847); rev. ed. (Amsterdam: Höveker, 1868). For an English abridgment, see Dyke, *Groen van Prinsterer's Lectures*, 293–539.
291. Cf. my "'Geen muziek om van het blad te zingen [No Music for Sight-Reading]': Groen van Prinsterer's *Ongeloof en Revolutie* (1847)," in F. G. M. Broeyer and D. Th. Kuiper, eds., *Is 't waar of niet? Ophefmakende publicaties uit de "lange" negentiende eeuw* (Zoetermeer: Meinema, 2005), 111–31.
292. Gefken, *Herinneringen* [*Memoirs*]; Réveil Archives, Collection J. W. Gefken.
293. Groen, *Ongeloof en Revolutie* (1847), 5.
294. Groen, *Ongeloof en Revolutie*, 26.
295. About this ahistorical element in the revolution and Enlightenment thought: J. A. Schlebusch *Strategic Narratives: Groen van Prinsterer as Nineteenth-Century Statesman-Historian* (University of Groningen, 2018), 110.

Endnotes

296. Groen, *Ongeloof en Revolutie*, xi.
297. Groen, *Ongeloof en Revolutie*, 319.
298. Groen, *Ongeloof en Revolutie*, 416–17.
299. Groen, *Ongeloof en Revolutie*, 420.
300. Groen, *Ongeloof en Revolutie*, 179.
301. Groen, *Ongeloof en Revolutie*, 423; see also 271.
302. Groen, *Ongeloof en Revolutie*, 43.
303. Groen, *Ongeloof en Revolutie*, 43.
304. Groen, *Ongeloof en Revolutie*, 51.
305. This quotation was circulated in occupied Holland during World War II and persuaded many Reformed people that resistance to the Nazi authorities was permissible, if not obligatory.
306. Groen, *Ongeloof en Revolutie*, 26.
307. Groen, *Ongeloof en Revolutie*, 224.
308. Groen, *Ongeloof en Revolutie*, 68, 83.
309. Groen, *Ongeloof en Revolutie*, 423.
310. Mackay to Groen, 26 August 1847; Groen, *Briefwisseling*, 2:810.
311. The "Mackay Notebook" is now deposited in the Free University Library in Amsterdam.
312. G. Groen van Prinsterer, "Over het gestadig protest der wetenschap tegen het staatsregt der Revolutie" ["On the Continuous Protest of Science Against the Political Theory of the Revolution"], *Christelijke Stemmen* [*Christian Voices*] 1 (1846–47) 1–9, 65–71, 129–34. Later that year he contributed "Het goddelijk regt der Overheid" ["The Divine Right of Government"], 747–55.
313. Wormser to Groen, 7 October 1847; Groen, *Brieven van Wormser*, 1:96.
314. See for the history of editions: Kuiper, "'Geen muziek om van het blad te zingen,'" 211–12. One of these editions was issued by Herman Bavinck. See James Eglinton, *Bavinck: A Critical Biography* (Grand Rapids: Baker Academic, 2005), 230–231.
315. Beets to Groen, 8 September 1847; Groen, *Briefwisseling*, 2:812.
316. Prince William III of Orange is known in British history as King William I for his role in the Glorious Revolution of 1688–89 and his subsequent reign with his consort Mary Stuart, daughter of King James II.
317. Groen wrote a French summary of the work under the title *Le parti anti-révolutionnaire et confessionnel dans l'Église réformée des Pays-Bas* (Amsterdam: Höveker, 1860), esp. 31–81.
318. G. Groen van Prinsterer, *Het regt der Hervormde Gezindheid* (Amsterdam: Müller, 1848).
319. G. Groen van Prinsterer, *Vrijheid, gelijkheid, broederschap; toelichting van de spreuk der Revolutie* [*Liberty, Equality, Fraternity: Elucidation of the Motto of the Revolution*] (The Hague: Roering, 1848); reprinted in *Verspreide Geschriften*, 1:254–326.
320. G. Groen van Prinsterer, *Grondwetherziening en eensgezindheid* [*Constitutional Revision and National Concord*] (Amsterdam: Müller, 1849), in nine installments.
321. Groen to Rev. H. J. Veldwijk, 4 February 1848; Groen, *Briefwisseling*, 2:863.

322. Groen to Mackay, 11 October 1847; Groen, *Briefwisseling*, 5:161.
323. Groen, *Essay on Truth*, 60.
324. Groen, *Het regt der Hervormde Gezindheid*, 46.
325. Groen, *Het regt der Hervormde Gezindheid*, 28.
326. Bos, *In dienst van het Koninkrijk*, 122.
327. Groen, *Het regt der Hervormde Gezindheid*, 1.
328. G. Groen van Prinsterer, "Over het verwijt van werkeloosheid aan de Christenen in de kerk," *Christelijke Stemmen* [*Christian Voices*] 1 (1846–47) 469–90, at 471.
329. Groen, "Over het verwijt van werkeloosheid aan de Christenen in de kerk," 471.
330. Groen, *Ongeloof en Revolutie*, 59.
331. Koenen to Groen, 31 August 1847; Groen, *Briefwisseling*, 2:810.
332. Groen to Koenen, 4 September 1847; Groen, *Briefwisseling*, 2:811.
333. Beets to Groen, 26 March 1848; Groen, *Briefwisseling*, 2:867; see also 836, 848, 851, 859, and 862.
334. Cf. D. P. D. Fabius, *Het Reglement van '52* (Amsterdam: n.p., 1888), 171.
335. R. B. Evenhuis, *Ook dat was Amsterdam*, 5 vols. (Amsterdam: Ten Have, 1965–78), 5:281.
336. "Lake Harlem" is today the home of many farms as well as Schiphol International Airport.
337. To wit, Jan Adriaensz. Leeghwater (1575–1650), Nicolaus Samuel Cruquius (1678–1758), and Frans Godard baron van Lijnden van Hemmen (1761–1845).
338. Cf. Jan de Vries, *Barges and Capitalism: Passenger Transportation in the Dutch Economy, 1632–1839* (Utrecht: Studia Historica, 1981), 201–7.
339. H. J. Broers, "De cholera," in J. P. de Keyser, *Neerland's Letterkunde in de negentiende eeuw; bloemlezing ten gebruike bij de beoefening onzer letterkunde* [*Dutch Literature in the Nineteenth Century: Anthology for Use in the Study of Our Literature*], 2 vols. (The Hague: Thieme, 1877), 1:688–94.
340. Groen, *Grondwetherziening en eensgezindheid*, 41.
341. Cf. the parallel drawn by James C. Kennedy in his study of the 1960s: *Building New Babylon: Cultural Change in the Netherlands During the 1960s* (Diss., University of Iowa, 1994).
342. Quoted in de Keijser, *Neerland's letterkunde in de negentiende eeuw*, 2:702. "Bij 't dagen van d'orkaan, die Koningen deed vlieden, / Gezeteld op den Troon van 't Nederlandsche Volk, / Weet hij, met kloek beleid, den storm het hoofd te bieden / En stoot de Hydra neer in 's afgronds gruwelkolk."
343. Groen to Aeneas Mackay, 4 November 1848; Groen, *Briefwisseling*, 5:184.
344. J. P. Duyverman, *Uit de geheime dagboeken van Aeneas Mackay, dienaar des Konings (1806–1876)* [*From the Secret Journals of Aeneas Mackay, Minister of the King*] (Houten: De Haan, 1987), 40.
345. Groen, *Grondwetherziening en eensgezindheid*, 33.
346. Isaac da Costa, *Het Oogenblik; een woord over het "Ontwerp van Grondwetherziening"* [*The Moment: A Word About the Proposed Constitutional Revision*] (Amsterdam: N.p., 1848), 4–6.
347. Koenen, *Autobiografie*, 154; Réveil Archives, Collection Koenen.

Endnotes

348. Da Costa to Mackay, undated; Algemeen Rijksarchief, Collection Mackay, nr. 312.

349. See also Roel Kuiper, *Zelfbeeld en wereldbeeld: Antirevolutionairen en het buitenland, 1848–1905* [*Self-Identity and Worldview: Antirevolutionaries and International Affairs, 1848–1905*], diss., Free University of Amsterdam (Kampen: Kok, 1992), 42ff.

350. Groen to Da Costa, 28 May 1848; Groen, *Brieven van Da Costa*, 1:320.

351. Groen to Da Costa, 23 June 1848; Groen, *Brieven van Da Costa*, 1:323.

352. Groen, *Grondwetherziening en eensgezindheid*, 1–556, at 50. The tract was dedicated "To the Voters of Districts Gorinchem and Harderwijk."

353. Groen to Da Costa, 29 September 1848; Groen, *Brieven van Da Costa*, 1:345.

354. Groen, *Grondwetherziening en eensgezindheid*, 58: it was not "heil belovend" but "onheilspellend."

355. Groen to Da Costa, 29 September 1848; Groen, *Brieven van Da Costa*, 1:345.

356. Cf. Groen, *Grondwetherziening en eensgezindheid*, 3; see also 84–92.

357. Boreel to Groen, 8 January 1849; Groen, *Briefwisseling*, 3:16.

358. Cf. D. J. Wolffram, *Bezwaarden en verlichten; verzuiling in een Gelderse provinciestad, Harderwijk 1850–1925* [*The Aggrieved and the Enlightened: Pillarization in Harderwijk, a Provincial Town in Gelderland, 1850–1925*], diss., City University of Amsterdam (Amsterdam: Het Spinhuis, 1993), 53ff.

359. C. A. Nairac to Groen, 14 November 1848; Groen, *Briefwisseling*, 3:4.

360. Queen Wilhelmina (1880–1963; r. 1898–1948).

361. Cf. Thys Booy, *Het is stil op het Loo; overpeinzingen in memoriam koningin Wilhelmina* [*All's Quiet at Loo Palace: Musings in Memory of Queen Wilhelmina*] (Amsterdam: Ten Have, 1963), 153.

362. Duyverman, *Uit de geheime dagboeken van Mackay*, 63.

363. G. Groen van Prinsterer, *De ministeriën De Kempenaer en Thorbecke, in hun politieke verwantschap beschouwd* [*The De Kempenaer and Thorbecke Ministries Viewed in Their Political Affinity*] (Amsterdam: Müller, 1849); reprinted in *Verscheidenheden over staatsregt en politiek* [*Sundry Writings About Constitutional Law and Politics*] (Amsterdam: Müller, 1850), 1:52.

364. *Briefwisseling van Thorbecke*, 4:11.

365. Cf. Jonathan Israel, *The Dutch Republic: Its Rise, Greatness and Fall, 1477–1806* (Oxford: Clarendon, 1998), 1067–121; Kossmann, *Low Countries, 1780–1940*, 34–47, 82–102; Schama, *Patriots and Liberators*, 100–210.

366. L. C. Suttorp, *F. A. van Hall en zijn constitutioneele beginselen* [*F. A. van Hall and His Constitutional Principles*], diss. Leyden (Amsterdam: H. J. Paris, 1932), 98.

367. Cf. D. P. D. Fabius, "Groen van Prinsterer over staatkundige partijen" ["Groen van Prinsterer on Political Parties"], in G. M. den Hartog, ed., *Schrift en Historie. Gedenkboek bij het vijftigjarig bestaan der georganiseerde Antirevolutionaire Partij, 1878–1928* [*Scripture and History; Memorial Book on the Occasion of the Fiftieth Anniversary of the Organized Antirevolutionary Party*] (Kampen: Kok, 1928), 214.

368. Cf. R. Kuiper, "Antirevolutionaire partijvorming en de grondwetswijziging van 1848" ["Antirevolutionary Party Formation and the Constitutional Revision of 1848"], in G. J. Schutte en J. Vree, eds., *Om de toekomst van het protestantse Nederland. De*

gevolgen van de grondwetsherziening van 1848 voor kerk, staat en maatschappij [*For the Future of Protestant Holland: The Consequences of the Constitutional Revision of 1848 for Church, State and Society*] (Zoetermeer: Meinema, 1998), 160.

369. Orig.: *"kiesverenigingen"*: associations of voters in electoral districts or ridings, usually active only during election campaigns; hereafter referred to as "voters' clubs."
370. Gefken, *Autobiografie*, 33; Réveil Archives, Collection Gefken.
371. N. Beets and A. H. Raabe, eds., *Bloemlezing uit de werken van mr. J. J. L. van der Brugghen* [*Anthology from the works of J. J. L. van der Brugghen*], 2 vols. (Nymegen: Ten Hoet, 1888-89), 2:320.
372. Quoted in Diepenhorst, *Groen van Prinsterer*, 1st ed., 350.
373. Cf. J. C. van der Does, *De vrijheid voorgestreên. Gedenkschrift ter gelegenheid van het eeuwfeest van de kiesvereniging 'Nederland en Oranje' te Amsterdam* [*Contending for Liberty; Memorial Book on the Occasion of the Centennial of the Amsterdam Voters' Club "Netherlands and Orange"*] (Hoorn: Edecea, 1950), 11.
374. Does, *De vrijheid voorgestreen*, 12.
375. Minutes of the Weeshuiscommissie [directors of the orphanage], 14 June 1852; Gemeentearchief, The Hague.
376. See also Da Costa to Betsy Groen, 9 July 1852; Groen, *Brieven van Da Costa*, 2:89.
377. Groen, *The Netherlander*, 8 September 1852; cf. Kuiper, *Zelfbeeld en wereldbeeld*, 54.
378. G. Groen van Prinsterer, *Adviezen in de Tweede Kamer der Staten-Generaal* [*Speeches in the Second Chamber of the States General*], 2 vols. (Utrecht: Kemink, 1856-57), 1:349-54, at 353 (Speech of 12 May 1851).
379. J. P. Duyverman, *Thorbecke debatteert; een bloemlezing* [*Thorbecke Debates: An Anthology*] (The Hague: V.U.G.A., 1988), 15.
380. J. Vree, "P. Hofstede de Groot," in J. de Bruijn et al., eds., *Geen heersende kerk, geen heersende staat; de verhouding tussen kerk en staat, 1796-1996* [*No dominant church, no dominant state: the relation between church and state, 1796-1996*] (Zoetermeer: Meinema, 1998), 262.
381. D. Langedijk, *Groen van Prinsterer en de schoolkwestie* [*Groen van Prinsterer and the Struggle for the Christian School*] (The Hague: Voorhoeve, 1947), 33.
382. Thus Rev. J. J. van Oosterzee to Groen, 28 September 1851; Groen, *Briefwisseling*, 3:86.
383. Via Elout van Soeterwoude; cf. Elout to Groen, 31 December 1849; Groen, *Briefwisseling*, 3:40.
384. Quoted in C. H. E. de Wit, *Thorbecke en de wording van de Nederlandse natie* [*Thorbecke and the Evolution of the Dutch Nation*] (Nymegen: S.U.N., 1980), 129.
385. Cf. J. C. Boogman, *Rondom 1848; de politieke ontwikkeling van Nederland, 1840-1858* [*In and Around 1848: The Political Development of the Netherlands, 1840-1858*] (Bussum: Unieboek, 1983), 127.
386. Raak, *In naam van het volmaakte*, 78.
387. Da Costa to Groen, Open Letter of August 1854; in Groen, *Brieven van Da Costa*, 2:206-74, at 240.
388. Groen to G. W. Vreede, 26 March 1853; Groen, *Briefwisseling*, 3:113.

Endnotes

389. R. J. Fruin, *Het antirevolutionaire staatsregt van Mr. Groen van Prinsterer ontvouwd en beoordeeld* (Amsterdam: Gebhard, 1853); repr. in R. J. Fruin, *Verspreide Geschriften*, 10:76–167.
390. Fruin, *Verspreide Geschriften*, 10:77.
391. J. Brouwer, *Het binnenste naar buiten; beginselen en activiteiten van mr. J. J. L. van der Brugghen* (1804–1863) [*Out with the Innermost: Principles and Activities of J. J. L. van der Brugghen*], diss., Nymegen (Zutphen: Walburg, 1981), 165.
392. Van Lynden to Groen, 10 May 1853; Groen, *Briefwisseling*, 3:122.
393. Van der Brugghen to Groen, 15 June 1854; Groen, *Briefwisseling*, 3:158.
394. Da Costa to Groen, August 1854; Groen, *Brieven van Da Costa*, 2:206–74, at 207.
395. A. C. Honders, *Doen en laten in Ernst en Vrede; notities over een Broederkring en een Tijdschrift* [*Action and Non-Action in Earnestness and Peace: Notes on a Brotherhood and a Periodical*], diss., City University of Amsterdam (The Hague: Boekencentrum, 1963).
396. Quoted in Honders, *Doen en laten in Ernst en Vrede*, 8.
397. *De Nederlander*, 15 August 1853. The sentence is a typical sample of Groen's style.
398. Wormser to Groen, 16 December 1850; Groen, *Brieven van Wormser*, 1:166.
399. Wormser to Groen, 11 March 1850; Groen, *Brieven van Wormser*, 1:115–16.
400. Wormser to Groen, 27 June 1852; Groen, *Brieven van Wormser*, 1:188, 3:101.
401. Wormser to Groen, July 1854; Groen, *Brieven van Wormser*, 2:81; see also Groen, *Brieven van Wormser*, 1:188.
402. Wormser to Groen, 27 August 1851; Groen, *Brieven van Wormser*, 2:238.
403. Van Toorenenbergen to Groen, 27 September 1854; Groen, *Briefwisseling*, 3:168.
404. Wormser to Groen, 13 December 1854; Groen, *Brieven van Wormser*, 2:138.
405. Cf. the title of his apologia, *Parti anti-révolutionnaire et confessionnel*.
406. Cf. Honders, *Doen en laten in Ernst en Vrede*, 113.
407. Groen to Da Costa, 13 February 1855; Groen, *Brieven van Da Costa*, 2:333.
408. Da Costa to Groen, 15 February 1855; Groen, *Brieven van Da Costa*, 2:338.
409. Wormser to Groen, 14 May 1855; Groen, *Brieven van Wormser*, 2:169.
410. Kemink to Groen, 12 June 1855; Groen, *Briefwisseling*, 3:192.
411. G. Groen van Prinsterer, *Narede van vijfjarigen strijd* (Utrecht: Kemink, 1855).
412. Van Raak, *In naam van het volmaakte*, 115–24.
413. De Geer to Groen, 1 October 1855; Groen, *Briefwisseling*, 3:205.
414. De Geer to Groen, 27 October 1855; Groen, *Briefwisseling*, 3:207–8.
415. Groen to De Geer; 4 January 1856; Groen, *Briefwisseling*, 3:214–15.
416. *Staatkundig en staathuishoudkundig jaarboekje* (Amsterdam, 1852), 31, and Groen, *Briefwisseling*, 3:46.
417. Van der Brugghen to Groen, 13 October 1854; Groen, *Briefwisseling*, 3:171.
418. Rev. L. J. van Rhijn to Groen, 20 December 1855; Groen, *Briefwisseling*, 3:213.
419. Brouwer, *Het binnenste naar buiten*, 177.

Endnotes

420. *Hoe de onderwijswet van 1857 tot stand kwam: historische bijdrage* [*How the Education Act of 1857 Came to Be: An Historical Contribution*], ed. G. Groen van Prinsterer (Amsterdam: Höveker, 1876), 12.
421. For the text of Groen's letter to Cousin, see his *Verspreide Geschriften*, 2:205–12.
422. Groen, *Adviezen in de Tweede Kamer* (1857), 2:172.
423. A. Goslinga, "Het conflict Groen–Van der Brugghen," in *Christendom en Historie; lustrumbundel van het Gezelschap van Christelijke Historici* (Amsterdam: Uitgeversmaatschappij Holland, 1925), 289.
424. Groen, *Hoe de onderwijswet van 1857 tot stand kwam*, 18–26.
425. Groen, *Hoe de onderwijswet van 1857 tot stand kwam*, 26.
426. Schlebusch. *Strategic Narratives*, 185–98.
427. Groen, "Aanteekeningen over de kabinetsformatie van 1856" ["Notes on the Cabinet Formation of 1856"] (1876), in *Bescheiden*, 2:548–55, at 549.
428. Singendonck to Groen, 5 June 1856; Groen, *Briefwisseling*, 3:230. The entire episode surrounding Groen's candidature for prime minister is narrated by Gera Kraan-Van den Burg on 186–239 of *De Spiegelklok* (Kampen: Kok, 1947), a historical novel about the life of Jan Singendonck.
429. Groen, *Bescheiden*, 2:549.
430. Groen, *Hoe de onderwijswet van 1857 tot stand kwam*, 32.
431. Groen, *Hoe de onderwijswet van 1857 tot stand kwam*, 40.
432. Groen, *Verspreide Geschriften*, 2:127.
433. Groen, *Hoe de onderwijswet van 1857 tot stand kwam*, 102.
434. Duyverman, *Uit de geheime dagboeken van Mackay*, 69.
435. Koenen to Groen, 25 June 1856; Groen, *Briefwisseling*, 3:235.
436. D. Chantepie de la Saussaye, "De optreding van het nieuwe ministerie," *Ernst en Vrede* 4 (1856) 299–309.
437. Groen, *Hoe de onderwijswet van 1857 tot stand kwam*, 48.
438. Groen, *Hoe de onderwijswet van 1857 tot stand kwam*, 48.
439. Da Costa to Groen, 18 August 1856; Groen, *Brieven van Da Costa*, 3:48.
440. Groen won by 1126 vs. 844 votes; Groen, *Briefwisseling*, 3:241 no. 3.
441. Van der Brugghen to Groen, 20 August 1856; Groen Archive, nr. 124A15. The letter was not included in the published correspondence.
442. Beets to Van der Brugghen, 25 June 1856; Groen, *Briefwisseling*, 3:944. See also Brouwer, *Het binnenste naar buiten*, 191.
443. Quoted in Brouwer, *Het binnenste naar buiten*, 197.
444. For the exchange of letters between Van der Brugghen and Groen at this time, see Groen, *Hoe de onderwijswet van 1857 tot stand kwam*, 98–110. See also Groen, *Adviezen in de Tweede Kamer* (1857), 2:195–207.
445. For the exchange of letters between Chantepie de la Saussaye and Groen at this time, see Groen, *Hoe de onderwijswet van 1857 tot stand kwam*, 112–18, 121–24, 126–29.
446. Groen, *Hoe de onderwijswet van 1857 tot stand kwam*, 116.
447. Groen, *Hoe de onderwijswet van 1857 tot stand kwam*, 122.

Endnotes

448. Groen, *Hoe de onderwijswet van 1857 tot stand kwam*, 145–47, with a reference to A. P. Stanley, *The Life and Correspondence of Thomas Arnold*, 2 vols. (London: Fellowes, 1845).
449. Groen, *Hoe de onderwijswet van 1857 tot stand kwam*, 208–9.
450. Rev. J. P. Hasebroek to Groen, 30 September 1857; Groen, *Briefwisseling*, 3:292.
451. In his *Hoe de onderwijswet van 1857 tot stand kwam*, in which Groen as late as 1876 published the correspondence of these years, the number of Reformed pastors is disproportionately high, yet only a few supported Groen on principle.
452. Wormser to Groen, 27 August 1857; Groen, *Briefwisseling*, 3:284.
453. Groen to Wormser, undated [1858]; Groen, *Brieven van Wormser*, 2:232.
454. Groen to Van Assen, 2 April 1858; Groen, *Briefwisseling*, 3:311.
455. P. A. S. van Limburg Brouwer, "De ontknooping" ["The Denouement"], *De Gids* 10 (1857) 305–30.
456. Groen to Heldring, 5 December 1858; Groen, *Briefwisseling*, 3:338.
457. G. Groen van Prinsterer, ed., *Archives ou Correspondance inédite de la Maison d'Orange-Nassau*, 2nd series, 5 vols. (Utrecht: Kemink, 1857–61).
458. Groen to King William III, 3 December 1850; Groen, *Briefwisseling*, 3:68.
459. Groen to King William III, 20 January 1857; Groen, *Briefwisseling*, 5:342–43.
460. Quoted in L. C. Suttorp et al., eds., *Groen's 'Ongeloof en Revolutie'; een bundel studiën* [*Groen's "Unbelief and Revolution": A Collection of Essays*] (Wageningen: Zomer & Keuning, 1949), 160–61.
461. See G. Groen van Prinsterer, *Antwoord aan Mr. M. C. van Hall* [*Reply to M. C. van Hall*] (Leiden: Luchtmans, 1844).
462. Robert Fruin, *Tien jaren uit den Tachtigjarige Oorlog, 1588–1598* [*Ten years in the Eighty Years' War, 1588–1598*] (Leiden: N.p., 1857–58).
463. The controversy revolves around two questions. First, were Oldenbarnevelt's measures in favor of the Arminians against the orthodox Calvinists constitutional or arbitrary, fueled by his aim to have Holland dominate the Union and the state dominate the church? Second, was Maurice's defense of the orthodox inspired by genuine religious considerations or by plain political ambition and rivalry?
464. Groen, *Archives*, 2nd series, 2:cxxii.
465. Da Costa to Groen, 23 July 1858; Groen, *Brieven van Da Costa*, 3:154–55; see also 160.
466. Cf. Groen to Da Costa, 26 July 1858; Groen, *Brieven van Da Costa*, 3:157.
467. See Motley's preface to *The Rise of the Dutch Republic*, 3 vols. (Amsterdam: Binger Brothers, 1855).
468. Groen, *Archives*, 2nd series, 1:vi.
469. G. Groen van Prinsterer, *Heiligerlee en Ultramontaansche kritiek* (Amsterdam: Höveker, 1868). Heiligerlee was the location of an early battle in the Dutch Revolt, in which a Spanish force was defeated.
470. G. Groen van Prinsterer, *1813 in het licht der Volkshistorie herdacht* (The Hague: Gerretsen, 1863).
471. Groen to Da Costa, September 1858; Groen, *Brieven van Da Costa*, 3:170.

472. Groen to Da Costa, September 1858; Groen, *Brieven van Da Costa*, 3:170-71.
473. Kuiper, *Zelfbeeld en wereldbeeld*, 81.
474. Kuiper, *Zelfbeeld en wereldbeeld*, 82.
475. Da Costa to Groen, 7 June 1859; Groen, *Brieven van Da Costa*, 3:215.
476. Groen to Mackay, 18 July 1859; Groen, *Briefwisseling*, 5:406.
477. Groen, *Verspreide Geschriften*, 2 vols.
478. Groen, *Verspreide Geschriften*, 1:vii-xii.
479. Groen, *Verspreide Geschriften*, x.
480. J. P. Trottet, "Quelque mots sur l'état religieux de la Hollande," in *Chrétien Évangélique du 19e siècle* (Lausanne), 25 October 1859.
481. Groen, *Parti anti-révolutionnaire et confessionnel*.
482. Groen, *Parti anti-révolutionnaire et confessionnel*, 30.
483. Groen, *Parti anti-révolutionnaire et confessionnel*, v.
484. Groen, *Parti anti-révolutionnaire et confessionnel*, 104-5.
485. Groen, *Parti anti-révolutionnaire et confessionnel*, 105.
486. Groen to Mrs. Wormser, 2 November 1862; Wormser died November 1. Groen, *Brieven van Wormser*, 2:271.
487. Groen, *Brieven van Da Costa*, 3:247.
488. Groen, *Brieven van Da Costa*, 3:252.
489. D. Langedijk, *De schoolstrijd in de eerste jaren na de wet van 1857* [*The schools struggle in the first years after the Act of 1857*] (Kampen: Kok, 1937), 46.
490. J. Kuiper, *Geschiedenis van het Christelijk Lager Onderwijs in Nederland* [*History of Christian Primary Education in the Netherlands*], 2nd rev. ed. (Amsterdam: H. A. van Bottenburg, 1904), 130.
491. Langedijk, *De schoolstrijd*, 67.
492. Cf. Stahl to Groen, 5 August 1860; Groen, *Briefwisseling*, 3:420-21.
493. G. Groen van Prinsterer, *Ter nagedachtenis van Stahl* (Amsterdam: Höveker, 1862); reprint, with notes and an epilogue, of the necrology in *Nieuwe Bijdragen voor Regtsgeleerdheid en wetgeving* 12.1 (1862) 161-212.
494. Groen, *Ter nagedachtenis van Stahl*, v; see also 46n1.
495. Groen to Schwartz, 16 December 1861; Groen, *Briefwisseling*, 3:516.
496. Groen, *Ter nagedachtenis van Stahl*, 27.
497. Groen, *Ter nagedachtenis van Stahl*, 55, 63, 72.
498. De Geer to Groen, 25 July 1862; Groen, *Briefwisseling*, 3:553.
499. O. W. Star Numan to Groen, 15 September 1862; Groen, *Briefwisseling*, 3:645n1.
500. Cf. Groen, "Historische brieven." (1875), in *Bescheiden*, 2:540-41.
501. Van Lynden to Groen, 6 June 1862; Groen, *Briefwisseling*, 3:546.
502. Groen, *Hoe de onderwijswet van 1857 tot stand kwam*, 196.
503. Quoted in J. A. de Wilde and C. Smeenk, *Het volk ten baat. Geschiedenis van de Antirevolutionaire Partij* [*For the Benefit of the Nation: History of the Antirevolutionary Party*] (Groningen: Haan, 1949), 29-30.

Endnotes

504. G. J. Laman, *Groen van Prinsterer als volksvertegenwoordiger, 1862–1865* [*Groen van Prinsterer as a Representative of the People*], diss., Free University of Amsterdam (Franeker: Wever, 1949), 42.
505. Van Lynden to Groen, 31 May 1863; Groen, *Briefwisseling*, 3:611.
506. G. Groen van Prinsterer, *De Tweede Kamer en de volksopvoeding in 1863* [*The Second Chamber and Public Education in 1863*] (The Hague: Gerretsen, 1864), part 1.
507. *Briefwisseling van Thorbecke*, 6:526.
508. Cf. the commentary by former minister J. B. van Son, in Groen, "*Eenige staatkundige aanteekeningen, 1860 en volgende jaren*," in *Bescheiden*, 2:267–74, at 271–72.
509. Groen to Mackay, 9 November 1864; Groen, *Briefwisseling*, 3:697.
510. J. D. W. Pape to Groen, 5 July 1864; Groen, *Briefwisseling*, 3:697.
511. Van Lynden to Mackay, 31 January 1865; Algemeen Rijksarchief, Collection Mackay.
512. That was how Beets saw Groen; cf. Groen, *Briefwisseling*, 5:806.
513. G. Groen van Prinsterer, *Aan de Kiezers* [*To the Voters*], nos. I–XX, in *Parlementaire Studien en Schetsen* (The Hague: Van Cleef, 1866).
514. G. Groen van Prinsterer, *Parlementaire Studiën en Schetsen*, 3 vols. (The Hague: Van Cleef, 1866). The three volumes collected forty-nine issues totaling over six hundred pages and dated from 23 October 1865 to 15 November 1866.
515. G. Groen van Prinsterer, *Leervrijheid of kerkbewustzijn?* [*Doctrinal Freedom or Ecclesiastical Consciousness?*] (The Hague: Gerretsen, 1864).
516. J. H. Gunning Jr., *Waartoe verwonderd?* [*Why surprised?*] (The Hague: Visser, 1864).
517. Chantepie to Groen, 11 March 1862; Groen, *Briefwisseling*, 3:533.
518. Gunning to Groen, 18 April 1863; Groen, *Briefwisseling*, 3:601.
519. Groen, "Lijden en strijden" (1864), Groen Archive, nr. 97; now published in *Bescheiden*, 2:455–69.
520. Groen, *Bescheiden*, 2:463.
521. Groen, "*Opstel inzake de Vereeniging tot verschaffing van hulp en raad aan gemeenten en personen in de Nederlandsche Hervormde kerk.*" [*Essay Regarding the Association for Furnishing Aid and Counsel to Congregations and Individuals in the Dutch Reformed Church*] (1865), in *Bescheiden*, 2:470–75, at 471–72.
522. Groen Archive, nr. 100; see also *Bescheiden*, 2:470n1.
523. Gunning, *Waartoe verwonderd?*, iv.
524. This research had led to Kuyper's prize-winning essay on the church polity of the Polish reformer Johannes a Lasco, recently published as *Abraham Kuyper's Commentatio* (1860): *The Young Kuyper About Calvin, a Lasco and the Church*, edited by Jasper Vree and Johan Zwaan, 2 vols. (Leiden: Brill, 2005).
525. Kuyper to Groen, 5 April 1867; Groen, *Briefwisseling*, 5:669.
526. See Kuyper to Groen, 11 April 1867; Groen, *Briefwisseling*, 5:671.
527. That is, Jan Heemskerk (1818–97). The extension Azn stands for "Abrahamszoon" or "son of Abraham [Heemskerk]." He is to be distinguished from his cousin, Jan Heemskerk Bzn [son of Bysterus Heemskerk] (1811–80), who was a member of the Second Chamber almost without interruption from 1849 to 1872.

Endnotes

528. Groen to Van Zuylen,12 June 1866; Groen, *Briefwisseling*, 3:828–29.
529. J. P. J. A. van Zuylen van Nijevelt, *Agitatie of pligtsbetrachting?* [*Agitation or Doing One's Duty?*] (Utrecht: N.p., 1866).
530. Schimmelpenninck to Groen, 22 October 1866; Groen, *Briefwisseling*, 5:660.
531. Groen to Van Lynden van Sandenburg, 9 October and 16 October 1866; Groen, *Briefwisseling*, 5:658–60.
532. *Dagblad van Zuid-Holland en 's-Gravenhage*, 27 October 1866.
533. Cf. R. Janssens, *De opbouw van de Antirevolutionaire Partij, 1850–1888* [*Building the Antirevolutionary Party, 1850–1888*] (Hilversum: Verloren, 2001), 44.
534. Groen to Van Otterloo, 18 November 1866; Groen, *Briefwisseling*, 5:662.
535. Groen to King William III, 28 August 1866; Groen, *Briefwisseling*, 3:849.
536. Smitskamp, *Groen van Prinsterer als historicus*, 14.
537. Cf. M. E. Kluit, *Nader over het Réveil; vijf schetsen* [*Further About the Réveil: Five Sketches*] (Kampen: Kok, 1977), 130–31.
538. Betsy Groen to Singendonck, 24 August 1864; Groen, *Briefwisseling*, 3:708.
539. G. Groen van Prinsterer, *La Prusse et Les Pays-Bas; à mes amis de Berlin* (Amsterdam: Höveker, 1867); twice reprinted that same year. London's *Pall Mall Gazette* of 27 April 1867, pp. 4ff., summarized its thrust in these words: "The little pamphlet which we have before us ... expresses the feeling of the most advanced, most patriotic, most thoroughly national portion of [Holland] on a question of intense importance to them—that of their 'annexation'—will they, will they [not]? to North Germany."
540. About these Stahlian views of Groen: Jelle Bijl, *Een Europese Antirevolutionair. Het Europabeeld van Groen van Prinsterer in tekst en context* (VU University Press, 2011), 535–42.
541. G. Groen van Prinsterer, *L'Empire Prussien et l'Apocalypse; à mes amis de Berlin. Essais historiques sur les événements d'Allemagne en 1866* (Amsterdam: Höveker, 1867).
542. Groen, *Empire Prussien et l'Apocalypse*, 19.
543. Said in his improvisation at the Fifth General Assembly of the Evangelical Alliance, Amsterdam, 1867; in M. Cohen Stuart, *In memoriam Guillaume Groen van Prinsterer; notice biographique* (Utrecht: Kemink, 1876), 50.
544. G. Groen van Prinsterer, *La nationalité religieuse en rapport avec la Hollande et l'Alliance Évangélique* (Amsterdam: Höveker, 1867); reprinted in M. Cohen Stuart, *In memoriam Groen van Prinsterer*, 47–51.
545. Quoted in Gerard Fafié, *Friedrich Julius Stahl; invloeden van zijn leven en werken in Nederland, 1847–1880* [*Friedrich Julius Stahl: Influences of His Life and Works in the Netherlands, 1847–1880*], diss., City University of Amsterdam (Rotterdam: Bronder-Offset, 1975), 142.
546. Groen, "Aanteekeningen van in Duitschland gevoerde gesprekken" ["Notes of Conversations in Germany"] (1867), in *Bescheiden*, 2:477–82, at 477 no. 9a.
547. Groen, *Februari 1868* (Amsterdam: Höveker, 1868), 5.
548. Groen, *Februari 1868*, 4–5.
549. Quoted in R. Kuiper, *Herenmuiterij; vernieuwing en sociaal conflict in de antirevolutionaire beweging, 1871–1894* [*Mutiny of the Gentry: Renewal and Social Conflict in the Antirevolutionary Movement, 1871–1894*] (Leiden: J. J. Groen, 1994), 17–18.

Endnotes

550. Cf. T. de Vries, *Mr. G. Groen van Prinsterer in zijne omgeving* [*Groen van Prinsterer in His Milieu*] (Leiden: Sijthoff, 1908), 68.

551. Cf. Groen to Mackay, 13 June 1868; Groen, *Briefwisseling*, 5:717.

552. Original: "Ik zing een man, die vroom en vroed / Tot hier zijn dagen sleet / Geen mensch wien 't heil van kerk en staat / In Nederland ter harte gaat / Die ooit die man vergeet. "Dien man, schoon grijs en lichaamszwak/ Vol geest- en krachtbetoon/ Dien strijder voor ons Heilgerlee/ Rijze onze dank, rijze onze bee/ Wees, Heere, zelf zijn loon."

553. Quoted in M. J. A. de Vrijer, *Gunning Tragicus* (The Hague: Daamen, 1946), 104.

554. A. Kuyper, *Het beroep op het volksgeweten* [*The Appeal to the National Conscience*] (Amsterdam: Blankenberg, 1869).

555. Groen, *Februari 1868*, 4.

556. G. Groen van Prinsterer, *Nederlandsche Gedachten*, 1872, no. 7.

557. Groen to Kuyper, 15 May 1870; Groen, *Briefwisseling*, 6:134.

558. Hans Knippenberg and Ben de Pater, *De eenwording van Nederland; schaalvergroting en integratie sinds 1800* [*The Unification of the Netherlands: Increase of Scale and Integration Since 1800*] (Nymegen: Socialistiese Uitgeverij, 1992), 61.

559. Janssens, *De opbouw van de Antirevolutionaire Partij*, 21–22.

560. G. Groen van Prinsterer, *Bij de stembus*, 5 vols. (Amsterdam: Höveker, 1869).

561. Johan Snel, *Abraham Kuyper, een leven in de journalistiek*. (Amsterdam: Boom, 2023).

562. G. Groen van Prinsterer, *Nederlandsche Gedachten*, second series, 6 vols. [257 pamphlets] (Amsterdam: Höveker, 1869–76).

563. Groen, *Nederlandsche Gedachten*, 2nd ser., 1873, no. 1.

564. Groen, *Nederlandsche Gedachten*, 2nd ser., 1873, no. 2.

565. Reprinted in G. Puchinger, ed., *Aandacht voor Groen van Prinsterer* (Kampen: Kok, 1976), 22–33. Busken Huet was then living in voluntary but lonely "exile" in Batavia, in the Dutch East Indies. His essay came in two parts and appeared in the issues of 15 and 16 April 1870. Busken Huet was a Reformed minister from 1851 to 1863 but resigned his pastorate when he came to the conclusion that it was incompatible with his theological modernism.

566. Gefken to Koenen, 21 January 1871; Réveilarchief, Collection Koenen.

567. D. Chantepie de la Saussaye, *Het protestantisme als politiek beginsel* [*Protestantism as a Political Principle*] (Rotterdam, 1871), 2.

568. Groen, *Nederlandsche Gedachten*, 2nd ser., 1869, no. 12.

569. Groen, *Nederlandsche Gedachten*, 2nd ser., 1871, no. 72.

570. Van Bylandt to Groen, 29 September and 21 December 1870; Groen, *Briefwisseling*, 6:181–84, 198–200.

571. Elout to Groen, 30 March 1871; Groen, *Briefwisseling*, 4:457.

572. *De Heraut*, 1871, no. 9.

573. *De Heraut*, 1871, no. 4.

574. Groen to C. Mulder, 19 February 1871; Groen, *Briefwisseling*, 4:454, no. 1.

575. See Kuiper, *Zelfbeeld en wereldbeeld*, passim.

Endnotes

576. Groen to Kuyper, 10 January 1870; Groen, *Briefwisseling*, 6:206.
577. Kuyper to Groen, 13 January 1870; Groen, *Briefwisseling*, 6:208.
578. Kuiper, *Herenmuiterij*, 18.
579. Groen, *Nederlandsche Gedachten*, 2nd ser., 22 March 1871, no. 77.
580. Groen, *Nederlandsche Gedachten*, 2nd ser., 1874, no. 50.
581. Kuyper to Groen, 24 May and 25 May 1871; Groen, *Briefwisseling*, 6:235-38.
582. Gefken, *Herinneringen*, 27 May 1871; Réveil Archives, Collection Gefken.
583. Cf. Janssens, *De opbouw van de Antirevolutionaire Partij*, 82-91.
584. Van Otterloo to Groen, 26 July 1871; Groen, *Briefwisseling*, 4:490-93, at 492.
585. In an article in *De Bazuin*, 16 June 1871; quoted in *Nederlandsche Gedachten*, 2nd ser., 27 June 1871, 49-50.
586. Quoted in Kuiper, *Herenmuiterij*, 22.
587. Quoted in G. M. den Hartogh, *Groen van Prinsterer en de Verkiezingen van 1871; een keerpunt in de wordingsgeschiedenis der Antirevolutionaire Partij* [*Groen van Prinsterer and the Elections of 1871: A Turning Point in the Genesis of the Antirevolutionary Party*], diss., Free University of Amsterdam (Kampen: Kok, 1933), 183-86, at 184.
588. Gefken, *Herinneringen*, July 1871; Réveilarchief, Collection Gefken.
589. Elout to Groen, 6 August 1871; Groen, *Briefwisseling*, 6:259.
590. Quoted in J. C. Rullmann, *Onze voortrekkers* [*Our Pioneers*] (Delft: Meinema, 1931), 65.
591. Groen, *Nederlandsche Gedachten*, 2nd ser., 1872, no. 1.
592. Groen to Kuyper, 7 June 1872; Groen, *Briefwisseling*, 6:344.
593. Groen, *Nederlandsche Gedachten*, 2nd ser., 1872, no. 26.
594. The idea for such a league came from the example of the Anti-Corn Law League in Britain; cf. A. Houkes and M. Janse, "Foreign Examples as Eye-Openers and Justification: The Transfer of the Anti-Corn Law League to the Netherlands," *European Review of History* 12 (2005) 321-44.
595. See A. Goslinga, ed., *Briefwisseling van Mr. G. Groen van Prinsterer met Dr. A. Kuyper, 1864-1876* (Kampen: Kok, 1937). This volume was prepared and published on the occasion of the centennial of Kuyper's birth; its contents have been re-edited and seeded into *Briefwisseling*, vols. 5 and 6 (1980 and 1992).
596. Groen to Kuyper, [early] August 1872; Groen, *Briefwisseling*, 6:364.
597. Groen, *Briefwisseling*, 6:363.
598. They consistently used the English word.
599. G. Groen van Prinsterer, *Maurice et Barnevelt; étude historique* (Utrecht: Kemink, 1875). The book was a French-language publication, and the publisher had arranged simultaneous publication in Brussels with the firm of C. Muquardt and in Leipzig with the firm of T. O. Weigel. The book was divided into three parts: the debate (pages i-ccxxii), the relevant Introductions by Groen in the Archives (pages 1-102), and the supporting documentation (pages 1-170).
600. J. L. Motley, *The Life and Death of John of Barneveld, Advocate of Holland: With a View of the Primary Causes and Movements of the Thirty Years' War*, 2 vols. (The Hague: Nijhoff; New York: Harper and Brothers, 1874).

Endnotes

601. Groen to King William III, 18 February 1875; Groen, *Briefwisseling*, 4:763.
602. Groen to Motley, 2 June 1874; Groen, *Briefwisseling*, 6:546.
603. Motley to Groen, 17 June 1874; Groen, *Briefwisseling*, 6:546.
604. Groen, *Maurice et Barnevelt*, 1–54 and 1–76, respectively.
605. Groen, *Maurice et Barnevelt*, xxxiv–xlvi and lxxi–cxxiv, respectively.
606. Conrad Busken Huet, *Litterarische fantasieën en kritieken*, 25 vols. (Haarlem: Tjeenk Willink, 1868–88), 5:21.
607. Groen, *Nederlandsche Gedachten*, 2nd ser., 1873, no. 2.
608. G. Groen van Prinsterer, ed., *Brieven van Mr. Isaac da Costa*, 3 vols. (Amsterdam: Höveker, 1872–76).
609. G. Groen van Prinsterer, ed., *Brieven van Thorbecke* (Amsterdam: Höveker, 1873).
610. Groen van Prinsterer, ed., *Brieven van J. A. Wormser*, 2 vols. (Amsterdam: Höveker, 1874–76).
611. *Je maintiendrai*: I shall maintain.
612. Groen, *Hoe de Onderwijswet van 1857 tot stand kwam*.
613. Witness, struggle, suffer: a frequent combination in Groen's Dutch prose: *belijden, strijden, lijden*.
614. Betsy to J. A. Wormser Jr., 1 May 1876; Groen, *Briefwisseling*, 6:703.
615. P. J. Elout van Soeterwoude, *Enkele herinneringen uit Mr. Groen van Prinsterer's laatste dagen* [*Some Recollections of Groen van Prinsterer's Final Days*] (The Hague: privately printed, 1885), 10–11.
616. "*Heer, waar dan heen? Tot U alleen!*" ("Lord, whither shall I go? To you alone!")—lines from a hymn by C. F. D. Schubert, translated by Ahasverus van den Berg (1733–1807).
617. Elout, *Enkele herinneringen*, 13–14.
618. Betsy to De Savornin Lohman, 15, 16, 17, and 19 May 1876; Groen, *Briefwisseling*, 6:704–5.
619. "*Amen, Jezus Christus, Amen!*"—line from a hymn by J. E. van de Velde nee Helmcke (1762–1844).
620. Reprinted in C. Bremmer and M. N. G. Kool, eds., *Een staatsman ter navolging*, 34.
621. Rullmann, *Onze voortrekkers*, 65–66, relates that the other wreath was a simple one made by a nine-year-old girl out of thankfulness to the old gentleman who once had stopped and spoken to her as she was playing on the street while convalescing in The Hague. He had asked her in a kindly voice if she went to school and if she had ever heard of the Lord Jesus who loved children so. Then he had said, "I see you are not well, but the same Lord Jesus is so powerful that He even raised the young man of Nain from the dead, and so He can also make you better." The girl had fully recovered and was much moved by the news of the kind man's death.
622. [J. H. Gunning, Jr., ed.], *Bij het graf van Mr. Groen van Prinsterer, 23 Mei 1876* [*At the Graveside of Mr. Groen van Prinsterer, 23 May 1876*] (Amsterdam: Höveker, 1876), 22. This slim volume of thirty-two pages reproduces the texts of the ten speeches given at Groen's open grave.
623. J. P. de Valk and M. van Faassen, eds., *Dagboeken en aantekeningen van Willem Hendrik de Beaufort, 1874–1918* [*Journals and Notes of Willem Hendrik de Beaufort, 1874–1918*], 2 vols. (The Hague: Instituut voor Nederlandse Geschiedenis, 1993), 1:6.

624. H. J. A. M. Schaepman, "*Mr. Groen van Prinsterer,*" *Onze Wachter* (June 1876), 2:65–74; reprinted in G. Puchinger, ed., *Aandacht voor Groen van Prinsterer*, 34–43, at 37–38.
625. *Mannen van beteekenis in onze dagen* [*Men of significance in our time*] (Haarlem: Kruseman & Tjeenk Willink, 1868).
626. N. C. Balsem, *G. Groen van Prinsterer*, vol. 7, no. 9 in the series *Mannen van beteekenis in onze dagen* (Haarlem, 1877), 358–408, at 408.
627. Janssens, *De opbouw van de Antirevolutionaire Partij*, 92–130; Rienk Janssens, "Antirevolutionaire organisatievorming, 1871–1879," in George Harinck, Roel Kuiper, and Peter Bak, eds., *De Antirevolutionaire Partij, 1829–1980* (Hilversum: Verloren, 2001), 53–72; Johan G. Westra, *Confessional Political Parties in the Netherlands, 1813–1946*, diss. University of Michigan (Ann Arbor, MI: University Microfilms, 1972), 152–58; McKendree R. Langley, *Emancipation and Apologetics: The Formation of Abraham Kuyper's Anti-Revolutionary Party*, diss., Westminster Theological Seminary (Ann Arbor, MI: University Microfilms, 1995), 114–32, 249–73.

Images

Father and mother, P. J. Groen van Prinsterer (1764–1837) and A. H. Groen van Prinsterer-Caan (1772–1832). By C. H. Hodges, painted in 1823 on the occasion of their twenty-fifth anniversary of marriage.

Coat of arms of the family Groen van Prinsterer.

Vreugd en Rust, the mansion of the family Groen van Prinsterer in Voorburg where Willem was born.

Willem and his sister Mimi (M. C. Philipse-Groen van Prinsterer, 1806–68). Painted by C. H. Hodges in 1823.

PROSOPOGRAPHIA

PLATONICA,

AUCTORE

GULIELMO GROEN VAN PRINSTERER,

*PHIL. THEOR. MAG., LIT. HUM. ET
JUR. ROM. ET HOD. DOCT.*

LUGDUNI BATAVORUM,
APUD H. W. HAZENBERG JUNIOREM,
MDCCCXXIII.

First page of Groen van Prinsterer's dissertation on Plato.

Sister Keetje (C. A. Hoffmann-Groen van Prinsterer, 1799–1858) and her husband M. A. F. H. Hoffmann (1795–1874).

Sister Mimi and her husband J. A. Philpse (1800–1884).

Betsy (E. M. M. Groen van Prinsterer-Van der Hoop, 1807–79), around 1845.

Letter of Betsy to Willem de Clercq, January 15, 1830.

Far left the house at Plein Square in The Hague where Willem and Betsy lived from 1832 to 1837.

In dark stone the house at the Korte Vijverberg where Willem and Betsy lived from 1837 until their deaths in 1876 and 1879.

Oud Wassenaer, the mansion of Willem and Betsy in Wassenaar in the years 1845–71.

Portrait of King William I. Painting by W. B. van der Kooij, 1818.

King William II, after a painting of J. A. Kruseman.

Cartoon of King William I regretting the loss of Belgium in 1830.

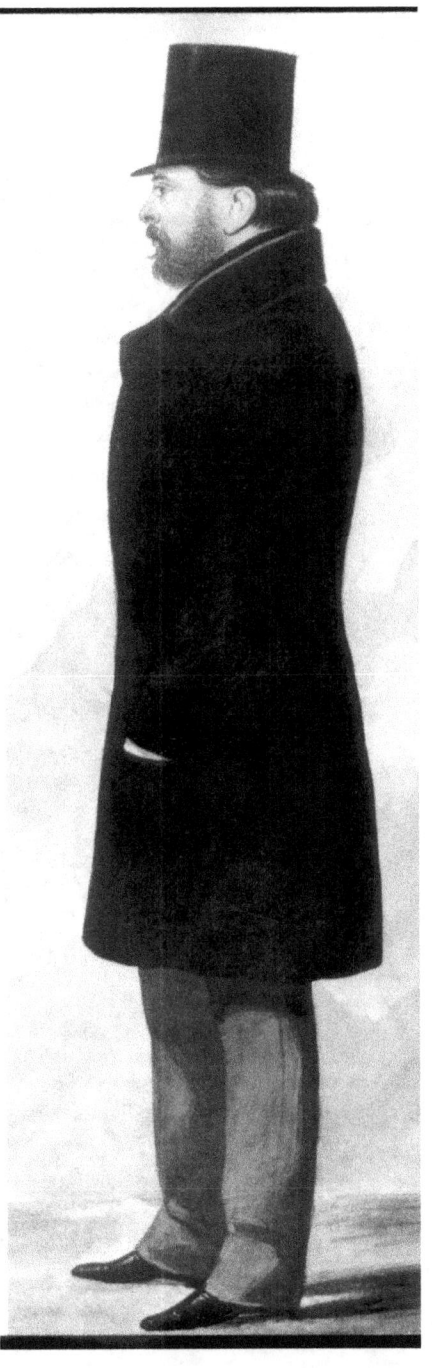

King William III in 1849.

Mr. W. Bilderdijk (1756–1831). Painting by C. H. Hodges.

J. H. Merle d'Aubigné (1794–1872).

Mr. I. da Costa (1798–1860).
W. de Clercq (1795–1844).

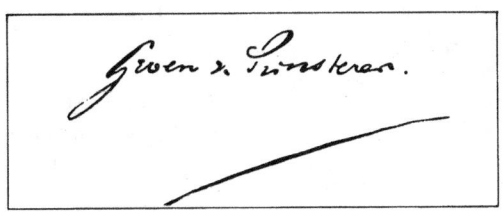

Willem Groen van Prinsterer around 1845.

Title page of *Measures Against the Seceders*, 1837.

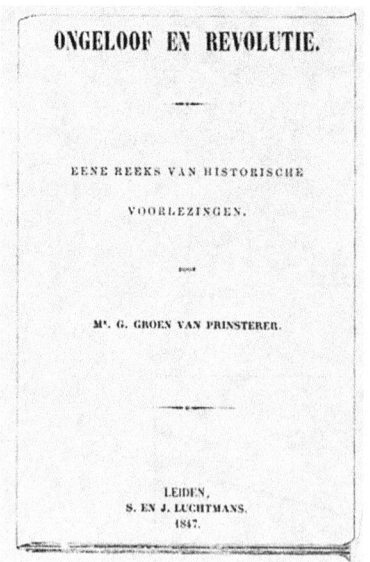

Title page of *Unbelief and Revolution*.

De predikant wekt zijn hoorders op.

Ook ouden van dagen gaan mee.

De landverhuizers, zingend een straatliedje van den tijd vertrekken naar de kust.

Cartoons about the seceders, making their way to America under the leadership of Rev. H. P. Scholte.

Portrait of J. R. Thorbecke (1798–1872). Painted by Jozef Israels.

Riots in Amsterdam, March 24, 1848. Inspired by European revolutions, workers start an uprising at Dam Square.

Pictures of Willem and Betsy, around 1860.

De Kiezers worden ok thans dringend verzocht, om bij de nieuwe stemming voor een lid der *Tweede Kamer van de Staten-Generaal*, op aanstaanden Dingsdag 12 Augustus, niet te verflaauwen in hunner ijver, maar op nieuw in grooten getale hunne stem uit te brengen op

M^r. G. GROEN VAN PRINSTERER,

den uitstekenden, echt Nederlandschen Staatsman, den trouwen Vriend van Koning en Vaderland.

Het groot aantal stemmen vroeger reeds op dien Heer uitgebragt, maakt thans alle verdere aanbeveling overbodig.

KIEZERS! stemt op nieuw

M^r. G. GROEN VAN PRINSTERER.

Zegt het voort.

Electoral pamphlet of Groen van Prinsterer.

Three antirevolutionary leaders: Groen van Prinsterer, Elout van Soeterwoude, and Aeneas Mackay.

Little personal note to the chairman of the Chamber, announcing Groen's immediate withdrawal from Parliament after the acceptance of the law of 1857.

This cartoon depicts the reluctance of the Roman Catholics to participate in Groen's struggle for the Christian school (published in *The Dutch Spectator*, 1867).

"Who is leading and who is suffering. Groen van Prinsterer denies the conservatives his help in Parliament" (published in *The Dutch Spectator*, 1869).

D. Chantepie de la Saussaye (1818–74).

J. A. Wormser (1807–62), close friend in Amsterdam.

Abraham Kuyper (1837–1920) as a pastor in his first congregation.

Willem Groen van Prinsterer when he was sixty-six.

'sGravenhage, den 19 Mei 1876.

Heden ontsliep mijn dierbare echtgenoot Mr. GUILLAUME GROEN VAN PRINSTERER, in het onwrikbaar geloof aan zijn Heer en Heiland, wien hij zijn leven gewijd had.

De scheiding eener echtverbindtenis van 48 jaren met zulk een man, vervult mijne ziele met diepen rouw.

Alleen de troost des Evangelie's en de hope eener zalige hereeniging lenigt mijne smart.

1 Cor. XV : 55—57.
E. M. M. GROEN VAN PRINSTERER,
VAN DER HOOP.

Announcement of the death of Groen van Prinsterer, May 19, 1876.

Graves of Willem and Betsy. In 1884 the Association of Christian Teachers and the Association for Christian-National School Education placed a stone in commemoration of Groen's efforts for Christian schools.

Bibliography

UNPUBLISHED PRIMARY SOURCES

Archives G. Groen van Prinsterer. Algemeen Rijksarchief, The Hague.
Archives E. Mackay. Algemeen Rijksarchief, The Hague.
Archives P. J. Elout van Soeterwoude. Algemeen Rijksarchief, The Hague.
Collection H. J. Koenen. Reveil Archives, Amsterdam.
Collection J. W. Gefken. Reveil Archives, Amsterdam.
Collection Sophie van Württemberg. Koninklijk Huisarchief, The Hague.
Collection W. de Clercq. Reveil Archives, Amsterdam.
Minutes of the directors of the orphanage, Waals-Hervormde Gemeente. Gemeente Archief, The Hague.
Minutes of the Waals-Hervormde Gemeente. Gemeente Archief, The Hague.
Pieces regarding the Royal Archives. Koninklijk Huisarchief, The Hague.

PUBLISHED PRIMARY SOURCES

De Briefwisseling van J. R. Thorbecke. Vols. 3–6. Edited by G. J. Hooijkaas. The Hague: Instituut voor Nederlandse Geschiedenis, 1988–98.
Gedenkschriften van Anton Reinhard Falck. Edited by H. T. Colenbrander. The Hague: Nijhoff, 1913.
Groen van Prinsterer, G., ed. *Brieven van J. A. Wormser.* 2 vols. Amsterdam: Höveker & Zoon, 1874–75.
———, ed. *Brieven van J. Thorbecke, 1830–1832.* Amsterdam: Höveker & Zoon, 1873.
———, ed. *Brieven van Mr. Isaac da Costa.* 3 vols. Amsterdam: Höveker & Zoon, 1872–76.
———. *Schriftelijke nalatenschap Groen van Prinsterer. Bescheiden 1: 1821–42.* Edited by J. Zwaan. Rijksgeschiedkundige Publicatiën 209. The Hague: Instituut v. Nederlandse Gesch., 1990.
———. *Schriftelijke nalatenschap Groen van Prinsterer. Bescheiden 2: 1842–76.* Edited by J. Zwaan. Rijksgeschiedkundige Publicatiën 210. The Hague: Instituut v. Nederlandse Gesch., 1991.

Bibliography

———. *Schriftelijke nalatenschap Groen van Prinsterer. Briefwisseling 1: 1808–33*. Edited by C. Gerretson. Rijksgeschiedkundige Publicatiën 58. The Hague: Nijhoff, 1925.
———. *Schriftelijke nalatenschap Groen van Prinsterer. Briefwisseling 2: 1833–48*. Edited by C. Gerretson and J. L. van Essen. Rijksgeschiedkundige Publicatiën 114. The Hague: Nijhoff, 1964.
———. *Schriftelijke nalatenschap Groen van Prinsterer. Briefwisseling 3: 1848–66*. Edited by H. J. Smit. Rijksgeschiedkundige Publicatiën 90. The Hague: Nijhoff, 1949.
———. *Schriftelijke nalatenschap Groen van Prinsterer. Briefwisseling 4: 1866–76*. Edited by A. Goslinga and J. L. van Essen. Rijksgeschiedkundige Publicatiën 123. The Hague: Nijhoff, 1967.
———. *Schriftelijke nalatenschap Groen van Prinsterer. Briefwisseling 5: 1827–69*. Edited by J. L. van Essen. Rijksgeschiedkundige Publicatiën 175. The Hague: Nijhoff, 1980.
———. *Schriftelijke nalatenschap Groen van Prinsterer. Briefwisseling 6: 1869–76*. Edited by J. L. van Essen. Rijksgeschiedkundige Publicatiën 219. The Hague: Nijhoff, 1992.
Hoe de Onderwijswet van 1857 tot stand kwam: historische bijdrage. Edited by G. Groen van Prinsterer. Amsterdam: Höveker & Zoon, 1876.
Valk, J. P. de, and M. van Faassen, eds. *Dagboeken en aantekeningen van Willem Hendrik de Beaufort, 1874–1918*. 2 vols. The Hague: Instituut voor Nederlandse Geschiedenis, 1993.

JOURNALS

Ernst en Vrede: Maandschrift voor de Nederlandsche Hervormde Kerk. Utrecht. 1853–58.
De Heraut. Amsterdam. 1869–72.
De Nederlander. Utrecht. 1850–55.
Nederlandsche Gedachten. The Hague. 1829–32.
Nederlandsche Gedachten. 2nd series. The Hague. 1869–76.
De Reformatie; tijdschrift ter bevordering van Gods Koningrijk in Nederland. Amsterdam. 1841–47.
De Standaard. Amsterdam. 1872–76.
De Vereeniging: Christelijke Stemmen. Amsterdam. 1847–75.

WORKS BY G. GROEN VAN PRINSTERER

Groen van Prinsterer, G. *1813 in het licht der Volkshistorie herdacht*. The Hague: Gerretsen, 1863.
———. *Aan de Kiezers*. Nos. 1–20. The Hague: Van Cleef, 1866.
———. *Adres aan de Algemeene Synode der Nederlandsche Hervormde Kerk over de Formulieren, de Academische opleiding der predikanten, het onderwijs en het Kerkbestuur*. Leiden: Luchtmans, 1842.
———. *Adviezen in de Tweede Kamer der Staten-Generaal in dubbelen getale*. Leiden: Luchtmans, 1840.
———. *Adviezen in de Tweede Kamer der Staten-Generaal, zitting van 1849*. Amsterdam: Müller, 1850.
———. *Adviezen in de Tweede Kamer der Staten-Generaal, zitting van 1849–50*. Amsterdam: Müller, 1851.

Bibliography

———. *Adviezen in de Tweede Kamer der Staten-Generaal*. 2 vols. Utrecht: Kemink, 1856–57.
———. *Antwoord aan Mr. M. C. van Hall*. Leiden: Luchtmans, 1844.
———, ed. *Archives ou Correspondance inédite de la Maison d'Orange-Nassau*. 1st series. 9 vols. Leiden: Luchtmans, 1835–47.
———, ed. *Archives ou Correspondance inédite de la Maison d'Orange-Nassau*. 2nd series. 5 vols. Utrecht: Kemink, 1857–61.
———. *Beschouwingen over Staats- en volkerenregt. Deel 1, Proeve van de middelen waardoor de waarheid wordt gekend en gestaafd*. Leiden, 1834.
———. *Bij de stembus*. 5 vols. Amsterdam: Höveker, 1869.
———. *Bijdrage tot herziening der Grondwet in Nederlandschen zin*. Leiden: Luchtmans, 1840.
———. *L'Empire Prussien et l'Apocalypse. À mes Amis de Berlin. Essai historique sur les événements d'Allemagne en 1866*. Amsterdam: Höveker, 1867.
———. *Februari 1868*. Amsterdam: Höveker, 1868.
———. *Grondwetherziening en Eensgezindheid*. Amsterdam: Müller, 1849.
———. *Handboek der Geschiedenis van het Vaderland*. Leiden: Luchtmans, 1846.
———. *Heiligerlee en Ultramontaansche kritiek*. 3 vols. Amsterdam: Höveker, 1868.
———. "Het goddelijk regt der Overheid." *Christelijke Stemmen* 1 (1846–47) 747–55.
———. *Het regt der Hervormde Gezindheid*. Amsterdam: Müller, 1848.
———. *Is er geen oorzaak? Eene wedervraag . . . aan ds. J. H. Gunning, Jr.* The Hague: Gerretson, 1864.
———. *Is het goed niet bevreesd voor de cholera te zijn?* The Hague: Roering, 1832.
———. *Kort Overzigt van de geschiedenis der vaderlands*. Leiden: Luchtmans, 1841.
———. *Leervrijheid of Kerkbewustzijn? Naar aanleiding van een protest van Ouderlingen te Parijs*. The Hague: Gerretson, 1864.
———. *De Maatregelen tegen de Afgescheidenen aan het staatsregt getoetst*. Leiden: Luchtmans, 1837.
———. *Maurice et Barnevelt; étude historique*. Utrecht: Kemink, 1875.
———. *Narede van vijfjarigen strijd*. Utrecht: Kemink, 1855.
———. *La nationalité religieuse en rapport avec La Hollande et l'Alliance Évangélique*. Amsterdam: Höveker, 1868.
———. *Natuurlijk of Ongerijmd? Aan ds. J. H. Gunning, Jr.* The Hague: Gerretson, 1864.
———. *Ongeloof en Revolutie; eene reeks van historische voorlezingen*. Leiden: Luchtmans, 1847.
———. "Over het gestadig protest der wetenschap tegen het staatsregt der Revolutie." *Christelijke Stemmen* 1 (1846–47) 1–9, 65–71, 129–34.
———. "Over het verwijt van werkeloosheid aan de Christenen in de kerk." *Christelijke Stemmen* 1 (1846–47) 469–90.
———. *Parlementaire Studiën en Schetsen*. 3 vols. The Hague: Van Cleef, 1865–66.
———. *Le Parti Anti-révolutionnaire et Confessionnel dans l'Église Réformée des Pays-Bas. Étude d'histoire contemporaine*. Amsterdam: Höveker, 1860.
———. *Proeve over de middelen waardoor de waarheid wordt gekend en gestaafd*. Leiden: Luchtmans, 1834.
———. *Proeve over de middelen waardoor de waarheid wordt gekend en gestaafd*. 2nd ed. Amsterdam: Höveker, 1858.
———. *La Prusse et Les Pays-Bas; À mes Amis de Berlin*. Amsterdam: Höveker, 1867.
———. *Redevoering over Willem I, gelijk hij uit zijne briefwisseling nader gekend wordt*. Amsterdam: Müller, 1842.

BIBLIOGRAPHY

———. *Ter Nagedachtenis van Stahl*. Amsterdam: Höveker, 1862.
———. *De Tweede Kamer en de volksopvoeding in 1863*. The Hague: Gerretsen, 1864.
———. *Vaderlandsche zangen*. Leiden: Luchtmans, 1841.
———. *Verscheidenheden over staatsregt en politiek*. Amsterdam: Müller, 1850.
———. *Verspreide Geschriften*. 2 vols. Amsterdam: Höveker, 1859–60.
———. *Vrijheid, Gelijkheid, Broederschap; toelichting van de spreuk der Revolutie*. The Hague: Roering, 1848.
———. *Vrijheid van Christelijk-Nationaal Onderwijs in verband met Scheiding van Kerk en Staat; Parlementair Fragment*. Amsterdam: Höveker, 1863.

SELECTED MONOGRAPHS IN DUTCH

Barnhoorn, J. G. *Amicitia Christiana: Da Costa en Groen van Prinsterer in hun briefwisseling (1830–1860)*. Apeldoorn: De Banier, 2011.
Boogman, J. C. *Rondom 1848. De politieke ontwikkeling van Nederland, 1840–1858*. Bussum: Unieboek, 1978.
Bosch, J. *Groen van Prinsterer en de kerkelijke strijd van heden*. Kampen: Kok, 1935.
Bremmer, C., and M. N. G. Kool, eds. *Een staatsman ter navolging. Groen van Prinsterer herdacht*. The Hague: Stichtingen Kader- en Vormingswerk ARP-CHU-KVP, 1976.
Bremmer, R. H. *Er staat geschreven! Er is geschied! Introductie tot het leven en werk van Groen van Prinsterer als getuigend historicus*. Apeldoorn: Willem de Zwijgerstichting, 1981.
Brouwer, J. *Het binnenste naar buiten. Beginselen en activiteiten van mr. J. J. L. van der Brugghen*. Zutphen: Walburg Pers, 1981.
Brugmans, I. J. *Thorbecke*. 2nd rev. ed. Haarlem: Bohn, 1948.
Bruijn, J. de, et al. *Geen heersende kerk, geen heersende staat. De verhouding tussen kerk en staat, 1796–1996*. Zoetermeer: Meinema, 1998.
Chantepie de la Saussaye, D. *Het protestantisme als politiek beginsel*. Rotterdam: Wenk, 1871.
Colenbrander, H. T. *Willem I, Koning der Nederlanden*. 2 vols. Amsterdam: Meulenhoff, 1931–35.
Cramer, N., et al. *Het Kabinet der Koningin. Geschiedenis van het instituut en het huis aan de Korte Vijverberg*. The Hague: Monumentenzorg Gemeente's-Gravenhage, 1993.
Dijk, D. J. H. van, and H. Massink, eds. *Groen en de grondwet. De betekenis van Groen van Prinsterers visie op de grondwet van 1848*. Heerenveen: J. J. Groen en Zoon, 1980.
Dijk, D. J. H. van, and C. G. van der Staaij, eds. *Vonken van heilig vuur. Groen van Prinsterer tweehonderd jaar*. Heerenveen: J. J. Groen, 2001.
Duyverman, J. P. *Uit de geheime dagboeken van Aeneas Mackay, dienaar des konings*. Houten: De Haan, 1987.
Elout van Soeterwoude, P. J. *Enkele herinneringen uit Mr. Groen van Prinsterers laatste dagen*. The Hague, privately printed, 1885.
Essen, J. L. van. *Een ziel van vuur. Opstellen over Groen van Prinsterer en zijn omgeving*. Leiden: J. J. Groen en Zoon, 1992.
Fafié, G. *Friedrich Julius Stahl. Invloeden van zijn leven en werken in Nederland, 1847–1880*. Rotterdam: Bronder-Offset, 1977.
Fortman, B. de Gaay. *Figuren uit het Réveil*. Kampen: Kok, 1980.

Bibliography

Fruin, R. *De antirevolutionaire bezwaren van Mr. Groen van Prinsterer tegen onzen staat en onze maatschappij overwogen.* Amsterdam: Gebhard, 1854.

———. *Het antirevolutionaire staatsrecht van Groen van Prinsterer ontvouwd en beoordeeld.* Amsterdam: Gebhard, 1853.

———. *Politieke moraliteit. Open Brief aan mr. G. Groen van Prinsterer.* Leiden: Sijthoff, 1864.

Goslinga, A. "Het conflict Groen–Van der Brugghen." In *Christendom en Historie; lustrumbundel van het Gezelschap van Christelijke Historici,* 265–374. Amsterdam: Uitgeversmaatschappij Holland, 1925.

———. *Koning Willem I als verlicht despoot.* Baarn: Bosch, 1918.

Gunning, J. H., Jr. *Eén doel, twee wegen. Antwoord op de wedervraag "Is er geen oorzaak?" van Mr. G. Groen van Prinsterer.* The Hague: Visser, 1864.

———. *Waartoe verwonderd? Een kort woord tot toelichting van de jongste bewegingen op kerkelijk gebied, inzonderheid te 's-Gravenhage.* The Hague: Visser, 1864.

Harinck, G., and R. Kuiper, eds. *Groen van Prinsterer en de geschiedenis.* Kampen: Kok, 1994.

Honders, A. C. *Doen en Laten in Ernst en Vrede. Notities over een broederkring en een tijdschrift.* The Hague: Boekencentrum, 1963.

Janssens, R. *De Opbouw van de Antirevolutionaire Partij, 1850–1888.* Hilversum: Verloren, 2001.

Kamphuis, J. *De hedendaagse kritiek op de causaliteit bij Groen van Prinsterers als historicus.* Groningen: De Vuurbaak, 1971.

Kluit, M. Elisabeth. *Het Protestantse Réveil in Nederland en daarbuiten, 1815–1865.* Amsterdam: H. J. Paris, 1970.

Knetsch, F. R. J. "Groen van Prinsterer over Bismarck." *Documentatieblad voor de Nederlandse Kerkgeschiedenis na 1800* 32 (nov. 1990).

Kuiper, R. "Antirevolutionaire partijvorming en de grondwetswijziging van 1848." In *Om de toekomst van het Protestantse Nederland. De gevolgen van de grondwetsherziening van 1848 voor kerk, staat en maatschappij,* edited by G. J. Schutte and J. Vree, 152–72. Zoetermeer: Meinema, 1998.

———. "'Geen muziek om van het blad te zingen.' Groen van Prinsterer's *Ongeloof en Revolutie* (1847)." In *Ophefmakende publicaties uit de "lange" negentiende eeuw,* edited by F. G. M. Broeyer en D. Th. Kuiper, 111–31. Zoetermeer: Meinema, 2005.

———. "G. W. Vreede, conservatisme en agitatie." In *Drie protestantse conservatieven uit de 19e eeuw,* edited by R. E. de Bruin and G. J. Schutte, 67–88. Amsterdam: VU Uitgeverij, 1994.

———. *Herenmuiterij. Vernieuwing en sociaal conflict in de antirevolutionaire beweging, 1871–1894.* Leiden: J. J. Groen, 1994.

———. *"Tot een voorbeeld zult gij blijven." Mr. G. Groen van Prinsterer (1801–1876).* Amsterdam: Buijten & Schipperheijn, 2001.

———. *Zelfbeeld en wereldbeeld. Antirevolutionairen en het buitenland, 1848–1905.* Kampen: Kok, 1992.

Langedijk, D. *Groen van Prinsterer en de schoolkwestie.* The Hague: Voorhoeve, 1947.

Meulen, Dik van der. *Koning Willem III 1817–1890.* Amsterdam: Boom, 2013.

Mulder, H. W. J. *Groen van Prinsterer: staatsman en profeet.* Franeker: Wever, 1973.

Pierson, A. *Oudere tijdgenooten. 1888.* 3rd impr. Amsterdam: Van Bottenburg, 1922.

Puchinger, G. *Aandacht voor Groen van Prinsterer.* Kampen: Kok, 1976.

Raak, R. van. *In naam van het volmaakte. Conservatisme in Nederland in de negentiende eeuw van Gerrit Jan Mulder tot Jan Heemskerk Azn.* Amsterdam: Wereldbibliotheek, 2001.
Rasker, A. J. *De Nederlandse Hervormde Kerk vanaf 1795.* Kampen: Kok, 1974.
Rhijn, L. J. van. "Wassenaarsche herinneringen aan Mr. G. Groen van Prinsterer." *Magdalena* 25 (1877) 148–53.
Roessingh, K. H. *Het modernisme in Nederland.* Haarlem: Bohn, 1922.
Rullmann, J. C. *Onze voortrekkers.* Delft: Meinema, 1931.
Schutte, G. J. *Mr. Groen van Prinsterer.* Goes: Oosterbaan & Le Cointre, 1976.
Steur, J. "De geldelijke nalatenschap van Groen van Prinsterer." *Tot Vrijheid Geroepen* 22 (1976) 78–87.
Suttorp, L. C., et al., eds. *Groen's "Ongeloof en Revolutie." Een bundel studiën.* Wageningen: Zomer en Keuning, 1949.
Vries, T. de. *Handleiding tot de kennis van het leven en de werken van Mr. G. Groen van Prinsterer.* Appingedam: Van der Ploeg, 1899.
———. *Mr. Groen van Prinsterer in zijne omgeving.* Leiden: Sijthoff, 1908.

DOCTORAL DISSERTATIONS DEVOTED TO ASPECTS OF GROEN VAN PRINSTERER

Bijl, Jelle. *Een Europese Antirevolutionair: Het Europabeeld van Groen van Prinsterer in tekst en context.* VU University Press, 2011 [on Groen as European antirevolutionary].
Brants, J. L. P. *Groen's geestelijke groei: Onderzoek naar Groen van Prinsterer's theorieën tot 1834.* Amsterdam: Van Soest, 1951 [on Groen's spiritual growth up to his conversion; English summary included].
Bruins Slot, J. A. H. J. S. *Groen van Prinsterer bij het herstel der hiërarchie in de Roomsch-Katholieke Kerk in Nederland.* 1935 [about Groen's response to the re-establishment of the Roman Catholic clergy].
Dengerink, J. D. *Critisch-historisch onderzoek naar de sociologische ontwikkeling van het beginsel der "souvereiniteit in eigen kring" in de 19e en 20e eeuw.* Kampen: Kok, 1948 [on Groen and the development of the theory of sphere-sovereignty; English summary included].
Diepenhorst, P. A. *Groen van Prinsterer.* 1st ed. Kampen: Kok, 1932 [on Groen and the theory of the Christian state, at 21–61].
———. *Groen van Prinsterer.* 2nd ed. Kampen: Kok, 1941.
Fokkema, F. J. *De Godsdienstig-wijsgerige beginselen van Mr. G. Groen van Prinsterer.* Grijpskerk: Riemersma, 1907 [on Groen's Platonizing philosophy].
Hartogh, G. M. den. *Groen van Prinsterer en de Verkiezingen van 1871; een keerpunt in de wordingsgeschiedenis der Antirevolutionaire Partij.* Diss., Free University of Amsterdam. Kampen: Kok, 1933 [about Groen's conduct during the election campaign of 1871].
Kirpenstein, J. W. *Groen van Prinsterer als belijder van Kerk en Staat in de negentiende eeuw.* Leiden: J. J. Groen, 1993 [about Groen on church and state; English summary included].
Koorders, D. *De antirevolutionaire staatsleer van Mr. Groen van Prinsterer uit de bronnen ontwikkeld.* Utrecht, 1860 [about Groen's antirevolutionary political doctrine].

BIBLIOGRAPHY

Laman, G. J. *Groen van Prinsterer als volksvertegenwoordiger, 1862–1865.* Diss., Free University of Amsterdam. Franeker: Wever, 1949 [on Groen as a member of parliament, 1862–65].
Schlebusch, Jan Adriaan. *Strategic Narratives: Groen van Prinsterer as Nineteenth-Century Statesman-Historian.* University of Groningen, 2018 [about Groen and his political narratives].
Smitskamp, H. *Groen van Prinsterer als historicus.* Amsterdam: H. J. Paris, 1940 [on Groen van Prinsterer as historian].
Tazelaar, C. *De jeugd van Groen, 1801–1827.* Amsterdam: Uitgeversmaatschappij Holland, 1925 [about Groen's formative years].
Thomassen a Thuessink van der Hoop van Slochteren, M. P. Th. A. *Kerk en staat volgens Groen van Prinsterer.* Groningen: Oppenheim, 1905 [about Groen on church and state].
Vliet, W. G. F. van. *Groen van Prinsterers historische benadering van de politiek.* Hilversum: Uitgeverij Verloren, 2008 [about Groen's historical approach to politics; English summary included].
Zwaan, J. *Groen van Prinsterer en de klassieke oudheid.* Amsterdam: Hakkert, 1973 [on Groen van Prinsterer as a classicist; English summary included].

SOME ENGLISH-LANGUAGE PUBLICATIONS

Dyke, Harry Van. "Groen van Prinsterer's Appreciation of Classical Antiquity." In *In the Phrygian Mode: Neo-Calvinism, Antiquity and the Lamentations of Reformed Philosophy*, edited by Robert Sweetman, 13–39. Lanham, MD: University Press of America, 2007.
———. "Groen van Prinsterer's Interpretation of the French Revolution and the Rise of 'Pillars' in Dutch Society." In *Presenting the Past: History, Art, Language, Literature*, edited by Jane Fenoulhet and Lesley Gilbert, 83–98. London: Centre for Low Countries Studies, 1996.
———. *Groen van Prinsterer's Lectures on Unbelief and Revolution.* Jordan Station, ON: Wedge, 1989.
———. "Groen van Prinsterer: Godfather of Bavinck and Kuyper." *Calvin Theological Journal* 47 (2012) 72–97.
Eglinton, James. *Bavinck: A Critical Biography.* Grand Rapids: Baker Academic, 2020.
Essen, J. L. van. "Guillaume Groen van Prinsterer and His Conception of History." *Westminster Theological Journal* 44 (1982) 205–49.
Essen, J. L. van, and H. Donald Morton. *Guillaume Groen van Prinsterer: Selected Studies.* Jordan Station, ON: Wedge, 1990.
Groen van Prinsterer, Guillaume. *Unbelief and Revolution.* Translated by Harry van Dyke. Bellingham, WA: Lexham Press, 2018.
Hospers, G. H. "Groen van Prinsterer and His Book." *Evangelical Quarterly* 7 (1935) 267–86.
Klapwijk, J. "Calvin and Neo-Calvinism on Non-Christian Philosophy." *Philosophia Reformata* 38 (1973) 43–61.
Langley, McKendree R. "The Legacy of Groen van Prinsterer." *Reformed Perspective* (Jan. 1985) 25–28.
———. "Pioneers of Christian Politics I." *Vanguard* (Apr. 1971) 7–9.

———. "What Does It Mean to Be a Christian in the World?" *The Presbyterian Guardian* (Jan. 1976) 8–13.
———. "The Witness of a World View." *Pro Rege* 8.2 (1979) 2–11.
Lloyd-Jones, D. Martyn. "The French Revolution and After." In *The Christian and the State in Revolutionary Times*, 94–99. London: Westminster Conference, 1975.
Runner, H. Evan. *Scriptural Religion and Political Task*. Toronto: Wedge, 1974.
Sap, J. W. *Paving the Way for Revolution: Calvinism and the Struggle for a Democratic Constitutional State*. Amsterdam: VU Uitgeverij, 2001.
Van Zylstra, B. "Voegelin on Unbelief and Revolution." In *Een Staatsman ter navolging: Groen van Prinsterer herdacht (1876–1976)*, edited by C. Bremmer and M. G. Kool, 191–200. The Hague, 1976.

GENERAL

Aerts, Remieg. *Land van kleine gebaren. Een politieke geschiedenis van Nederland 1780–1990*. Nijmegen: Sun 1999.
Alphen, H. van. *De gronden mijner geloofsbelijdenis, opengelegd voor mijne kinderen*. Utrecht: N.p., 1786.
Appeltere, A. W. van. *Het Staatsregt in Nederland, vooral met betrekking tot de kerk, en de handelingen der regeering ten opzigte der Afgescheidenen, nader toegelicht*. The Hague and Amsterdam: Van Cleef, 1837.
Baggen, Peter. *Vorming door wetenschap; universitair onderwijs in Nederland, 1815–1960*. Delft: Eburon, 1998.
Balsem, N. C. *G. Groen van Prinsterer*. Vol. 7, no. 9 of *Mannen van beteekenis in onze dagen*. Haarlem: Kruseman & Tjeenk Willink, 1877.
Beets, N., and A. H. Raabe, eds. *Bloemlezing uit de werken van mr. J. J. L. van der Brugghen*. 2 vols. Nymegen: Ten Hoet, 1888–89.
Belien, H. M. D. Van der Horst, and G. J. van Setten, red. *Nederlanders van het eerste uur. Het ontstaan van het moderne Nederland 1780–1830*. Amsterdam: Uitgeverij Bert Bakker, 1996.
Bilderdijk, Willem. *Geschiedenis des Vaderlands*. Edited by H. W. Tydeman. 12 vols. Leiden: Warnars, 1832–53.
Booy, Thys. *Het is stil op het Loo; overpeinzingen in memoriam koningin Wilhelmina*. Amsterdam: Ten Have, 1963.
Bos, David. *In dienst van het Koninkrijk; beroepsontwikkeling van hervormde predikanten in het negentiende-eeuwse Nederland*. Amsterdam: B. Bakker, 1999.
Brouwer, P. A. S. van Limburg. "De ontknooping." *De Gids* 10 (1857) 305–30.
Chantepie de la Saussaye, D. "De optreding van het nieuwe ministerie." *Ernst en Vrede* 4 (1856) 299–309.
Costa, Isaac da. *Het Oogenblik; een woord over het "Ontwerp van Grondwetherziening."* Amsterdam: N.p., 1848.
Cousin, V. *De l'instruction publique en Hollande*. Paris: Levrault, 1837.
Does, J. C. van der. *De vrijheid voorgestreên. Gedenkschrift ter gelegenheid van het eeuwfeest van de kiesvereniging "Nederland en Oranje" te Amsterdam*. Hoorn: Edecea, 1950.
Duyverman, J. P. *Thorbecke debatteert; een bloemlezing*. The Hague: V.U.G.A., 1988.
Evenhuis, R. B. *Ook dat was Amsterdam*. 5 vols. Amsterdam: Ten Have, 1965–78.
Fabius, D. P. D. *Het Reglement van '52*. Amsterdam: n.p., 1888.

BIBLIOGRAPHY

Fruin, Robert. *Tien jaren uit den Tachtigjarige Oorlog, 1588-1598.* Leiden: n.p., 1857-58.

———. *Verspreide Geschriften.* 10 vols. Leiden: n.p., 1905.

Gewin, E. *In den Reveilkring.* Baarn: Hollandia Drukkerij, 1920.

Glenn, Charles L., Jr. *The Myth of the Common School.* Amherst: University of Massachusetts Press, 1988.

Gunning, J. H., Jr., ed. *Bij het graf van Mr. Groen van Prinsterer, 23 Mei 1876.* Amsterdam: Höveker, 1876.

Harinck, George, Roel Kuiper, and Peter Bak, eds. *De Antirevolutionaire Partij, 1829-1980.* Hilversum: Verloren, 2001.

Hartogh, G. M. den, ed. *Schrift en Historie. Gedenkboek bij het vijftigjarig bestaan der georganiseerde Antirevolutionaire Partij, 1878-1928.* Kampen: Kok, 1928.

Heusde, Ph. W. van. *De Socratische school, of wijsbegeerte voor de negentiende eeuw.* 4 vols. Utrecht: Altheer, 1834-39.

Houkes, A., and M. Janse. "Foreign Examples as Eye-Openers and Justification: The Transfer of the Anti-Corn Law League to the Netherlands." *European Review of History* 12 (2005) 321-44.

Huet, Conrad Busken. *Litterarische fantasieën en kritieken.* 25 vols. Haarlem: Tjeenk Willink, 1868-88.

Israel, Jonathan. *The Dutch Republic: Its Rise, Greatness and Fall, 1477-1806.* Oxford: Clarendon, 1998.

Keijser, J. P. de. *Neerland's Letterkunde in de negentiende eeuw; bloemlezing ten gebruike bij de beoefening onzer letterkunde.* 2 vols. The Hague: Thieme, 1877.

Kemp, C. M. van der. *De eere der Nederlandsche Hervormde Kerk gehandhaafd tegen Ypey en Dermout.* 3 vols. Rotterdam: Van der Meer & Verbruggen, 1830-33.

Kennedy, James C. *Building New Babylon: Cultural Change in the Netherlands During the 1960s.* Diss., University of Iowa, 1994.

Kluit, M. E. *Nader over het Réveil; vijf schetsen.* Kampen: Kok, 1977.

———. "Uit de briefwisseling van C. M. van der Kemp (1799-1861) en H. J. Koenen (1809-1874)." *Bijdragen en Mededelingen van het Historisch Genootschap* 63 (1942) 1-290.

Knippenberg, Hans, and Ben de Pater. *De eenwording van Nederland; schaalvergroting en integratie sinds 1800.* Nymegen: Socialistiese Uitgeverij, 1992.

Kossmann, E. H. *The Low Countries, 1780-1940.* Oxford: Clarendon, 1978.

Kraan-Van den Burg, Gera. *De Spiegelklok.* Kampen: Kok, 1947.

Kuiper, J. *Geschiedenis van het Christelijk Lager Onderwijs in Nederland.* 2nd rev. ed. Amsterdam: H. A. van Bottenburg, 1904.

Kuyper, Abraham. *Het beroep op het volksgeweten.* Amsterdam: Blankenberg, 1869.

Langedijk, D. *De schoolstrijd in de eerste jaren na de wet van 1857.* Kampen: Kok, 1937.

Langley, McKendree R. *Emancipation and Apologetics: The Formation of Abraham Kuyper's Anti-Revolutionary Party.* Diss., Westminster Theological Seminary. Ann Arbor, MI: University Microfilms, 1995.

Lohman, W. H. de Savornin, ed. "Groen's reis naar Parijs en Besançon in 1836 ten behoeve der Archieven." *Bijdragen en Mededelingen van het Historisch Genootschap* 42 (1921) 1-106.

Lummel, A. J. van. *Register op het Handboek der Geschiedenis van het Vaderland van Mr. G. Groen van Prinsterer.* Utrecht: Kemink, 1877.

Motley, J. L. *The Life and Death of John of Barneveld, Advocate of Holland: With a View of the Primary Causes and Movements of the Thirty Years' War.* 2 vols. New York: Harper and Brothers, 1874.

Bibliography

———. *The Rise of the Dutch Republic*. 3 vols. Amsterdam: Binger Brothers, 1855.
Nijevelt, J. P. J. A. van Zuylen van. *Agitatie of pligtsbetrachting?* Utrecht: N.p., 1866.
Opzoomer, C. W. *Onze godsdienst*. Amsterdam: N.p., 1874.
Pater, J. C. H. de. "Burke en Groen van Prinsterer." *Stemmen des Tijds* 14 (1925) 68–99.
Pierson, A. *Willem de Clercq naar zijn dagboek*. 2 vols. Haarlem: N.p., 1888.
Schama, Simon. *Patriots and Liberators: Revolution in the Netherlands, 1780–1813*. London: Collins, 1977.
Schutte, Gerrit J. *Het Calvinistisch Nederland; mythe en werkelijkheid*. Hilversum: Verloren, 2000.
Sheeres, Janet Sjaarda. *Son of Secession: Douwe J. Vander Werp*. Grand Rapids: Eerdmans, 2006.
Smits, A. *1830 Scheuring in de Nederlanden*. Deel 3. Heule-Kortrijk: UGA, 1999.
Snel, Johan. *Abraham Kuyper, een leven in de journalistiek*. Amsterdam: Boom, 2023
Steur, J. "Staatssecretarie en Kabinet des Konings onder Willem I." *Bijdragen en Mededelingen Betreffende de Geschiedenis der Nederlanden* 84 (1969) 88.
Stuart, M. Cohen. *In memoriam Guillaume Groen van Prinsterer; notice biographique*. Utrecht: Kemink, 1876.
Suttorp, L. C. F. *A. van Hall en zijn constitutioneele beginselen*. Diss., Leiden. Amsterdam: H. J. Paris, 1932.
Tamse, C. A. *Queen Sophie 1818–1877*. Zutphen: Walburg, 1984.
TenZythoff, Gerrit J. *Sources of Secession: The Netherlands Hervormde Kerk on the Eve of the Dutch Immigration to the American Midwest*. Grand Rapids: Eerdmans, 1987.
Thorbecke, J. R. *Aanteekeningen op de grondwet*. Amsterdam: Müller, 1839.
Trottet, J. P. "Quelques mots sur l'état religieux de la Hollande." *Chrétien Evangélique du 19e siècle* (Oct. 25, 1859).
———. *Le parti orthodoxe pur dans l'Église Wallonne de la Haye. Réponse B la brochure de Mr. G. Groen van Prinsterer intitulée: Le parti anti-révolutionnaire et confessionnel dans l'Église Réformée des Pays-Bas*. The Hague: Visser, 1860.
Vree, Jasper, and Johan Zwaan, eds. *The Young Kuyper About Calvin, a Lasco and the Church*. 2 vols. Leiden: Brill, 2005.
Vries, Jan de. *Barges and Capitalism: Passenger Transportation in the Dutch Economy, 1632–1839*. Utrecht: Studia Historica, 1981.
Vrijer, M. J. A. de. *Gunning Tragicus*. The Hague: Daamen, 1946.
Westra, Johan G. *Confessional Political Parties in the Netherlands, 1813–1946*. Diss., University of Michigan. Ann Arbor, MI: University Microfilms, 1972.
Wilde, J. A. de, and C. Smeenk. *Het volk ten baat. Geschiedenis van de Antirevolutionaire Partij*. Groningen: Haan, 1949.
Wit, C. H. E. de. *Thorbecke en de wording van de Nederlandse natie*. Nymegen: S.U.N., 1980.
Witlox, J. H. J. M. "Groen van Prinsterer." In *Varia Historica*, 114. Hertogenbosch: Teulings, 1936.
Woelderink, B. "Groen van Prinsterer's First Years at the Royal Archives (1831–1841)." *Jaarboek Oranje-Nassau Museum* (1993) 93–101.
Wolffram, D. J. *Bezwaarden en verlichten; verzuiling in een Gelderse provinciestad, Harderwijk 1850–1925*. Diss., University of Amsterdam. Amsterdam: Het Spinhuis, 1993.
Ypey, A., and I. J. Dermout. *Geschiedenis der Nederlandsche Hervormde Kerk*. 4 vols. Breda: Van Bergen, 1819–27.

Index

Alphen, Hieronymus van, 10, 94
America, 114, 119
Assen, C.J. van, 13, 18, 19, 21, 29, 32, 36, 37, 39, 46, 47, 54, 55, 61, 75, 81, 88, 93, 122, 155, 171

Beets, Nicolaas, 101, 110, 116, 117, 134, 143, 144, 156, 158, 159, 161, 162, 171, 172, 193, 194, 213, 214
Belgian Revolt, 32, 40–42, 46, 74
Bilderdijk, Willem, 3, 12, 13, 16, 40, 45, 48, 63, 72, 93, 94, 96, 127, 213
Bismarck, Otto von, 188–90, 200–202
Brugghen, Justinus Jacob Leonard van der, 91, 132, 133, 141, 142, 149–51, 154–62, 170, 173, 213, 214
Bunyan, John, 64, 215
Brummelkamp, Anthony, 79, 204
Burke, Edmund, 28, 39, 45, 103
Busken Huet, Conrad, 188, 199, 211

Calvinism, 65, 138
Capadose, Abraham, 10, 61, 86, 102, 111, 116, 167, 169
Chambers of Parliament
    Second Chamber, 14, 25, 28, 72, 73, 82, 120, 127, 131–37, 140–45, 149–53, 156–63, 167, 169, 170, 176–80, 183–86, 191, 198, 203, 205, 217
    First Chamber, 25, 109, 124, 125, 127, 128, 130

Chantepie de la Saussaye, Daniel, 143, 146, 151, 156–59, 170, 181, 194, 200, 205, 207, 213, 214
Christian Reformed Churches, 79
Cicero (Roman statesman), 8, 11, 160
Clerq, Willem de, 34, 35, 39, 47, 49–52, 54, 60, 64, 66, 67, 69, 71, 90, 99, 100, 213, 215
Clerq, Caroline de, 34, 35, 49–51, 66, 215
Costa, Isaac da, vii, ix, 10, 12, 13, 34, 35, 39, 60, 63, 65, 66, 70, 80, 81, 93, 94, 99, 103, 112, 116, 123, 124, 126, 127, 133, 139, 140, 142, 143, 147, 157, 159, 160, 161, 165, 166, 169, 171, 181, 182, 207, 212, 213
Cock, Hendrik de, 65, 66

Dermout, Isaac Johannes, 8, 9, 63, 64, 66, 85
Donker Curtius, Dirk, 128, 130, 131
Dutch Indies, 25, 179, 184
Dutch Reformed Church, viii, 9, 74, 76, 78, 79, 108, 111, 113–17, 146, 165, 181, 182, 193
Dutch Republic, 25, 30, 78, 95, 96, 164, 190

Education Act, 86, 90, 91, 150, 151, 163, 177, 178, 191, 193, 208, 213
Elout, Pieter Jacob van Soeterwoude, 63, 86, 99, 103, 109, 111, 123, 141, 149, 157, 160, 163, 167, 177, 185, 189, 201, 216
Enlightenment (thought), viii, 28, 45, 105

Index

Europe, 19, 119, 136, 164, 165, 169, 188, 201, 205, 206
Evangelical Alliance, 101, 189

French Revolution, 19, 28, 31, 40, 44, 52, 102–5, 108, 125, 135
Fruin, Robert, 141, 165, 179, 210

Geer van Jutphaas, Barthold Jacob Lintelo, 133, 140, 148, 149, 151, 157, 163, 174, 176, 185, 191, 193, 197, 202, 203
Gefken, Jan Willem, 61, 73, 77, 81, 103, 132, 157, 168, 200, 204
Gerlach, Ludwig von, 190
Glorious Revolution, 164, 175
Great Powers, 40, 41, 42, 53, 83, 168, 169
Groen van Prinsterer, Petrus Jacobus, 1–5, 8, 16, 20, 27, 32, 50, 52, 53, 66, 70, 71, 73, 75, 98
Groen van Prinsterer-Caan, Adriana Hendrika, 1, 2, 8, 49
Groen van Prinsterer- Van der Hoop, Elisabeth Maria Magdalena (Betsy), 22–24, 28, 32–35, 49–54, 62–64, 66, 68–72, 80, 90, 94, 97, 98, 110, 121, 122, 129, 134, 135, 147, 168, 169, 171, 182, 187, 188, 191, 192, 206, 215–18
Guizot, Franz, 68, 103, 119
Gunning, Johannes Hermanus, 172, 181, 182, 193

Haldane, Robert, 28
Hall, Floris Adriaan van, 132, 144, 148, 152, 154
Haller, Carl Ludwig von, 28, 45, 52, 108
Hegel, Georg Wilhelm Friedrich, 58
Heldring, Ottho Gerhard, 56, 90, 91, 100, 101, 112, 116, 146, 151, 156, 158, 159, 163, 172, 213
Herder, Johann Gottfried, 20
Heusde, Philip Willem van, 7, 11, 16, 60, 87, 138
Historical School of Law, 13
Hodges, Charles Howard, painter, 14, 245, 247, 256

Hofmann, Mari, 14, 49, 71, 103, 149
Hofstede de Groot, Petrus, 102, 113, 161
Hogendorp, Gijsbert Karel, 6
House of Orange, 12, 25, 39, 46, 61, 62, 70, 74, 84, 85, 95, 96, 126, 129, 130, 133, 139, 163, 205

Justinian Code, 13, 15

Kappeyne van de Coppello, J, 7, 8, 15, 16, 19, 21, 24, 29, 52, 218
Kemp, Carel Maria van der, 56, 60, 61, 64, 66, 67, 81, 86, 89, 93, 103, 111, 123, 143, 167, 171, 181
Keuchenius, Levinus Wilhelmus Christiaan, 184, 185, 203, 204
Kock, Frederik Lodewijk Willem (Frits), de, 148, 152, 154, 155
Kögel, Rudolf, 168
Koenen, Hendrik Jacob, 35, 39, 47, 60, 61, 67, 70, 79, 80, 87, 97, 101, 103, 115, 124, 156
Kuyper, Abraham, vii, 109, 183, 192, 193, 195, 197, 198, 201–5, 207–9, 211, 214, 217, 218

Leo, Heinrich, historian, 68
Liefde, Jan de, 146, 173
Louis Philippe, king of France, 119
Lynden, Willem van, 125, 132, 141, 149, 157, 160, 163, 169, 176–78, 180, 185
Louis Napoleon, king of the Netherlands, 3, 40

Maanen, Cornelis Felix van, 25, 35, 37, 38, 40, 41, 74, 77
Mackay, Aeneas, 86, 102, 103, 109, 112, 116, 123–25, 129, 132, 136, 141, 149, 156–58, 160, 163, 167, 169, 177, 179, 185, 189, 205, 214
Marnix of St. Aldegonde, 176
Maurice, prince of Orange, 110, 164, 165, 210, 211
Merle d'Aubigné, Jean-Henri, 28, 34, 35, 43, 69, 79, 171, 207
Michelet, Jules, historian, 68, 96

Index

Monod, Frédéric Joel Jean Gérard, 69
Motley, John Lothrop, historian, 166, 210, 211, 213
Mulder, Gerrit Jan, 138–40, 148, 149, 151, 183
Metternich, Klemens Wenzel Lothar von, 119

Napoleon Bonaparte, emperor of France, 6, 7, 31, 168
Napoleon III, emperor of France, 136, 168, 169, 200

Oldenbarneveld, Johan van, 164–66, 210, 211
Otterloo, Michiel Derk van, 172, 203, 204, 208

Pascal, Blaise, philosopher, 28
Plato, philosopher, 7, 11, 15, 59, 72
Pope of Rome, 137–39, 142

Raalte, Albertus Christiaan van, 114
Ranke, Leopold von, historian, 68, 187
Rappard, Anthony Gerhard Alexander van, 36, 39, 42–44, 67, 77, 129, 137, 148
Rhijn, Leendert Johannes, viii, 159, 172, 192, 217
Robespierre, Maximilien de, 105
Rousseau, Jean-Jacques, 11–13, 20, 28
Reformation, 62, 95, 208
Reformed seminary, 144
Renaissance, 105
Restoration, 2, 75, 91
Reveil (movement), viii, 28, 35, 51, 52, 54, 56, 61–66, 69, 70, 73, 80, 81, 86, 96, 97, 99–102, 111, 112, 114–16, 123, 124, 129, 142, 143, 160, 162, 167, 190, 209
Risorgimento, 168
Romanticism, 20

Savigny, Friedrich Carl von, 13, 45
Savornin Lohman, Alexander Frederik de, 215

Schimmelpenninck, Rutger Jan, 3, 4, 8
Schaepman, Herman, 217
Scholte, Hendrik Pieter, 65, 66, 73, 77, 114
Schwartz, Carl, 175, 198, 201
Seceders, 9, 73–77, 79, 81, 112–14, 119, 125, 144, 145, 173, 201, 208, 209, 216, 218
Secession (of 1834), 64–66, 73, 75, 83, 114
Secrétan, Jean Charles Isaac, 34, 44, 50, 53, 63, 81, 116, 168
Singendonck, Johan Anne, 103, 109, 111, 123, 124, 134, 154, 155, 159, 167, 188, 205, 213
Sophie von Württemberg, queen, 85, 128, 129, 187, 216
Stahl, Friedrich Julius, 103, 125, 127, 132, 171, 174–76, 188, 189
Synod of Dordt, 9, 64, 164

Tholuck, August, 29, 82
Thorbecke, Johan Rudolf, vii, 11, 18, 19, 41, 42, 44, 61, 78, 79, 82, 84, 88, 94, 106, 120, 122, 125, 126, 128, 130, 131, 136, 139–41, 152, 155, 157, 159, 165, 177–79, 183, 203, 207, 212, 216, 217
Trottet, Jean Pierre, 170

Unbelief and Revolution (book), ix, 44, 56, 103, 109, 110, 115, 116, 123, 124, 145, 183
United Kingdom of the Netherlands, 17, 26, 29, 30, 42, 83
University of Groningen, 24, 176
University of Leyden, 8, 9, 17, 18, 74, 122, 130
University of Utrecht, 138

Vondel, Joost van den, 94
Vinet, Alexandre Rodolphe, 115, 133

Wassenaer van Catwijck, Otto van, 171, 184, 185, 197, 203–6
Wilhelmina, queen of the Netherlands, 129

Index

William I, king of the Netherlands, 6, 18, 21, 22, 25, 26, 31, 32, 35, 36, 38, 40, 45, 46, 53–55, 61, 62, 67, 68, 70, 73–75, 80, 83–85, 118, 128, 167, 187, 207

William II, king of the Netherlands, 83–85, 90, 92, 119, 128, 183, 187

William III, king of the Netherlands, 128, 129, 139, 149, 152–54, 185, 187, 206

William of Orange (William the Silent, prince), 32, 61, 62, 67, 95, 166, 176

William III of Orange (prince and king of Engeland), 95, 110, 164, 165, 174

Wormser, Johan Adam, 109, 134, 144–47, 160–63, 171, 180–82, 207, 212, 213

Zaalberg, Johannes Cornelis, 180, 181

Zuylen van Nijevelt, Julius Philip Jacob Adriaan, 168, 183–86

www.ingramcontent.com/pod-product-compliance
Lightning Source LLC
Chambersburg PA
CBHW061433300426
44114CB00014B/1668